God (in) Acts

God (in) Acts

The Characterization of God
in the Acts of the Apostles

Christine H. Aarflot

PICKWICK *Publications* • Eugene, Oregon

GOD (IN) ACTS
The Characterization of God in the Acts of the Apostles

Copyright © 2020 Christine H. Aarflot. All rights reserved. Except for brief quotations in critical publications or reviews, no part of this book may be reproduced in any manner without prior written permission from the publisher. Write: Permissions, Wipf and Stock Publishers, 199 W. 8th Ave., Suite 3, Eugene, OR 97401.

Pickwick Publications
An Imprint of Wipf and Stock Publishers
199 W. 8th Ave., Suite 3
Eugene, OR 97401

www.wipfandstock.com

PAPERBACK ISBN: 978-1-5326-9349-6
HARDCOVER ISBN: 978-1-5326-9350-2
EBOOK ISBN: 978-1-5326-9351-9

Cataloguing-in-Publication data:

Names: Aarflot, Christine H., author.

Title: God (in) Acts: The Characterization of God in the Acts of the Apostles / by Christine H. Aarflot.

Description: Eugene, OR: Pickwick Publications, 2020 | Includes bibliographical references and index.

Identifiers: ISBN 978-1-5326-9349-6 (paperback) | ISBN 978-1-5326-9350-2 (hardcover) | ISBN 978-1-5326-9351-9 (ebook)

Subjects: LCSH: Bible. Acts—Criticism, interpretation, etc. | God—Biblical teaching.

Classification: BS2625.2 A27 2020 (print) | BS2625.2 (ebook)

Scripture citations are, unless otherwise noted, from the New Revised Standard Version Bible, copyright © 1989 the Division of Christian Education of the National Council of the Churches of Christ in the United States of America. Used by permission. All rights reserved.

A few other citations are taken from:

The Holy Bible, New International Version®, NIV® Copyright © 1973, 1978, 1984, 2011 by Biblica, Inc.® Used by permission. All rights reserved worldwide.

New American Bible with Revised New Testament and Revised Psalms © 1991, 1986, 1970 Confraternity of Christian Doctrine, Washington, DC, and are used by permission of the copyright owner. All Rights Reserved.

Manufactured in the U.S.A.   06/24/20

*To my parents, Hilde Marie and Jan-Olav, who first taught me
to see God in my own story.*

Contents

Acknowledgments | xi
List of Abbreviations | xiii

Chapter 1: **Introduction** | 1

    1.0 Problem and Purpose   1
    1.1 Research History   3
        1.1.1 From Neglected Factor to Central, Acting Character   5
        1.1.2 Salvation History: God's Plan, Purpose, and Providence   8
        1.1.3 Characteristics of God   14
    1.2 The Way Forward   19

Chapter 2: **Method and Material** | 24

    2.0 A Narrative Approach: Preliminary Observations   24
    2.1 Reading God in Acts   27
        2.1.1 Discerning God's Actions   27
        2.1.2 Reading as a Competent Reader   31
        2.1.3 What about the Gospel of Luke?   35
        2.1.4 The Question of Genre: Reading Acts as Biblical History   38
    2.2 The Character and Characterization of God in Acts   44
        2.2.1 God as Character: Who is "God" in Acts?   45
            2.2.1.1 Distinguishing God from Jesus and the Spirit   45
            2.2.1.2 God and Jesus   46
            2.2.1.3 God and the Holy Spirit   53
        2.2.2 God as Character: The Characterization of God   57
            2.2.2.1 Story and Discourse   60
            2.2.2.2 Settings   61
            2.2.2.3 Plot   62

2.2.2.4 The Implied Author, Narrators, Narration, and Focalization   63
2.2.2.5 Modes of Characterization   65
2.3 Delimitation and Project Outline   66

Chapter 3: **The God of the Last Days** (Acts 2:1–41) | 70

3.0 Introduction   70
3.1 A Theophany of Sound, Flame, and Spirit (2:1–13)   71
3.2 Peter's Speech (2:14–36)   78
    3.2.1 "'And in the last days it will be,' says God" (2:14–21)   78
    3.2.2 God's Works through Jesus (2:22–28)   84
    3.2.3 The Lord's Lord (2:29–36)   86
3.3 God's Universal Promise of Salvation (2:37–41)   90
3.4 Concluding Observations   91

Chapter 4: **The God of Glory and Heaven: Stephen's Speech and Vision** (Acts 6:8—7:60) | 94

4.0. Introduction   94
4.1 Stephen as a Reliable Narrator of God's Actions   96
4.2 Stephen's Speech: The God of Glory Revealed (7:2–53)   98
    4.2.1 God and Abraham (7:1–8)   98
        4.2.1.1 The God of Glory Revealed   98
        4.2.1.2 The Settings of God's Revelation   100
    4.2.2 God and Joseph: God Acting as Savior in Egypt (7:9–16)   101
    4.2.3 God and Moses (7:17–43)   102
        4.2.3.1 The Revelatory Descent of the Holy God   102
        4.2.3.2 God Liberates and Gives the Law   104
    4.2.4 God Transcends the Temple (7:44–50)   105
    4.2.5 Stephen's Accusation (7:51–53)   112
4.3 Stephen's Vision: The Glory of God Revealed (7:54–60)   114
4.4 Concluding Observations   117

Chapter 5: **"Who are you, Lord?"** (Acts 9:1–19; 22:1–21; 26:1–23) | 119

5.0 Introduction   119
5.1 "Who are you, Lord?" (Acts 9:1–19)   120
5.2 The God of Our Fathers (Acts 22:1–21)   130

5.3 The God of Life (Acts 26:1–23)   135
5.4 Concluding Observations   140

Chapter 6: **God's Impartiality (Acts 10:1—11:18; 15:1–21)** | 142

6.0 Introduction   142
6.1 Cornelius and Peter (10:1—11:18)   143
  6.1.1 Two Visions: God's Enigmatic Orchestration (10:1-23a)   144
  6.1.2 Peter in Cornelius's House: Interpreting God's Directions (10:23b-48)   152
    6.1.2.1 Peter and Cornelius (10:23b-33)   152
    6.1.2.2 Peter's Speech and the Descent of the Spirit (10:23b-48)   153
6.2 Peter in Jerusalem: God's Gift to the Gentiles (11:1-18)   159
6.3 The Apostolic Council (15:1-21)   160
  6.3.1 A Problem and Dispute (15:1-5): Contending Views of God   161
  6.3.2 The Council at Jerusalem (15:6-21)   163
    6.3.2.1 Peter's Speech (15:7-11): God's Testimony to the Gentiles   163
    6.3.2.2 Barnabas and Paul's Reports (15:11-12): "All That God Had Done With Them"   165
    6.3.2.3 James's Speech (15:13-21): "A People for His Name"   166
6.4 Concluding Observations   171

Chapter 7: **The Faithful God: Paul's Proclamation in Pisidian Antioch (13:13–52)** | 175

7.0 Introduction   175
7.1 Setting the Stage (13:13-16a)   176
7.2 Paul's Speech (13:16b-41)   177
  7.2.1 God's Actions in Israel's History (Exordium and Narratio, 13:16b-25)   177
  7.2.2 God's Message of Salvation (Propositio and Probatio, 13:26-37)   181
  7.2.3 Forgiveness and Warning (Peroratio, 13:38-41)   184
7.3 In the Face of Opposition (13:42-52): Continued Proclamation   185
7.4 Concluding Observations   191

Chapter 8: **God as Savior at Sea (27:1–44)** | 192

    8.0 Introduction   192
    8.1 Setting the Scene: A Problem and a Warning (27:1–12)   192
    8.2 The Journey: Hope is Lost (27:13–20)   193
    8.3 God in the Deep (27:21–26)   196
    8.4 Complications (27:27–32)   197
    8.5 Food (27:33–38)   198
    8.6 Firm Ground (27:39–44)   201
    8.7 Concluding Observations   202

Chapter 9: **The God of Power and Wonder** | 204

    9.0 Introduction   204
    9.1 Acts of Restoration   206
        9.1.1 Signs, Wonders, and Deeds of Power   206
        9.1.2 Release from Prison   217
    9.2 Acts of Infliction   220
        9.2.1 Death as Divine Judgment   220
        9.2.2 The Blindings of Paul and Elymas   225
    9.3 Concluding Observations   227

Chapter 10: **The Portrayal of God in Acts** | 229

    10.0 Introduction   229
    10.1 God of the Past, Present, and Future   230
        10.1.1 A Changing God, or Changing Perceptions?   231
        10.1.2 God as Faithful, Judge, and Savior   232
            10.1.2.1 God as Faithful   233
            10.1.2.2 God as Judge   235
            10.1.2.3 God as Savior   236
    10.2 God and Jesus   238
    10.3 Outlook   241

Bibliography | 245
Author Index | 261
Subject Index | 265
Scripture Index | 269

Acknowledgments

This is a slightly revised version of my doctoral dissertation, which was successfully defended at MF Norwegian School of Theology in March 2018.

There are many to whom I owe my gratitude for their support and constructive criticism while I was writing this dissertation. First of all, I am grateful to MF Norwegian School of Theology for taking me on as a research fellow so that I could pursue this project. Working as a scholar and teacher was a dream come true, and I count myself lucky to have been able to realize it in a school with so many supporting colleagues, students, and staff.

My parents and brother, Hilde Marie, Jan-Olav, and Andreas, have always been an unfailing source of support. I could not have done this without their love and interest in my work. Their encouragement is only equal to that of Maja Leonora Olsen Skålvold. She, together with Annette K. Dreyer, Maria S. Ånonsen, Marissa A. Ortiz, Ruth Eva Sollie, and Kristian Myklebust, deserve a special mention for the many ways in which they, directly or indirectly, have made my life as a scholar better.

I owe thanks to Geir Otto Holmås, who supervised the initial writing stages. Under his guidance, this project found much of its present form. The Norwegian-Swedish "doctoral days" has offered an annual venue for fellowship and constructive criticism. Samuel Byrskog's interest in my work encouraged me more than he might be aware of. My thanks also go to Maria Sturesson, who read and provided feedback on my chapter on method. Marianne Bjelland Kartzow has played a valuable and valued role in my scholarly life; our coffee dates have been a source of laughter, support, and inspiration.

I am particularly grateful to Joel B. Green for his hospitality, feedback, and mentoring during my stay at Fuller Theological Seminary in 2014–2015. I am also indebted to Steve Walton, who read my entire first draft and provided invaluable comments in the final stages of the writing process. Loveday C. A. Alexander and Matthew L. Skinner were both on my examination committee. They have my sincere thanks for engaging with my work, offering constructive feedback, and further broadening my insights into Acts.

I had wonderful colleagues during my time at MF. The library staff was exceptionally helpful. No matter how busy they were, their service was always kind and prompt. Our PhD-coordinator organized an excellent dissertation seminar. I am also particularly grateful to all my former colleagues in the New Testament department: Hanne Birgitte Sødal Tveito, Hilde Brekke Møller, Per Kristian Sætre, Glenn Wehus, and Reidar Hvalvik for all the conversations we have had, the help they have provided, and the fun we have shared. To Glenn I owe special thanks for proofreading my Greek.

Ole Jakob Filtvedt came on board as co-supervisor during the second half of my project. His insightful questions and observations have unquestionably made this study better, and made me reach further than I thought I could. I am truly grateful that he took me up on the challenge of challenging me.

Last, but not least, my heartfelt gratitude goes to Karl Olav Sandnes, my *Doktorvater*. Karl Olav first guided me into the world of the New Testament as a student, and later encouraged me to pursue this path further. In my time as a research fellow, he offered constructive and thoughtful criticism of my work, and demonstrated by example what it means to be a scholar of integrity. His unwavering encouragement and warm hospitality mean more than I could say.

Abbreviations

AB	Anchor Bible
ABD	*The Anchor Bible Dictionary*
	Freedman, David Noel, ed. *The Anchor Bible Dictionary*. 6 vols. New York: Doubleday, 1992.
ACNT	Augsburg Commentary on the New Testament
AcBib	Academia Biblica
AGJU	Arbeiten zur Geschichte des antiken Judentums und des Urchristentums
AmUSt.TR	American University Studies. Series 7, Theology and Religion
AnBib	Analecta Biblica
AnGr	Analecta Gregoriana
ANRW	*Aufstieg und Niedergang der römischen Welt*
ANTC	Abingdon New Testament Commentaries
BBR	*Bulletin for Biblical Research*
BECNT	Baker Exegetical Commentary on the New Testament
BETL	Bibliotheca Ephemeridum Theologicarum Lovaniensium
Bib	*Biblica*
BibInt	*Biblical Interpretation*
BibInt	Biblical Interpretation Series
BHT	Beiträge zur historischen Theologie
BLS	Bible and Literature Series
BSac	*Bibliotheca Sacra*
BZNW	Beihefte zur Zeitschrift für die neutestamentliche Wissenschaft
CBQ	*Catholic Biblical Quarterly*
CurBR	*Currents in Biblical Research*

DJG	*Dictionary of Jesus and the Gospels*
	Green, Joel B., Jeannine K. Brown, and Nicholas Perrin, eds. *Dictionary of Jesus and the Gospels*. 2nd ed. Downers Grove, IL: InterVarsity, 2013.
EKKNT	Evangelisch-katholischer Kommentar zum Neuen Testament
EpC	Epworth Commentary Series
ESEC	Emory Studies in Early Christianity
EvQ	*Evangelical Quarterly*
ExpTim	*Expository Times*
FC	The Fathers of the Church
HThKNT	Herders Theologischer Kommentar zum Neuen Testament
HTR	*Harvard Theological Review*
ICC	International Critical Commentary
Int	*Interpretation*
JBL	*Journal of Biblical Literature*
JETS	*Journal of the Evangelical Theological Society*
JPT	*Journal of Pentecostal Theology*
JPTSup	Journal of Pentecostal Theology Supplement Series
JSHRZ	Jüdische Schriften aus hellenistisch-römischer Zeit
JSOTSup	Journal for the Study of the Old Testament Supplement Series
JSNT	*Journal for the Study of the New Testament*
JSNTSup	Journal for the Study of the New Testament Supplement Series
JSS	*Journal of Semitic Studies*
JTS	*Journal of Theological Studies*
KEK	Kritisch-exegetischer Kommentar über das Neue Testament (Meyer-Kommentar)
LCL	Loeb Classical Library
LEC	Library of Early Christianity
LHBOTS	The Library of Hebrew Bible/Old Testament Studies
LSJ	*Liddell-Scott-Jones Greek English Lexicon*
	Liddell, Henry George, et al. *The Online Liddell-Scott-Jones Greek-English Lexicon*. Irvine: University of California, 2011. http://www.tlg.uci.edu/lsj.

LNTS	The Library of New Testament Studies
MNTS	McMaster New Testament Studies
Neot	*Neotestamentica*
NIDNTT	*New International Dictionary of New Testament Theology*
	Brown, Colin, ed. *New International Dictionary of New Testament Theology*. Translated by Hans Bietenhard, et al. 4 vols. Exeter: Paternoster, 1975–1986.
NovT	*Novum Testamentum*
NovTSup	Supplements to Novum Testamentum
NICNT	New International Commentary on the New Testament
NSBT	New Studies in Biblical Theology
NTD	Das Neue Testament Deutsch
NTL	New Testament Library
NTS	*New Testament Studies*
PBM	Paternoster Biblical Monographs
PRSt	*Perspectives in Religious Studies*
QD	Quaestiones Disputatae
RAC	*Reallexikon für Antike und Christentum*. Edited by Theodor Klauser et al. Stuttgart: Hiersemann, 1950–
ResQ	*Restoration Quarterly*
RSR	*Recherches de science religieuse*
R&T	*Religion and Theology*
SBLDS	Society of Biblical Literature Dissertation Series
SBLMS	Society of Biblical Literature Monograph Series
SBLRBS	*Society of Biblical Literature: Resources for Biblical Study*
SBLSP	Society of Biblical Literature Seminar Papers
SBR	Studies of the Bible and Its Reception
SEÅ	*Svensk exegetisk årsbok*
SNTG	Studies in New Testament Greek
SNTSMS	Society for New Testament Studies Monograph Series
SNTW	Studies of the New Testament and Its World
SP	Sacra Pagina
ST	*Studia Theologica*
SBT	Studies in Biblical Theology
StBibLit	Studies in Biblical Literature (Lang)

TJ	*Trinity Journal*
TDNT	*Theological Dictionary of the New Testament*
	Kittel, Gerhard, and Gerhard Friedrich, eds. *Theological Dictionary of the New Testament*. Translated by Geoffrey W. Bromiley. 10 vols. Grand Rapids: Eerdmans, 1964–1976.
TNTC	Tyndale New Testament Commentaries
TynBul	*Tyndale Bulletin*
WBC	Word Biblical Commentary
WTJ	*Westminster Theological Journal*
WUANT	Wissenschaftliche Untersuchungen zum Alten und Neuen Testament
WUNT	Wissenschaftliche Untersuchungen zum Neuen Testament
WW	*Word and World*
ZNW	*Zeitschrift für die neutestamentliche Wissenschaft und die Kunde der älteren Kirche*

Chapter 1: **Introduction**

1.0 Problem and Purpose

Who is God? The Bible may be read as one or several accounts of experiences of an acting God, a God whose agency brings God into contact with humanity and constitutes a history of God's saving works. Regardless of whether one conceives of the Bible as presenting several, multifaceted images of God, or one unified image, each book of the Bible adds to what has become the canonical witness to God in the church.[1] To explore the Bible's discourse(s) of God is, therefore, to enter into dialogue with texts that still inform people's understanding of God today. At a fundamental level, this is what the following study aims to do in looking at the characterization of God in The Acts of the Apostles.

The Acts of the Apostles is the only book "in the New Testament to *narrativize* how the God of Israel becomes the God of all."[2] It thus offers a valuable foundation for studying one of the New Testament's presentations of God.[3] Acts reveals a God at work. Indeed, as we shall see, God's actions are of such central importance to this book that a more fitting name might have been "The Acts of God."[4] In Acts, God is presented as the agent of Jesus's resurrection (e.g., Acts 2:24; 3:15; 4:10; 5:30; 10:40; 13:30, 37; 17:31),[5] as being behind the promises to Israel and the early church (e.g., 1:4–5;

---

1. I try, as far as possible, to avoid using personal pronouns for God. On occasion, however, the literary flow of an argument has resulted in my following the biblical tradition and using masculine pronouns. I do so, however, with caution; well aware that most theological conceptions of God cannot and should not be constrained by or limited to gendered language.

2. Marguerat, *First Christian Historian*, 36–37 (emphasis original). Cf. François Bovon, "Le Dieu," 296. In citing these words, I do not wish to imply Jewish theology does not suggest that even if God is the god of Israel, God is not also god of the world. Acts does, however, narrativize a movement uparallelled in Israel's Scriptures, through which Israel's God moves beyond the borders of Israel to both Jews and gentiles.

3. "The New Testament" is obviously an anachronistic term, but I use it here for the sake of simplicity.

4. Cf. the title of Steve Walton's article: "Acts—of God?," 291–306.

5. All biblical references from this point onwards refer to Acts, unless otherwise indicated.

2:30, 33, 39; 7:5; 13:23, 32; 26:6–7), and as a helper in the apostolic mission (e.g., 2:47; 15:7–9). God frequently becomes a starting point in the apostles' proclamation to both Jews and gentiles (2:17; 3:13; 5:29–30; 7:2–3; 10:34–36; 13:17; 14:15; 17:22–24), and is the initiator of the mission to the gentiles (Acts 10:1—11:18).[6] In short, God's past and continued works are portrayed to be of the highest significance to the activities of the followers of the Way and the spread of the gospel. At the same time, the one whom we here call "God," and who in Acts appears under the various designations of "Lord" (κύριος, δεσπότης), "God" (θεός), "highest" (ὕψιστος), and "Father" (πατήρ), frequently acts through others, and is not always easily distinguished from Jesus, who is also called "Lord" (κύριος) in Acts. In sum, it is quite clear *that* God is at work in Acts. At the same time, because God's actions are often mediated, and God and Jesus not always easily distinguished from each other, the text invites the active participation of the reader in discerning where and how God is at work.

As we shall soon see, several scholars have made a note of the centrality of God in Acts. Fewer scholars, however, have asked for a more comprehensive image of God in Acts. In fact, in *Centering on God* (1990), Robert L. Brawley asserts that a search for a so-called epitomization of God's character in Luke-Acts would be a futile venture:

> To inquire into the character of God is an effort to fix that character. But it remains elusive. For one thing, it is complex. . . . For another, with all the complexity there are gaps that render God's character indeterminate. Thus, all efforts to epitomize the character of God in Luke-Acts will be frustrated.[7]

The character of God in Acts is, as Brawley notes, indeed complex. In Acts, there is a dialectic between the "omnipresence" of God's character, whose hand may be seen behind the development of the Jesus movement, and the emergence of God's character through specific events. An investigation into the characterization and portrayal of God in Acts can therefore never hope to fully epitomize that character, but must make its investigation in the tension between the "actor behind the scenes" and the concrete actions mentioned or narrated in the story. Yet I would argue that this search nevertheless remains worthwhile: In seeking to understand how the text speaks of God lies the potential for both (re)new(ed) understanding and confrontation with our own preconceptions of whom this God is presented as.

6. It is debated whether the Ethiopian eunuch is the first gentile convert, see sec. 5.1, n. 2.

7. Brawley, *Centering on God*, 123.

Among recent scholars on Acts, Daniel L. Marguerat is one of two who have explicitly sought to examine the image of God in Acts.[8] He notes that while previous research has enumerated the characteristics given to God in the Lukan narrative, it has not paid sufficient attention to the narrative form through which the image of God is constructed.[9] The present work takes these observations as its point of departure. It aims to further the scholarly conversation on God in Acts by answering the following question: *How is God portrayed through God's actions in the Acts of the Apostles?* In answering this question, I offer a narrative-critical analysis that aims to pay attention not only to *what* is said about God in Acts, but also to the unique manner of *how* and *where* God's character is presented through God's actions, so as to bring out a portrayal of *who* this God is.

Two things in particular make the image of God in Acts distinctive: 1) the impact of Jesus's character on the characterization of God, and 2) the development of a gentile mission. As the following survey will demonstrate, previous scholarship has done much to bring God and God's actions in Acts to the fore. However, even though it is frequently noted that the God of Israel becomes the "God of all" in Acts, surprisingly little attention has been paid to the question of how Acts itself presents God through God's actions in Israel's past in comparison with how this God is depicted in Israel's present. The present study seeks to remedy this neglect.

While our main question seeks to discover how God is portrayed through God's actions in Acts, two further questions shape the focus of our investigation: 1) *In what ways do the actions and characterization of God in the story-time relate to the actions of God spoken of in Jesus's life and ministry and Israel's more distant past?* and 2) *How does Jesus's ascension into heaven impact the characterization of God?* Through its analyses of the characterization of God through God's actions, this book demonstrates how the answers to these questions are key to the distinctive portrayal of God in Acts. We will return to these questions towards the end of this chapter. First, however, we will situate the study in relationship to previous research on God in Acts.

1.1 Research History

The present study stands in a tradition of New Testament research focusing on God. In the last four decades, a number of articles and monographs have

---

8. Marguerat, *First Christian Historian*, 85–108. The other one to examine the image of God in Acts is Ling Cheng. See Cheng, *Characterisation of God*. Her study will be addressed as part of research history below, and Marguerat's will be treated in sec. 2.1.1.

9. Marguerat, *First Christian Historian*, 85–86.

responded to Nils Alstrup Dahl's famous claim that God is the neglected factor in New Testament theology.[10] Upon analyzing the situation, Dahl suggested that there are three main reasons why "it is hard to find any comprehensive or penetrating study"[11] on this theme: a dominating Christocentric perspective on the New Testament, the existence of few thematic formulations about God in the New Testament, and the fact that God is only referred to "in contexts that deal with some other theme."[12] Scholars who seek to write about New Testament theo-logy today still face these challenges.[13] However, Dahl's original claim that God is neglected in New Testament theology no longer rings true.[14] In the years following the publication of Dahl's article, a number of scholars have sought to redress the situation and recover "God" as a central topic in New Testament research.[15] The result has been a growing appreciation of the importance of the discourse(s) on God in the New Testament writings, and a demonstration of the value of returning to the question of "Who is the God of the New Testament?" in order to communicate the foundation and initiative on which the gospel message rests. When the present study makes "God" its object of study, it therefore does so as one among several studies that have responded to Dahl's claim.

While interest in God in New Testament studies in general, and Lukan scholarship in particular, is surging, the latter has generally focused on God's plan and purpose in history, or described how and how frequently God acts. Additionally, a few studies have looked at some of the distinctive features of God's portrayal in Acts, using different foci and methods. Among these, Ling Cheng's study, *The Characterisation of God in Acts* (2011), resembles the present project in terms of focus and aim. There are nevertheless also significant differences between the two studies, which we will return to below. So far, however, Lukan scholarship lacks a larger investigation into how God is characterized *through God's actions* in the narrative of Acts. The current book aims to fill that gap.

---

10. Cf. the title of Dahl's article, "The Neglected Factor in New Testament Theology," 153–63. Originally published under the same title in *Reflections* 73.1 (1975) 5–8.

11. Dahl, "Neglected Factor," 154.

12. Dahl, "Neglected Factor," 156.

13. Theo-logy is here simply used about *what is said about God*.

14. When the back cover of *The Unrelenting God*, the festschrift to Beverley R. Gaventa, asks if God is still the neglected factor in NT theology, this seems to be a rhetorical question expecting a negative answer. See Downs and Skinner, *Unrelenting God*.

15. Scholars who explicitly take up Dahl's challenge include, e.g., Donahue, "Neglected Factor," 563–94; Thompson, *God of the Gospel of John*; Smith, "Theology of the Gospel of Mark"; Chen, *God as Father*; Hurtado, *God in New Testament Theology*; Carter, *God in the New Testament*.

A survey of central aspects in the research history on God in Acts will bring more clearly into view how this book joins the conversation of previous studies. Moreover, this survey will pave the way for the investigation at hand by alerting us to questions and observations that are of significance to the study of the characterization of God in Acts. We will first consider some scholars who have put God and God's actions on the agenda in Lukan scholarship in the years after Dahl's claim. We will then look at studies concerning the interrelated themes of God's salvation history, plan, purpose, and providence. Finally, we will turn to scholarship that has shed light on some distinctive aspects of God's character in Acts.

1.1.1 From Neglected Factor to Central, Acting Character

A number of scholars have put God in Acts on the agenda. Only six years after Dahl made the perceptive observation about the lack of scholarship on God in the New Testament, François Bovon's "Le Dieu de Luc"[16] addressed some themes that are still important in scholarship on God in Luke-Acts today. Among these, we may particularly note Bovon's stress on how God's message is transmitted through intermediaries, and the function of Jesus as the one through whom God can be known. Furthermore, Bovon notes that Acts depicts a "universal explosion" of the mission to the gentiles in a narrative manner.[17] This focus on Acts as a narrative has, as we have already noted, shaped the present project. More importantly, that God is known through Jesus also suggests that Jesus's character greatly impacts *how* God is known. As we shall see later, our study identifies a moment in time which is crucial to the way God is portrayed in Acts: The ascension of Jesus. As a result of the ascension, God's characteristics come to characterize Jesus more and more. It is the central contribution and claim of this book that this also influences the way *God* is presented.

A few years after Bovon, in three papers presented at the Society of Biblical Literature, Robert L. Mowery brought God's actions to the fore by looking at different ways in which God's agency is expressed in Acts. In his first paper, "Direct Statements Concerning God's Activity in Luke-Acts," he offers an account of the contexts in which God's activity is directly mentioned in connection with verbs and participles.[18] While Mowery notes that some of these statements are of a more timeless character,[19] most of what is said about God

---

16. Bovon, "Le Dieu," 296.
17. In the original: "explosion universaliste," see Bovon, "Le Dieu," 296.
18. Mowery, "Direct Statements," 196–211.
19. See Acts 7:48; 17:24; 7:49; 17:25a; 17:27, 29, cf. Mowery, "Direct Statements," 210.

is in fact related to God's actions in events,[20] both ones that take place in and before the story-time of Acts' narrative. Significantly, Mowery remarks that sometimes the speeches in Acts directly name God as the agent of an event, whereas the *narration* of the same incident does not necessarily do so.[21] The speech thus interprets the event. In this way, Mowery points to the intrinsic relationship between the different ways, both directly and indirectly, in which God and God's actions are presented.

In his second paper, "The Divine Hand and the Divine Plan in the Lukan Passion," Mowery looks at God's role in Jesus's passion.[22] In the part of this paper devoted to Acts alone, Mowery observes that Jesus's passion was both a part of God's plan, and that God in fact fulfilled this plan through Jesus's opponents.[23] In his third paper, Mowery provides an overview of where the designations "Lord," "God," and "Father" occur in Luke-Acts and how these designations are used as subjects of clauses.[24] In line with the observations from his first two papers, he notes that when God appears—whether it is with the designation "Lord," "God," or "Father"—it is as the subject of an action. In sum, Mowery's observations reveal that the presence of God in Acts is closely related to God's actions.

While Acts does contain some of what Dahl might have considered "thematic formulations" about God (cf. e.g., 7:48; 10:34; 17:24–29),[25] God is mainly presented through God's agency in events, which is pointed to by characters in their speeches. These events—whether they take place in the story-time of Acts' narrative, before its beginning, or are foreseen to come to pass after it—are therefore key to anyone who wants to investigate how God is presented in Acts. We may also note this means that God is characterized in much the same way as other characters in Greco-Roman literature who are also presented through actions.[26]

In *Centering on God*, Robert L. Brawley approaches Luke-Acts as a narrative with literary qualities. In doing so, he employs theory from various literary critics in demonstrating that God in Acts may be studied as a character. Building on Ian Watt's assertion that "character can be individualized only if set in a particular time and place,"[27] Brawley establishes God as

---

20. Mowery, "Direct Statements," 211.
21. Mowery, "Direct Statements," 202–3.
22. Mowery, "Divine Hand," 558–75.
23. Mowery, "Divine Hand," 569.
24. Mowery, "Lord, God, and Father," 82–101.
25. Mowery, "Direct Statements," 210.
26. Thompson, *Keeping the Church in its Place*, 18.
27. Brawley, *Centering on God*, 110; quoting Watt, "Realism and the Novel," 68.

a character by locating God in the place Acts calls "heaven," and points to the narrative to show that God has "a past, present, and future" and is thus located in time.[28] Using a term from Roland Barthes and Jonathan Culler, Brawley also notes that God's character is identifiable by the reader, who is able to construct this character on the basis of the information—so-called "semes"—connected to God's different names in the text.[29] Finally, it should be noted that Brawley's study, unsurprisingly, yields the conclusion that Luke-Acts is a theocentric work.

In establishing God as a character, *Centering on God* offers an important stepping stone for this study. The ontological existence of *God* arguably cannot be proven and therefore cannot be studied, but the way "God" is presented in a text can. The literary category "character" and how it is constructed therefore open up ways of seeing how Acts invites an understanding of God. There are, however, certain challenges related to treating God as a character, and we will return to these in the chapter on method (ch. 2).

Centering on God is not the only work to assert God's centrality. Just as the title of Brawley's book reveals where his conclusion is headed, so does the name of Steve Walton's article, "The Acts—of God? What is the 'Acts of the Apostles' all about?" Walton's survey shows that God is the subject of different clauses, is connected to words implying divine action, is the center of attention in the speeches, and the key agent at other key points in the narrative. As the title of his article indicates, Walton concludes that "God is the key actor in Acts."[30] Walton's valuable insights resemble those presented by Robert Mowery. Thus, Walton's contribution solidifies the observation that God and God's actions are of central importance to the Acts of the Apostles. Walton's observations, however, have met with objections from Richard A. Burridge, who distinguishes between the speeches in Acts and the rest of the narrative: He argues that while God may be an important subject in the speeches, "this does not mean that God is the subject of the book itself."[31] Thus for Burridge, in contrast to Walton, the conclusion is that "Luke, as author, does *not* depict God doing things as the 'key actor'; rather, he depicts his key actors, namely Peter, Stephen, Paul and the other disciples, *interpreting* what is happening as the activity of God."[32] I would question, however, whether this distinction between the narrator's presentation of events as the activity of God, and the key actors' presentation of events as the activity of

---

28. Brawley, *Centering on God*, 110.
29. Brawley, *Centering on God*, 111.
30. Walton, "Acts—of God?," 303.
31. Burridge, "Genre of Acts," 15.
32. Burridge, "Genre of Acts," 15.

God, is a meaningful one to the reader, given that both represent the perspective of the implied author.[33] In the present study, I find it more fruitful to distinguish between what is said by the key actors and their opponents than between the key actors and the narrator.

In sum, the studies of the abovementioned scholars reveal God's centrality in Acts. In this way, they have moved away from what Dahl in his day perceived of as a dominating Christocentric perspective on the New Testament. Just as importantly, while Mowery does find a few thematic formulations about God, he and the other scholars reveal that God appears in Acts primarily through God's actions, as these are recounted both as part of the narrative that takes place in Acts (the "narrative present" or "story-time") and in the history of Israel that Acts refers to. These observations therefore strengthen my thesis question that God's portrayal must primarily be sought through God's characterization through actions. That God in Acts may, in fact, be approached as a character is something that Brawley's work confirms, and is a matter to which we will return to in our chapter on method.

The above scholars have treated the topic of "God" and "God's actions" in Acts more broadly. However, God's actions have also been treated as part of the broader theme of salvation history, to which such concepts as God's plan, purpose and providence belong. To this we now turn.

1.1.2 Salvation History: God's Plan, Purpose, and Providence

Ever since the publication of Hans Conzelmann's *Die Mitte der Zeit* (1954), "salvation history" has been recognized as a major theme in Luke-Acts. Positing that Luke-Acts was written in response to the problem caused by the delay of the parousia, Conzelmann divides salvation history into three stages: The period of Israel, the period of Jesus's ministry, and the period after the ascension, with the parousia representing the fulfillment of salvation history.[34] These stages are held together by God's plan.[35] I. Howard Marshall, however, criticizes Conzelmann for separating Jesus's ministry from the time of the church, arguing that both belong to the time of fulfillment.[36] In

---

33. In terms of this debate, it might be helpful to distinguish between what the narrator focuses on, and what the implied author focuses on. Burridge's words about whom are presented as key actors in Acts are true if we speak of whom the *narrator* focuses on; then, Peter, Stephen, Paul, and the other disciples easily come into view. However, the *implied author* focuses on God both through the narrator and the protagonists throughout Acts.

34. Conzelmann, *Die Mitte der Zeit*, 5–11.

35. Conzelmann, *Die Mitte der Zeit*, 139–57.

36. Marshall, *Luke*, 120–21.

Marshall's scheme, there are consequently two epochs in salvation history rather than three, with the era of salvation extending from the time of Jesus's ministry and onwards.[37] In thus emphasizing salvation history as a theme, Conzelmann and Marshall simultaneously put God as savior on the agenda.[38] Moreover, these scholars' distinction between past and present pave the way for the question this study asks, about how the actions and characterization of God in the story-time relate to the actions of God spoken of in Jesus's life and ministry and Israel's more distant past.

Closely related to salvation history is the theme of God's plan or purpose. Keeping in mind that the present study seeks to investigate how God is portrayed through actions, it is important to note that scholarship over the last four decades has emphasized that *God's actions point towards God's plan and purpose*. In other words, it has been the *functions* of these actions as the goal and driving force behind the events narrated in Luke-Acts that have received attention. The terms "plan" and "purpose" have been used more or less interchangeably by scholars, and are rarely explicated beyond the fact that they point towards God's salvific intentions. This plan and purpose have constituted a framework within which God's actions have been understood: When God acts, it is to direct the fulfillment of this plan and purpose.

The theme of God's plan/purpose/providence has been used and approached in different ways by different scholars. In his seminal article, "The Divine Dei in Luke-Acts" (1984), Charles Cosgrove sets out to discuss the theme of divine providence in its relation to the uses of δεῖ ("it is necessary") in Luke-Acts. He criticizes previous approaches to this theme which from the outset assume that the Lukan understanding of providence must be classified as either "Jewish" or "Hellenistic." Instead, he calls attention to the texts' own use of δεῖ. As he himself pursues this method, Cosgrove discovers that even though δεῖ cannot be classified as a "*terminus technicus* for divine necessity,"[39] there is good reason to understand it as a "divine must" and part of the Lukan vocabulary of divine providence. Taking a step further and looking at the wider vocabulary of divine providence in Luke-Acts, Cosgrove notes that the Lukan assumption that "God planned events long ago and brings them to pass without fail"[40] is not worked out in a conceptually coherent manner in Luke-Acts. Instead, the notion of providence has different functions in the story: As divine attestation or authentication of events (Acts 2:23–24; 3:18;

---

37. Marshall, *Luke*, 119–21.

38. Thus Conzelmann (*Die Mitte der Zeit*, 161): "Der Heilsplan ist ausschließlich Gottes Plan"; Marshall (*Historian and Theologian*, 103): "Luke views God the Father as the ultimate source of salvation."

39. Cosgrove, "Divine Dei," 189.

40. Cosgrove, "Divine Dei," 185.

7:52; 10:41–42); as encouragement, because God will intervene to ensure the fulfillment of God's plan (Acts 4:28); and as divine command or imperative (20:28; 22:10).[41] These discoveries pave the way for the observations which make up the final part of Cosgrove's conclusion. Here he argues that fulfillment of God's plan is guaranteed by God through God's continuous interventions. These interventions reveal that history lies open with the possibility of change.[42] Cosgrove further highlights history as the place where God's saving miracles take place and reverse human conditions.[43]

Cosgrove's article offers insights of importance for the present study. First of all, the observation that God's actions are placed within the framework of "God's plan" is significant. God's plan, within which history is seen to unfold according to God's will and through God's continuous interventions, is the wider framework within which God's actions take place and come to fruition. When God intervenes, it is to ensure the fulfillment of God's plan. In this way, history becomes the arena of God's saving actions, which bind together the story of Jesus and the early church. When God's actions are analyzed in the present study, they must therefore be seen as part of the broader presentation of God in Acts, which includes the language of divine providence.

Secondly, Cosgrove demonstrates that God's actions are interrelated with characters' actions. Actors of significance, such as Jesus (in Luke) and Paul (in Acts) follow the divine imperative and summons to obedience. Their actions thus correlate with God's plan and follow from God's initiative as it is revealed through Scripture,[44] disclosed through visions, etc. Accordingly, God's actions impact the plot; they move along events and create or influence the storyline. This is an important function of God's actions in Acts.

The plan and purpose of God are also emphasized as a narrative theme by a number of scholars. The works of Robert C. Tannehill, Joel B. Green, and Beverly R. Gaventa are illustrative: Robert C. Tannehill's *The Narrative Unity of Luke-Acts* (1986, 1990) broke new ground in producing the first larger work to analyze Luke-Acts by using the tools of narrative criticism. The "narrative unity" asserted by Tannehill is to be found in the theme of God's salvific purpose: "Luke-Acts is a unified narrative because the chief human characters (John the Baptist, Jesus, the apostles, Paul) share in a mission which expresses a single controlling purpose—the purpose of

---

41. Cosgrove also mentions a couple of examples with an "apocalyptic usage" of the vocabulary of divine providence (Acts 1:7 and 17:31). See Cosgrove, "Divine Dei," 185.
42. Cosgrove, "Divine Dei," 184.
43. Cosgrove, "Divine Dei," 190.
44. Cosgrove, "Divine Dei," 174–76.

God."⁴⁵ Or, in other words: "It is finally the plan or purpose of God which gives shape and meaning to the story of Jesus and his witnesses."⁴⁶ This observation guides Tannehill's reading of Luke-Acts. Here he discovers a God of surprises, who overrules human purpose, and works through ironic reversals of events and fortunes in service of God's purpose.⁴⁷ In its fullness, this purpose includes salvation for the entire world, and it is in light of this that the gentile mission must be understood.⁴⁸

Because Tannehill considers God's purpose a unifying theme that binds together Luke-Acts, God becomes a central agent in the narrative. Moreover, because Tannehill understands characters in terms of role, God becomes a character insofar as God acts towards God's purpose.⁴⁹ God may be a character hidden from human view,⁵⁰ but God's presence, Tannehill notes, is signalled through "angels, visions, messages from the Spirit, and so forth."⁵¹ It follows from Tannehill's view of characters, therefore, that God's actions are what constitute God's character.

Tannehill states that the speeches in Acts in particular affirm God's activity in the story of Jesus.⁵² This observation is shared by Joel B. Green. In "Salvation to the End of the Earth: God as the Savior in the Acts of the Apostles" (1998), Green notes two things in particular that will remain with us throughout our study of Acts. First, Green explicates how God's salvific purpose is acted out through Jesus. In this sense, Luke's soteriology is Christocentric. Yet because the story of Jesus is only one part of the greater purpose and history of God with God's people, salvation is theocentric at its heart and origin; it is *God's* salvific purpose that is acted out through Jesus.⁵³ Secondly, and closely related, is Green's observation that the speeches in Acts locate the story of Jesus within the wider story of God's redemptive purposes with Israel, and further inscribe the story of the church within the framework of the story of Jesus.⁵⁴ In contrast to Cosgrove, whose main focus on the Lukan use of Scripture is on its revelation of the divine will and imperative, Green

---

45. Tannehill, *Narrative Unity of Luke-Acts*, 1:xiii; Green, "'God My Savior,'" 26; Gaventa, *Acts*, 31.

46. Tannehill, *Narrative Unity of Luke-Acts*, 1:29.

47. E.g., Tannehill, *Narrative Unity of Luke-Acts*, 1:30–31, 194, 261, 283, 288; Tannehill, *Narrative Unity of Luke-Acts*, 2:3, 77.

48. Tannehill, *Narrative Unity of Luke-Acts*, 2:257. See also Gaventa, *Acts*, 219.

49. Tannehill, *Narrative Unity of Luke-Acts*, 1:1.

50. Tannehill, *Narrative Unity of Luke-Acts*, 1:29.

51. Tannehill, *Narrative Unity of Luke-Acts*, 2:72.

52. Tannehill, *Narrative Unity of Luke-Acts*, 2:72.

53. Green, "Salvation," 97–98.

54. Green, "Salvation," 102.

emphasizes the Lukan use of the Septuagint as a means of creating narrative continuity between the history of Israel and the story of Luke-Acts.[55] The story of Israel, the story of Jesus, and the story of the early church are thus closely connected, and point toward the same common purpose of God's. Even Scripture, however, is subordinated to God's redemptive purpose and gains its authority from being aligned with it.[56]

Beverly R. Gaventa, unlike Tannehill and Green, prefers "God's plan" to "God's purpose." It is, however, clear that Gaventa's focus on God's plan as constitutive for the story in Acts is similar to these other two scholars' view of God's purpose:

> "Plan of God" refers to God as the one whose intention and oversight governs the events that unfold, encompassing both the events from Jesus' own life and the way in which the witness moves throughout the cities of the Mediterranean world, stretching in Acts from the Jerusalem ascension of Jesus to the testimony of Paul in Rome (e.g., 2:23; 4:28; 5:38; 20:27).[57]

Like Tannehill and Green, Gaventa views God's actions in and for the church as part of God's plan and activity.[58] This is also true of God's actions in the crucifixion: Resembling Tannehill, who sees a God of irony at work in Jesus's death[59] because the purposes of those who executed him are overturned, Gaventa maintains the culpability of those who killed Jesus and the fact that the crucifixion was part of God's plan.[60] In this way, Tannehill and Gaventa's observations about God's plan move to include not only those who willingly follow God's purpose, like Jesus and Paul, but the actions of those who attempt to thwart it. In this perspective, God's own actions are not the only ones to advance God's plan.

Another work that merits attention is John T. Squires's reworked doctoral dissertation, *The Plan of God in Luke-Acts* (1993). Here Squires elucidates the theme of God's plan in Luke-Acts through comparative analysis with Hellenistic histories of the time. Squires's analysis is based on an understanding of Luke-Acts as historiography. His central thesis is that "The plan of God is a distinctively Lukan theme which undergirds the whole of Luke-Acts."[61] According to Squires, God's plan in Luke-Acts comes to

---

55. Green, *Gospel of Luke*, 52.
56. Green, "'God My Savior,'" 28.
57. Gaventa, *Acts*, 31.
58. Gaventa, *Acts*, 39.
59. Tannehill, *Narrative Unity of Luke-Acts*, 1:283.
60. Gaventa, *Acts*, 82.
61. Squires, *Plan of God*, 1.

expression in five different ways, or "strands." He names these by using five different categories from Acts' contemporary context: Providence, portents and signs, epiphanies, prophecy, and fate. These terms are used to structure Squires's analysis of the various strands of God's plan in Luke-Acts, and to compare these to expressions of divine providence in the histories of Diodorus Siculus, Dionysius of Halicarnassus, and Flavius Josephus. In short, Squires asserts that God's providence, or guiding activity, encompasses all of history, from creation until final judgment.[62] The speeches in Acts in particular locate history within the framework of God's plan.[63] He further notes that the passion of Jesus and the gentile mission are especially emphasized as part of this plan.[64] Divine providence in Luke-Acts, he argues, is apologetic in the sense that it defends the Christian understanding of the passion and gentile mission by making it clear that these key points in the history of the Jesus movement do not diverge from, but are in fact part of, God's consistent plan.[65] In this way, Squires's study seeks to locate Luke-Acts in the first century discussion on divine providence, and to uncover the understanding of providence that underlies the Lukan project.

The above scholars' understandings of God's plan or purpose as a narratively unifying theme in Luke-Acts intimately connect God's actions to God's purpose. When the present investigation focuses on God's actions, its discoveries will—at least implicitly—touch upon the question of whether the functions of all these actions are to promote this theme. Do, as Squires suggests, the various elements that express God's plan reinforce each other and locate the events they are connected to within God's plan? Or does a more multifaceted view of these strands—and the functions of God's actions—emerge from our reading? Our answer to this question is anticipated by a second observation: While the theme of God's purpose is an important element in understanding the characterization of God in Luke-Acts as, e.g., savior and master of history, the understanding of how God is portrayed becomes limited when all of God's actions are seen to point in the same direction—towards God's one and only purpose. It is this project's assertion that the portrayal of God in Acts contains a complexity which is not immediately contained by the theme

---

62. Squires, *Plan of God*, 2.
63. Squires, *Plan of God*, 189.
64. Squires, *Plan of God*, 76.
65. Squires, *Plan of God*, 76–77. Note David Peterson, who traces the pattern of fulfillment throughout Luke and Acts. He engages with Squires mainly in order to show that the apologetic dimension of the Lukan work ("to explain and defend Christianity to hellenised Christians," 103) cannot be discounted. Unlike Squires, Peterson concludes that the work's purpose is edification. See Peterson, "Motif of Fulfilment," 83–104, engaging with Squires on pages 100–104.

of "God's purpose" alone. Instead, the image of God must be sought in the dynamic interaction between God and other characters, including the interaction between God, Jesus, and the Spirit, and in the ways in which both the narrator and different characters speak of God. This dynamic complexity is something the present study aims to bring to the fore.

The above scholars also show that God's plan and purpose are not only realized by God, but also by other characters. This means that nearly every action in Acts may be understood in relation to God's purpose, and that the entire story may be read through a theocentric interpretive lens. It is, however, not possible within the scope of this investigation to analyze every action in accordance with God's purpose as an action that characterizes God. Further delimitation of what may be counted as "God's action" is necessary, and is therefore a matter I will return to in sec. 2.1.1.

Finally, of chief significance to this study is Green's observation that the speeches in Acts serve to outline and interpret history in a way that reveals both the overarching agenda of God's purpose, and also serve to insert the experiences of the Jesus believers into a larger meta-narrative in which God is the main agent. For the present inquiry, this means that an investigation into the presentation of God in Acts as a narrative not only relies on what is happening in present events in the story-time of Acts. As we shall see, the characterization of God is also part of a narrated history that spans from creation to the day of judgment. Secondly, Green observes that Scripture both reveals the purpose of God and is subordinate to this purpose. This means that it is not merely the Lukan use of Scripture that reveals God's purpose, but that Scripture's authority is evaluated against the sum of the narrative strategy of the implied author. It will therefore be necessary to ask not only what Scripture says, but who quotes Scripture, and how this lends authority to what is said about God.[66]

1.1.3 Characteristics of God

In recent years, three published studies in particular elucidate aspects of the character of God in (Luke-)Acts: Diane G. Chen's *God as Father in Luke-Acts* (2006); Ling Cheng's *The Characterisation of God in Acts: The Indirect Portrayal of an Invisible Character* (2011); and Scott Shauf's *The Divine in Acts and in Ancient Historiography* (2015).[67]

---

66. Cf. Green, "'God My Savior,'" 27.

67. Matthew L. Skinner's *Intrusive God, Disruptive Gospel* (2015) also deserves mention. In this publication, Skinner explores how God is depicted in Acts. While I do not include the book in the above survey of research history, however, it is not because

In her study, which is a revised version of her doctoral dissertation at Fuller Theological Seminary, Diane G. Chen focuses on the father image of God in Luke-Acts. Arguing that God as father has been neglected in Lukan studies and that far more attention has been paid to God as savior and Lord, Chen explores how the father metaphor in Luke-Acts may be understood on the background of Greco-Roman thought, the Old Testament, and Second Temple Judaism. Her conclusion is summarized as follows:

> The father metaphor brings to the foreground the authority, faithfulness, mercy, and tenacious love of God. As Father, God rises above the best of human fathers and the most powerful of Roman *Patres Patriae*. Based on these fatherly characteristics of God that Luke has presented to us, we further surmise that Luke holds out at the end of Acts the hope that all Israel will yet be saved. Indeed, in Luke-Acts there is no other metaphor for God that can better convey the persistence and attentiveness in God's dealings with those whom he loves than the image of God as Father.[68]

Chen's study is helpful in elucidating characteristics associated with the father image in the ancient world, but her thesis is more convincing in terms of Luke than it is of Acts. In Acts, God is mentioned as father only thrice, each time by (1:4, 7) or in relation to (2:33) Jesus. To be fair, in her treatment of the OT material,[69] Chen herself admits that Luke "hardly makes any direct reference to the above materials that explicitly identify YHWH as the Father of Israel in the Old Testament,"[70] but argues that the way Luke talks about God nevertheless fits with this picture of God as father presented in the Old Testament.[71] I do not dispute that Chen's observations may cohere with a picture of God as father, and that there are even elements in Acts that are best understood in light of this metaphor for God. I do, however, question the weight this metaphor is given when Acts rarely uses familial language for God, Israel, or the gentiles. The present study will not neglect to look at how God is characterized as father in Acts. It will do so by looking more closely at which of God's actions are related to the use of this designation, and at how

---

it does not provide any useful insights (it does, and these will be engaged with later!), but because it does not fit comfortably into the genre of *research* history. Skinner readily admits that "This book is different from what I usually write. . . . I am more interested in exploring the story Acts tells to us today and how that story prompts us to consider who God is and how God operates" (Skinner, *Intrusive God*, viii).

68. Chen, *God as Father*, 240–41.
69. "The Old Testament" (OT) is the term used by Chen.
70. Chen, *God as Father*, 148.
71. Chen, *God as Father*, 148.

this relates to what Chen appears to consider as familial language throughout the narrative (2:33; 7:34–35; 13:17–19).

Ling Cheng's study, *The Characterisation of God in Acts: The Indirect Portrayal of an Invisible Character* (2011), employs narrative criticism in order to look at how God is characterized through other characters and in relation to the plot in Acts. Cheng's project is, unmistakably, in many ways similar to the present one, but I should make clear that the latter has been developed independently of the former.[72] In her conclusion, Cheng summarizes how God is portrayed in the narrative. In doing so, she emphasizes traditional themes to be found in the study of God in Acts, i.e., God as the ruler and director of salvation history, who as faithful and omnipotent savior works to realize God's universal promise of salvation to all.[73] God is, moreover, portrayed as an "invisible-but-perceivable character"[74] who acts from "backstage" through others. Importantly, Cheng also suggests that in Acts, the image of God changes and is transformed through the fulfillment of God's promise of salvation in Jesus.[75]

One of the strengths of Cheng's study is the comprehensiveness with which she approaches the portrayal of God. In looking at how God is characterized through divine, major, and minor characters, and by also reviewing God's role in the plot, hardly any stone is left unturned. This results in a thorough overview of just how significant God's character is in Acts. However, the comprehensiveness of Cheng's study comes at a cost: Important discussions in research on Acts are not entered, significant insights are occasionally left undeveloped, and sometimes Cheng's Christian background produces theological statements that cannot be deduced from Acts alone. Consequently, Cheng writes about Paul's "conversion" without problematizing the concept,[76] elaborates on Peter's characterization of God without suggesting why the reader should consider his words reliable or not,[77] makes the heavily theologically loaded statement that "Jesus himself

---

72. I did not learn of Cheng's study until the first draft of my dissertation was being completed in March 2017. My own project has therefore been shaped independently from and without knowledge of Cheng's study.

73. Cheng (*Characterisation of God*), highlights such aspects as God as the "supreme and sovereign Lord of salvation" (225); "God's determined providence of universal salvation and his authoritative faithfulness in fulfilling his promise of salvation" (225); God as "super director" of other characters and incidents in Acts, but no puppeteer (226–28); God as "sovereign and omnipotent Savior of all" (226); "Lord God who is the gracious and faithful ruler of the heavenly kingdom" (226).

74. Cheng, *Characterisation of God*, 227.

75. Cheng, *Characterisation of God*, 228.

76. Cheng, *Characterisation of God*, 22.

77. Cheng, *Characterisation of God*, 44–92.

becomes the Word of God,"[78] and infers from Jesus's being handed over according to God's plan and foreknowledge in 2:23 that the earthly Jesus "submits himself fully to God's will."[79] Moreover, in the conclusion referred to above, Cheng suggests that the image of God in Acts is transformed through the realization of God's promise of salvation in Jesus. But although Cheng does address Jesus as the realization of this promise throughout her study, she does not explicitly elaborate on how the image of God is transformed through it.[80] The result is that Acts is read in a manner which points to God's activity and elucidates the manner in which God is characterized, but which does not reflect any struggle with what is potentially ambiguous or tension-filled within Acts' narrative. Nor is it always apparent, in spite of the fact that Cheng's study is well-researched, what is at stake in scholarly discussions of important passages in Acts.

Cheng's study will be a conversation partner throughout this book. The present project, however, differs from hers in three significant ways: First, whereas Cheng aims to read Acts through a more strictly text-centered approach in which "one constructs the narrative world without regard to its historical world,"[81] the present study takes the cultural encyclopedia of the reader into account (see ch. 2). Secondly, the present study takes God's *actions* as its main point of departure for looking at the characterization of God. This does not mean that I disregard the multiple perspectives from which God is presented by different characters in the narrative, but it is God's actions rather than their points of view which is the starting point. Finally, the present investigation will look more closely at how the image of God is maintained or differs from the way God is presented in Israel's past and in the story-time of Acts. This makes the present study's contribution more dynamic in terms of how it explicates the portrayal of God in this narrative.

Shauf's book, *The Divine in Acts and in Ancient Historiography*, looks at how Acts understands and portrays divine involvement in comparison

---

78. Cheng, *Characterisation of God*, 41.

79. Cheng, *Characterisation of God*, 34.

80. Against Cheng, I would argue that it is difficult to suggest how the image of God is transformed when the narrative is read without regards to its "historical world," as Cheng purports to do (see Cheng, *Characterisation of God*, 3).

81. Cheng, *Characterisation of God*, 3. Cheng does, however, stray from this method on occasion. Note, e.g., that she speaks of the OT concept of God (79), and mentions the belief of God as creator as a thought which "pervades Judaism and permeates every single Jew" (195). One may also ask what kind of narrative reading would allow the reader to speak of "God's inner world," even when this is delineated "as expressed in the narrative world" (Cheng, *Characterisation of God*, 20, 41, 198, 225)

with other ancient historiographical works.[82] This is an impressive survey, which makes comparisons with Greco-Roman, biblical, Jewish, and Hellenistic Jewish historiographies. Shauf essentially holds that Acts follows Jewish historiography in its portrayal of the divine,[83] but that the divine is depicted in more ways than in both Jewish and Greco-Roman historiography.[84] In fact, Acts shows "an intensity of divine presence and action unparalleled in its intense focus on such a small group of people."[85] In terms of genre, Shauf argues that Acts differs from Greco-Roman historiography in its focus on divine rather than human causation (but he notes that human motives also play a part),[86] presents simple rather than complex sequences, pays little attention to human motives, and does not offer critical reflection upon the events that are narrated.[87]

Shauf's observations are particularly important in terms of the question of genre, and we will return to these in sec. 2.1.4. Here, however, I wish to make a note of a few of his observations that are of particular importance to the present study: First of all, Shauf's investigation into divine involvement reveals that Acts' portrayal of the divine builds on a distinctively Jewish portrayal of the divine established early on in the Gospel of Luke.[88] The Gospel establishes this portrayal "through references to the religious heritage of Israel, distinctively Jewish divine figures and expressions, and religious institutions specific to Judaism."[89] This portrayal is then developed in Acts: "Luke couples a firm sense of the particularity of God—God as the God of Israel—with an expanding sense of divine partiality. God is still partial to his people, but inclusion in the people of God is now open to all."[90] In short, Shauf's study significantly points to the portrayal of a particular god, the God of Israel, who is impartial in the sense of a developing partiality that comes to include gentiles.[91] This is a useful nuance which conditions in what ways we can speak of God as "universal" or "impartial" in Acts. Even more importantly, Shauf's observation puts words to how Acts holds in balance

---

82. Shauf, *Divine in Acts*, 1.
83. Shauf, *Divine in Acts*, 262–63.
84. Shauf, *Divine in Acts*, 264.
85. Shauf, *Divine in Acts*, 264.
86. Shauf, *Divine in Acts*, 280. Shauf notes that human motives are particularly important in Acts 15 and 21–28.
87. Shauf, *Divine in Acts*, 267–82.
88. Shauf, *Divine in Acts*, 181–85.
89. Shauf, *Divine in Acts*, 183.
90. Shauf, *Divine in Acts*, 264.
91. Shauf, *Divine in Acts*, 197, cf. 202: "Acts displays divine impartiality in the form of an expanding partiality tied to a strong particularity."

the tension between continuity and development in how God is depicted in Israel's past and in the story-time of Acts. This relationship between how Acts portrays God in the past and in the narrative present is, as we have noted, of central interest to our study.

1.2 The Way Forward

It seems only fitting that the way forward is pointed out in conversation with some of the challenges Dahl once posited to a study of "God" in the New Testament. In applying Dahl's insights to Acts, we note that with a few exceptions, Acts' narrative contains few thematic formulations, or "direct statements," about God. Moreover, God is only referred to in contexts dealing with some other theme. But this is the case precisely because God is not presented as a "dogma"; rather, God is woven into the story as a character.[92] As we saw above, the main way through which God is characterized in Acts is through God's actions. Because the God in Acts has no physical form and rarely speaks, it is these actions as they are narrated either by the narrator or referred to by the story's characters which become the primary means of describing God's character.[93] That is why these actions will be the focus of this study in approaching the characterization of God.

The narrative form of Acts means that God's actions are always contextualized, i.e., they always relate to someone or something. In other words, when we look at how God is characterized, this characterization happens within the dynamics of a narrative where points of view, plot, settings, other characters, etc., fundamentally shape our interpretation of how God is presented. As God frequently acts through others in Acts, the present study will have to clarify on what terms it considers something an action of *God's*. It is only when we have looked at "how" the characterization of God happens that we can begin to speak of the nature of God's character in Acts, i.e., "who" God is characterized as. The former is a necessary means to the latter, but it is the latter which shapes the primary focus of this investigation. While I will sometimes use "portrayal" and "presentation" synonymously with "characterization," I also use portrayal in a summative

---

92. In this way, the present study overlaps somewhat with those versions of narrative theology which hold that God must always be understood on the basis of the stories of which God is a part. See, e.g., Navone, "'Seeing God,'" 205–8.

93. This is perhaps not so strange, given that Acts was written in antiquity: "for ancient characterization in general it certainly seems one's character (ēthos) is revealed through one's action" (Burnett, "Characterization," 11). Burnett references Russell, "On Reading Plutarch's Lives," 144; Stanton, *Jesus of Nazareth*, 122; Köster, "φύσις, φυσικός, φυσικῶς," 253; Robbins, *Jesus the Teacher*, 114.

sense about *whom* God is presented as. The portrayal of God is then meant as the *sum* of the characterization of God through actions in Acts that coheres with the implied author's point of view.

If we take a step back and look at the entire discourse of God in Acts, then on the one hand, we see what we have observed in our research history survey, namely that the portrayal of God in Acts emerges from specific actions in the time of the story: God acts through visions, angelophanies, christophanies, theophanies, the Spirit, signs, wonders,[94] and in response to prayer. Thus, God is, both explicitly and implicitly, part of the unfolding of most of the narrative's events. In short, God becomes an actor behind the scenes, whose presence may be discerned behind the developing mission and the growing number of believers.[95] At the same time, the speeches in Acts draw up a greater narrative of God's actions that extends beyond the time of the story, reaching as far back as creation (cf. 4:24; 7:50; 14:15; 17:24–26), and as far into the future as the time of judgment (cf. 2:21–22; 17:31). Together, God's actions in the past, present, and future of the story-time make up the greater part of the discourse of God in Acts.

On the other hand, the discourse of God in Acts consists of more than God's actions. The present study therefore cannot hope to say all there is to say about God's character in Acts. In focusing on God's actions, we are primarily focusing on how God is characterized as an agent. However, there are a number of elements which influence the ways in which the reader comes to perceive of God in Acts which are not based on actions. For instance, it is important to acknowledge that God in Acts is not only an acting subject, but an *object*—of prayer (e.g., 1:24; 4:24–30; 6:6; 8:15–24; 9:11, 40; 10:2–4, 9, 30–31; 11:5; 12:5, 12),[96] lies (5:4, cf. 8:21), and praise (2:47; 3:8–9; 4:21; 11:18;

---

94. I include exorcisms and resurrection miracles here with wonders.

95. God as an "actor behind the scenes" or an absent character is a common way of presenting God's character in biblical literature. See, e.g., some of the introductory observations in Freedman, *God as an Absent Character*, 1–3.

96. Some argue that the Lord in 1:24 should be understood as Jesus. See e.g., Talbert, *Reading Acts*, 21. Talbert's argument is based on the observations that the Lukan Jesus is the one to choose the disciples; prayer to Jesus does not seem to be outside the horizon of Acts (see 7:59), and the Lukan Jesus is—similarly to the God of Israel in Scripture—also a knower of human hearts. I would also add that Talbert's argument has some literary merit, seeing as the only "Lord" mentioned thus far in Acts is Jesus. However, although Talbert offers some valid arguments, I disagree with some of his claims. While it is true that the Lukan Jesus chooses the disciples, he does so only after a night of prayer (Luke 6:12), which makes it natural to presume that the disciples in Acts are following Jesus's example of praying to God. Moreover, although prayer to Jesus does take place within Acts (cf. 7:59), and Jesus is even worshipped after the ascension in Luke (24:52), it seems strange that if the first prayer in Acts is directed to Jesus, Jesus is not specifically mentioned if this is the reading that the implied

21:20). By presenting God as the object of these actions, the implied author indicates how the characters perceive of God, which in turn influences the way in which the reader perceives of God's character.

In addition to God's actions, a number of phrases throughout Acts open up the "associative field" connected to God. Throughout the story we find a number of phrases associated with designations for God, but which do not always have God as their referent. These phrases include, but are not limited to, God's kingdom (ἡ βασιλεία τοῦ θεοῦ, 1:3, 6; 8:12; 14:22; 19:8; 20:25; 28:23, 31), God's great works (τὰ μεγαλεῖα τοῦ θεοῦ, 2:11), God's will and God's foreknowledge (see above), the word of God/the Lord (ὁ λόγος τοῦ θεοῦ / κυρίου, e.g., 4:31; 6:2; 8:14, 25; 11:1, 16;[97] 12:24; 13:5, 7, 44, 46, 48, 49; 15:35–36; 16:32; 17:13; 18:11; 19:10), God's glory (δόξα θεοῦ, 7:55), God's power (ἡ δύναμις τοῦ θεοῦ, 8:10), God's way (ἡ ὁδὸς τοῦ θεοῦ, 18:26), God's congregation (ἡ ἐκκλησία τοῦ θεοῦ, 20:28), and God's salvation (τὸ σωτήριον τοῦ θεοῦ, 28:28). By linking designations for God with different words, God is to some extent associated with what these phrases refer to. These phrases thus constitute part of the construction of God's character in Acts, because they—in a number of ways—open up the associative field connected to "God." In what way and to what extent depends on the narrative contexts in which they occur. When these phrases are found in contexts where God's actions are related, they may be helpful guides for interpreting the significance of these actions. Consequently, even though these phrases as such are not the focus of this study, it is worth acknowledging that they influence the way in which God in Acts may be perceived.[98]

By now, this chapter should have made clear that God's actions are of utmost importance both to Acts and to the characterization of God. However, it is not thereby said that other points of departure for studying the portrayal of God would not have been feasible. It might, e.g., have been possible to primarily investigate the difference between the perspectives

---

author seeks to invite. Finally, while the passages Talbert uses in support of Jesus as the "knower of hearts" (Luke 5:20–23; 7:39–43) do refer to Jesus as someone who knows something about a person's character without having been told of it, the term καρδιογνώστης is not used in any of them. It is, however, used of *God* in Acts 15:8. All this is to say that I maintain "God" as the object of the disciples' prayer in 1:24. I do, however, grant that the different interpretations of the object of the prayer make it meaningful to see it as part of the ambiguous discourse of God in Acts (see sec. 2.1.1), which blurs the lines between God and Jesus.

97. 11:16: τὸ ῥῆμα τοῦ κυρίου.

98. For instance, when the phrase "God's plan" (ἡ βουλὴ τοῦ θεοῦ) is used in connection with significant moments in Israel's history and Acts' plot, i.e., the life of David (13:36), the treason against Jesus (2:23; 4:27–28), and Paul's proclamation (20:26–27), it is suggested that the God of Acts is also the Lord of history.

from which God is presented throughout Acts,[99] and in this way, perhaps pay more attention to the "polyphony" of voices that speak of God than we will do in the present study. Rather than doing this, however, this study will primarily consider texts that express the implied author's perspective, which means we will be looking at texts where God and God's actions are presented through "reliable" narrators (see sec. 2.2.2.4). Yet another way of approaching the characterization of God in Acts might have been to look more specifically at how God relates to Jesus and the Spirit, or at how other characters relate to God, etc. I would claim, however, that these aspects are not neglected by the present study, but are considered as part of our investigation into how God's actions characterize God.

Previous research has done much in terms of bringing God and God's actions in Acts to the fore. As we have seen in this chapter, however, the majority of scholarship has focused more on the "what" of God's actions than on the relationship between these and God's character, more on God's plan than on the agent behind it. Even if some of the distinctive traits of God in Acts have been pointed out, to date there exists no monograph-length study that looks at the portrayal of God in Acts *through actions*. Our main question throughout this book will consequently be how God is characterized through actions in Acts. As previous research has shown, however, these actions are part of a larger history of salvation, into which the story of the early Jesus movement is inscribed. God's promises in Israel's past significantly impact the Jesus believers' proclamation and understanding of what takes place in the story-time. In order to focus the study somewhat more, we will therefore also be asking:

> *In what ways do the actions and characterization of God in the story-time relate to the actions of God spoken of in Jesus's life and ministry and Israel's more distant past?*

This question seeks to further open up the dynamics described by Shauf above: "Luke couples a firm sense of the particularity of God—God as the God of Israel—with an expanding sense of divine partiality. God is still partial to his people, but inclusion in the people of God is now open to all."[100] In other words, how does the story of Acts deal with this relationship between "old" and "new," past and present, in its depiction of God? The emphasis of this question is on its latter half. When it comes to what is said about God's actions in Jesus's life and ministry in Acts, this is also

---

99. Cheng's study, *Characterisation of God in Acts*, pays attention to how different characters characterize God in Acts, but not so much to the difference between their perspectives.

100. Shauf, *Divine in Acts*, 264.

important, but limited by Acts' own focus on the deeds of power, signs, and wonders performed by Jesus (e.g., Acts 2:22).

Another significant aspect of the depiction of God in Acts, is how closely the characterization of God is linked to that of Jesus. This observation will be more thoroughly developed in our next chapter (ch. 2), but for now we note that Acts often makes it difficult to distinguish between God and Jesus after Jesus's ascension into heaven. We therefore also ask:

> *How does Jesus's ascension into heaven impact the characterization of God in Acts?*

This second question turns upside down the question so often asked in studies on New Testament Christology, namely, in what ways Jesus resembles and relates to God. To the best of my knowledge, however, biblical scholars rarely, if ever, ask what happens to the characterization of *God* when Jesus comes to resemble God. As we shall see, in Acts, God and Jesus's characters primarily become difficult to distinguish from each other after the ascension. This is why we ask how Jesus's ascension into heaven impacts the characterization of God.

Before putting these questions to the material, however, we must further clarify the method and hermeneutical presuppositions on which this study rests. This will be dealt with in our next chapter, "Method and Material." Here we will also further delimit our material and finally present the outline of this book.

Chapter 2: **Method and Material**

2.0 A Narrative Approach: Preliminary Observations

As a narrative project which seeks to understand the portrayal of God as it emerges on the basis of the story of Acts, the present study employs tools and insights from narrative criticism as its chief methodological strategy. In this chapter, I clarify some of the grounds on which I approach Acts as a narrative and God as a character. I should state from the outset that even though my method is influenced by narrative criticism, the hermeneutical presuppositions with which I approach Acts as a whole move beyond strictly narratological concerns.[1] This will, I hope, be made clear throughout the different sections of this chapter. Nevertheless, I have chosen to retain the term "narrative criticism" because I, like Matthew Sleeman, find that it has "heuristic value as a collective label for the broad raft of narrative-based approaches to the biblical texts."[2]

Based on the insights of narratology, narrative criticism was born as part of the literary turn in biblical studies in the 1980s and early 90s. In contrast to historical criticism, form criticism, redaction criticism, and source criticism, which investigated smaller sections of biblical texts "in terms of probable origins and compositional history,"[3] scholars now turned to focus on the literary qualities and narrative unity of the gospels and Acts.[4] In Lukan studies, Robert C. Tannehill's two-volume commentary, *The Narrative Unity of Luke-Acts* (1986/1991), was among the first to approach Luke-Acts as a unified narrative, and use "selected aspects of narrative criticism to

---

1. I state this quite clearly because even though narrative criticism today is not the same as it was at its conception, it has nevertheless come under criticism both for being "ignorant of recent developments in literary studies and ahistorical despite the numerous reevaluations and supplementations provided by contemporary users of the method" (Henrichs-Tarasenkova, *Luke's Christology*, 27). Whether this critique is always warranted is a different debate.

2. Sleeman, *Geography and the Ascension Narrative*, 7n31.

3. Powell, "Emergence of a Prominent Reading Strategy," 19.

4. E.g., Rhoads and Michie, *Mark as Story*. The second edition, published in 1999, was revised and includes contributions from Joanna Dewey. See also Culpepper, *Anatomy of the Fourth Gospel*; Kingsbury, *Matthew as Story*.

gain new insights into Luke-Acts."[5] In the nearly three decades following his work, a number of other commentaries on Luke and Acts also came to include literary perspectives as part of their approach.[6] These commentaries balance historical perspectives with literary ones, but are nevertheless testimony to the influence of narrative criticism within the field. For the present project, the main inheritance from narrative criticism is its use of literary categories, and the fundamental observation that it is possible to approach and read Acts as a unified narrative.[7]

Narrative theory, then, is part of the theoretical foundations on which the present study rests. Citing James Phelan, Cornelis Bennema observes that, "narrative theory now takes as its objects of study narrative of all kinds occurring in all kinds of media throughout history."[8] In other words, narrative theory's applicability is not limited to "modern" genres, but encompasses many different kinds of narrative from many different times in history, including the Acts of the Apostles. The usefulness of a narrative approach to Acts may be recognized through the observation that the history Acts purports to be an attestation to is *emplotted*,[9] that is, the events it relates are located in a narrative account that contextualizes them in multiple ways.[10] God's character is therefore presented to us in ways that cannot be understood apart from this emplotment: The actions of God's character

---

5. Tannehill, *Narrative Unity of Luke-Acts*, 1:1.

6. Notable among these are the following commentaries: Johnson, *Acts of the Apostles*; Gaventa, *Acts*; Spencer, *Journeying through Acts*; Green, *Gospel of Luke*.

7. I am not hereby making claims to Acts' inherent unity, only to the possibility of reading it as unified. A reader's mind will always be expecting "texts to provide them with sufficient data and guidance . . . to construe a narrative world that hangs together and makes sense" (Darr, *On Character Building*, 31). In avoiding making an empirical claim about the text, and instead making one about the reader, I am trying to avoid the circular assumptions made by David Rhoads, which have been pointed out by Petri Merenlahti: "To prove, empirically, that the gospels are unified narratives is to prove that they qualify as literature, which will legitimate a literary approach" (Merenlahti, *Poetics for the Gospels?*, 19).

8. Bennema, *Theory of Character*, 55.

9. Todd Penner argues that ancient historians saw it precisely as their task to create a "unitary, focused, well-plotted, and persuasive narrative" (*In Praise of Christian Origins*, 220). If, as we shall see, the prologue to the Gospel of Luke may also function as a prologue to Acts, then καθεξῆς ("in order," Luke 1:3) may refer to what was commonly perceived to be the historian's task, i.e., to create an orderly account of his material. See Penner, *In Praise of Christian Origins*, 220; Holmås, *Prayer and Vindication*, 52–53. For more on καθεξῆς, see sec. 2.1.4.

10. These events are contextualized socially, culturally, theologically, etc. See, e.g., Green arguing in part on the basis of insights from Paul Veyne in Green, "Narrative Criticism," 87.

are portrayed from specific points of view, in specific settings, in relation to specific events, and in relation to specific actors. It is from the interaction between God and these elements that the portrayal of God in Acts arises. To approach the portrayal of God in Acts from a narrative perspective, as the present study does, therefore has some advantages. It allows us to approach Acts as a whole, and use literary categories such as plot, character, and setting. These make it possible to investigate more closely the why and how of how God's character emerges as it does within the literary dynamics of the text. In chapter 2.2.2, we look more closely at which literary categories come into play when looking at the characterization of God.

The fact that Acts may be approached as emplotted history means that this narrative cannot be understood apart from history. As Joel B. Green has aptly noted,

> narrative criticism of the Gospels and Acts cannot be reduced to consideration of literary devices and textual artistry. Historical, readerly, and theological concerns must be integrated with elements typically associated with narratology—theme, plot, characterization, point of view, and so on.[11]

When the present study employs tools and insights from narrative criticism, it therefore does so with awareness that both text and actual reader are influenced by several contexts. This makes knowledge of the ancient world in which the text came into being and transparent reflection on the reader's contextual location and theological assumptions imperative for understanding the text and how it is read. If the recognition of Acts as biblical history (see sec. 2.1.4) is to be taken seriously, insights from other methodological approaches must also be invited into conversation. Awareness of, e.g., social conventions and different kinds of symbols—in short, sociocultural information—provides an important key to reading because it entails knowledge that enables the reader to better understand and interpret the text. Most of these issues will be treated in the following section on the *reader*.

Finally, in its approach to Acts as a unified narrative, this study will take its point of departure in the critical edition to Acts found in *Novum Testamentum Graece* (28th ed). In the case of Acts, whose transmission is largely represented by "Alexandrian" and "Western" forms of the text, NA28 favors the former. Where differences in the manuscript tradition influence the way God is presented, I will discuss how they impact the portrayal of God. I consider these differences to be of interest in their own right, and therefore do not make it my primary goal to establish "the older" version of

---

11. Green, "Narrative Criticism," 92.

the text. In some cases, however, it will be necessary to clarify which text I proceed to base the rest of my interpretation upon. In those cases, I follow standard principles of traditional textual criticism.

The remainder of this chapter is divided into three main parts. The first part deals with some of the fundamental perspectives from which I approach Acts. I begin by addressing how God's actions may be implicitly, explicitly, and ambiguously discerned in the narrative, and define what the present study considers an "action" of God's (2.1.1). This part clarifies the understanding of my project's method, and why narrative criticism is so appropriate for making sense of Acts and the theology of Acts. I then continue by explicating my concept of the reader (2.1.2), and clarify how this study relates to the Gospel of Luke (2.1.3). After this, I consider the question of genre (2.1.4). The second part of this chapter then narrows in on characterization: After a brief introduction (2.2), I clarify how God's character may be delineated in Acts. and on what terms I consider God's character differentiated from those of Jesus and the Holy Spirit (2.2.1). I then look at some of the more theoretical aspects of characterization and the literary terms I will be employing in the present study (2.2.2). Finally, in the third part of this chapter, I present this project's delimitation and outline (2.3).

2.1 Reading God in Acts

2.1.1 Discerning God's Actions

In chapter 1, we observed that the God of Acts is first and foremost a God who acts. It is primarily from these actions that the portrayal of God emerges. These actions are presented in a number of ways. Daniel Marguerat perceptively observes how Acts uses both implicit and explicit language in its presentation of "God." He notes that "the implicit language corresponds to the theophanies of the Greek Bible,"[12] and includes messages from angels, visions, the casting of lots, the Spirit's address of the believers, wonders and the power of the apostles to heal, perform exorcisms and resuscitate the dead, and their ability to "punish those guilty of fraud and escape from vipers."[13] The implicit actions of God are therefore also to a large extent based on God's work *through others*. The explicit language, on the other hand, is the language through which God is directly named. Mainly found in the speeches, the explicit "god-language" or "discourse of God" points to a significant characteristic of the Acts narrative: "Except for a few rare

---

12. Marguerat, *First Christian Historian*, 87.
13. Marguerat, *First Christian Historian*, 87.

occasions, the narrator never directly ascribes the action of the narrative to God. In other words, God becomes a subject only in the words of a character."[14] Thus, according to Marguerat,

> The examination of the language required to speak of 'God' in the book of Acts reveals a systematic control on the part of the narrator, who chooses narrative language when God manifests himself by mediation, which conceals him, and who chooses discursive language when God is mentioned by name as an agent of history. In the technical terms of narrative analysis: the implicit language is reserved for the narrator (extra-diegetic authority), while the explicit language characterizes the speech of the characters of the story (intra-diegetic authorities).[15]

These observations are helpful for a number of reasons. For one, the distinction between implicit and explicit language puts words to why God's character is, in Marguerat's words, "concealed," yet nevertheless also a distinct and acting presence within the narrative. Secondly, to speak of "God" in Acts relies upon an interpretive process, where the explicit is allowed to interpret the implicit.[16] It is through this dialectic that God is allowed to emerge as a character at all. Relatedly, it is not possible to speak of "God's actions" solely as actions where God is explicitly *named* as the subject of a verb. Rather, to speak of "God's actions" entails a process of discernment: How is God's involvement in the lives of the believers traced, when the God of Israel does not have any physical form? The reader of Acts must learn to see through the eyes of the (reliable) characters that explicitly name God's involvement, and must also activate the cultural encyclopedia that provides the lenses to see where God is at work (see sec. 2.1.2).

I owe much to Marguerat's keen insights, but nevertheless find it useful to nuance some of his observations. While Marguerat mainly distinguishes between the narrator's implicit language and the characters' explicit language, there are times when we find implicit language about God in characters' speeches too. Judas's death is one example (cf. 1:16–20). God is never named the agent of his death, yet the Scripture cited by Peter and the literary tradition of death as divine punishment in the first century[17] both allow the reader to discern God's unseen hand.[18] Another example

---

14. Marguerat, *First Christian Historian*, 90.
15. Marguerat, *First Christian Historian*, 91–92.
16. Cf. Marguerat, *First Christian Historian*, 91.
17. Cf. Josephus's depictions of Catullus's (*J.W.* 7.451–53) and Herod Agrippa's deaths (*Ant.* 19.345–50).
18. Cf. the deaths of Ananias and Sapphira (5:1–10) and Herod (12:20–23).

of implicit discourse of God in the mouths of characters may be found in their references to Jesus's ascension and forgiveness of sins. The white-clad men tell the disciples about "Jesus who was taken up from you" (ὁ Ἰησοῦς ὁ ἀναλημφθεὶς ἀφ' ὑμῶν, 1:11).[19] They do not name God, but the participle should be understood as a divine passive: God is the one who lifts Jesus up into heaven. In the same vein, God is never explicitly said to be the one who will forgive the sins of the repentant believers in Acts. That this is the case is nevertheless a fundamental, but implicit element of the apostles' proclamation. However, whereas in Israel's Scriptures, God alone forgives sins,[20] in Acts this forgiveness is offered *through* Jesus (cf. 10:43; 13:38; 26:18). Accordingly, Jesus's character becomes a mediator of forgiveness, but he is nevertheless not the one with whom this forgiveness originates.

Finally, I would like to supplement Marguerat's categories of implicit and explicit god-language with the notion of *ambiguous* god-language. Specifically, I have in mind the occasions on which God is *possibly* named or acting. One example of this is those occasions where "the Lord" is mentioned, but where it is unclear whether it is God, Jesus, or both whom the narrator is referring to. Examples of this will be given and treated in our analyses. In short, the "ambiguous god-language" is a category located in tension between the explicit and the implicit discourse of God, because it only *potentially* names God explicitly, and implicitly indicates that God's character is woven together with Jesus's.

The discourse from which the portrayal of God in Acts emerges is, in sum, explicit, implicit, and ambiguous. This is true not only of the discourse in its entirety, but also of God's actions. The following will therefore function as a working definition for "actions" in the present study:

> *God's actions are here defined as those happenings referred to in Acts, where God's character is either explicitly or implicitly to be understood as the main agent behind a promise, an alteration, decision, event, or accomplishment. These actions may take place within the story-time of Acts, or they may be past or professed future actions referred to in the narrative.*

This definition takes into account that God's actions are both explicit and implicit parts of the narrative, and that these actions are often mediated through others even though God may also be understood as the agent. Actions that may only "ambiguously" be ascribed to God are neither

---

19. My translation.

20. This exclusivity is, to the best of my knowledge, never explicitly claimed, but nevertheless an implicit part of Jewish theology, especially as it relates to the theology of atonement. See, e.g., Luke 5:21; Ps 103:3; Mic 7:18–19; Lev 16; Ezra 9.

specifically included nor excluded by this definition; they are ambiguous, and defy classification beyond this. On the rare occasion that God is mentioned as speaking, this is considered an action; however, I broadly consider references to the word of God/the Lord as a reference to the contents of the apostles' proclamation, and not an action in itself.[21] Moreover, this definition of actions does not depend on whom the action is referred to by: It may be narrated by the narrator, or referred to by a character narrator in, e.g., one of Acts' many speeches.

Importantly, the above definition maintains the broad timeline, from creation till judgment, on which God's actions in Acts are painted: God's actions are both analeptically and proleptically referred to, but a number of them also take place in the story-time. This means that the image of God in Acts does not merely rely on God's actions in the present, but on how these relate to the past and are linked to what the characters say about the future. Finally, the definition maintains the manifold aspects of God's actions. Some are *punctual* and take place at a specific point in time, as when Jesus was raised from the dead (e.g., 3:15); some are *part of a process* that alters conditions or intentions (e.g., Acts 10); or they may be defined as the *result* of something God has done, for example the fulfillment of God's promises in the coming of the Spirit on Pentecost (1:4–5 and 2:1–4.).

As we have seen above, God's actions are many, and may be discerned in different ways. However, the question remains how, and which actions, may be fruitfully studied as part of a narrative reading of Acts. I will return to this question in sec. 2.3. In anticipation of my observations there, however, I will note that I propose to study Acts primarily from a perspective that considers how God is depicted at the *turning points* of the narrative, i.e., the events in the story-time with the most significant bearings on the plot. One example of such a turning point would be the descent of the Spirit on Pentecost (Acts 2), which is followed by the apostles' mission; another is the story of Stephen's martyrdom (Acts 7), followed by the persecution of the Jesus believers and their scattering from Jerusalem. By focusing on those of God's actions that are narrated or mentioned at turning points, we ensure that the actions we look at are tied to some of the most significant themes and turns of the story. This makes it possible to see how the image of God develops, and helps bring out what is distinctive about Acts' portrayal of God.[22]

---

21. See ch. 7, n. 57.

22. Other interpretive strategies might focus on the characterization of God from the perspectives of different narrators (like Cheng, cf. sec. 1.1.3), or simply extract all of God's actions from the narrative and then analyze what they can tell us about God's character in Acts. I do consider it important to consider how God's actions are related

2.1.2 Reading as a Competent Reader

There are many ways of reading a text. In biblical scholarship, the readers whose reading are under consideration are sometimes real, but more often than not, they are historical or text-based constructs. These readers function as heuristic lenses through which a text is read; they are hermeneutical constructs that explain what criteria a text is read according to. In the present study, I designate my reader a "competent" reader. To borrow words from Brittany Wilson, this is "a product of the interaction between the Lukan text and its ancient cultural context, as well as my own cultural context and perspective as a biblical scholar."[23] Some aspects of what I hope to maintain by approaching Acts through this lens may be derived from the definition just cited: 1) Acts must be treated as a product of a different time and place than our own. 2) As a consequence of this, Acts must be read on the background of sociocultural knowledge of the time around the first century, which we here call the "cultural encyclopedia." 3) The reading, even when it is done through a constructed reader, will inevitably be conditioned by my own embeddedness in a multitude of contexts. A fourth matter will be further elucidated below, i.e., 4), the ways in which I perceive of the relationship between text and reader.

In the following, I will begin to explicate my concept of the competent reader, hereafter simply referred to as "the reader." First, however, I pause to make one disclaimer. We have noted that a study of Acts should take seriously both the irrevocable influence of the critic's embeddedness in multiple contexts, at the same time as knowledge of the first century is imperative in order to understand Acts. However, with this follows a recognition that the majority of those first to become acquainted with the biblical texts, and in this case the Acts of the Apostles, were *listeners* rather than *readers*.[24] It can therefore be questioned whether "reader" is a suitable term for anyone who wishes both to "respect the role reserved for the

---

by different (extradiegetic and intradiegetic) narrators in Acts, but this perspective will not be missing from my analyses. However, if I were to make my focus the characterization of God from the perspectives of different narrators, I would not only be repeating the work of Ling Cheng, but run the risk of placing equal value on each of God's actions by failing to take into account which aspects of God are emphasized through the development of the plot. A strategy of extraction, in turn, would run the risk of untying the actions from their narrative context, thereby failing to take into account that God's character is not only characterized by what God does, but by whom the action is narrated, whom the action affects, and in which contexts God does what.

23. Wilson, *Unmanly Men*, 37. This comes very close to the hybrid reader posited in Darr, *On Character Building*, 26–29.

24. Cf. Rhoads, *Reading Mark*, 35–36.

'reader' or 'lector' who 'performs' the text by reading (or reciting) it aloud, but also to underscore the aural and communal context within which Luke expected his work to be experienced."[25] In order to better appreciate this way of becoming acquainted with the text, it has now become popular to speak of Acts' *audience* rather than a group "readers." However, I cannot escape the fact that the present study is based on a *reading* of Acts rather an auditory performance. While I appreciate that hearing the text might bring out different nuances and perceptions of the God whom Acts portrays than the ones that will result from my own research, making e.g., a performance critical analysis of Acts would not be possible to do within the scope of this study. Therefore, I will continue to speak of the "reader" rather than "audience." I will, however, make note of auditory elements in the text which might influence the way God is perceived.[26]

What is the relationship between text and (competent) reader? This question may be answered in two different ways: 1) By looking at how the implied author of Acts invites the reader to read the story, and 2) by an appreciation of the reading process. The first of these is specific to Acts: The preface to Acts (1:1–11) immediately throws the reader back to the Gospel of Luke. It is quite possible, if not necessary, from a readerly perspective to consider the gospel prologue (Luke 1:1–4) to have implications for Luke-Acts as a whole. If we do so, we see that the narrator invites the reader to accept the reliability or truthfulness (ἀσφάλεια, Luke 1:4) of his narrative, but also shapes and conditions a *willing* reader: This is a reader who accepts the words of the implied author as true, and who is partial to the implied author's perspective.[27] We will say more about this in sec. 2.1.4. For now, however, we can note that a willing reader resembles what Mark Allan Powell describes as an implied reader, i.e., a reader who "actualizes the potential for meaning in a text, who responds to it in ways consistent with the expectations that we may ascribe to its implied author."[28] A willing reader is consequently someone who "goes along with the text," rather than being suspicious of it or disagreeing with the author. The same text may nevertheless still invite polyvalent readings. In the cases where potential readings differ greatly and influence the understanding of Acts' presentation of God, I will discuss them.

---

25. Parsons, *Acts*, 5.

26. The ekphrastic language in Acts 2:1–4 is one example. See sec. 3.1 for more on this.

27. See sec. 2.2.2.4 for more about the implied author.

28. Powell, "Narrative Criticism," 242.

A second way of looking at the relationship between text and reader is through appreciation of the more theoretical aspects of the reading *process*. Rather than detailing the many aspects of the reading process here, however, I refer my reader to John A. Darr's summary in *On Character Building* (1992, 29–32), which is largely influenced by Wolfgang Iser. I do wish to note, however, that I look at Acts from the perspective of a reader who has read Acts several times, as an "experienced" reader. The reading process is, as Darr notes, a constant act of anticipation and retrospection. Thus the initial preconceptions of God that the reader brings to Acts create expectations, which may be "reaffirmed, negated, revised, and supplemented" throughout the course of reading.[29] This insight is of particular importance to Acts, because this book constantly negotiates how actions are conceived of as God's as the story progresses. It is therefore important to note *where* and *how* expectations about God and God's actions are revised or maintained in the narrative.

This, in turn, leads us to the question of *what* expectations about God the reader brings to the text. When we speak of expectations, we touch upon what we here call the "cultural encyclopedia" of the reader. Originating with Umberto Eco, the "cultural encyclopedia" is an expression that seems to have taken on a life of his own in biblical studies.[30] In short, the cultural encyclopedia refers to the knowledge an author would presuppose to be available to her reader in order to interpret a text: "The author has thus to foresee a model of the possible reader (hereafter Model Reader) supposedly able to deal interpretatively with the expressions in the same way as the author deals generatively with them."[31] In this study, we further define this as the amount of cultural data *implied* by the text in Acts, and available to implied reader and author alike. In other words, there are clues within Acts that show us what knowledge an audience would need in order to offer an informed reading of the text. It would, for instance, be difficult to understand Peter's vision in Acts 10 without an awareness of Jewish customs regarding clean and unclean meat. At the same time, it must be acknowledged that what we consider to be *implied* is dependent on our modern knowledge of the ancient world, and is therefore also a construct influenced by my context as a biblical scholar. Another consequence of using the cultural encyclopedia is that we are using material in our reading which we do not know whether the actual reader(s) had access to. Our

29. Darr, *On Character Building*, 30.

30. Eco speaks of an "encyclopedia" and a shared "encyclopedic competence" between author and model reader; see Eco, *Role of the Reader*, 7. However, I have yet to discover where Eco uses the exact term "cultural encyclopedia."

31. Eco, *Role of the Reader*, 7.

reading thus runs the risk of being less, or better, informed than any actual historical reader's. Even so, there is value in employing the concept of the cultural encyclopedia, for it elucidates how scholarship continues to critically read, interpret, and pass on historically informed knowledge of a text which is still in use in religion and society today.

It is clear from Acts' frequent use of the LXX that at least some of Israel's Scriptures must be considered part of the cultural encyclopedia of the reader.[32] This leads me to consider the reader to be familiar with different accounts of various ways in which God has been depicted to intervene in the history of Israel. Closely connected to this are the preconceptions I assume in this study, namely that this God's identity is largely defined by God's relationship with Israel, and the understanding of God as one. In addition to moulding preconceptions about God, the cultural encyclopedia of the "competent reader" assumes further content. In general, I postulate a reader with basic knowledge of Jewish beliefs and traditions, a general understanding about the history, geography and political system of the Roman Empire, and familiarity with general customs and ideas of the Greco-Roman world,[33] and elements of Homeric mythology. I also presuppose familiarity with the Gospel of Luke and other early Jesus traditions. Finally, I see the question of genre as part of the cultural literacy of the reader of Acts, and I will return to this further below.[34] In sum, the employment of this extratextual knowledge provides the basis for an informed reading of Acts. Please note, however, that this overview is intentionally generic and should not be taken as an exhaustive list. Rather, it is an attempt to mention some of the more significant presuppositions which this book assumes on the part of the competent reader. Where further specification of this knowledge is called for, it will be provided in conjunction with our analyses of the texts that speak of God's actions.

---

32. In this book, I use the "LXX" / "Septuagint" when referring to specific texts. I use "Israel's Scriptures" in a slightly broader sense. It is not entirely clear *which* texts the author of Acts would have regarded as Scripture. However, to borrow the words of Ole Jakob Filtvedt for the purposes of this study, it is quite clear that the author of Acts "does relate to a body of tradition, regarded as sacred and authoritative, which in many ways resembles what came to be canonized as Scripture. Thus, I will continue to use the term 'Scripture,' although with due caution" (Filtvedt, *Identity of God's People*, 2n3.

33. My brief and all-too-general summary owes greatly to Tyson, Darr, and Parsons, who each offer a suggested overview of the extratextual repertoire of the implied reader/reader/authorial audience, respectively. I have also been influenced by the article of Vernon K. Robbins on the implied author. See Tyson, "Implied Reader," 23–35; Darr, *On Character Building*, 26–29; Parsons, *Acts*, 20; Robbins, "Social Location," 305–32.

34. For the competent reader, genre is among the preconceptions with which the text is approached.

In sum, my "competent reader" should be seen as a heuristic lens, and is not to be confused with an actual, historically reconstructed reader. It is, however, a reader who reads Acts in its ancient cultural and literary context, and pays due attention to the literary dynamics of the text. In the following chapters, we turn to further unpack the implications of this for reading Acts. First, however, we must ask the following question.

2.1.3 What about the Gospel of Luke?

In reading Acts, how does this study relate to the Gospel of Luke? To date, there is no surviving evidence that suggests the Gospel of Luke and the Acts of the Apostles were read as one work in two volumes in the first centuries of the common era.[35] In this sense, the present study could be argued to read Acts in the way it was read by early Christians; as an individual book, rather than as part of a two-volume work.[36] Arguments made from silence can be dangerous, however, and I do not seek to claim that Luke and Acts were never read together. Nor am I making any claims against the literary unity of Luke-Acts. Instead, I simply wish to suggest that our earliest available reception history of Acts shows us that it is *possible* to read this book as an individual entity, rather than as an inseparable part of Luke-Acts. This, then, is precisely what our study does: It looks at the characterization of God in Acts. As this book will hopefully demonstrate, focusing specifically on Acts' contribution to the characterization of God yields some interesting results. Nevertheless, as we shall see below, reading Acts as an individual entity does not mean that the book or our reading is completely independent of the Gospel of Luke.

---

35. Andrew Gregory concludes his survey of reception history before the time of Irenaeus by stating that "This investigation of the evidence for the reception of *Luke* and *Acts* in the period before Irenaeus has found no evidence other than that of Irenaeus and the Muratorian fragment to demonstrate that *Luke* and *Acts* were read as two volumes of one work" (Gregory, *Reception of Luke and Acts*, 352). C. Kavin Rowe, however, contests the part of his conclusion that suggests Luke and Acts were actually read as one literary work by Irenaeus and in the Muratorian fragment. Rowe convincingly argues that in the case of the former, Acts is not only read together with Luke, but the fourfold gospel (44–45, cf. *Haer.* 3.1.1), and that the Muratorian fragment can only be used as evidence of common authorship, not of a reading of Luke-Acts as a literary whole (45–46). See Rowe, "History, Hermeneutics," 131–57.

36. I am here specifically dealing with Acts' relation to the Gospel of Luke. However, $\mathfrak{P}^{45}$ suggests that Acts has been read as a continuation of the *fourfold* gospel. Moreover, a number of later manuscripts have Acts introduce the Epistles—seemingly offering a narrative framework for their reading. This in turn adds force to the argument that Acts does not *necessarily* have to be read together with the Gospel of Luke.

Acts' contribution to the characterization of God emerges on the basis of a story with its own unique characteristics. Acts is distinguished from the Gospel of Luke through a change in style, plot and protagonists. Whereas God in the Gospel of Luke is mainly presented through God's relation to the events of Jesus's life, death and resurrection, the main plot of Acts unfolds after Jesus's ascension. As this study hopes to explicate, Jesus's resurrection, ascension, and the coming of the Spirit bring a new dimension to the image of God, which Acts, unlike the Gospel of Luke, addresses through its narrative of the spread of the gospel. That is not to say that the image of God is not a matter of debate in the Gospel of Luke: Jesus's interaction with people who were considered unclean, sinners or of low standing in Jewish society, not to mention Jesus's discussions with the scribes and Pharisees do, indirectly, challenge different Jewish perceptions of God. It is, however, only after Jesus's ascension in Acts that God gives the Spirit to the gentiles and the mission of the Jesus movement crosses the borders of Israel. The fact that Acts presents an image of God "on the move" thus merits a reading of Acts alone.[37] This does not mean, however, that significant aspects of the characterization of God in Acts do not depend on the story that is told in Luke.[38] Acts actively makes events from the Gospel of Luke an explicit part of its own narrative by speaking of God's role in the ministry, death and resurrection of Jesus.[39] In doing so, Acts shows its dependence on the Gospel, but also its independence from it because it interprets Gospel events in service of its own narrative about the mission and development of the early Jesus movement. I will say more about the competent reader's relationship to the Gospel of Luke below.

The delimitation and choice of the present study to focus on Acts also relies on pragmatic and hermeneutical concerns. In terms of the former, the scope and necessary limits of this project do not permit a study of both books. In terms of the latter, our study of Acts takes its point of departure in the theory that meaning is constructed in the interaction between text and reader, and therefore does not rely upon knowledge of either author or original intention in order to make sense.[40] This hermeneutical stance

---

37. This does not mean that God is not "on the move" at all in the Gospel of Luke; traveling is an important motif in Luke's Gospel. See, e.g., Barreto, "Gospel on the Move," 175–87. Moreover, Jesus crosses into the borderlands between Samaria and Galilee (17:11) and the worldwide mission is foreshadowed in 24:47.

38. I do not *equate* this story with the Gospel of Luke, as it is quite possible to say that Acts also depends on the story told in, e.g., the Gospel of Mark, oral traditions, etc.

39. Cf. especially Acts 2:22–28, 36; 10:36–43.

40. Two clarifications are necessary here: First, I do not believe the author's original intention with his or her work is insignificant for what kind of meaning is

means that I approach the question of unity in Luke-Acts from a different perspective than the traditional debate on unity, which has until recently been dominated by a focus on the "intended" or "original" relationship between the two texts.[41] Because the focus of the present study is on what portrayal of God emerges in the interaction between Acts and the reader, the question of authorship is of little importance when it comes to whether Luke-Acts should be read as a single text or not. Not only does the literary turn question the possibility of discovering the original author; common authorship does not necessitate unity in either form or content. One author may write two completely different books, and two different authors may write two very similar books. However, this does not mean that it does not matter what kind of author the text *implies*—the implied author greatly influences the reading of the text. Nor should our study be taken to

---

generated between text and reader in the end. However, this meaning is primarily accessed through the text, not through knowledge of the original author. Secondly, the above is not to say that information about the text's historical context is not valuable; it is, as we shall see in our next chapter.

41. See, e.g., Verheyden, "Unity of Luke-Acts," 4–10. As he begins his examination of how previous scholars have conceived of the unity of Luke and Acts, Verheyden refers to four of I. H. Marshall's models for looking at the relationship between Luke and Acts. All of these (possibly with the exception of 2a: "these are autonomous works with their own topic and concerns") take their point of departure in the question of authorship and how the author conceived of his work. See Verheyden, "Unity of Luke-Acts," 4–5.

The discussion on unity has been advanced somewhat in later years. In an article in the *Journal for the Study of the New Testament* in 2005, C. Kavin Rowe calls for a further distinction between the actual reception of Luke and Acts, where the two texts were read separately, and the narrative reading of the texts, which allows for a view of Luke-Acts as a single work. In the same issue of *JSNT*, Markus Bockmuehl responds to Rowe's article, arguing that reception history is a better indication of the intention of the work than narrative unity. He further suggests that it would be profitable to distinguish between the Luke of history and the implied author's relation to the narrative unity of the work, because it is not immediately clear that "the evangelist designed the two volumes as an integral whole from the start, or that he meant them to be read as a single work even by the time he wrote Acts." This claim, Bockmuehl argues, can only be made on literary grounds; see Bockmuehl, "Why Not?," 164. The assertions of these two scholars demonstrate that, firstly, it is impossible to say whether Luke and Acts were originally intended to be read as Luke-Acts: reception history has read them separately, so there is no historical evidence to suggest that they *must* be read together. This supports the present study's decision to read Acts alone. Secondly, it follows from Bockmuehl's claim that the unity of Luke-Acts can only be made as a literary judgment, that in a narrative approach to Acts, the reader may be understood to see connecting lines and echoes between the two texts. Consequently, the implied reader may still be understood to have read the Gospel of Luke. See Bockmuehl, "Why Not?," 163–66; Rowe, "History, Hemeneutics," 131–57. See also Rowe, "Literary Unity," 449–57. Now found in Gregory and Rowe, *Rethinking the Unity and Reception*.

dispute the authorial unity of Luke-Acts; it simply suggests that the identity of the original author is not decisive for how the present study reads these texts. Instead, this study is based on the theory that it is from the interaction between the text and the reader that an understanding of the presentation of God emerges.

It is when we speak of the reader that Acts' relation to the Gospel of Luke resurfaces. As we have noted, the preface to Acts (1:1–11) immediately directs the reader back into a recollection of the gospel narrative through the mention of the "first book" (1:1). While it is debated to what extent the prologue to Luke (1:1–4) should be considered to control the aims and genre of Acts too,[42] the prefaces to both Luke and Acts must at the very least be said to have a uniting function. This leaves us with the question of how the Gospel of Luke is employed when we analyze our texts in Acts. First, the obvious must be stated: Because awareness of the Gospel of Luke is implied by the preface to Acts, it must be considered part of the "cultural encyclopedia" of the reader, i.e., as something the reader is familiar with. In looking at the portrayal of God in Acts, however, the sections we analyze are chiefly viewed in light of the narrative of Acts, rather than the entire narrative of Luke-Acts. By this I mean that, for instance, I do not read the punishment miracles in Acts in light of Zechariah's muteness in Luke 1. Instead, I consider Judas's death the first divine punishment that conditions further readings of such punishments in Acts. The *primary* narrative reference for the texts I analyze will thus be Acts. The gospel narrative is, however, *secondarily* employed in my argument where it helps shed light on difficult questions, or aids in substantiating an argument. This maintains Acts as the primary interpretive context for reading, while simultaneously recognizing the book's relationship to the Gospel of Luke.

2.1.4 The Question of Genre: Reading Acts as Biblical History

What kind of literary endeavor is the characterization of God part of? While genre may be defined as a category of literature that conforms to a set of stylistic criteria, it is equally essential that these criteria function to express a specific kind of content. In the history of scholarship on Acts, a number of genre proposals have been made.[43] These include ancient

---

42. Cf. Alexander, *Acts in its Ancient Literary Context*, 23–25.

43. Note that some of these proposals have since been revised, and do not necessarily reflect the present views of the authors. Thus, e.g., Talbert in a 1998 SBL paper argues that Acts must be a blending of genres. See Talbert and Stepp, "Succession in Mediterranean Antiquity," 178–79.

biography,[44] theological history,[45] ancient novel,[46] ancient epic,[47] ancient historiography,[48] biographical monograph,[49] and biblical history.[50] Today, however, the tendency in scholarship seems to be moving towards seeing Acts as a blending of different genres.[51] When we approach the question of genre here, it is because it is closely related to the question of the reader. As Marianne Palmer Bonz succinctly puts it, "genre is fundamental to interpretation. Genre provides the initial key to understanding what an author actually means by what he has written. Are his words to be taken literally, figuratively, satirically, or hyperbolically?"[52] Although we will employ a more reader-oriented perspective on genre below, Bonz's point stands: Genre guides reader perceptions and expectations.

The reader's understanding of genre results in a choice of perspective in terms of how Acts is read: Locating Acts together with ancient biographies will result in a sharper focus on the apostles in Acts than, e.g., reading it as theological history, which may result in a stronger emphasis on God. Furthermore, the classification into a generic family determines what kind of material one considers Acts to be more easily compared to. These are all good reasons why the question of genre ought to be addressed. With regards to this study, however, I would maintain that the question of genre is informative, but not crucial, in terms of how Acts invites the reader to understand the characterization of God. It is informative to the extent that it allows us to look at and determine reader expectations. This in turn touches upon the question of what expectations would have been possible for a first-century reader, and what kind of "cultural encyclopedia" Acts is read on the background of. The question of genre is not crucial, however, because none of the genres proposed for Acts above create "rules"

---

44. In Talbert's case, Acts is more specifically considered a succession narrative that follows the "biography" of Jesus in the Gospel of Luke. See Talbert, *Literary Patterns*. In newer times, an argument to read Acts as a "collected biography" has been put forward in Adams, *Genre of Acts and Collected Biography*.

45. Maddox, *Purpose of Luke-Acts*.

46. Pervo, *Profit with Delight*.

47. Bonz, *Past as Legacy*; MacDonald, *Does the New Testament Imitate Homer?* It is not entirely clear whether MacDonald suggests that parts of Luke-Acts imitate Homeric epic, or whether he considers the book as a whole to belong to this genre.

48. E.g., Aune, *New Testament in its Literary Environment*; Sterling, *Historiography and Self-Definition*; Penner, *In Praise of Christian Origins*.

49. Burridge, "Genre of Acts," 3–28.

50. Rosner, "Acts and Biblical History," 65–82. That Acts should be read as biblical history is now also claimed by Alexander, see ch 2.1.4.

51. Phillips, "Genre of Acts," 383–85.

52. Bonz, *Past as Legacy*, 183.

for reading Acts, where the reader is invited to be sceptical of the implied author's presentation of God, or to interpret God's character as fundamentally satirically or hyperbolically presented, etc. In other words, the characterization of God in Acts would be approached in much the same way regardless of any of the above genre proposals.

This being said, the present study considers Acts to belong to the genre of biblical history, but considers the method and aims of its author to be aligned with some of the principles of ancient history writing. In the following, I will briefly expound on these observations.

The principles of ancient history writing may be detected through recourse to the prologues to both Luke and Acts. We have already noted that the reader's first encounter with Acts is its preface, which immediately points back to the Gospel of Luke. The gospel preface (1:1–4), in turn, introduces some of the fundamentals of the Lukan project: We see here that the primary goal of the Lukan narrative is to convince Theophilus of the truth, or certainty (ἀσφάλεια, 1:4), about the things he has been told. In Lucian of Samosata's *How to Write History*, written ca. 166–168CE (hereafter referred to as *HWH*), Lucian states that the primary purpose of history is for it to be both useful (τὸ χρήσιμον) and truthful (ὅπερ ἐκ τοῦ ἀληθοῦς μόνου συνάγεται, Lucian, *HWH*, 9). While Acts is an earlier composition than Lucian's text, "there are nevertheless strong reasons to think that this pamphlet . . . fixes a much earlier scholarly tradition."[53] Luke's purpose is therefore in line with what Lucian defines as one of the main aims of historians.[54]

The intention of the (implied) author, which we hereafter call Luke, to write a truthful account, is also joined by a rhetorical appeal to its reliability.[55] The opening verses make clear that the author is familiar with "the events that have been fulfilled among us" (Luke 1:1),[56] and states that accounts of these events have been handed down by both eyewitnesses and ministers of the word (1:2). On the basis of this material, Luke constructs his narrative, which he aims to write in both a careful and orderly manner (ἀκριβῶς καθεξῆς, Luke 1:3). A source awareness similar to that of Luke may be found

---

53. Marguerat, *First Christian Historian*, 13.

54. Thucydides also demonstrates a concern with facts (and by implication, with truth). Of his reader, he writes: "He should regard the facts as having been made out with sufficient accuracy, on the basis of the clearest indications, considering that they have to do with early times" (Thucydides, *Hist.* 21.2).

55. For a more detailed account of the ways in which the Lukan prologue reveals Luke's affiliation with history writing at the time, see Penner, *In Praise of Christian Origins*, 219–22.

56. All citations from the Bible follow the NRSV's translation unless otherwise stated.

in Thucydides. He also writes that he uses eyewitnesses, and has investigated "with the greatest possible accuracy each detail, in the case both of the events in which I myself participated and of those regarding which I got my information from others." (Thucydides, *Hist.* 1.22.2 [Forster Smith, LCL]). The gathering of information through eyewitnesses continues to be an ideal for historians in the centuries that follow, as exemplified by a similar sentiment found in Lucian: He claims that the historian should "for preference be an eyewitness, but, if not, listen to those who tell the more impartial story" (Lucian, *HWH*, 47 [Kilburn, LCL]). The fact that Luke explicitly mentions the sources behind his account therefore furthers the impression that he is writing with the intention of recording history.

Finally, Luke's endeavor to present his material in a careful and orderly manner (ἀκριβῶς καθεξῆς) could possibly also point to another value shared by ancient historians. This is expressed through Lucian's considerations about the historian's task of arranging his series of notes into order (εἶτα ἐπιθεὶς τὴν τάξιν, Lucian, *HWH*, 48 [Kilburn, LCL]), and "to give a fine arrangement to events" ("εἰς καλὸν διαθέσθαι τὰ πεπραγμένα," Lucian, *HWH*, 51 [Kilburn, LCL]). It is, however, debated within Lukan studies what καθεξῆς means. Perhaps we can come no closer than noting with Penner, that "this does not necessarily imply 'chronological order,' but, in line with the rest of the terminology, represents the means by which Luke will achieve an 'accurate' narrative portrayal of the events, which, ultimately, means a 'convincing' account."[57] The use of the word does, in other words, suggest a rhetorically convincing order, "a narrative sequence (καθεξῆς) that will provide a firm(er) understanding of the significance of the events (ἵνα ἐπιγνῷς [. . .] τὴν ἀσφάλειαν)."[58]

I would contend, however, that even if the above suggests that Luke writes according to some of the principles of ancient history writing, he does not write using the *genre* of Greco-Roman historiography. Shauf's observations are particularly important here: He argues that Acts differs from Greco-Roman historiography, perhaps most importantly in its focus on divine rather than human causation, in its presentation of simple rather than

---

57. Penner, *In Praise of Christian Origins*, 220. I find David P. Moessner's observation about the use of καθεξῆς in Acts 11:4 particularly enlightening: "Peter's recounting καθεξῆς is neither a chronological improvement nor an abbreviated, simplified version of the narrator's account. Peter begins with his own vision of 'the sheet with unclean food' (11:5-10) over against the narrator's depiction of Cornelius at prayer and the visitation by an angel / messenger (10:1-3)" (Moessner, "Appeal and Power of Poetics," 100).

58. Cf. Moessner, "Appeal and Power of Poetics," 112.

complex sequences, and in its lack of critical reflection on the material.[59] Thus, although the prefaces to Luke and Acts have been considered by many as a signal that Acts belongs to the genre of ancient historiography, a survey of the narrative discourse of Acts tells a different story. I therefore follow Loveday Alexander, who has recently come to argue that the prologue(s) may not be genre indicators for Luke and Acts after all. Here, Alexander's perspective has shifted: In her earlier works, Alexander argued against reading the Gospel prologue in terms of Greco-Roman historiography,[60] but suggested that it has more in common with *Fachprosa*.[61] However, at a recent SBL meeting in San Antonio (2016), Alexander introduced a developed version of her earlier position, this time in specific relation to the preface to Acts.[62] According to Alexander, this preface may not be indicative of genre as such, for *Fachprosa* is not a genre. It is a linguistic register, which serves a specific purpose in a specific setting. In the case of Acts' preface, its linguistic register serves the function of beginning the book (which requires formality and solemnity of language), and of positioning the written text in relation to oral traditions. This, however, is not the same as indicating genre.

The preface nevertheless provides a stepping stone for Alexander to further discuss the question of genre: The preface to Acts explicitly presents itself as a continuation of the Gospel of Luke, the "first book." But if the reader expects the preface to explain the contents of Acts, (s)he will be disappointed. Rather than explaining what the following story will be about, the narrator identifies a resurrected leader, Jesus. In terms of genre, this could suggest a biography. However, any resemblance to this genre disappears together with the initial explanatory framework that Acts begins with: The narrator's voice suddenly gives way to Jesus (1:4), who presents a perspective that embraces no less than the whole world (1:8). This is not a convention familiar to readers of Greco-Roman literature, and differs from ancient historiography where the primary focus is national or civic. Furthermore, a number of elements appear in Acts for which no explanation is offered: Who is John? What is the Holy Spirit? What are apostles?

---

59. Shauf, *Divine in Acts*, 267-82.

60. Alexander, *Preface*, 200.

61. Alexander, *Acts in its Ancient Literary Context*, 3.

62. Loveday Alexander, "Gospel of Luke: Luke: Historian and Theologian: Engaging the Work of David Moessner and Loveday Alexander. Luke, Historian—and Theologian: A Conversation with Loveday Alexander." 21st of November 2016. SBL Annual Meeting 2016. What is presented above is based on my own notes made during the talk. Any shortcomings or potential misunderstandings are my own, but Alexander did read through the the above prior to submission.

With the disappearance of familiarity, the reader is left to seek out conventional clues to understand what kind of work (s)he is reading. These conventions are found, Alexander argues, not in ancient historiographies, but in the Septuagint. This coheres well with Acts' rhetorical presentation of the content of the Jesus movement's proclamation as a continuation of the story found in Israel's Scriptures. Alexander is not the first to suggest that Acts resembles biblical history,[63] but her perspective breaks new ground because she shifts the focus from the author's intention in writing the text, to the question of whom the text is going to and *paideia*. This focus on the reader allows the insight that for a person to be able to conceive of something as belonging to a specific genre, she or he must be educated, and must through this education have been introduced to classic works that shape knowledge of different genres. The texts presented in education are primarily classic texts. These accordingly become the texts that control and mould reader expectations. In the case of Acts, Alexander argues, the controlling classic text does not belong to any of the ancient historians like Thucydides, Polybius, etc. Instead, Luke's classical text is the Septuagint. Luke is, in short, Alexander argues, writing "biblical history." This, in turn, is a genre flexible enough to accommodate other linguistic modes and literary codes, and with room for echoing other stories that would likely also have been recognizable to ancient readers through the classical works read in their education.[64]

How do the above observations add to our concept of the reader? First of all, we do well to acknowledge that the prologue to Luke's Gospel signals that the method and intention of the author coheres with the values of ancient history writing. Luke 1:1–4 both locates Luke-Acts *in* history, and invites the reader to accept the author's truthfulness and reliability *about* history. Even if Acts may be closer to biblical history in terms of genre, its aim can be readily located among ancient historiographies. Through its claims to truth, the prologue thus moulds a "willing" reader, who is ready to accept and follow the author's literary cues. When we read Acts, these cues are closely related to the literary world of the LXX. The Septuagint is part of the reader's cultural encyclopedia, and is the classical text which allows the reader to pick up literary cues about how and where God is at work; and it is similarly these texts that shape the expectations of how God will come to act.

These expectations about whom Israel's God is and how this God acts, include an emphasis on the particularity of the God of Israel as sharply

---

63. Cf. Rosner, "Acts and Biblical History," 65–82.

64. Hellenistic and Greco-Roman education's focus was on Homer. See e.g., Hezser, "Torah Versus Homer," 10. Thus, e.g., as we will see in chapter 8, the shipwreck story in Acts closely resembles the shipwreck story in another classical work in antiquity, i.e., the *Odyssey*.

distinguished from other gods. They also include a notion of the partiality of this God towards Israel, which in contrast to the partiality of the gods in Greco-Roman historiography is based on election rather than merit and virtue. Direct divine speech is expected rather than speech uttered through oracles. The existence of God's Spirit and angels is assumed; as is God's affirmative response to prayer. Moreover, divine retribution is understood as a response to the countering of God's demands, rather than as punishment for hubris or impiety.[65] Through the author's writing of biblical history, the reader is invited to see the events of the Jesus movement's recent past as a continuation of Israel's history, and to not only accept, but positively evaluate God's interference. Acts can therefore neither be expected to be hyperbolic nor tragic in its portrayal of God, but seeks to demonstrate the "truth" about the emergence of the Jesus movement as the continuation of God's story with God's people, as part of a world in which God acts and reigns.

2.2 The Character and Characterization of God in Acts

Much has changed since 1992 when John A. Darr pointed out the neglect of work on biblical characterization in Lukan scholarship.[66] As recently as 2016, an entire monograph was dedicated to *Characters and Characterization in Luke-Acts*.[67] Here, thirteen contributors showcase a number of narratological approaches to characterization in Luke-Acts, each of which is combined with other theories and perspectives. The contributors focus on characterization in conversation with elements as diverse as genre, cognitive narratology, sociolinguistics, intertextuality, and reception history.[68] Thus the book as a whole exemplifies how characterization in Lukan scholarship has grown into an area of interest that opens up for a number of conversations and perspectives.

As characterization is gaining ground in biblical studies, it is important to stay alert to the fact that there are different approaches to "characterization," and that these are in turn embedded in different theoretical frameworks. A pertinent question for our study of Acts is whether terms and categories from modern literary theory can be used on an ancient text at all, or whether we should restrict our perspective to the use of ancient

---

65. Shauf, *Divine in Acts*, 75–91; 93–96.
66. Darr, *On Character Building*, 11.
67. Dicken and Snyder, *Characters and Characterization*.
68. See the contributions by Sean A. Adams, Joel B. Green, Julia A. Snyder, Stephen E. Fowl, and Frank E. Dicken. The examples mentioned above do not cover all the contributions in the book, but are illustrative of its range.

literary categories in order to do justice to Acts as a product of a time different from our own. The answer one gives would ultimately depend on a number of considerations, including the purpose of one's study. If my intention had been to present a hypothesis of what ancient techniques of characterization were employed by the actual author of Acts, it would have been appropriate to make ancient literary theory my point of departure. As it is, however, I approach the characterization of God in Acts from the perspective of a "competent reader," which, in simplified terms, means that I consider how a character can be meaningfully understood in the present based on "cultural encyclopaedic knowledge" from/about the past. In this context, modern literary categories become the means of perceiving and expressing "what is going on" in Acts; but by stating this I am not making the claim that an ancient reader would have perceived the exact same things without access to the same categories.[69]

Having made these observations, we now turn to God as a character in Acts. Before we can begin to discuss the characterization of God, we must begin by asking who "God" in Acts is (sec. 2.2.1). This will then take us to the question of how God is characterized in Acts, and what literary categories elucidate this characterization (sec. 2.2.2). Finally, we look at how the reader may discern the actions on which most of the characterization of God in Acts is based (sec. 2.2.3).

2.2.1 God as Character: Who is "God" in Acts?

2.2.1.1 Distinguishing God from Jesus and the Spirit

This study argues that it is possible, and even meaningful, to speak of the portrayal of "God" in the Acts of the Apostles. But who is "God" in Acts? The answer to this question is not immediately obvious. In working on this project, it has become clear that for many, my research question evokes associations to the church's Trinitarian reading of the Bible. These reactions signal the importance of stating that when I refer to "God," I do not refer to what the church has come to call "the Trinity." Equally important, however, is the corollary observation that to most people it is not entirely clear whom I am referring to when speaking of "God" in Acts at all. If a character is mainly defined by its designations and actions, then the "God" of Acts is not so easily delineated. One problem is that God's actions are frequently performed through others. We have already addressed the task of discerning

---

69. Cf. Bennema, who dispels the charge of anachronism in employing modern terms on ancient texts, "provided we remember that the terms or categories we use may be unknown to the ancient authors and audiences" (Bennema, *Theory of Character*, 55).

God's actions in sec. 2.1.1. The challenges we will address here, however, include the fact that both God and Jesus[70] are referred to as (ὁ) κύριος, and that God, Jesus, *and* the Holy Spirit are referred to as subjects of the same action (cf. Acts 16:6–10). Therefore, to say that by "God" I mean the character referred to mainly through variations of "Father" (πατήρ), "God" (θεός), and "Lord" (κύριος; δεσπότης), is only to offer a partial answer.[71]

The subsequent section sketches the beginning of an answer to the following questions: How is it possible to delineate God as a character when the actions of Jesus and the Holy Spirit are so bound up with God's purpose? In what ways do the actions of Jesus and the Holy Spirit influence the characterization of God? In answering these questions, I first look at how God's character is construed in relation to Jesus, and then on how God's character is construed in relation to the Holy Spirit. Ultimately, this will allow me to clarify on what terms I speak of "God" as a character in this book.

2.2.1.2 God and Jesus

In Acts, a tension between correlation and dissimilarity characterizes the relationship between God's and Jesus's characters: God and Jesus are both construed as distinct characters *and* as characters who are at times nearly impossible to distinguish from each other.[72] As a result, ambiguous discourse of God arises from the manner in which God and Jesus are presented in similar, and sometimes overlapping, ways.[73] The manner in which this impacts the characterization of God may be addressed both by employing christological vocabulary, and from a more literary approach. The focus of this chapter will be on the latter, but we begin with a few words on the Christology of Acts, as this allows us to clarify some of the present study's presuppositions.

---

70. Because κύριε denotes something along the lines of "sir," this term is also used by Cornelius when he addresses the angel in 10:4, and by Peter when he addresses the voice in 10:14 (some would argue that Peter recognizes the voice as Jesus, however, see sec. 6.1.1).

71. Because θεός is a generic term (cf. 17:23), I should specify that I am here talking about the θεός which has "The God of our ancestors" (ὁ θεὸς τῶν πατέρων ἡμῶν) as its referent.

72. See below. See also Hurtado, "God or Jesus?," 239.

73. This dynamic between correlation and difference is one of the ways in which the characterization of Jesus differs from that of other agents (e.g., the apostles, the Spirit, angels, etc.) through whom God works in Acts. It is, however, also one of the ways in which Jesus's character resembles other chief agent figures in ancient Jewish tradition. For more on this, see e.g., Hurtado, *One God*.

With the overlaps between the characterization of God and Jesus, there is little wonder that the Christological debate in Lukan studies has taken a turn from emphasizing a subordination Christology to a "high" or even "divine" Christology in Acts.[74] I would suggest that this shift has been aided by the narrative turn, which has enabled interpreters to consider more closely the similarities between the characterization of God and Jesus as agents in the narrative. Using the words of Andrew Chester, we may define and distinguish between,

> 'high' Christology, where Christ is seen as exalted and set in special relationship with God, and 'divine' Christology, with Christ being seen as on a level with God, representing in himself the divine Glory, and sharing the divine name, attributes and activity.[75]

If we employ the definitions of "high" and "divine" Christology used above, we will find that in many ways, both fit the characterization of Jesus in Acts: Jesus is not only exalted (2:22–24; 5:31) and set in a special relationship to God as God's son, Lord, judge, and Messiah (2:36; 9:20–22; 10:42; 17:31). Jesus is also, as will be pointed out throughout this book, characterized in many of the same ways as God (see esp. ch. 5).[76] Our study may therefore be said to be working from a perspective on Jesus that lies somewhere between high and divine Christology. I should make clear, however, that this position is not intended as a comment on the historical development of Christology, but as a way of clarifying how the characterization of Jesus in Acts can be expressed through christological language. Simply put, when we speak of the characterization of Jesus as located somewhere between the categories of "high" and "divine" Christology, it is a way of pointing out both that Jesus in Acts is, on a number of occasions, characterized in many of the same ways as God, but also that the characterization of Jesus inscribes him into other traditions of "chief agents" in ancient Jewish tradition, traditions of the Son of Man (7:56), the Messiah (e.g., 2:36), etc. It follows from this that, from a christological perspective, the present study does not consider Jesus as "being" God in Acts. However, it does acknowledge that Jesus is frequently

---

74. See Bovon's survey in Bovon, *Luke the Theologian*, 123–223. See also more recent publications emphasizing Jesus as divine, e.g., Turner, "Spirit of Christ and 'Divine' Christology," 413–36; Buckwalter, *Character and Purpose of Luke's Christology*; Henrichs-Tarasenkova, *Luke's Christology of Divine Identity*.

75. Chester, "High Christology," 33.

76. In chapter 5, we will see that Jesus is inscribed into the name theology of Israel's Scriptures. We will also observe how Jesus shares the designation κύριος with God, blinds Paul, and appears to Paul in a manner that resembles both that of God and/or God's intermediary figures.

presented *as* God, and that his character may in this capacity be said to be frequently identified *with* God.⁷⁷ With these observations, we anticipate our answer to the question of how God's and Jesus's characters are distinguished from each other in Acts.

From a literary perspective, an important question remains: To what extent is God characterized by Jesus in Acts? In order to illustrate potential answers to this question, we may draw up two positions: 1) Jesus's character is completely aligned with God's purpose. Everything Jesus does in Acts, Jesus does on behalf of God. Thus, everything Jesus does reveals God's purpose, and consequently who God is. This position sees little need of sharply distinguishing between God and Jesus's characters, and sees everything Jesus does as indirect characterization of God. The second position, while similar to the first in some regards, nevertheless distinguishes more clearly between God and Jesus's characters: 2) God and Jesus may share some of the same actions and the same purpose, but they are not entirely the same character—e.g., Jesus dies; God raises Jesus from the dead. It is not only the similarities between these two characters, but the dynamics between them, which put God's character into relief. These dynamics are based on difference. Not everything Jesus does provides indirect characterization of God.

At this point, it will come as no surprise to the reader that I prefer the second position. As we shall see in chapters 4 and 5 in particular, after the ascension it becomes far more difficult to differentiate between God's and Jesus's actions *in the story-time*. But to treat God and Jesus as the same character from this point onwards, may obscure the questions that arise precisely from the fact that two—initially distinct—characters now have so much in common. This is why our study maintains that it is fruitful to ask what happens to the portrayal of God, when Jesus's character comes to perform actions similar to God's and even takes on some of God's characteristics. Maintaining a distinction between "God" as a character and

---

77. It is perhaps possible to say that I position myself somewhere between Larry W. Hurtado and Richard Bauckham. Hurtado considers Jesus-devotion to involve an adaptation of principal-agent traditions in ancient Jewish monotheism. See Hurtado, *Lord Jesus Christ*, 53; cf. Hurtado, *One God*, esp. 17–40. Richard Bauckham views the "so-called divine functions which Jesus exercises . . . intrinsic to who God is. This Christology of divine identity is already a fully divine Christology, maintaining that Jesus Christ is intrinsic to the unique and eternal identity of God" (Bauckham, *Jesus and the God of Israel*, x). In short, whereas Bauckham considers the development of high Christology to have been "possible within a Jewish monotheistic context, not by applying to Jesus a Jewish category of semi-divine intermediary status, but by identifying Jesus directly with the one God of Israel" (Bauckham, *Jesus and the God of Israel*, 3), and Hurtado by contrast emphasizes the conceptual role of principal figures in the development of early high Christology, I am suggesting that the characterization of Jesus in Acts overlaps both with the ways in which God *and* God's intermediary figures are characterized.

"Jesus" as a character, then, opens up for a more nuanced picture of whom God in Acts is portrayed as, because it makes it possible to ask what *consequences* arise from the fact that God and Jesus are portrayed both similarly and differently. These dynamics of difference and similarity will be one of our focus areas in the following chapters. Here, we pause only to make some foundational, but initial observations about how God's character is construed in relation to Jesus's.

Acts shares a feature in common with most narratives, namely the significance of the beginning in terms of presenting important characters and laying the foundations for its plot. The first part of Acts' story establishes the characters of Jesus and God as separate characters. A closer look at the narrative yields some notable observations about how they are construed in relation to each other. First, the risen but not yet ascended Jesus orders his disciples to wait in Jerusalem "for the promise of the Father" (τὴν ἐπαγγελίαν τοῦ πατρός, 1:4). Jesus is thus the first one in the narrative to name God, with a designation used only by Jesus (or about his relation to God) in Acts: πατήρ.[78] The relationship between their characters is thus immediately presented as one between father and son, distinguishing the two characters from each other. In fact, the most obvious way in which God's and Jesus's characters are differentiated in Acts is through their separate designations: Jesus is mainly referred to as "Jesus" (Ἰησοῦς), "Christ" (ὁ χριστός), "Son of God" (ὁ υἱὸς τοῦ θεοῦ) and "Lord" (κύριος). God, on the other hand, is referred to mainly through variations of "Father" (πατήρ), "God" (θεός), and "Lord" (κύριος; δεσπότης). With the exception of κύριος, these terms distinguish God and Jesus from each other, but also define their mutual relation: Jesus is God's son and promised Messiah; God is Jesus's father. Thus, God's character is relationally defined from the beginning.

Before we continue, we must pause to address one problem raised by overlapping designations: What criteria are used to decide whether God or Jesus is the referent of (ὁ) κύριος? This kind of categorization has been attempted by others.[79] These attempts, however, seem to rely on a notion that the referent of κύριος is fixed, either as God or Jesus, or that it is deliberately ambiguous.[80] In line with the observations made above about reading as a process (see sec. 2.1.2), however, I would like to shift the perspective

78. Cf. Mowery, "Lord, God, and Father," 90.

79. See e.g., Schneider, "Gott und Christus," 161–74; Cheng, *Characterisation of God*, 237–39; Dunn, "Κύριος in Acts," 245–48. In terms of whom they consider the referent of κύριος, Cheng and Dunn distinguish between God, Jesus, and an ambiguous referent.

80. Note, however, that Schneider guards himself against ascribing any intentions to Luke. See Schneider, "Gott und Christus," 171.

from *intended* referent and instead speak of *interpreted* referent. I would like to propose that what to a first-time reader of Acts may appear to be a reference to God, could be understood as a reference to Jesus by a second-time reader; or perhaps one might say that at this point the referent has become ambiguous. In chapter 3, we will suggest that this dynamic is at play in Acts 2:21. Here κύριος initially seems to refer to God, but upon finishing Peter's speech, the reader could equally well understand it to refer to Jesus. In the present study, the choice of whether to interpret God or Jesus as the referent of κύριος in any given place will be argued based upon literary context. Where necessary, however, I will also distinguish between whom the referent appears to be to a first-time reader of Acts and a second-time or "experienced" reader. Finally, as these discussions will demonstrate, the periodic ambiguity in terms of whether God or Jesus is referred to, is part of what makes the portrayal of God in Acts distinctive.

The beginning of Acts also introduces Jesus as God's agent. This is initially done through the disciples' question in 1:6: "Lord, is this the time when you will restore the kingdom to Israel?" Their question assumes that Jesus will be the agent of the restoration. While the disciples' question points to Jesus, however, Jesus points to God: His father will ultimately be the one to decide when the times are right (1:7). Scholars disagree as to whether Jesus's cryptic response is meant as a postponement of the disciples' hopes for restoration, a rebuke because the disciples have not understood that Jesus's mission is universal, or an answer that includes both restoration for Israel and the gentiles.[81] However, I would agree with Alan J. Thompson that the context suggests that the disciples' question arises from the situation of Jesus's teaching. Thus Jesus's response, albeit vague with regards to when or where,

---

81. Thompson, *Acts of the Risen Lord Jesus*, 104–8. See also Turner, *Power from on High*, 299–302.

More recently, Jason Maston has attempted to "restore some honour to Jesus' earliest followers" ("How Wrong Were the Disciples?," 178) in the face of scholarly criticism of the disciples' question in 1:6 as ignorant. His article takes issue with those who assert the disciples were wrong for purportedly asking about a territorial, political, and national kingdom. Against these, Maston argues that the kingdom should be seen as territorial (the world and universe), political (God's kingdom clashes with human kingdoms, and calls for a cruciform way of life), and national (a national kingdom for Israel does not exclude blessings for non-Israelites). Maston's article touches upon a number of debates in Lukan studies within the limited scope of an article, which at times results in a lack of substantiation and nuance to his claims. However, we can note his general conclusion, namely that the disciples' question in 1:6 "does not betray complete ignorance. Rather, it reflects careful listening to their Lord's teaching" (178). Insofar as the disciples' question arises from a teaching situation, I would agree their question is not ignorant. However, the extent to which it reflects careful listening to Jesus's teaching is a much larger debate, and Maston has not completely convinced me of his view. See Maston, "How Wrong Were the Disciples?," 169–78.

does not deny that a restoration will take place. However, Jesus's words link the disciples' expectations to the power of the Spirit to bear witness to the ends of the earth (cf. 1:7–8), and thus to the entire mission in Acts—including the gentile mission. "Restoration" in this sense must, accordingly, encompass not only Israel, but the diaspora and gentiles too.[82] With respect to this study's topic, we observe that Jesus's words suggest that Jesus submits his own actions to God's will, hence submitting himself to God's authority. However, they also tie God and Jesus to the same purpose of bringing about restoration. As we shall see below, when Jesus and God come to share in a joint purpose, this has consequences for understanding the actions attributed to both Jesus and God later on in the narrative.

Jesus and God's characters are, perhaps, most fundamentally distinguished through Jesus's resurrection and his ascension.[83] The relationship between the resurrection and ascension has engendered much debate in Lukan scholarship, both in terms of historicity and what relation they bear to Jesus's exaltation.[84] To fully address this issue falls outside the scope of this inquiry, but some observations which directly impact our study must be addressed. In terms of our focus on God's actions, the resurrection as God's act is a central feature of the apostles' proclamation throughout Acts (e.g., 2:24; 13:33–34). Because it has taken place before the story-time, it is mentioned specifically only after Jesus's ascension (2:24 et al). The Gospel of Luke separates the resurrection (Luke 24:1–12; 24:50–51) and the ascension in time, and Jesus's appearance in Acts takes place after the resurrection and before his final departure from the disciples (1:1–11). But even if the two events happen at different moments in the Lukan narrative, we shall see in chapter 3 that both resurrection and ascension are *theologically held together* as part of the process of Jesus's exaltation in Acts (2:31–33). Therefore, I treat the resurrection and ascension as two separate acts of God, but nevertheless consider them both part of the process of Jesus's exaltation.[85] The fact that God is the agent of the resurrection (cf. e.g., 13:30) is one of the most distinctive ways in which God's character is set apart from Jesus's. The ascension of Jesus is God's first action in the story-time of Acts, narrated through divine passives that describe Jesus as being lifted up (ἐπήρθη, 1:9, cf. ὁ ἀναλημφθείς in 1:11) into heaven (1:9–11). Both resurrection and

---

82. Cf. Thompson, *Acts of the Risen Lord Jesus*, 104–8.

83. Gerhard Lohfink notes that the intense focus on sight-language in Acts 1:9–11 emphasizes the apostles as witnesses the the ascension. See Lohfink, *Die Himmelfahrt Jesu*, 186–87.

84. Kevin L. Anderson offers a helpful survey; see Anderson, *"But God Raised Him from the Dead,"* 6–10.

85. So also Walton, "'Heavens Opened,'" 65.

ascension may consequently be seen as acts of God which distinguish God's and Jesus's characters from each other.

Even though the *act* of the ascension presupposes a distinction between Jesus and God's characters, this study will show that the ascension makes it more difficult to distinguish between their characters.[86] This claim presupposes that there is a time when this difficulty has not yet arisen. We argued this above, when we observed that Jesus and God's characters are distinct at the beginning of Acts, but that Jesus's will is submitted to God's. Even though Acts places God behind every stage of Jesus's life and ministry, their characters are still distinguished in important ways throughout Jesus's ministry, such as by Jesus's eating and drinking with his disciples (10:41). If we move to the Gospel of Luke, the distinction between God and Jesus's characters can be even better illustrated. In Jesus's prayer on the Mount of Olives, Jesus asks that his father "remove this cup from me; yet, not my will but yours be done." (Luke 22:42). Not only does Jesus address God directly as πάτερ; Jesus and God's wills are portrayed as separable from each other. Jesus's ascension (1:1–9), however, marks the end of his earthly ministry (cf. 1:1–2),[87] and his departure from his disciples. From this moment on, Jesus does not remain with them for extended periods at the time. However, even though Jesus no longer stays with the disciples, he does appear in visions to both Stephen (7:55) and Paul (9:3–7; 22:17–21), and hence he does not disappear from the story.[88] As our study will demonstrate, the distinction that has been maintained between God and Jesus's characters throughout Jesus's ministry is not as clear in Acts after the ascension, when God and Jesus are located in the same place (1:1–2, 10–11). As we shall see, their shared location comes to pose a challenge in terms of distinguishing between God and Jesus in Acts, and this in turn impacts the characterization of God.

---

86. Cf. also Sleeman (*Geography and the Ascension Narrative*, 258), who notes that there is a "functional blurring of the activities and titles associated with God and Jesus brought about by Jesus' ascension."

87. Lohfink, *Die Himmelfahrt Jesu*, 251–56.

88. Lohfink notes that the way Jesus appears to his disciples after his resurrection and after his ascension is different: "Bei den Ostererscheinungen befindet sich Jesus mitten unter seinen Jüngern. Er wandert an ihrer Seite, er läßt sich von ihnen berühren, er ißt und trinkt mit ihnen.... Ganz anders die Erscheinungen *nach* der Himmelfahrt: Jetzt zeigt sich Jesus in seiner δόξα (Apg 9,3; 22,6.11; 26,13). Visionsterminologie taucht auf (Apg 18,9; 22,17f; 26,19). Vor allem aber wird nun klar zum Ausdruck gebracht, daß er vom Himmel her erscheint" (Lohfink, *Die Himmelfahrt Jesu*, 274).

2.2.1.3 God and the Holy Spirit

The characters of God and the Holy Spirit are closely intertwined in Acts. This makes it difficult to say whether they should be conceived of as separate characters, or whether the "Holy Spirit" should simply be seen as a metaphor or circumlocution for "God." The extratextual material outside of Acts does not help us much in this regard. The conceptual background of the Holy Spirit in Acts may be found in Israel's Scriptures and intertestamental literature,[89] but Acts itself appears to be testament to a changing conception of the Spirit simply through the fact that the Spirit is now a gift poured out by the exalted Messiah rather than by God (cf. 2:33).[90] While it is possible to assert that a first-century reader/audience would conceive of the Spirit within the framework of monotheism, it is difficult to define the reader's preconceptions beyond this. By necessity, therefore, I leave these questions aside, and focus on Acts' literary construction of the Holy Spirit: While I would assert that it is both possible (and warranted) to conceive of the Holy Spirit as a separate character,[91] it is also possible to perceive of all the Holy Spirit's actions as providing indirect characterization of God.[92] This, in turn, has important implications for the portrayal of God in Acts. In the following, I will unpack and substantiate these claims.

To claim that God and the Holy Spirit are separate characters in Acts implies that the Holy Spirit may be understood as a character in the first place. There are good literary reasons for this. Like God, the Spirit may be identified through a number of designations, which also function as direct definitions:[93] "Holy Spirit" ([τὸ] πνεῦμα [τὸ] ἅγιον,[94] 1:2, 5, 8, 16; 2:4, 33, 38; 4:8, 25, 31; 5:3, 32; 6:5; 7:51, 55; 8:15, 17, 19; 9:17, 31; 10:38, 44–45, 47; 11:15–16, 24; 13:2, 4, 9, 52; 15:8, 28; 16:6; 19:2, 6; 20:23, 28; 21:11;

---

89. In the Hebrew Bible and LXX, the term "Holy Spirit" is rare (it only appears in Ps 51:13 and Isa 63:10-11). "The Lord's/God's spirit" and pronominal variants thereof are more frequently used. See Horn, "Holy Spirit," 3:264.

90. See ch. 3.

91. Robert L. Brawley suggests that "the divine appellation 'Holy Spirit' may serve as nothing more than a convenient designation of God" (*Centering on God*, 115). It is not entirely clear whether Brawley intends this as a general statement about the Spirit in Luke-Acts, but it nevertheless does not seem to take into account the challenges this statement runs into by the fact that *Jesus* is said to pour out the Spirit on Pentecost (2:33).

92. Cf. William H. Shepherd: "The characterization of the Holy Spirit in Luke-Acts is an indirect characterization of God" (Shepherd, *Narrative Function*, 255).

93. I owe the insight that these expressions for the Spirit function as direct definitions to Hur, *Dynamic Reading*, 131.

94. The adjective is sometimes placed before the noun.

28:25), "my [God's] spirit" (τὸ πνεῦμα μου, 2:17–18), "the Lord's spirit" (τὸ πνεῦμα κυρίου, 5:9; 8:39), "Spirit of Jesus" (τὸ πνεῦμα Ἰησοῦ, 16:7), "the promise of my [Jesus's]/[the] Father" (ἡ ἐπαγγελία τοῦ πατρός, 1:4), "witness" (μάρτυς, 5:32), and "gift of God" (ἡ δωρεὰ τοῦ θεοῦ, 8:20). These designations make it possible to distinguish their referent as an agent whose actions impact the plot: The Spirit testifies, forbids travel, travels in space, appoints leaders, and speaks.[95] Thus William H. Shepherd argues that, "Insofar as Luke presents the Spirit as an actor in the plot, Luke presents the Spirit as a character. And inasmuch as Luke presents the Spirit in conflict with other characters, again, the Spirit can be considered a character."[96] While the Spirit is, arguably, only involved in conflict in Acts to a small degree,[97] numerous actions are ascribed to it.[98] It is mainly these actions that allow us to approach the Spirit as a character.

As a character, the Spirit is to some extent personified by the Spirit's actions. More than once, e.g., we read what "the Spirit says . . . " (8:29; 10:19; 13:2). This Spirit is not only personified in the likeness of a person, however. Ju Hur observes: "The Holy Spirit can be seen as a character who holds to dialectic paradigms of traits, i.e., those of 'person-likeness' *and* 'person-unlikeness'. In a word, the Holy Spirit in Luke-Acts is to be understood as a divine character."[99] While the Spirit's "person-likeness" is expressed through its words and directions to the believers, its "person-unlikeness" puts words to the fact that even though the Spirit may be presented as speaking and acting, it does not have any set physical form. Arguably, the only exception is when the narrator describes it to appear like, or accompanied by, tongues of flame at Pentecost (2:3).[100] The Spirit is, moreover, transcendent, not only in time, but in space: It spoke through the prophets in the past (cf. e.g., 4:25), and it is able to "fill" multiple

---

95. Shepherd, *Narrative Function*, 91.

96. Shepherd, *Narrative Function*, 66.

97. Shepherd argues that the Spirit is fundamentally part of the cosmic conflict between God and the devil in Luke-Acts (see Shepherd, *Narrative Function*, 94–95). I cannot see how this conflict is apparent in Acts, but I would agree that the Spirit could be seen as part of the "conflict" between Ananias, Sapphira, and the community, which results in the deaths of the former two (cf. 5:1–11, esp. v. 3).

98. Due to the argument about the Spirit's "person-likeness" and "person-unlikeness," I have tried to avoid using personal pronouns when referring to the Spirit. In some cases, however, where this has proven difficult or obstructive to the flow of the text, I refer to the Spirit as "it" in line with the gender of the Greek τὸ πνεῦμα.

99. Hur, *Dynamic Reading*, 130.

100. It appears in the shape of a dove in Luke (3:22). Cf. Hur, *Dynamic Reading*, 130.

characters at the same time (cf. 2:4; 10:44).[101] Thus the Spirit acts not only towards, but through other characters in the narrative.

To understand the Spirit's role in the presentation of God, we must look at how it is introduced at the beginning of the narrative. Here, Jesus is reported to be giving directions "by the Holy Spirit" (διὰ πνεύματος ἁγίου, 1:2), at the same time as he asks the disciples to wait in Jerusalem for the "Father's promise" (1:4, cf. 1:8). On the one hand, the Holy Spirit sanctions reliability to Jesus's words; on the other hand, Jesus's words foreshadow that the coming of the Spirit at Pentecost is the fulfillment of God's promise. This promise is, after the outpouring, confirmed by Peter through a Scripture citation from Joel (2:17–21, cf. Joel 3:1–5a). Peter then states that it is Jesus who has poured out the Spirit (2:33, see ch. 3). Already here, then, the Spirit is distinguished from God, because it is variously presented as an object of both God's and Jesus's action.[102]

The Spirit's descent heralds a new period in time (see 2:17 and sec. 3.2.1), and it enters the narrative to direct, encourage, and fill the followers of the Way. A key to understanding the Spirit's role in Acts is as the fulfillment of God's promise. As promise fulfillment, the Spirit's outpouring at Pentecost is an expression of God's will. Because this is how it is introduced in Acts, the remainder of the Spirit's activity should be viewed in light of this: The Holy Spirit's actions may be seen as expressions of God's purpose and reflect on God's character. In other words, the Holy Spirit indirectly characterizes God throughout Acts. This explains why similar actions may be accredited to God and the Spirit (3:18, 21), and why Peter presents lying to the Spirit as synonymous to lying to God (5:3–4). This also means that even though the Spirit can be distinguished from God as a character, its activity should be seen as God's activity. Nevertheless, we should not fail to note that the Spirit's actions in Acts are of a particular nature: On a number of occasions, the Spirit's descent inspires prophetic speech (e.g., 2:17–18; 11:28; 19:6), and its appearance is frequently associated with baptism (2:38; 8:12–16; 9:17–18; 10:47–48; 19:1–7).[103] Even though God may also be said to speak through the prophets (see 3:18), inspired or prophetic speech is in Acts primarily related to the Spirit's activity. In this sense, the Spirit in Acts

---

101. Hur, *Dynamic Reading*, 156–57.

102. God, on the other hand, is never the object of the Spirit's action.

103. The relation between baptism and the reception of the Holy Spirit has proved a bone of contention. Some would claim that Peter's statement in 2:38 should be perceived of as programmatic, and hence that baptism always precedes the gift of the Holy Spirit. Literarily speaking, however, Acts seems to emphasize the close relation between baptism and the reception of the Holy Spirit, rather than the order in which the two take place. See, e.g., 8:14–17; 10:44–48, cf. 11:16–17; 19:1–6.

is associated with the function of *God's spirit* in the LXX.[104] Furthermore, God's actions are not always the Spirit's actions. For instance, Acts does not once state that the Spirit created the world or raised Jesus from the dead. In this narrative, these actions are God's alone.

We have seen that the Spirit can be distinguished from God, and while its activity is of a particular nature, it should be understood as God's activity. The close connection between the Spirit's activity and God's purpose may be further substantiated by Shepherd's and Hur's insights. In their revised PhD dissertations, published seven years apart, both approach the Spirit in Luke-Acts as a character.[105] One of Shepherd's insights regarding the Spirit's function in Acts is that it ensures the reliability of God's promises in Acts, and as such, the reliability of God.[106] It does so, Shepherd suggests, by inspiring prophetic speech which is later fulfilled, and because it "intervenes directly to bring to pass what God has ordained (see especially Acts 10–15)."[107] It is not difficult to see that these observations weave the Spirit closely together with God's purpose. This close connection is further substantiated by Hur's observations. Hur, building on John A. Darr, argues that "a divine frame of reference" guides the reader in discerning the reliability of characters and events in Acts.[108] The Holy Spirit is part of this frame of reference,[109] and

> the reader is encouraged to grasp that not only the Holy Spirit (and other elements of the divine frame of reference), but also characters who are inspired and guided by the Holy Spirit are characterized as God's (divine and human) reliable agents revealing/initiating, developing and accomplishing/confirming his purpose/plan in the development of the narrative of Luke-Acts.[110]

The Spirit's function as a validator of God's purpose through people and events makes the Spirit little more than an agent of God's and a functionary of the plot. In this sense, the Spirit may indeed be seen as "the onstage representative of the offstage God,"[111] providing indirect characterization of God throughout the story.

---

104. Cf. Turner, *Power from on High*, esp. 86–138; 348–52.
105. Shepherd, *Narrative Function* (1994); Hur, *Dynamic Reading* (2001).
106. Shepherd, *Narrative Function*, 246–47.
107. Shepherd, *Narrative Function*, 246.
108. Hur, *Dynamic Reading*, 100–1.
109. Hur suggests that "the Lukan narrator's ideology is theocentric, christocentric and pneumocentric, and he evaluates or judges any characters and incidents in these terms" (Hur, *Dynamic Reading*, 113).
110. Hur, *Dynamic Reading*, 114.
111. Shepherd, *Narrative Function*, 40.

What, then, are the consequences of distinguishing between God and the Spirit, while nevertheless maintaining their interrelatedness as described above? If the Spirit is the "onstage representative of the offstage God," then the Spirit brings God's agency into the narrative, at the same time as God remains concealed "offstage," as an acting but hidden God. The Spirit is gift and promise fulfillment; as gift, however, the Spirit points to and is revelatory of its origin (God). Moreover, the coming of the Spirit allows the reader to better observe Jesus's power as the exalted Messiah: We have already noted that he is the one to pour out the Spirit on Pentecost (2:33). From this point onwards, the Spirit is also Jesus's spirit (cf. 16:7). The fact that Jesus is the one to pour out the Spirit, means that Jesus's role in the fulfillment of God's promises in Acts can not only be found in his resurrection and exaltation as God's Messiah. Jesus also brings about the fulfillment of his father's promise (cf. 1:4) as he pours out the Spirit (2:33). Thus, the "discourse of God" in Acts indissolubly links the characters of Jesus and the Holy Spirit to the activity of God and God's plan, and hence to how God is portrayed.

2.2.2 God as Character: The Characterization of God

The basis for answering how God is portrayed through actions is the investigation into how God's actions *characterize* God. We must therefore look at "how" the characterization of God happens before we can speak of "whom" God is characterized as. While it is necessary to establish the former in order to say something about the latter, it is ultimately the latter that this study is concerned with. My perspective on characterization is both text- and reader-oriented: "Texts are necessary for characters to exist and subsist; individual minds are needed to actualize them."[112] To borrow words from Richard P. Thompson, "Characterization, as presented in this study, refers *both* to the textual images and descriptions of characters *and* to the reader's construction, evaluation, and reevaluation of those characters."[113] In other words, characterization is here considered the construction of character based on the text, i.e., the reader's analyses of the ways in which the implied author presents a character. The *portrayal* is the resultant image of a character that the competent reader is left with after having read the entire narrative. The portrayal we are talking about in this study will be the product of the characterization of God *through actions* in the story.

---

112. Margolin, "Character," 67. Cf. e.g., Burnett, "Characterization," 5.
113. Thompson, *Keeping the Church in its Place*, 28.

My thesis question relies upon an approach to God as a character. Because θεός is a generic term (cf. 17:23), I should specify that I am here talking about the θεός who has variations of "The God of our fathers" (ὁ θεὸς τῶν πατέρων ἡμῶν), "Father" (πατήρ), "highest" (ὕψιστος), and "Lord" (κύριος, δεσπότης) as its referent. Like Robert L. Brawley, I would argue that, in the narrative world of Acts, God exists as a character because God can be located in the space and time of the story, and it is possible for the reader to attribute different signifiers, such as specific actions and traits, to God's designations.[114] In short, God is a character because God can be individualized and is described to act in the story world.[115] This is further supported by Mark A. Powell's character definition: "Characters are the actors in a story, the ones who carry out the various activities that comprise the plot."[116] Because it is the reader who connects the actions and traits to God's designations,[117] and in this way individualizes God as a character, we may say that God's character is "an *effect* of reading."[118]

God in Acts may be defined as a character, but in doing so, this study adopts some of the challenges faced by literary critics. One of these is the question of what characters are—"people" or "words." The question reflects the basic positions of mimetic criticism and semiotic criticism. In the former view, characters are fictive people; they imitate reality, so that in order "to understand characters, readers tend to resort to their knowledge about real people."[119] In the second view, character is understood "as mere words or a paradigm of traits described by words."[120] In this view, character "dissolves into textuality,"[121] and are at most "patterns of recurrence, motifs which are continually recontextualized in other motifs."[122] The problem with both, however, as summarized by Weinsheimer, is that "the former [semiotic criticism] cannot account for the interchange, even

---

114. Brawley, *Centering on God*, 110–11.

115. Cf. Margolin, "Character," 66: "Character can be succinctly defined as storyworld participant."

116. Powell, *What is Narrative Criticism?*, 51.

117. It is sometimes difficult to discern whether it is God or Jesus who should be considered the referent when κύριος is used. Where this is the case, a close reading and analysis of the contexts and sequence in which this designation occurs might shed some light on whom the referent is; and, where this fails to elucidate the matter, it may be equally fruitful to highlight the ambiguity in the narrative, cf. sec. 2.2.1.2.

118. Burnett, "Characterization," 5.

119. Jannidis, "Character," para. 7.

120. Jannidis, "Character." See also Rimmon-Kenan, *Narrative Fiction*, 31–34.

121. Rimmon-Kenan, *Narrative Fiction*, 33.

122. Weinsheimer, "Theory of Character," 195.

identity, between the world and the text; the latter [mimetic criticism] cannot account for their difference."[123]

If we apply the above views to God's character in Acts, then two observations become acute: First of all, it is impossible to say whether God in Acts imitates "God," for it is debatable whether one can even talk about the ontological existence of "God" in the first place. If Acts' God were to imitate "reality," then it would be an imitation of religious conceptions, dogmas, narratives, and experiences of God. Moreover, because a number of approaches to characterization inevitably take as their "norm human characters who, in some respect or another, are like 'real people,' one wonders whether the best we can ever do is to offer a characterization of God in terms that we usually use to characterize human beings."[124] At the same time, God is *not* characterized in the same way as human characters. Because the characterization of God lacks such elements as social location, physical description, or descent, what is not said about God also becomes an important aspect of the narrative's portrayal of God.[125]

Secondly, to speak of "God" merely as "words" seems, to my mind, to overlook the observation that this character, while embedded into the discourse of the narrative, is nevertheless a product of the interaction between text and reader, and hence a construct that cannot immediately be constrained merely by its textuality—for the character arises through this text–reader interaction.[126] Perhaps it is wise then, having acknowledged that the mimetic and semiotic views pertain to the ontological status of characters, to make a move from ontology to pragmatism. By this I mean that the present study acknowledges that theories of character, rather than speaking of ontological status, may function as "cognitive instruments, tools, or points of vantage, all of which coexist at any given time as options for the theorist."[127] This allows our investigation to focus on "God" as textualized, but also leaves room for what it means for the reader's preconceptions to interact with this somewhat textually constrained entity.

Moving on from this debate, we note that the lack of such elements as, e.g., physical description makes it important to ask what the characterization of God does in fact rely on. We have made a case for suggesting that,

---

123. Weinsheimer, "Theory of Character," 208.
124. Thompson, "'God's Voice,'" 187.
125. Thompson, "'God's Voice,'" 186–87.
126. Cf. also Burnett ("Characterization," 6), who argues that while a character may be reduced to textuality, "character as an *effect* of the reading process can 'transcend' the text" (emphasis original).
127. Margolin, "The What, the When," 455.

in Acts, the characterization of God primarily relies on God's actions.[128] We will say more about how God's actions may be discerned below (ch. 2.3). For now, however, it is important to repeat and clarify that when this study speaks of God's actions, it refers both to God's actions as they are mentioned or narrated by the narrator (and take place in the story-time of the narrative), *and* actions of God as they are presented by different characters in the story (and take place in the past, present, and prospective future of the story-time). Because our study seeks to discover what image of God the narrative communicates to its readers in relation to the development of its plot, we will primarily consider texts that express the implied author's point of view. This means we will be looking at texts where God and God's actions are presented by "reliable" narrators. Furthermore, actions mediated through others will also be considered among actions of God in those cases where God is also credited with said action. In order to approach the characterization of God through actions in Acts, however, certain literary tools and categories will be employed. To these we now turn.

2.2.2.1 Story and Discourse

With the above observations as a backdrop, we now turn to the tools and terms we will be employing in our approach to the characterization of God through actions. First of all, as this is a narrative study, it will pay attention to elements pertaining both to the narrative's *story* and *discourse*: "Story refers to the content of the narrative, what it is about.... *Discourse* refers to the rhetoric of the narrative, how the story is told."[129] This distinction should not obscure the fact that both the "what" and the "how" of the narrative are intimately connected, but story and discourse nevertheless remain useful categories in distinguishing the focus of the questions that will be asked

---

128. The different character types frequently employed by narrative criticism seem to me to be unsuitable categories for this study. For instance, to say that God is a "round" character would indicate that God is characterized as complex, dynamic, and capable of surprise, which may in fact be how certain readers would interpret God's characterization as a result of the descent of the Spirit on "all flesh" (2:17). It seems to be one of the concerns of the implied author to clarify that God does not change, however, but that what God does is foretold in Israel's Scriptures (see sec. 6.3). Rather than classifying God's character as either this or that kind of character, then, the present study finds it more useful to discuss how God is characterized in the past in comparison with how God is characterized in the characters' present, rather than restricting this discussion to pre-made categories. In my treatment of the Spirit (2.2.1.3), however, I have used the term "functionary," which applies to characters who "are there for the effect that they have on the plot or its characters" (Berlin, *Poetics and Interpretation*, 32).

129. Powell, *What is Narrative Criticism?*, 23.

of the text: What does God do (story)? How are God's actions presented (discourse)? By whom are these actions focalized and narrated (discourse)? What are their settings (story)?

2.2.2.2 *Settings*

Settings indicate where, when, and how God's actions occur.[130] That God created the world (4:24; 7:50; 14:15; 17:24) and acts in the present by sending an angel to free the apostles from prison (5:17–21; 12:6–11), are examples of first a temporal, and then a both temporal and spatial setting, which reveal the variation and potency of God's actions. More significantly, the emergence of the mission in Jerusalem and its movement out into the world and towards Rome impacts the way God's character is presented and thus demonstrates the way in which settings play a part in broadening the image of God.[131] We may also observe that social settings are significant; for instance, when God in Acts sends his angel to the house of a gentile (10:1–6), this has different implications for the characterization of God than sending an angel to the house of a Jew might have.

With regard to temporal settings, we have previously noted that Acts refers to actions of God which extend beyond the time of the events depicted in Acts. At this point it may therefore be useful to distinguish more clearly between *the story-time* or *narrative present*, which refers to the events that take place within the chronology of the events narrated in Acts; *the time before the story-time*, which designates God's actions from creation until Jesus's ascension; and *the time after the story-time*, which refers to the future and day of judgment. In Acts, it is primarily the direct discourse of the apostles that brings together these three temporal times.[132] It follows from this that the actions that take place in the story-time must be understood as part of a larger narrative of God's actions with the world from creation until judgment. The actions that characterize God are therefore not only the actions that take place in the story-time. They also include the actions

---

130. Cf. Powell, *What is Narrative Criticism?*, 69. Given how Powell continues (70–75), this seems to refer to spatial, temporal, and social settings. Cf. also Marguerat and Bourquin, *How to Read Bible Stories*, 77–84. Marguerat and Bourquin also write that settings can be everything from a geographical, to a cultural, or a social setting.

131. Note, e.g., the differences between which of God's actions are presented in Peter's speech to the Jews in Jerusalem and which ones are referred to in Paul's speech to the Greeks at Areopagus.

132. Note, e.g., the believers' prayer (4:24–30); Stephen's speech (7:1–53); Paul's speech in Athens (17:22–31).

which Acts refers to that reach beyond the time of the first Jesus believers, and into their past and future.

2.2.2.3 Plot

Literary criticism has long discussed the relationship between plot and character, or character and actions. The debate goes all the way back to Aristotle, who in his discussion of tragedy subordinates character to action in the plot (Aristotle, *Poetics*, 6:15–30/1450a [Halliwell, LCL]). Nowadays, Henry James is often cited as a mediator between this and the opposite view:[133] "What is character but the determination of incident? What is incident but the illustration of character?"[134] Naturally, James's observation goes hand in glove with the present study, where incident—or actions—are seen to illustrate God's character, and God's character, in turn, will be seen to determine most of the incidents in Acts.

The above is simply another way of saying that God's actions relate to and impact the plot of Acts. "The plot in a dramatic or narrative work is constituted by its events and actions, as these are rendered and ordered towards achieving particular emotional and artistic effects."[135] This definition reveals that a plot is about more than a sequence of events; it is about the manner in which these events are related and connected to each other, and *how* the way they are recounted initiates a response from the reader. The sequence of the events, the conflicts around which they are organized,[136] how the events and themes are presented—all of these contribute to the formation of the plot. Moreover, through the ordering and presentation of events, causality is revealed, tension created, and emphases made. In Acts, God's actions are intimately connected to the causality of the plot and the tension in the story. For instance, the extension of the mission to the gentiles may be seen as a causal consequence of God's "action" in Peter's vision, and to lead to a tension between the view of those who assert that the baptized should also be circumcised, and those who believe that they need not be (see Acts 15).

The plot of Acts may be described as follows:

> *The Acts of the Apostles tells the story of how, after he has instructed his apostles for forty days, the resurrected Jesus is raised by God to heaven. From here, the Holy Spirit is poured out. This*

---

133. See, e.g., Rimmon-Kenan, *Narrative Fiction*, 35; Burnett, "Characterization," 5; Bennett and Royle, *Introduction to Literature*, 63.

134. James, "Art of Fiction," 80.

135. Abrams, *Glossary of Literary Terms*, 159.

136. Amit, *Reading Biblical Narratives*, 46–47.

event initiates the apostles' mission from Jerusalem, to Samaria, and onwards. Through their witness, the apostles meet with a mixed reception, and face many trials and persecution. God, however, frequently intervenes in their hardships, and gradually reveals what it entails for their witness to be taken to the ends of the earth—to both Jews and gentiles.

The plot in Acts is episodic, which means that the story consists of events or "episodes" that are held together by its characters and main themes. Because the protagonists shift throughout Acts, the common theme of bearing witness becomes one of the most important connecting links. Additionally, Scott Shauf rightly argues that programmatic prophecies and the divine plan "are the central causes that drive the rest of the narrated happenings."[137] In our own words, the plot in Acts is driven forward by divine causation. This means that even where human causality is lacking as a means of binding the different episodes together, the motive of God's plan connects the different scenes together and creates progression.[138] This progression can, as suggested above (and in 1:8) be geographically traced from Jerusalem, to Judea, Samaria, and beyond.

2.2.2.4 *The Implied Author, Narrators, Narration, and Focalization*

The *implied author* is not the historical author, but the author suggested by the text. (S)he, or rather, this principle, is the "subject of the narrative strategy"[139] and may be constructed by paying attention to such elements as the text's style, presentation of characters, and values.[140] The "voice" of the implied author, the one who addresses the reader, is the *narrator*. The "persona" of Acts' narrator shifts throughout the course of the narrative: from a first person singular narrator who directly addresses the *narratee*, Theophilus (1:1–5), to an omniscient narrator (most of the story), and a "we-narrator" who on a few occasions intrudes into the account (16:10–17; 20:5–15; 21:1–18; 27:1—28:16). Much can and has been said in research on Acts about the function of the different narrators that cannot be repeated here.[141] However, in my analyses, I will pay attention to the narrator's role in the characterization of God.

---

137. Shauf, *Divine in Acts*, 279–80.
138. See Shauf, *Divine in Acts*, 286–87.
139. Marguerat and Bourquin, *How to Read Bible Stories*, 13.
140. Marguerat and Bourquin, *How to Read Bible Stories*, 13.
141. See e.g., Kurz, *Reading Luke-Acts*; Campbell, "Narrator," 385–407.

The narrator of Acts is what may also be called an extradiegetic narrator, who (with the exception of the we-passages) narrates the story from a perspective outside of the story. I will normally refer to the extradiegetic narrator simply as the *narrator*. The characters in the story can be considered intradiegetic narrators when they offer accounts to other characters in the narrative.[142] This is the case with, e.g., the speeches. For the sake of simplicity, I will refer to the intradiegetic narrators as *character narrators* throughout this study.

In addition to narration, *focalization* also plays a part in mediating the story, and hence in shaping and guiding the reader's reading: "Narration is the telling of a story in a way that simultaneously respects the needs and enlists the co-operation of its audience; *focalization* is the submission of (potentially limitless) narrative information to a perspectival filter."[143] The term *focalization* first arose as a result of the wish to distinguish between the theoretical questions of "who speaks" and "who sees" in a narrative.[144] Focalization happens either through character focalizers or external focalizers: "When focalization lies with one character which participates in the fabula as an actor, we could refer to internal focalization."[145] External focalization, on the other hand, happens when "an anonymous agent, situated outside the fabula, is functioning as focalizer."[146] When it comes to Acts, this means that the narrator *can* be the focalizer, but need not be. In the case of e.g., Stephen's vision (Acts 7:55–56), what Stephen sees is *focalized* through Stephen's character, but it is the narrator who first *tells* what Stephen sees. Hence Stephen's character becomes an internal focalizer, but his vision is initially narrated by the narrator (7:55), before the narration is taken over by Stephen (7:56).

By means of narration and focalization, the implied author invites the reader to positively or negatively evaluate other characters and their points of view. Because who says and sees what matters, it will be our task

---

142. See the explanation of what extradiegetic and intradiegetic narrators are, in Marguerat and Bourquin, *How to Read Bible Stories*, 25.

143. Jahn, "Focalization," 94.

144. Genette, *Narrative Discourse*, 186. The concept of focalization was originally introduced to literary theory by Genette. Since then, however, *focalization* has been debated and conceptualized differently among literary critics. The term has, most notably, been critiqued and developed by Mieke Bal. See, e.g., Bal and Lewin, "Narrating and the Focalizing," 234–69; Bal, *Narratology*, 145–63. For the purposes of the present study, we adhere to a concept of focalization closer to that of Bal than that of Genette. Simply put, we consider focalization as "the relation between the 'vision,' the agent that sees, and that which is seen" (Bal, *Narratology*, 149).

145. Bal, *Narratology*, 152.

146. Bal, *Narratology*, 152.

throughout this study to consider who speaks of God and through whom God's character is focalized. Is it the respected Peter, or an opponent of the apostles? How does this affect our understanding of the portrayal of God? In Acts, the narrator is always trustworthy, and so are Jesus and God.[147] This means that any character aligned with their values and perspective may be considered authoritative. For instance, the manner in which Peter is characterized makes it easy to accept his words about God, while the words of the apostles' opponents must be considered more carefully.

2.2.2.5 Modes of Characterization

It is in the interaction between direct and indirect characterization and the reader that the portrayal of God emerges. Because the primary characterization of God in Acts takes place through actions, it is to a large extent *indirect* characterization that is used. In contrast to direct characterization, where the reader is given direct information about someone by the narrator, "indirect characterization is the product of an analysis of the persona's discourse and his/her actions and conduct."[148] The difference between the two modes of characterization may be illustrated with examples from the larger biblical narrative: The Deuteronomist's statement that "the Lord your God is a merciful God" (Deut 4:31) is direct characterization of God, whereas the description of God's action in giving the Israelites manna in the desert (Exod 16) characterizes God indirectly. Both modes of characterization reveal a merciful God, but in the case of the latter, it is the action that reveals the mercy and not any explicit statement.

Regardless of how they are recounted, God's actions in Acts characterize God indirectly. This is true both when these actions are spoken of in speeches (where God's deeds are related and God's words cited), and when God intervenes in narrative events. It is worth noting that, to some extent, the analyses made in this study will involve a move similar to a move from indirect characterization to direct characterization. In asking what the indirect characterization reveals about God, the answer seeks to make the

---

147. See sec. 2.1.4: It follows from the concept of the reader as "willing" that (s)he considers the narrator trustworthy and reliable. "The narrator is reliable in that his perspective is always borne out in the text and he always speaks in accord with the norms of the work (he fully and faithfully represents the implied author)" (Darr, *Herod the Fox*, 80n53). This reliability may be further exemplified by the fact that the narrator never provides false information, what the narrator foreshadows comes to pass, etc. As the ascended "hero" of the story, Jesus must also be considered reliable, and so is God, the one whose plan is coming to fruition throughout the narrative.

148. Darr, *On Character Building*, 74.

implicit explicit. Even as we make this observation, it is important to be aware that because "readers rely upon their knowledge of the trait-name in the real world, traits are culturally coded."[149] Where possible, I will try to use language native to a first-century setting in describing God's character. However, in inferring traits or choosing words to describe God's character based on the indirect characterization of God, I must acknowledge that I am to some extent at the mercy of the vocabulary of my own time.

Indirect and direct characterization are often referred to as "tell" (direct characterization) and "show" (indirect characterization). However, while these designations frequently overlap, the comparison is somewhat imprecise. Although "telling" may indeed include direct characterization, i.e., direct statements made about God's character, "telling" may also refer to those accounts of God's deeds that are informative rather than descriptive. Peter and the other apostles' statement that "The God of our ancestors raised Jesus" (5:30) is one example of "telling." The reader is informed about the fact, but there is no description of how it happened. In Acts, God's actions are mostly "told" of in the speeches. Outside the speeches, however, we find examples of "showing." The appearance of the Spirit at Pentecost (Acts 2:1–4) and Peter's vision (10:11–16) are illustrations of this. Here, the reader is not only informed of God's actions, but these actions are described in enough detail that the reader may picture them. It follows from this that in Acts, "showing" coincides with indirect characterization. Interestingly, it also coincides with what we, influenced by Marguerat, label implicit discourse of God (see sec. 2.1.1).

2.3 Delimitation and Project Outline

In these past two chapters, we have looked at previous research on God in Acts and defined our own project as a study of the characterization of God through God's actions. By studying God as a character, we are looking at how this character is constructed through God's actions within the narrative of Acts as a whole, and how a resultant portrayal of God emerges in the dynamic between text and reader. However, by this point it has become clear that God's actions are so many and presented in so different ways that it would be impossible to analyze them all. A selection must suffice, and so we turn to the question of delimitation. We must then ask: Which of God's actions are so representative of the presentation of God in Acts and of such significance to the unfolding of the plot so as to merit focus and attention?

---

149. Bennema, *Theory of Character*, 45, following Chatman, *Story and Discourse*, 123–25.

The following provides the justification for the material we have chosen to look at in the following chapters.

The majority of the chapters in this book will look at how God is depicted, either by the narrator or characters, at decisive moments or *turning points* in the narrative plot. "Turning point" is here used quite broadly about events with significant causal consequences for the further development of the plot. This also brings some necessary limitations to this study. To look at how God is depicted "at the turning points" does, however, also safeguard a number of concerns that make sure we do justice to the characterization of God. As the chapters delineated below reveal, this kind of selection ensures that God's actions are always connected to *significant themes* in the story, and illustrate a *variety* of actions. It also allows us to look at how God—through God's actions—is presented from *different perspectives*: The narrator's, Peter's, Stephen's, Cornelius's, and Paul's. As will be made clear throughout the course of this study, these all represent the implied author's point of view, at the same time as their voices combine to elucidate God's character from different angles. Finally, the themes introduced in these texts, such as the descent of the Spirit, the persecution of the Jesus movement, the proclamation of the word, etc., run as common and recurrent themes throughout the narrative. This suggests that the selection below is *representative* of the narrative as a whole. It is my hope, therefore, that the choice of texts below will—if not perfectly, then to a respectable degree—do justice to the characterization of God through actions in Acts.[150]

In our section about Acts' plot (2.2.2.3), we noted that God's first action in the story-time is Jesus's ascension. However, we have already touched upon this in sec. 2.2.1.2, and will return to the ascension's implications throughout this book. Our first chapter (ch. 3) therefore deals with the outpouring of the Spirit on Pentecost (Acts 2:1–41). This event is interpreted by Peter as both God's and the ascended Jesus's action, which allows us to start looking at the ascension's impact on the characterization of God. Importantly, this event is the first major turning point in the narrative, from which the apostolic mission springs. The Spirit's descent is, moreover, something which is repeated throughout the story, which both adds significance

---

150. Delimitation always comes at a cost, and some may wonder why I have not, for instance, included Paul's Areopagus speech among the above texts. However, although Paul's visit to Athens is certainly part of the plot, it is not decisive to its development. Simply put, it would have been possible to remove the speech from Acts without impacting either the course of Paul's journey, his proclamation, or any of the plot's conflicts. Furthermore, many of the things Paul says about God (e.g., God is creator and judge) are covered by texts included in our above selection, so these aspects of God are not neglected by our study.

to its descent, and makes God's role in its outpouring fundamental to the portrayal of God in Acts.

Our next chapter (ch. 4), takes us to the accusations against Stephen, followed by Stephen's speech and God's revelation to him (Acts 6:8—7:60). This is Acts' depiction of the culmination of the conflict between the Jesus believers and Jewish authorities; after Stephen's death, the Jesus believers are persecuted and spread into Judea and Samaria (8:1). How God is presented in Acts 6:8—7:60, both by Stephen and through his vision, is therefore of great interest insofar as it comes at a decisive point in the mission. The points of contact between Stephen's speech and his vision do, moreover, allow us to observe how a character narrator's depiction of God in Israel's past relates to Acts' depiction of God in the narrative present.

In term of Acts' plot, the mission to the gentiles is momentous. It is possible to observe at least three starting points for the gentile mission in the story: Philip's encounter with the Ethiopian eunuch (8:26-40), Paul's encounter with the risen Jesus (9:1-19), and Peter and Cornelius's visions and encounter (10:1-48). For the sake of delimitation, we do not look at the first of these, because after Philip's encounter with the eunuch, they both disappear from the story. The last two accounts, on the other hand, are of greater significance to the plot: The first account introduces Paul as an apostle to the gentiles and paves the way for his role as a protagonist, and the Cornelius account illustrates the descent of the Spirit on the gentiles and becomes part of the argument presented at the apostle meeting (Acts 15:1-21). In chapter 5, we therefore look at how God is characterized at some decisive moments in Paul's life and mission, at the same time as we review how God is portrayed by Paul through God's actions in Israel's history (Acts 9:1-19; 22:1-21; 26:1-23). In chapter 6, we then turn to look at God's implicit role and characterization in orchestrating Peter and Cornelius's encounter. We also consider how God's character is interpreted, first by Peter, and later by a number of the apostles at the apostle meeting (Acts 10:1—11:18; 15:1-21).

In chapter 7, we look at an example of the apostles' proclamation and turn to Paul's speech in Pisidian Antioch (13:13-52). Here, we survey how God is characterized through God's actions in Israel's past and how these are related to the narrative present. The speech and its aftermath prove a decisive moment in the narrative, illustrated by Paul and Barnabas's declaration that they from now on will take the gospel to the gentiles (13:46-47). In other words, this chapter allows us to address a question that arises for the reader as (s)he reads Acts, namely how God's character must be understood to relate to the Jews now that the gospel is also proclaimed to the gentiles. In order to answer this question, this chapter also addresses the ending of Acts.

In chapter 8, the final chapter to offer an in-depth analysis of the characterization of God in a specific passage, we turn to look at Paul and the ship crew's rescue from the storm (Acts 27:1–44). Without God's intervention through an angel, Paul would not have reached Rome. This makes both God's action and the passage decisive for the unfolding of the plot. This story does, moreover, illustrate well how God is (implicitly) depicted in the story-time.

In our second to last chapter, ch. 9, we look summarily at how God is characterized through a number of God's actions that have not yet been covered. These are actions which are largely mediated through others but accredited to God: They include the signs, wonders, and deeds of power performed by the apostles, their miraculous releases from prison chains; the deaths of Judas (1:16–25), Ananias and Sapphira (5:1–11), and Herod (12:21–23), and the blindings of Paul (9:1–19) and Elymas (13:4–12). This part does not add anything new to research on these acts, but suggests how their frequency and significance are constructive elements of the portrayal of God in Acts, and how they relate to our previous discoveries.

In our final and concluding chapter, ch. 10, we synthesize our findings and look at the sum of the characterization of God in Acts, asking what kind of portrayal of God is drawn through God's actions. Here we return to our initial questions, and explicate in what ways the actions and characterization of God in the story-time relate to the actions of God spoken of in Jesus's life and ministry and Israel's more distant past, and answer the question of how the characterization of Jesus post-ascension impacts the characterization of God.

Chapter 3: The God of the Last Days (Acts 2:1–41)

3.0 Introduction

This chapter looks at the characterization of God in Acts 2:1–41. In these verses, the promise of the Father (ἡ ἐπαγγελία τοῦ πατρός), anticipated by both John the Baptist (Luke 3:16) and Jesus (Luke 24:49; Acts 1:4), is fulfilled in the coming of the Spirit. Throughout our analysis, three observations of direct relevance to our thesis will be developed in particular: First of all, the passages describing the events at Pentecost have a programmatic function. Not only do they introduce central aspects of God's character, Peter's speech also frames the entire narrative in the temporal setting of the eschatological age, points forward to the universal mission, and introduces salvation as a fundamental theme. Secondly, the events at Pentecost allow us to observe some foundational elements in terms of how God is characterized in relation to Jesus after his ascension. Thirdly, the theophany and Peter's subsequent speech are illustrative of how God is characterized both explicitly, implicitly, and ambiguously in Acts.

This is the first time in Acts that God is explicitly said to be acting in the story-time.[1] The scene moves from implicit characterization of God through the theophany (2:1–4), to explicit affirmation of God's actions in Peter's speech (2:14–41). As the speech continues, however, the reader's understanding of God as an agent at Pentecost is negotiated when Peter first states that it is God, but later that it is Jesus, who pours out the Spirit. This, together with Peter's statements about God's involvement in Jesus's life, death, and resurrection, allows us to make some initial observations about how the relationship between God and Jesus is construed in this speech.

---

1. God is by no means absent from Acts' beginning, however. God is the agent behind Jesus's ascension (1:2, 9), and responds to prayer in the election of a new apostle (1:24–26). Jesus's words to the disciples also foreshadow God's future actions: God has given the promise of the Spirit (1:4) and will give the disciples power to witness when the Spirit arrives (1:8). God is, moreover, said to have acted in the past by establishing the times and seasons of history (1:7).

This, in turn, provides a backdrop for how we talk about "God's actions" and hence the characterization of God later on in this book.

The narrator in Acts 2 does not characterize God directly, but the indirect characterization of God in these verses is expressed in different ways. The implicit discourse (i.e., the theophany) in 2:1–4 is followed by Peter's speech, in which the implied author employs the words of Peter as a character narrator, and Scripture in Peter's mouth, to name God and point to God's actions (θεός, 2:17, 22–24, 30, 32, 36, 39; κύριος, 2:25, 34; πατήρ, 2:33), both in the theophany in the story-time, and in moments in Israel's history. Peter's speech is then followed by the reaction of the crowd and the subsequent baptism of 3,000 people. Together, these elements are typical of Acts in the way they call attention to and communicate God's presence and activity from different perspectives.[2] They do, moreover, place God's portrayal within a framework in which the experience and words of the believers, Scripture, God's promises throughout Israel's history, and Jesus's life, death, and resurrection all play a significant role.

The following analysis of the presentation of God in Acts 2 takes its point of departure in the following structure:

>   2:1–13: A Theophany of Sound, Flame and Spirit
>   2:14–36: Peter's Speech
>   2:14–21: "'And in the last days it will be,' says God"
>   2:22–28: God's Works through Jesus
>   2:29–36: The Lord's Lord
>   2:37–41: God's Universal Promise of Salvation

3.1 A Theophany of Sound, Flame, and Spirit (2:1–13)

The sudden appearance of the sound of a driven, violent wind from heaven (2:2) implies God's presence, but God is not mentioned explicitly. The audition is followed by a vision of tongues of fire, which are divided[3] only to settle on the apostles (2:3). These receive the Spirit, which enables them to speak in different languages. In the text itself, the origin of the sound from heaven, the place of God, implies God's presence.[4] The suddenness or im-

---

2. Cf. e.g., 12:6–11, where the angel of the Lord leads Peter out of prison, but the Lord is credited with the escape (12:17), and all of Paul and Barnabas's signs and wonders (Acts 13–14), which are interpreted as God's work through them (15:4, cf. the Lord's testimony to them in 14:3).

3. Gr. διαμεριζόμεναι (Act 2:3), literally "dividing themselves."

4. Alan J. Thompson suggests that after Jesus's ascension, "readers are prepared to understand . . . the risen and ascended Lord Jesus of Acts 1 is behind the events of

mediateness of the event is also typical of how Acts points to divine interference (cf. παραχρῆμα, 3:7, 5:10; 12:23; 13:11; ἄφνω, 2:2; 16:26).[5] But the sound of wind and the vision of flames are also recognizable elements of nature theophanies in Israel's Scriptures, where God's presence and/or power is manifested through natural phenomena.[6] Of direct interest to our reading is the observation that God's presence, and sometimes more explicitly God's glory, is sometimes associated with wind, fire, and flame in these Scriptures (e.g., Exod 19:17-18; 24:17; Deut 4:11-40; Pss 18:8; 21:8-9; 29:7; 104:1-4, etc.). The key word is "associated," however: For the most part in this kind of theophany, "in the strict sense God does not 'appear' at all; it is only the consequences that are visible, and only they are described in detail."[7]

Mikeal A. Parsons suggests that the theophany in Acts 2 is so vividly described that it merits the designation *ekphrastic* language, which denotes a graphic description. The function of *ekphrasis* is, in short, "to draw attention to the significance of the event thus described for the overarching argument of the narrative."[8] So also here: The theophany and gift of the Spirit are of fundamental importance to the narrative; not only does

---

Acts 2" (Thompson, *Acts of the Risen Lord Jesus*, 130). To some extent, I agree with Thompson, because it is not unproblematic to understand the phenomena accompanying the descent of the Spirit as a theophany rather than a christophany. I do not believe, however, that the reader is prepared to interpret this as the ascended Jesus's action from heaven *just yet*. I nevertheless do believe that the events at Pentecost and Peter's speech together prepare the reader to observe the ascended Jesus's actions from heaven at a *later* stage in the narrative. I will develop this argument in the following chapters.

5. Cf. Larsson, *Apostlagärningarna 1-12*, 38.

6. "Theophany" is a term widely used by scholars "for descriptions of the appearance of God in the Hebrew Scriptures. . . . God is understood by Israel to be a reality different from the world and unlimited by it (1 Kgs 8:27; Amos 9:2-4; Ps 139). Yet in theophanies God is revealed by self-limitation to specific places and particular forms within the world itself. The distinctive places and forms within the world which become modes of divine manifestation in Israel are to be found in the realm of nature and of human society" (cf. Hiebert, "Theophany in the OT," 6:505).

7. Schmidt, *Faith of the Old Testament*, 163.

The citation above deserves further clarification: The theophanies listed in the main text exemplify theophanies in which God's presence or glory is associated with wind, fire, and flame. However, they do not all exemplify theophanies where merely the "consequences" of God's appearance are visible. They differ in terms of whether God is "seen" directly: The Exodus account suggests that Moses and his entourage "saw" God (Exod 24:9-10); the account in Deuteronomy is clear that God's form is not seen (see Deut 4:12). Even within the biblical material, however, there is a tendency to qualify assertions that someone "saw God" "so as to deny that anyone actually sees God directly, or face to face" (Thompson, *God of the Gospel of John*, 111-13). The "theophany" in Acts resembles those theophanies in Israel's Scriptures in which God's form is not directly seen.

8. Parsons, *Acts*, 38.

it spark the earliest mission in Jerusalem (cf. 2:14–41), but the gift of the Spirit also becomes the main argument in favor of a universal mission later on (cf. Acts 10:1—11:18; 15:1–21). We will return to these observations in chapter 6. For now, however, we note that in Acts 2:1–4, the reader is initially invited to observe God's presence in the theophany, through which God is characterized as master of both sound and flame. By employing imagery familiar to the reader as imagery associated with Israel's God, the narrator paves the way for Peter's declaration that it is indeed this God who is at work (2:17–36).

Acts 2:1 identifies the temporal setting as Pentecost or the Feast of Weeks.[9] The festival suggests why so many Jews from the diaspora have gathered in Jerusalem (2:5),[10] and why the disciples "were all together in one place" (2:1). The sound of wind, vision of flames, and resulting xenolalia takes place at a Jewish festival in Israel's cultic capital, which is full of Jews from both the city and the diaspora, and alert the reader to the presence of Israel's God. This temporal setting, in addition to some of the literary features of the text, has raised the question of whether the theophany and subsequent speech should be understood to evoke the Sinai event (Exod 19–24). With regards to our focus on God's actions, we can reframe the question to ask whether Acts 2 evokes the Sinai event so as to present God as offering a new covenant.

The answer to this question has been debated along two different, but intersecting lines: On the one hand, the question of setting evokes a *historical* question which pertains to how we consider the cultural encyclopedia: Was the Feast of Weeks connected to the commemoration of the covenant given on Sinai around the first century CE?[11] At stake when it comes to the present study's question is, in short, whether this connection should be considered part of the reader's cultural encyclopedia so as to invoke Sinai as a likely

---

9. The time is introduced by the typically Lukan ἐν τῷ + infinitive. The verb συμπληρόω usually denotes something that is already over, but in the present context it must refer to the arrival of Pentecost. See Schneider, *Die Apostelgeschichte 1,1—8,40*, 247–48.

10. The verb κατοικέω (2:5) leaves room for asking whether the Jews were living in Jerusalem permanently (as the verb, if read on its own, seems to indicate), or whether they were merely residing there during the festival. Given the Pentecost setting with people coming up to the city because of the festival, it seems likely that the latter is the case. Contra, e.g., Jervell, *Die Apostelgeschichte*, 134; Witherington, *Acts of the Apostles*, 135.

11. The connection between Pentecost and the the covenant given on Sinai is argued by, e.g., Pesch, *Die Apostelgeschichte (Apg 1–12)*, 108; Talbert, *Reading Acts,* 23; Jervell, *Die Apostelgeschichte,* 132; Spencer, *Journeying through Acts,* 42; Parsons, *Acts,* 36; Park, *Pentecost and Sinai,* 176–246.

frame of interpretation. On the other hand, we have the question of whether the *literary* features of Acts 2 invite the reader to read the Pentecost account in light of Sinai. Both questions relate to whether the Spirit's descent should be understood as God's action of making a new covenant.

Arguably, one of the strongest arguments in terms of both a historical and a literary connection to Sinai, is found in the similarities between Acts' description of Pentecost and Philo's description of how God passed on the commandments:

> I should suppose (μοι δοκεῖ) that God wrought on this occasion a miracle of a truly holy kind by bidding an invisible sound to be created in the air more marvellous than all instruments and fitted with perfect harmonies, not soulless, nor yet composed of body and soul like a living creature, but a rational soul full of clearness and distinctness, which giving shape and tension to the air and changing it to flaming fire, sounded forth like the breath through a trumpet an articulate voice so loud that it appeared to be equally audible to the farthest as well as the nearest. (Philo, *Decal.* 9.33 [Colson, LCL])

Here, in Philo's imagination, sound in air changed to flaming fire accompany God's speech. But precisely because Philo introduces this as imagery arising from his own considerations (μοι δοκεῖ), it seems unreasonable to consider that his portrayal of God's speech at Sinai represents so common imagery for this event that the competent reader of Acts would immediately associate the theophanic signs at Pentecost with the theophany at Sinai. This, however, seems to be the argument that Max Turner attempts to make in a literary comparison between the passage from Philo with Acts 2.[12] Claiming to be unconvinced by the argument posited by Robert P. Menzies, namely that the imagery employed by both Luke and Philo is common theophanic imagery,[13] Turner uses the correspondences between the Lukan text and Philo to suggest it is "difficult to see how anyone can say the Pentecost account would not 'remind' a reader of Jewish Sinai traditions."[14] In further support of this observation, Turner suggests that in Peter's Pentecost speech, Jesus (especially in 2:33–34a) in the deep structures of the text is in fact presented as Moses who "ascends" to receive the Torah and give it to Israel.[15]

---

12. Turner, *Power from on High*, 283–85.

13. Turner, *Power from on High*, 283. See Menzies, who suggests that the language used is "not unique to Sinai traditions but characteristic of theophanic language in general" (Menzies, *Empowered for Witness*, 196; see also 194–96). See also Krodel, *Acts*, 75.

14. Turner, *Power from on High*, 285.

15. Turner, *Power from on High*, 286–88.

If we review Turner's arguments, however, it is somewhat difficult to grasp the logic of his first claim: Turner states there is no genetic parallel between the Lukan text and Philo,[16] emphasizes that they are describing two different events,[17] but concludes from the correspondences between their structural features that Acts 2 evokes Jewish Sinai traditions.[18] In fact, Turner's argument may just as easily be used in support of the claim he rejects from Menzies, namely that Philo and Luke both employ stock theophanic imagery. This does not exclude the possibility that the imagery employed in Acts 2 potentially evokes associations to the Sinai event for the reader, but it does not necessarily include it either. In terms of his second argument, Turner admits that the Jesus–Moses parallels are not found "in the surface structure of the argument, but they may inform the story's deep structure."[19] This argument does present the *possibility* that the Moses tradition influences the way Jesus is presented in Peter's Pentecost speech. Even if this were to be the case, however, the implied author primarily and *explicitly* invites the reader to view Jesus in light of his Davidic descent (2:30–36).[20] It is therefore to overstate the evidence to say that Peter presents Jesus as Moses, and that this links Pentecost to Sinai.

In terms of the historical question posed, Pentecost was eventually connected to the Sinai event, but the time during which this connection was made—and became widespread—is notoriously difficult to date. When looking at writers reasonably contemporary with Luke, i.e., Philo and Josephus, neither of them connect Pentecost to Sinai.[21] Instead, Philo describes "the feast which is held when the number 50 is reached" (Philo, *Spec. Laws* 2.179 [Colson, LCL]) as a harvest festival;[22] much in the same

16. Turner, *Power from on High*, 283.
17. Turner, *Power from on High*, 284.
18. Turner, *Power from on High*, 285.
19. Turner, *Power from on High*, 286.

20. See also Robert O'Toole, who argues that the Pentecost speech focuses on the promises made to David rather than on the covenant given to Moses. See O'Toole, "Acts 2:30," 245–58, esp. 248–56.

21. See Philo, *Spec. Laws* 2.179–87. Josephus (*Ant.* 3.252–54) mentions the offerings and sacrifices made on this festival (a loaf, two lambs, and whole burnt offerings). The other places where Pentecost is mentioned (*Ant.* 13.252, 14.337, 17.254; *J.W.* 1.253, 2.42, 6.299) do not mention the reasons behind the festival, though Josephus's works indicate, like Acts, that it drew many Jews to Jerusalem.

22. "The feast which is held when the number 50 is reached has acquired the title of 'first-products'. . . . One explanation of the name 'Feast of First-products' is that the first produce of the young wheat and the earliest fruit to appear is brought as a sample of offering before the year's harvest comes to be used by men" (Philo, *Spec. Laws* 2.179). "Another reason for the name may be that wheaten grain is pre-eminent as the first and

way that Israel's Scriptures describes Shavuot, or the Feast of Weeks (Exod 23:16; 34:22; Lev 23:15-22; Num 28:26-31; Deut 16:9-12). Jubilees, which is difficult to date,[23] connects the date both to the covenant on Sinai (Jub. 1:1) and God's covenant with Noah (Jub. 6:17-19). I do concede that Sejin Park may be right in suggesting that "it is impossible to think of covenant without law and vice versa, since the law represents the stipulations which are the heart of the covenant itself,"[24] and that Jubilees may consequently be read as evidence of a connection of the Sinai event with Pentecost. But even so, the counterevidence of the Pentecost-Sinai connection in both Philo and Josephus does not allow us knowledge of how widespread this assumption was by the time Acts was written. In conclusion, this makes it difficult to argue that the Sinai event should crucially inform the reader's understanding of the temporal setting.[25] It would seem then, that the tenuous connection between Sinai and Acts' Pentecost does not allow us to answer the question of whether God is presented as offering a covenant through the descent of the Spirit. However, we shall explore this question a little further in section 3.4 below.

Arguably, a more reasonable background on which to read Luke's depiction of Pentecost may be found in the story of Babel (Gen 11:1-9).[26] The focal point of this intertextual connection is the apostles' sudden ability to speak in different tongues; multiple languages[27] characterize the events of Pentecost and Babel alike.[28] For those who uphold the similarities between the two accounts, the question is whether Pentecost represents a reversal of Babel or a parody of it. Richard I. Pervo is a modern representative of the former view,[29] observing that "By reversing linguistic

---

best product, all the other sown crops ranking in second class in comparison"; Philo, *Spec. Laws* 2.181).

23. Jubilees as a complete work is known from Ethiopic sources from the fourteenth century, and what was likely a complete copy in Latin from the sixth century. All other evidence remains fragmentary.

24. Park, *Pentecost and Sinai*, 200-1.

25. See also Menzies, *Empowered for Witness*, 189-201. Note also Bock, *Acts*, 96: "Luke's lack of appeal to this idea means that the debate over the background for Acts is not of such great significance for interpreting Acts, even though it may well have been at work in the cultural backdrop to the event."

26. Cf., e.g., Spencer, *Journeying through Acts*, 43; Pervo, *Acts*, 61-62.

27. Given the geographical locations from which Peter's audience comes, both languages and dialects could be in view. See Green, "'In Our Own Languages,'" 201.

28. More similarities can be traced, see the summary of the linguistic similarities to the LXX in Davies, "Pentecost and Glossolalia," 228-29.

29. The view that Pentecost represents a reversal of Babel goes back at least as early as to the fourth century, (see e.g., Cyril of Jerusalem, *Catechetical Lectures* 17.17),

disunity, the experience is revealed as both an eschatological event of new creation and a utopian restoration of the unity of the human race."[30] It is not entirely clear what Pervo means by a reversal of linguistic disunity here, but he seems to refer to a recovery of the unity of the languages dispersed at Babel. He further emphasizes that the gift of the Spirit is "for the entire human race,"[31] which arguably suggests that the unity is also a result of the universal gift of the Spirit.

While unity is an important keyword here, Acts 2 does not, like Pervo suggests, "reverse linguistic disunity" unless one refers to the unified *comprehension* of the apostles' words in the vernacular. In fact, this very disunity is the central feature of the account (cf. 2:4, 7–11).[32] But to what end? In "In Our Own Languages," Joel B. Green reads Babel's "one language" as a "metaphor in the Ancient Near East for the subjugation and assimilation of conquered peoples by a dominant nation."[33] Without repeating his entire argument here, we can note that Green proposes to read Acts 2:1–13 as displacing visions of empire ("Babel- and Jerusalem- and Rome-centered visions of a unified world").[34] This displacement, however, is not a replacement of unity, but a different unity than one created by language: "Unity is found at Pentecost, but not by reviving a pre-Babel homogeneity. With the outpouring of the Spirit, koinonia is possible not by the dissolution of multiple languages but rather by embodiment in a people generated by the Spirit, gathered in the name of Jesus Christ."[35] Accordingly, both Green and Pervo appear to suggest that the gift of the Spirit creates unity at Pentecost. This is a fruitful observation. When this study reads Acts 2 from this perspective, a contrast between Babel and Pentecost emerges through which the reader, as (s)he continues to read or listen, is invited to see God as someone who reaches out to unify people through the Spirit. In this sense, the apostles' speaking in different languages reflects God's

---

persists throughout the Middle Ages (as evidenced in Bede, *Venerable Bede*, 2.4) and is still argued today (see below).

30. Pervo, *Acts*, 61–62.

31. Pervo, *Acts*, 62.

32. Cf. Krodel, *Acts*, 76: "On the contrary, Luke assumed that the disciples spoke in a multitude of languages." Dunn also observes that this poses a problem in terms of viewing Acts 2 as an allusion to Babel; for him, however, the problem of different tongues seems to result in a lack of pursuit of further connections to the Babel story. See also Dunn, *Acts of the Apostles*, 24. Dunn's conclusion may be a bit premature. As we note above, there are other reasons to view the Pentecost story as alluding to Babel.

33. Green, "'In Our Own Languages,'" 209.

34. Green, "'In Our Own Languages,'" 199.

35. Green, "'In Our Own Languages,'" 199.

reaching out to different people. Although the people present at Pentecost are primarily Jews and proselytes, the events at Pentecost, when read in light of Acts as a whole, arguably foreshadow the inclusion of the gentiles as people of God, not through their shared customs with the Jews, but through the gift of the Spirit (cf. 10:44–48).

The apostles' sudden ability to speak in different languages astonishes the listeners (2:8). They describe what they are hearing about as *God's deeds of power* (τὰ μεγαλεῖα τοῦ θεοῦ, 2:11). At this point, the specific contents of these deeds are not unpacked. The listeners' statement therefore comes to function as a summary of Peter's speech, or alternatively, as a preview to it: Peter focuses on God's deeds of power, and specifically links these to God's actions through Jesus (δυνάμεις, 2:22b). The main function of the theophany, however, is to alert the reader to the coming of the Spirit. Through its arrival, the "promise of the Father" (1:4, cf. Luke 3:16; 24:49) is fulfilled at last. The main function of this fulfillment with regards to the portrayal of God is, above all, to point to God's faithfulness.[36] What God has promised in the past, is realized in the present: God is a God who fulfills God's promises. This theme of faithfulness continues to be important in the speech that follows. As we shall see, that Jesus is made Lord and Messiah by God is also an expression of God's faithfulness, and this continues to be a significant aspect of God's portrayal throughout the entire narrative of Acts.

3.2 Peter's Speech (2:14–36)

Peter's speech makes God's actions explicit for the first time in Acts. As Peter interprets the experiences of Pentecost by quoting Scripture that directly names God as the sender of the Spirit (λέγει ὁ θεός, ἐκχεῶ ἀπὸ τοῦ πνεύματός μου, 2:17), God initially emerges as an agent in the unfolding events. However, this changes with the introduction of Jesus, whom Peter credits with the outpouring of Spirit (2:33). As we shall see, the way the Spirit's descent is credited to two different agents, plays a central role in how the speech introduces some of the fundamental dynamics between God and Jesus as characters in Acts.

3.2.1 "'And in the last days it will be,' says God" (2:14–21)

The first part of the speech (2:14–21) is focused around a citation from the prophet Joel, and provides a temporal frame within which the subsequent narrative of Acts may be understood: These are the "last days," whose

36. Cf. Cheng, *Characterisation of God*, 54.

CHAPTER 3: THE GOD OF THE LAST DAYS (ACTS 2:1–41)

beginning is signalled by the outpouring of the Spirit and which end with the arrival of the Day of the Lord (2:17, 20). As we shall see, the speech can be said to have a programmatic function for Acts, as it both interprets the events of Pentecost and foreshadows some of what later comes to pass in the story.[37] In doing this, the speech also demonstrates how the plot of Acts is dependent on God's actions, because both the outpouring of the Spirit and the signs which signal the last days have their origin in God. Finally, we shall see that in using Scripture to interpret the Pentecost events as proof-from-prophecy, Peter's interpretation takes its basis in God's faithfulness.

Prior to the point where Peter raises his voice (2:14), the narrator has already indicated his prominence among the apostles through the placement of his name as first on the list of the eleven (1:13), and then through his central role in electing a new apostle (1:15–26).[38] His character may therefore be considered to offer both a reliable and authoritative point of view on God's actions in the unfolding events. Denying some of the onlookers' charge of drunkenness (2:15), Peter interprets the arrival of the Spirit and the xenolalia through words from the prophet Joel (Acts 2:17–21, citing Joel 3:1–5a). The scriptural citation differs from the manuscripts of the Septuagint that we have access to today: In Acts, λέγει ὁ θεός is added, and ἐν ταῖς ἐσχάταις ἡμέραις (2:17) replaces the LXX's μετὰ ταῦτα. At this point, we also run into variant readings in the manuscripts to Acts. Θεός is replaced by some witnesses with κύριος,[39] and ἐν ταῖς ἐσχάταις ἡμέραις is replaced by ἐν ταῖς ἡμέραις ἐκείναις.

It does not make much difference to our interpretation of the text if θεός is replaced by κύριος (2:17): Because the "Lord" is said to be speaking

---

37. Stanley E. Porter calls Peter's speech a "programmatic statement for the book," and Richard F. Zehnle calls it a "keynote address." See Porter, "Scripture Justifies Mission," 104–26; Zehnle, *Peter's Pentecost Discourse*, 95, 130–31.

38. Needless to say, it is from his role as an apostle that Peter's character gains its greatest authority. Like the other apostles, he has accompanied Jesus throughout his ministry, "beginning from the baptism of John until the day when he was taken up from us" and is a witness to Jesus's resurrection (1:21–22). While Peter had a prominent role among the disciples in the Gospel of Luke too, it is worth noting that Acts, in contrast to the Gospel of Luke, portrays Peter as trustworthy. His reliability in Acts may be observed through the way he speaks on behalf of the Twelve, proclaims the gospel, and interprets Scripture. By way of contrast, Peter's character in Luke failed Jesus (Luke 22:54–62). This shift in characterization of Peter's character is, in my opinion, one of the arguments for why Acts may be read as an individual narrative.

For the use of Scripture as a means of characterizing Peter as a leading character, see Arnold, "Luke's Characterizing Use," 308–9.

39. Most notably, Codices Bezae and Laudianus here have κύριος. Θεός, however, is better attested among the textual witnesses and is less conventional; see Pervo, *Acts*, 77n26.

through a prophet (Joel), the subject is better understood as God than Jesus, independently of whether God is designated θεός or κύριος. The difference between ἐν ταῖς ἐσχάταις ἡμέραις and μετὰ ταῦτα is greater. In those cases where the text is assimilated to the μετὰ ταῦτα in the Septuagint's Joel 3:1 ("after these things") in Vaticanus, Ephraemi Rescriptus, 076 and some Sahidic traditions (and with the reading μετὰ ἡμέραις ἐκείναις [after those days] in 1175), the initial emphasis on an "eschatological age" disappears. Nevertheless, the eschatological imagery is retained in the rest of the citation, and still designates a timeline that ends with the Day of the Lord.[40] One challenge here is that it is not immediately clear from Peter's words what "after these things" would refer to.[41] What "these things" refer to is clearer in the majority of, including some of the oldest, textual witnesses.[42] These begin the citation with "in the last days." This reading is also explanatory of the eschatological language in the rest of the citation (2:17–21). Thus both the internal and external evidence favor this reading. We therefore follow it in the rest of our interpretation of Peter's speech. In this form of the quote beginning with "in the last days," which differs from extant versions of Joel, it is clear that it is God who is pouring out the Spirit and pronouncing the beginning of the last days. Pentecost is consequently theologically interpreted and God explicitly named by Peter. God thus emerges as an agent whose actions are unfolding in the present events.

The beginning and ending of the scriptural citation from Joel thus frame the events that unfold in Acts and situate them in the last days: The quote begins with a description of what is happening at Pentecost, ἐκχεῶ ἀπὸ τοῦ πνεύματός μου ἐπὶ πᾶσαν σάρκα (2:17), and ends with a promise of salvation, καὶ ἔσται πᾶς ὃς ἂν ἐπικαλέσηται τὸ ὄνομα κυρίου σωθήσεται (2:21). This provides an interpretive key for understanding the plot of Acts: The arrival of the Spirit is the catalyst of the mission, and later universal mission, in Acts, whose ultimate goal is to pave the way for God's salvation on the Day of the Lord. The Day of the Lord is here to be understood as the Day of Yahweh, which, in Israel's Scriptures is a day or judgment or deliverance: This judgment is variously depicted as judgment against foreign nations (e.g., Isa 24:21, Jer 25:33, Ezek 30:3–5, Joel 3:11–16), or either

40. Cf. Bock, *Proclamation*, 161.

41. The most immediate interpretation would be that "these things" refer to "the outpouring of the Spirit." This does not make sense, however, because the text would then mean something like "after the outpouring of the Spirit, I will pour out my Spirit." Nor is it likely that Peter should be understood to be talking about Jesus, for he has not yet introduced the Jesus story to his narrative audience.

42. These witnesses include, but are not limited 𝔓[56] and Codices Sinaiticus, Alexandrinus, and Bezae.

judgment against or deliverance of Israel (judgment: e.g., Amos 2:13–16; 3:14; 8:3,9; Hos 1:4–5; 5:9; Isa 3:18–4:1; 7:18–23; 10:3; 22:5; Mic 2:4; Ezek 7:7–12; Joel 1:15; 2; etc. / deliverance: e.g., Isa 2:2–4; 11:10–16; 12:1–4; 19:18–25; 25:6–9; Jer 23:5–6; Ezek 39:13; Mal 3:16–18).[43] Although all or either of these conceptions of the Day of Yahweh may be considered part of the cultural encyclopedia, we may note that in Acts' quote from Joel, the emphasis is on salvation. While God's role as judge could also be reflected (see below), in presenting salvation as the conclusion not only to the citation, but to "the last days," Acts as a whole may be viewed as a narrative which ultimately invites the reader to perceive of God as savior.

While I am submitting that the reader is initially led to understand God as savior here, it is not unambiguous whom the "Lord," whose name one must call upon to be saved (2:21) refers to. Several scholars read 2:21 in light of 2:36, and thus see Jesus rather than God as the obvious referent.[44] Their argument gains weight from the fact that Jesus has been referred to as Lord earlier in Acts (1:6, 21).[45] Also, the verb for "calling on" the name of the Lord in 2:21 is ἐπικαλέω, which is the same verb that is used when Stephen calls upon Jesus in 7:59. Furthermore, the title's referent could be considered to refer to Jesus in light of the Gospel of Luke, where "Lord" is frequently used about Jesus (see esp. Luke 2:11). In contrast to this conclusion, I instead argue for a potential ambiguity, which would allow a first-time reader to understand God as the referent of "Lord," only to have this comprehension negotiated later on. In support of a first-time reading of the referent as God, we observe that Jesus has not been mentioned so far in Peter's speech. There is therefore nothing in the text that points to Jesus as the "Lord" in question. God, however, is already in view (2:17, 20). Accordingly, Darrell Bock suggests that, "From the near context one might conclude initially that κύριος in Acts 2.21 refers to God. Thus the ambiguity would most certainly exist until the latter part of the speech."[46] Secondly, 2:21 follows from 2:20, which speaks of "the Lord's great and glorious day." As we have already noted, in Israel's Scriptures, this is the Day of Yahweh's judgment. Thus, it seems apparent that "Lord" in both 2:20 and 2:21 can initially be understood to have the same referent: God.[47] It is, however, important to observe that while

---

43. For more examples, see Hiers, "Day of the Lord," 82–83.

44. See, e.g., Schneider, *Die Apostelgeschichte 1,1—8,40*, 270; Pesch, *Apg 1–12*, 118; Hurtado, *Lord Jesus Christ*, 179; Fitzmyer, *Acts of the Apostles*, 254.

45. It is ambiguous whether Jesus or God is the object of the prayer in 1:24. See ch. 1, n. 97.

46. Bock, *Proclamation*, 165.

47. Barrett fails to note this nuance, and seems to have it both ways in his commentary. He suggests in one place that "salvation is offered to all who call upon God's name,"

"Lord" at this point seems to clearly denote God, this term is negotiated as Peter continues his speech.[48]

The Scripture citation from Joel ends with words that evoke God's salvation, but the largest portion of the quote in its entirety does not speak of salvation, but emphasizes the signs that herald the last days. We have already observed that through the citation from Joel, Peter interprets the theophany and ensuing speech as a result of God's outpouring of the Spirit in the last days (2:17). This action, initially presented as the first explicit action of God's in Acts, is purportedly done "on all flesh" (ἐπὶ πᾶσαν σάρκα, 2:17). Whether intended by Peter's character or not, his words come to foreshadow the universal mission, and as the narrative goes on, this phrase "on all flesh"—and the outpouring of the Spirit—come to indirectly characterize God as a universal God (cf. 10:44-48; 11:15-17; 15:8).

In addition to the coming of the Spirit, the signs heralding the last days include prophetic speech, visions and dreams, bestowed regardless of age, social status or gender (2:17-18). The quote further declares that God will place portents and signs on heaven and earth (2:19). Here, in contrast to the words in extant manuscripts to Joel (LXX), "Luke adds the words 'above,' 'signs,' and 'below,' emphasizing the inescapability of these events."[49] The words used for wonders and signs, τέρατα and σημεῖα (2:19), especially the addition of the latter, should not escape the reader's notice. The words sometimes appear nearly idiomatically together in the LXX, frequently functioning "as a formulaic depiction of YHWH's acts of delivering Israel from Egypt (Deut. 4.34; 6.22; 7.19; 26.8; 29.2; 34.11; Ps. 135.9)."[50] In Acts, the idiomatic expression serves to describe the work of God through Jesus (2:22), the apostles, Peter, Stephen, Paul, and other followers of the Way (cf. 2:43; 4:30; 5:12; 6:8; 8:6; 14:3; 15:12).[51] While this work is mainly centered on healing and exorcisms and thus differs from the signs specified in 2:19 as "blood, and fire, and smoky mist," it is difficult not to read the believers'

---

only to state later that the *name* in 2:21 refers to Jesus. See Barrett, Acts I-XIV, 129, 139.

48. By 2:36, Jesus has become the referent of κύριος. I would therefore suggest a distinction between a first reading of 2:21, in which God is clearly the referent, and a re-reading of 2:21 in light of the rest of Acts. In the latter reading, 2:21 becomes open for re-interpretation.

Ling Cheng seems to argue both that "the reference would be clearly to Yahweh" when the Jewish audience first heard the citation, *and* that "it is likely that God refers κύριος to a person other than himself" (Cheng, Characterisation of God, 51). For reasons suggested above, I find that this argument requires further nuance.

49. Gaventa, Acts, 77.

50. Moberly, "Miracles in the Hebrew Bible," 57-74, 58.

51. Cf. Parsons, Acts, 33-34.

CHAPTER 3: THE GOD OF THE LAST DAYS (ACTS 2:1–41)

"signs and wonders" as a reflection of the eschatological age heralded by God's own signs and wonders.[52]

So far, we have observed that the citation from Joel provides an interpretation of and temporal frame[53] for the events in Acts. This, together with its length and the fact that it begins one of the first and longer speeches in Acts,[54] allow us to regard it as *programmatic*. A few further examples will make this clear. First of all, the citation speaks of God's action of pouring out the Spirit. But Acts also speaks of the Spirit as descending on other occasions than on Pentecost; it fills and guides people, or is given, in a number of other places throughout the narrative (e.g., 4:8; 8:17; 10:44; 13:4, 52; 16:6–7; 19:6). In other words, the speech is also programmatic to the extent that it introduces the descent of the Spirit as a recurring and central motif.

A second example of the citation's programmatic function is Peter's speech. As Peter raises his voice, he himself is fulfilling the prophet's words that people will prophesy (2:17).[55] Not only the arrival of the Spirit, but Peter's words, may consequently be understood as proof-from-prophecy. Furthermore, both Peter's character, and later Paul's, are cast as prophets when they proclaim the gospel and what they perceive of as the will of God, and perform signs and wonders (see chapter 9.2.1).[56] They, and others, will be given visions and dreams (10:1–16; 27:23–36, cf. 2:17). These too, may in light of the citation be understood as originating with God, and can be understood as means by which God directs the Jesus movement. In sum, it is clear that later events in Acts may be read in light of the citation from Joel, as characteristics of the last days. Finally, it follows from the argument that this Scripture citation is programmatic for Acts, that *God's actions are programmatic for Acts*. God's actions are at the center of the words from Joel, and will remain central throughout Acts as God continues to send the Spirit and aid the apostles in their mission. These actions accordingly also seem to be part of the unfolding of God's purpose.

---

52. *Contra* Krodel, *Acts*, 81.
53. See Pervo, *Acts*, 79.
54. Cf. Spencer, *Journeying through Acts*, 45.
55. Parsons, *Acts*, 43. Note also that most manuscripts (Codex Bezae being the main exception) appear to add προφητεύσουσιν to the Joel citation in Acts 2:18. This is of interest mainly insofar as we regard Peter's speech as programmatic: In reemphasizing prophecy as one of the main results of the coming of the Spirit, the speech also foreshadows further "prophetic" proclamation in Acts.
56. Johnson, *Prophetic Jesus, Prophetic Church*, 32–33; McWhirter, *Rejected Prophets*, esp. 87–94. On Paul, see Najda, *Der Apostel als Prophet*, 237–41.

3.2.2 God's Works through Jesus (2:22–28)

When Peter addresses his audience once more (this time as Ἄνδρες Ἰσραηλῖται, 2:22), it marks a shift in focus. Jesus of Nazareth holds center stage in this part of Peter's speech. The presentation of Jesus, however, is heavily theologically founded:[57] *God* pointed him out, *God* attested to him through mighty deeds, wonders and signs (2:22),[58] it was through *God's* plan and foreknowledge that Jesus was delivered up and killed (2:23), and finally, *God* who released him from death (2:24). The rapid succession of these theological underpinnings of Jesus's life, death, and resurrection has as its key oratorical goal to convince Peter's listeners of Jesus's significance and legitimacy as God's agent: There is no point in the Jesus story that God did not will or bring about. It does, moreover, emphatically underscore the intimate connection between God and Jesus.

The interweaving of the Jesus story with God's actions significantly informs Acts' portrayal of God, so that "God is further characterized . . . through relationship and actions with Jesus."[59] In speaking of God as someone who worked deeds of power, wonders, and signs through Jesus (2:22), Peter presents God as someone who actively interferes in and through the lives of humans. This is also of interest to the larger story of Acts, as it reveals who is at work behind the apostles' signs and wonders. In this way, the way God acts through the life of Jesus reveals how Acts' God engages with the world through both Jesus and the Jesus movement.

God's plan, and thus the characterization of God as the master of history, is a central aspect of the characterization of God through the life of Jesus. Peter declares that Jesus was handed over to the Israelites "according to the definite plan [βουλῇ] and foreknowledge [προγνώσει] of God" (2:23). This statement is apologetic in content: Jesus's death was not a matter of failure of God's purpose, but was securely lodged in it.[60] Divine providence,

---

57. Cf., e.g., Bibb, "Characterization of God," 285.

58. It is interesting to read ἀποδείκνυμι (from ἀπόδειξις) in Acts 2:22 in light of ancient rhetoric: Read against this backdrop, the verb signifies that God is doing something convincing, demonstrating something to the world, through his deeds of powers, wonders, and signs. That this reading may have some merit is further suggested through the use of πίστις about Jesus's resurrection in 17:31: In ancient rhetoric, πίστις signifies *proof*, as does ἀπόδειξις. See e.g., Aristotle, *Rhetoric*, 1.11.

59. Bibb, "Characterization of God," 285.

60. Cf. Ling Cheng, referring to the contrast between God's and the Jews' role in the death of Jesus: "From such a literary strategy of contrast emanates God's overruling power which rules over the deadly force and amplifies God's omnipotent authority in keeping with his own plan" (Cheng, *Characterisation of God*, 53). Cheng's observation is to the point in terms of God's power. As a biblical scholar, however, it is important to be aware that it is both problematic and potentially dangerous to speak of "the Jews'

then, is explicitly expressed as a driving force in the story of Jesus. In some ways, this observation may seem to state the obvious. Its significance for Acts should not be overlooked, however, as *2:23 is the first time in Acts that Jesus's death is mentioned as part of God's plan.* As writers have observed throughout the centuries, Jesus's death was one of the potentially greatest stumbling blocks for the early church. If Jesus died, did he not then fail, and did not his claim to be sent by God fail with him?[61] In arguing that this was not the case, but that the point of "failure," i.e., Jesus's death, was inevitable, the text invites the reader to see the entire Jesus story under the purview of God's providence, and God is indirectly characterized as the lord of history. Christology thus becomes intertwined with theology, and God's purpose is inextricably linked to Jesus.

Even as we note that God's plan is explicitly mentioned in 2:23, we can pause to observe that the three citations from the LXX (in 2:17–21, 25b–28, and 34b–35) can also be read in service of this same theme.[62] Read as such, the plan of God according to Peter, is that God would resurrect his Messiah (2:25–28; cf. 2:31), enthroning him at his right hand side (2:34–35), and through him pour out his Spirit upon all flesh, promising salvation for everyone who calls upon the Lord's name (2:17–21). Thus Peter's speech, in addition to providing an interpretive lens through which the narrative of Acts is read as the time leading up to the Day of the Lord, also suggests that what is taking place is according to the plan of God and accordingly follows the designs of the lord of history.

The final verses of this part of the speech (2:24–28) focus on God as someone who ultimately desires life, not death. Death is personified: "the pangs of death"[63] and "death was not strong enough" (2:24) depict

---

role" in Jesus's death. This is due to a history of anti-semitism in which the Jews have been blamed for Jesus's death, but it is also problematic because Jesus and his disciples were themselves Jews.

61. See, e.g., 1 Cor 1:23–25 about Jesus as a stumbling block to Jews and a folly to the gentiles, and Origen, who refers to the same text (*Cels.* 1.13). See also Origen's reference to Celsus, who argues based on Jesus's betrayal: "*. . . and least of all could he, who was regarded as Savior, and son of the greatest God, and an angel, be deserted and betrayed by his associates*" (*Cels.* II.9, emphasis Chadwick's, see Origen, *Contra Celsum*). I do not claim that these are part of the "cultural encyclopedia" of the competent reader, but they add weight to the argument that it is highly significant when Acts claims that Jesus's death was part of God's plan.

62. This is basically the thesis argued in Moessner, "Luke's 'Plan of God,'" 223–38.

63. I join scholars in noting the oddness of "having eased the pangs of death" as an image of resurrection. It is possible that Peter is here referring to Ps 18:5, in which the MT lists "the cords of death" (מות חבלי) and the LXX "pangs of death" (ὠδῖνες θανάτου), and that the odd characterization arises from the LXX's misreading of חבל (which could mean "cords" if read with a different vocalization). See Pervo, *Acts*, 81–82

death as a power in opposition to God. Death's lack of strength, however, serves to indicate God's possession of strength. In releasing Jesus from the pangs of death, God is seen to have the power to restore life. In the verses that follow (2:25–28), Jesus's faith in God's power over death is brought to the fore through a citation from Ps 14:8–11 LXX. The Psalm is assigned to David, who here speaks on behalf of the Messiah.[64] The words uttered express complete confidence in God's presence ("he is by my right side"), and more importantly, in the fact that God will neither abandon the speaker to Hades, nor let his "Holy One experience corruption" (2:27). This faith in God's life-giving will and power has already received their reward in Jesus's resurrection (2:24). Thus, God is presented not only as a giver of life, but worthy of Jesus's trust.

3.2.3 The Lord's Lord (2:29–36)

In the third part of Peter's speech, God's fulfillment of his promise to David (cf. 2 Sam 7:8–16) takes center place in the indirect characterization of God. Through his final address of his listeners by means of a familial term, "Ἄνδρες ἀδελφοί" (2:29), Peter evokes the apostles' kinship with the crowd and allows him to make his argument by appealing to David as their common ancestor. The allusion to David establishes Jesus's Davidic descent as Peter recalls Nathan's promise to David: "God had sworn with an oath to him that he would put one of his descendants on his throne." (2:30, cf. 2 Sam 7:8–16). David is said to have foreseen (2:31) the fulfillment of this promise, and to therefore utter the words Peter cites from Ps 14:10 LXX (Acts 2:25–28) as words about Jesus's resurrection. Consequently, the resurrection is described as both enthronement and scriptural fulfillment of God's promise, and once more demonstrates the faithfulness of God. Moreover, as we shall see in our treatment of Acts 26:1–23 (in chapter 5), resurrection is in Acts depicted as the hope of Israel (26:6–8). Thus, Peter's words about Jesus's resurrection also pertain to a broader meta-narrative, where God is the one who promises life after death for Israel.

There is a close relationship between presenting Jesus's resurrection as proof-from-prophecy, and speaking of Jesus's death as part of God's plan: Proof and fulfillment may both be seen as part of the realization of God's will. When Peter borrows David's prophetic authority to speak of Jesus's resurrection, his words therefore further establish the foundation of Jesus's identity in divine providence. This is worth noting, as it provides the

---

This has no bearing on Acts' presentation of God, however.

64. Technically, the term "Messiah" does not appear until 2:31.

backdrop for the words that follow about the outpouring of the Spirit: Jesus was raised from the dead, exalted, received (or took) the promise of the Spirit by the Father, and poured out the Spirit (2:32–33). The verb which indicates the passing of the Spirit between the Father and Jesus is λαβών (2:33). Its meaning suggests a dynamic between God and Jesus's characters, for the verb could both suggest that Jesus is *given* (has received) the promise of the Spirit, or that he has *taken* the Spirit from the Father. When we appreciate this twofold meaning, Jesus does not become a passive object of his Father's action, but his co-agency together with God is emphasized. That the Spirit passes from God to Jesus is one of the most significant actions of God's in this speech. Peter's declaration that Jesus has poured out the Spirit, however, stands in contrast to the first part of his speech, where the citation from the prophet in 2:17–21 introduced God as the giver of the Spirit. In naming Jesus as the giver of the Spirit,[65] a shift takes place in the speech from the Spirit's exclusively theocentric origins, to Jesus as the exalted giver of the Spirit: "The Spirit of prophecy, promised through Joel, has become the Spirit of Jesus (Acts 16:7)."[66] From this time onwards, the activity of the Spirit in Acts may also be viewed as the activity of the ascended Jesus.[67]

This shift from the emphasis on God to Jesus as the giver of the Spirit is, I would argue, made possible in two ways. First, the two participles in 2:32–33 (ὑψωθείς, λαβών), followed by the indicative aorist, ἐξέχεεν, indicate that Jesus's exaltation and the Father's promise of the Holy Spirit are preconditions for Jesus's pouring out the Spirit.[68] That Jesus's exaltation is in fact a precondition for this action, is more clearly illustrated by Peter's use of Psalm 110 in 2:34. The quote from this Psalm, which seems to have been widely used in early Christological reflection (cf. e.g., Matt 22:44; 1 Cor 15:25; Heb 1:13), is linked to the outpouring of the Spirit by the conjunction γάρ (2:34), and the common imagery of being placed at God's right side (2:33, 34). Being put in this place of honor here signifies Jesus's enthronement as God's Messiah (2:30, 36; cf. Ps 110:1–2). This further

---

65. Note that this is the only instance in the Pentecost speech in which Jesus has been referred to "as an agent who performs an action extending beyond himself" (Martín-Asensio, *Transitivity-Based Foregrounding*, 160). This further highlights that God is presented as the main agent in the speech.

66. Turner, "Spirit of Christ and Christology," 180.

67. "The phrase 'to receive (the gift of) the Holy Spirit' denotes the beginning in a man's life or activity of some new nexus of functions of the Spirit" (Turner, "Spirit of Christ and Christology," 180).

68. Note that Jesus's resurrection (2:31–32) and exaltation (ὑψωθείς, 2:33) are here held together by the conjunction οὖν (2:33).

suggests that it is in the capacity of having been made God's acting regent that Jesus pours out the Spirit.[69]

Secondly, the shift in emphasis from God to Jesus as the giver of the Spirit is made possible by Peter's broader argument that Jesus is the fulfillment of God's plan and purpose as this is expressed in God's promises throughout Israel's history (cf. 2:30), because this closely links Jesus's role to God's will. Finally, we should note that in the pouring out of the Spirit, God is explicitly referred to as Jesus's father for the second time in Acts (2:33; cf. 1:4). While this familial language is not developed further here,[70] it does invite the reader to perceive of the relationship between God and Jesus as one between father and son. This double (or "doubly credited") agency in terms of who is said to pour out the Spirit (2:17, 33), which finds its foundation in God and Jesus's father–son relationship, Jesus as the fulfillment of God's plan and purpose, and God's resurrection and ascension of Jesus, means that the same action used to characterize God comes to characterize Jesus. It may, accordingly, be seen as part of the movement through which Jesus's character comes to take over more of God's characteristics in Acts. Thus Max Turner suggests that,

> If, for him [Peter], Jesus' functions have become so aligned with Yahweh's that both can be said to pour out the Spirit (*cf.* 2:17, 33), then there is nothing to prevent the Christological application of the Joel citation being carried through at every point. Jesus can barely be other than the one denoted by Joel's expression *to onoma kyriou*.[71]

The fact that Jesus pours out the Spirit, together with God's enthronement of him as Lord and Messiah (2:36; see below), accordingly provide a shift through which Peter's speech may be re-read in a way that allows the reader to understand Jesus as performing several of God's functions.

One might ask, at this point, whether the above observations mean that the theophany in 2:1-4 should rather be interpreted as a "christophany,"

---

69. Psalm 110:5-6 also depicts God's ruler in terms of one performing judgment, which is interesting in the light of Acts' depiction of Jesus performing judgment in God's stead (10:42; 17:31).

70. The familial language does not seem to be developed significantly in the rest of Acts either. Thus, Diane G. Chen seems to overstate the evidence when she writes that, "as children of God, Jesus's disciples are to participate in the saving work of their Father under the empowerment of the same Spirit" (Chen, *God as Father*, 51). I am not suggesting that it is impossible to argue that the disciples in Luke-Acts may be understood as children of God, but I *am* suggesting that this image of God as the father of the disciples, and the disciples as God's children, is not explicitly developed in Acts.

71. Turner, "Spirit of Christ and Christology," 184.

CHAPTER 3: THE GOD OF THE LAST DAYS (ACTS 2:1-41)

given that Jesus is said to be pouring out the Spirit.[72] To this, the text offers no definite answer. We may note, as we have already done, that Peter initially interprets what is happening as God's pouring out of the Spirit in the last days. This coheres with the imagery we initially observed as theophanic (2:1-4). But we have also seen that the rest of Peter's speech upsets the notion of what God does alone, versus what God does through Jesus. This reading is perhaps particularly relevant, if Acts is read in light of John the Baptist's promise in Luke 3:16: "he will baptize you with holy spirit and fire." Here, the fire imagery is explicitly connected to Jesus, and Acts 2:33b does suggest that Jesus is pouring out "this that you both see and hear." To conclude, however, it is perhaps more important to note that the text itself does not raise any questions about a theophany versus christophany, but that it allows such a question to be raised by the reader.

As the focus of the speech shifts from God to Jesus, Jesus's character is given some of the characteristics previously accorded to God. The citation from Ps 110 in Acts 2:34b-35 provides one example. This psalm is cited as a Davidic prophecy about God and Jesus. Here both God and Jesus are accorded the title "Lord," and Jesus is offered a place at the right hand of God (2:34).[73] This quote is then complemented and superseded by the conclusion to the entire speech: "Therefore let the entire house of Israel know with certainty that God has made him both Lord and Messiah, this Jesus whom you crucified." (2:36). In this way, Krodel notes, "Jesus' ascension is interpreted as his enthronement to his Davidic-messianic Lordship, the reason why everyone who calls on the name of the Lord shall be saved (2:21), and why his opponents shall become a stool for his feet (cf. 3:23)."[74] To be more specific, however, the fulfillment of the Davidic promise is also connected Jesus's resurrection (2:30-32), which means that Jesus's enthronement should be understood as a result both of his resurrection *and* ascension. One of the consequences of the statement that Jesus has been made Lord in 2:36, is that it invites a reinterpretation or negotiation of how the citation from the prophet Joel (in Acts 2:17-21) may be understood: Verse 21, which states that "everyone who calls on the name of the Lord will be saved," now gains a double meaning. "Lord" may now, on the basis of 2:34 and 2:36, be understood as both God and his anointed. This ambiguity in terms of the

---

72. Matthew Sleeman argues that 2:2 ought to be understood christologically in light of "the ordering of space established by 1:6-11" (*Geography and the Ascension Narrative*, 94).

73. As Barrett (*Acts I–XIV,* 149) observes, τῇ δεξιᾷ (2:33) is ambiguous, as the dative could signify either the instrument or the location. Cf. also Jervell, *Die Apostelgeschichte,* 148-49. In light of Acts 7:56, however, it should probably be interpreted as the latter.

74. Krodel, *Acts,* 88.

referent of "Lord" continues throughout Acts, at times creating confusion about whom the title is referring to.

In short, in the final parts of the speech, God's identity is firmly connected to the identity of his Messiah. This is also essential in terms of how God is presented. Although the messianic expectations in the first and second centuries of the common era varied in terms of specific content, a common feature is that they reveal an expectation of God as deliverer of Israel.[75] In providing a Messiah of Davidic descent, God is therefore here to be understood as a savior; a savior faithful to his promises of sending a Messiah to sit on the throne of David. This promise is in 2:36 portrayed as fulfilled through the resurrection of Jesus. This also corresponds to our previous observations that the final verse in the citation from Joel (in Acts 2:21) frames the plot in Acts by pointing to God's salvation.

3.3 God's Universal Promise of Salvation (2:37–41)

Peter concludes his speech by accusing his listeners of having executed Jesus ("this Jesus whom *you* crucified," 2:36; my emphasis). His words pave the way for his audience's reaction, both their regret, "they were cut to the heart," and their question, "Brothers, what should we do?" (2:37). The response from Peter is simple: He urges the crowd to repent and be baptised. If they do, they will receive both forgiveness and the Spirit. The reader and Peter's audience are consequently invited to see God as forgiving. Of further significance, moreover, are Peter's next to final words: "For the promise (ἡ ἐπαγγελία) is for you, for your children, and for all who are far away, everyone whom the Lord our God calls to him." (2:39). Dunn's observation that ἡ ἐπαγγελία is covenant language in Acts (and Paul, cf. Acts 2:39; 7:17; 13:23, 32; Rom 4:13, 16, 20; 9:8) is worth noting here: It evokes the history of Israel's past through which God's relationship with Israel is shaped by God's covenants with his people.[76] In light of this, we may say that in Acts, God's relationship to God's people comes to be shaped by the gift of the Spirit to the believers. While the promise has earlier referred to the gift of Spirit (1:4; 2:33), it here appears to be modified by what Peter has just said, and is consequently synonymous with both the consequences of baptism and repentance, i.e., both forgiveness and the gift of the Spirit.

According to Peter, the promise offered by God knows neither temporal nor geographical boundaries (2:40). In light of Peter's proclamation to the house of Israel (2:36) in this speech, this initially seems to indicate that

---

75. See, e.g., Charlesworth, "From Messianology to Christology," 3–35.
76. Dunn, *Baptism in the Holy Spirit*, 47.

"at least the 'all flesh' would include dispersed Jews,"[77] but for a second-time reader of Acts, it also points to the universality of God's call (cf. 2:17, 21).[78] In this way, verses 37–41 seem to mirror the foregoing speech, which has emphasized the Spirit's descent on "all flesh" (2:17) regardless of age, gender, and social class, and the salvation of everyone who calls on the name of the Lord (2:21). Read in this light, Peter's declaration that the promise is for everyone whom the Lord calls in this and future generations, further characterize God as savior. These verses, moreover, foreshadow the universalization of the apostolic mission, and when they are read in light of Acts as a whole, emphasize the universal sovereignty of God.

At the end of the day, 3,000 people join the disciples (2:41). The passive form "were added" should likely be understood as a divine passive.[79] It thus implies God's hand in the growth of the community of believers. Their number attests to the power of God's call. It does, moreover, provide a backdrop against which Gamaliel's words in Acts 5:39 may be read: "But if it is of God, you will not be able to overthrow them." This ironically makes Gamaliel a mouthpiece for the true origins of the mission, and allows for the growth of the Jesus movement to be understood as an attestation to God's purpose.

3.4 Concluding Observations

In the depiction of the events of Pentecost, the implied author maintains a strong focus on the continuation between Israel's past and the narrative present. What happens on this day provides a catalyst for the rest of the plot that unfolds in Acts. The Spirit is given, and the promise of the Father is thus fulfilled. In this way, God's faithfulness enables the mission of the Jesus movement. By characterizing God's presence through sound and flame in a way reminiscent of Israel's Scriptures, the implied author invites the reader to see the actions at Pentecost as a continuation of God's works with Israel. The apostles, who are now speaking in different tongues, reach out to people from "all over the world," and thus foreshadow a universal mission—and God's universal purpose of salvation.

---

77. Treier, "Fulfillment of Joel 2:28–32," 20.

78. Janusz Kucicki (*Function of the Speeches*, 64) suggests that the gentiles are also included "as object of God's promise" in 2:21. This, however, is a statement that can only be justified *after* a reading of the entire narrative: God's promise does indeed come to include the gentiles, but in Acts 2, Peter's speech is addressed to Jews and proselytes (cf. 2:5–11). It is only in 10:34 that Peter comes to understand God's impartiality.

79. Spencer (*Journeying through Acts*, 49) seems to interpret it similarly. So also Krodel, *Acts*, 23; Bock, *Acts*, 154.

While God is first characterized indirectly through the theophany, Peter soon names God's presence. Peter's speech provides both an interpretation of the events of Pentecost and has a programmatic function for the rest of Acts. By temporally locating the events that follow in Acts between the gift of the Spirit and the Day of the Lord, the apostolic mission is framed by God's actions of gift, judgment, and salvation. God may thus be understood as the uttermost foundation of the narrative movement. This movement has its origins in the gift of the Spirit, and its goal in God's salvific purpose. God is thus ultimately portrayed as the savior whose plan the apostles are moving to unfold as they spread the word of the gospel. Peter's speech is, moreover, programmatic in that it simultaneously interprets what happens at Pentecost and foreshadows events that later come to pass within the narrative. Peter's prophetic words are themselves a realization of the words of Joel (cf. ἀποφθέγγομαι, 2:14),[80] and the reader will encounter more prophetic words, visions, and dreams, as (s)he continues to read on.[81] When the words of God, expressed through the scriptural citation from Joel, are realized, the events of the narrative are revealed as standing under the purview of God.

Peter's speech centers on the life and destiny of Jesus of Nazareth and demonstrates God's presence behind every stage of the Jesus story. Through Jesus's *life*, God's salvific purpose in the lives of humans are revealed; Jesus's *death* is encompassed by God's plan and foreknowledge; through Jesus's *resurrection*, God is revealed as master of death and giver of life. In Peter's speech, it is, in short, first and foremost God's relation to Jesus that informs the portrayal of God. This relation is mainly described through a movement from promise to fulfillment. Reaching back into the history of Israel, Peter argues that Jesus's resurrection is the fulfillment of the Davidic covenant and God's promise of a Messiah. Thus, in the Jesus story, God's faithfulness to God's promises and purpose comes to expression.

In sending the Messiah, God is portrayed as the deliverer of Israel. However, as Peter continues his speech, the outpouring of the Spirit, originally accorded to God, is now accorded to Jesus through God. When the title "Lord" comes to be used about Jesus, textual ambiguity arises with regards to whom the referent of this title is. This ambiguity continues throughout Acts. It attests to an intimate connection between God and Jesus, which in turn encourages the reader to see God's purposes as realized through Jesus.

Finally, the events of Pentecost allow us to trace the beginnings of Acts' portrayal of a universal God. Peter declares to the Jews that God's promise is

---

80. Cf. Jervell (*Die Apostelgeschichte*, 141–42), who also designates Peter's speech "prophetic."

81. Cf. Pervo, *Acts*, 79.

for everyone "whom the Lord our God calls to him" (2:39), and states that this call knows neither generational nor geographical boundaries. In this way, God's purpose of a universal mission is both declared and foreshadowed. By the same token, God's promise of forgiveness and the Spirit should also be seen as universal. By the end of Pentecost, 3,000 people are baptized; the first among many to respond to God's call throughout the narrative.

Chapter 4: The God of Glory and Heaven: Stephen's Speech and Vision (Acts 6:8—7:60)

4.0. Introduction

Within its narrative context, Stephen's speech follows upon the accusations made against him in 6:11, 13-14. These accusations are first presented by men instigated by some diaspora Jews (6:11),[1] and later by false witnesses in front of the council, i.e., the Sanhedrin (6:13-14). The first set of charges is twofold: that Stephen speaks blasphemous words against Moses, and that he speaks blasphemous words against God (6:11). The second set of charges is presented by false witnesses who claim that Stephen speaks both "against this holy place" (κατὰ τοῦ τόπου τοῦ ἁγίου, 6:13, i.e., the temple) and the law by proclaiming that Jesus would tear down the temple and change the customs from Moses (6:14).[2] In short, he stands "accused of attacking the foundations of Jewish life: temple and Torah, God and Moses."[3]

---

1. The Greek is unclear in terms of how many groups of Jews there are: There could be as many as five (a synagogue of Freedmen and four others from different places), or as few as one (a synagogue of Freedmen from four places). Cf. e.g., Gaventa, *Acts*, 118-19; Parsons, *Acts*, 86.

2. These customs probably refer to "the oral traditions giving the scribal interpretation of the law" (Marshall, *Acts of the Apostles*, 130).

It is difficult to properly clarify the relationship between the charges in 6:13-14 and 6:11. It has been suggested that the accusations in 6:13-14 should be understood as a concretization of the charges in 6:11, and that speaking blasphemous words against Moses and God are equivalent to speaking against the customs from Moses and the temple. However, while Acts does on occasion equate Moses with the law (cf. e.g., 15:21; 21:21), there is no similar example of blasphemy against God as the same as speaking against the temple. Conversely, all the charges could be understood to be concerning blasphemy against God. In this case, speaking against the law and temple would be exemplifications of blasphemy against God, and the charges in 6:11 are synonymous. Perhaps we can come no further in this discussion than by pointing out the interrelatedness of all the charges, and suggesting that Stephen is accused of speaking of things that are perceived as theologically problematic, and which go to the very heart of Jewish life.

3. Tannehill, *Narrative Unity of Luke-Acts*, 2:85.

While it could be argued that the high priest's question of whether the charges are true (7:1) receives a "non-answer," and simply provides an occasion for Stephen to speak before the council, this does not do justice to the narrative context. To a large degree, Stephen's speech focuses on God, Moses, and the temple. This suggests that even if Stephen is not directly addressing the charges, his speech nevertheless *demonstrates* how he relates to them.[4] His speech does, moreover, build up to his own accusation against his accusers (7:51–53), which suggests that the rhetorical thrust of his foregoing words is to respond to their allegations.[5]

On this background, the accusations against Stephen provide the focal lens when we look at the characterization of God in the following chapter. Which of God's actions does Stephen speak of, how do they characterize God, and in what way do they relate to the temple and the law? We shall see that Stephen's speech theologically prepares the way for the spread of the gospel by deemphasizing the role of the temple and anchoring God's revelation throughout history beyond the land promised to Abraham[6]—and by extension beyond Jerusalem and the temple. We might say that even though the speech begins with God's revelation to Abraham in Mesopotamia, continues with God's care for Joseph in Egypt, and moves on to God's revelation to Moses on Mount Sinai, there is a steady movement towards Jerusalem in the speech.[7] Yet Stephen's death results in the opposite movement, when the Jesus believers are persecuted and scattered beyond Jerusalem (8:1).

---

4. Contra Dibelius, "Speeches in Acts," 167–69. Dibelius considers 7:2–34 irrelevant to the charges. See also Witherington (*Acts*, 258), who argues that "the speech of Stephen in the following chapter does not seem to address or answer these charges, or if it does it only speaks briefly and tangentially to the second charge"; and Haenchen, *Die Apostelgeschichte*, 238: "Stefanus soll die Frage beantworten, ob die Anklage gegen ihn zutrifft; aber ein sehr grosser Teil seiner Rede geht darauf gar nicht ein!"

5. This bears similarity to Witherington's argument (*Acts*, 260–61). Witherington considers the speech a coherent whole, and an example of judicial/forensic rhetoric.

6. As early as 1930, F. J. Foakes-Jackson observed that the object of the speech is "that the history of God's dealing with Israel is a continuous proof that He never confined Himself to one sacred spot but revealed Himself to patriarchs and prophets throughout the world in Mesopotamia, in Egypt and in the wilderness. This would emphasize the truth of what was declared by Solomon that the Most High does not dwell in houses made with hands, and that as the teaching of Jesus implied true worship was not bound up with the continuance of the Temple" ("Stephen's Speech in Acts," 283). This observation has later been taken up by a number of scholars.

7. I owe this observation to Edvin Larsson, who in his article on temple criticism and the Jewish heritage, suggests that even though the events related in the stories of Abraham, Joseph, and Moses take "place outside Israel, they nevertheless are aiming at the people's return to the Holy Land and the true place of their worship of God" (Larsson, "Temple-Criticism," 388).

When we turn to look at the characterization of God in Acts 7:1–60, the setting of God's actions therefore plays an important role. While *what* God does remains fundamental to our survey, *where* God acts is also significant. It may be that the settings of God's actions do not seem so important upon a first reading. However, the culmination of Stephen's speech with words from Isaiah asserting that "the Most High does not dwell in houses made by human hands" (7:48) makes this a central point, not only in characterizing God's presence, but in addressing the temple charge. Furthermore, this close connection between "what" and "where" in characterizing God allows us to discern how Stephen's vision (7:55–56) is connected to Stephen's speech, not only as a vindication of Stephen, but as a revelation of Jesus and God's presence in heaven.

The following chapter begins by addressing the basis for considering Stephen a reliable narrator. Following this, it looks at God's role and the characterization of God at moments in Israel's past, i.e., in the lives of Abraham (7:1–8), Joseph (7:9–16), and Moses (7:17–43). We then turn to address more fully the question of how Stephen's speech and his words about God relate to the temple charge (7:44–50). Finally, we look briefly at Stephen's own accusation (7:51–53), in preparation of reviewing how Stephen's vision characterizes God is in the story-time (7:54–60).

4.1 Stephen as a Reliable Narrator of God's Actions

Few characters in Acts, if any, are so thoroughly and positively introduced as Stephen. As one of the Jesus believers in Jerusalem, his reliability is first signalled by the trust placed in him by the apostles: Stephen, together with six others, is selected to distribute food among the believers, thus solving a conflict between the Hellenists and Hebrews by making sure the Hellenist widows are no longer neglected (6:1–6).[8] In this context, he is also directly characterized as "full of faith and the Holy Spirit" (6:5), which in Acts seems to favorably single out characters that are particularly pious (cf. 11:24). This description, could, moreover, be significant in that the Holy Spirit in Acts is connected to the apostles' power to witness and proclaim (cf. e.g., 1:8; 2:4). This foreshadows that Stephen, although initially chosen to do table service, also has the prophetic gift of the Spirit (cf. 2:17).[9] The reactions of

---

8. Given his Greek name, it is quite possible that Stephen should be considered to be one of the Hellenists. For a thorough survey of what "Hellenist" may actually refer to, and the historical problems associated with the distinction between Hebrews and Hellenists, see Penner, *In Praise of Christian Origins*, esp. 60–103.

9. In its most basic sense, prophesying can be understood as proclaiming "the revelation, the message of God, imparted to the prophet"; Meyer et al., "προφήτης κτλ," 829.

those who argue with him substantiate this observation: "They could not withstand the wisdom and Spirit with which he spoke" (6:10). This suggests that Stephen stands in the tradition of those believers who witness to God's works through the Holy Spirit.

Stephen is, moreover, said to be a worker of "wonders and signs" (τέρατα καὶ σημεῖα, 6:8). Accordingly, his character is depicted in the same way as Jesus (2:22, cf. 14:3), the apostles (2:43; 5:12), Moses (7:36), and Paul and Barnabas (15:4). In spite of the brief part he plays in the narrative, Stephen is thus characterized in a manner similar to some of its most significant characters. Moreover, because signs and wonders are from God (cf. 2:22; 15:4), his performance of them suggests that Stephen has God's favor.

In addition to the above, the narrator mentions how Stephen is perceived by the council he is brought before: To them, "his face was like an angel" (6:15). This observation evokes a number of possible connotations: Angels frequent the Acts narrative as messengers of God, bringing both release from captivity, words from God (e.g., 5:17–20), and death (12:20–23). However, because it is Stephen's physical features that are highlighted here, the expression should probably be seen to "convey the idea of a person reflecting some of God's glory and character as a result of being close to God and in God's very presence"[10] (cf. Exod 34:29; Luke 9:29). Read in this light, the characterization of Stephen contains a subtle irony, for not only does his opponents' observation cohere with the narrator's point of view, it also means that his accusers later stone the man in whose face they see a glimpse of the divine revealed.[11]

In short, the manner in which Stephen is characterized presents his point of view as reliable, and his words as empowered by the Spirit. This prepares the reader to see him as a character that speaks the truth with divine

---

However, with the imparting of the Spirit on "all flesh" in Acts, not only prophets, but "everyone" is able to proclaim through the Spirit (2:17–18). When I speak of "prophetic gift" here, I therefore mean the speech inspired by the Holy Spirit (cf. 2:17), which in its most basic sense can be understood as proclamation of God's message (cf. 2:14–36), but in Acts also comes to expression through xenolalia (2:4), prediction of the future (11:28), and speaking in tongues (19:6).

10. Witherington, *Acts,* 259.

11. Cf. Gaventa, *Acts,* 119: "What they see, the face of an angel, indicates God's presence with Stephen, a presence to which the council seems immune." It is also worth noting, with Fletcher-Louis, the possibility that 6:15 and 7:53 form an inclusio around Stephen's speech, which "is otherwise present in the fact that in Acts 7:53 Stephen counters the charge against him—that he speaks against the Torah (Acts 6:11, 13)—with the accusation that his accusers do not themselves keep the Torah" (Fletcher-Louis, *Luke-Acts,* 98).

authority,[12] in contrast to the false witnesses that accuse him. His innocence is thus foreshadowed from the outset.

4.2 Stephen's Speech: The God of Glory Revealed (7:2–53)

4.2.1 God and Abraham (7:1–8)

4.2.1.1 The God of Glory Revealed

Stephen's first words, "The God of glory revealed himself to our father Abraham" (Ὁ θεὸς τῆς δόξης ὤφθη τῷ πατρὶ ἡμῶν Ἀβραάμ, 7:2), immediately locate God at the center stage of Stephen's defense and sound a theme of revelation.[13] God's glory and revelation bridge past and present. They also frame Stephen's speech and vision in an inclusio, for what Stephen later sees as he looks towards the heavens is God's glory revealed (δόξα θεοῦ, 7:55).[14] Stephen is the only one in Acts to call God the God *of glory*. Not only does this phrase directly characterize God as glorious, but because it stands at the head of the speech, the following accounts of God's actions may be understood as exemplifications of this glory. Furthermore, because the designation is used so rarely,[15] it may be worth observing that in the Exodus account, after Moses ascends Mount Sinai to receive the commandments, ἡ δόξα τοῦ θεοῦ (Exod 24:16, δόξα κυρίου in 24:17) settles on the mountain. Stephen's initial words therefore do not only characterize God as glorious, but draw on imagery that forms a connecting line between the accusations against him (speaking against Moses) and what he is now about to say.

---

12. Parsons (*Acts*, 89) suggests that Stephen's angel-like appearance "emphasizes the divinely endowed authority of the speaker."

13. At this point it is important to distinguish between Stephen and the implied author. Whereas Stephen's character focuses more on God's revelation than on Jesus, the implied author focuses on Jesus through the parallels between Stephen and Jesus. Both are, e.g., presented as prophets in the tradition of Moses, performing wonders and signs (6:8 and 2:22), and Stephen's words as he is dying echo those of Jesus on the cross (7:59–60, cf. Luke 23:34, 46). For more on the Jesus-Stephen parallels, see esp. 233–34 in Moessner, "'Christ Must Suffer,'" 220–56.

It is worth noting that in Acts, Jesus's post-resurrection appearances are also described by the same verb (ὁράω) in the aorist passive: He was revealed (ὤφθη) to them (see e.g., 9:17; 13:31; 26:16). Although this could, on the surface, seem christologically significant, it is more likely that we are here dealing with the language of visions, for the verb is also used of the Macedonian man's appearance in a dream to Paul, calling him to preach the gospel in Macedonia (16:9).

14. Neudorfer, "Speech of Stephen," 283.

15. The only time ὁ θεὸς τῆς δόξης is used in the LXX is in Ps 28:3.

The God who reveals godself to Abraham directs and promises: Abraham is told where to go (7:3-4), and is promised a future in a land that will be given to his descendants (7:5). Thus God appears not only as Abraham's lord and god, but as someone with the power to direct or perhaps foresee the future. By promising judgment upon the nations that would enslave Abraham's posterity (7:7), and giving him the covenant of circumcision (7:8), God ties godself not only to Abraham, but to the following generations (cf. 7:7) by way of promise and sign. Relation is a means of identification: Through God's relation to Abraham, God is both characterized and known in a way that later allows God to be identified not as just any god, but as the "God of the fathers" (cf. 7:32). How this relation is maintained and the promises realized are demonstrated through the story that Stephen goes on to relate.

When Stephen speaks of God's appearances to Abraham (7:2-8), he reports God's words to him as direct speech: God speaks (ὁ θεὸς εἶπεν, 7:7, cf. 7:3). This is only the second time in Acts that God's words are reported without being offered through an intermediary (see 3:25). On all previous occasions, they are spoken through a prophet (see, e.g., 2:16-21, 34-35). Stephen's speech therefore stands out in that it portrays God as interacting directly first with Abraham, and then (arguably) with Moses (cf. 7:31-33).[16] Thus, we may say that God is here depicted as "near" in the past, in a manner that differs from how God's presence is presented in later theophanic mediations of God in Acts. Although the voice speaking to Peter in Acts 10:13-16 could be an exception, it is never explicitly identified as God's. Instead, God's activity in Acts relies mainly upon mediation by others, whether this be the apostles, the ascended Jesus, the angel of the Lord, or the Spirit. The few times God's presence is not mediated by a person-like character, it is through theophanies that resemble or influence tumultuous nature (2:1-4; 4:31; 16:26). In this sense, the fact that Stephen speaks of God as a talking agent fleshes out the portrayal of God in comparison with how God is otherwise presented in Acts. We might even say that through Stephen's words, God is depicted differently in Israel's past from the way God is depicted in the story-time.

---

16. This coheres well with Scott Shauf"s observation that "divine speech is not reported in postbiblical historiography, except when referring to the biblical period" (Shauf, *Divine in Acts*, 87).

4.2.1.2 The Settings of God's Revelation

As we shall see, the account of God's revelation to Abraham may be understood to build up to Stephen's later claims about God and the temple. In anticipation of this argument, we may note two observations that arise from God's revelation to Abraham. First, we may discern that Stephen references an event where God appears outside the borders of Israel, in Mesopotamia (7:2-3).[17] Even though the temple was not yet built in the days of Abraham, Stephen's words may accordingly remind the reader of the far-reaching presence of God beyond the land promised to Abraham.[18]

Secondly, while the setting in Mesopotamia serves as a reminder of God's presence beyond the temple, it is less clear how the account of God's words to Abraham in 7:7 should be understood in relation to the temple accusation. After Abraham has moved "to this country in which you are now living" (7:4), Stephen states that God's final words to Abraham are that his descendants "shall come out and worship me in this place" (7:7). These words are more or less similar to those to Moses in Exod 3:12, where the setting is explicitly "this mountain," i.e., Sinai. Accordingly, Stephen's words function as a "recontextualization" of words God spoke to Moses, because they are placed into a setting where God speaks to Abraham. This recontextualization has given rise to diverging opinions about how the citation relates to the temple accusation. On the one hand, we have F. Scott Spencer, who asserts,

> While such a statement may seem to support the centrality of the temple, in fact a check of Stephen's handling of scriptural sources reveals a different stance.... The original Exodus context leaves no room for doubt: 'this place' was 'this *mountain*,' namely Mt *Sinai*. Before the temple on Mt Zion came into existence and began to be venerated as *the* fixed holy place of Israel, the wandering children of Abraham found God perfectly well and re-established their covenant with him at a remote desert outpost.[19]

Spencer's words seem to suggest that Stephen's citation decentralizes the role of the temple, because it refers to a "remote desert outpost" rather than Mt Zion. Schneider and Barrett argue the opposite, however,

---

17. There is a difference here between the setting in Acts and in Genesis. In Genesis, God appears to Abraham while he is living in Haran (see Gen 12).

18. Cf. e.g., Witherington, *Acts*, 266; Marshall, *Acts*, 135; Frøvig, *Kommentar til Apostlenes gjerninger*, 141; Kim, "Explicit Quotations from Genesis," 352.

19. Spencer, *Journeying through Acts*, 81.

suggesting that "this place" rather signifies the temple.[20] While there is truth to Spencer's claim insofar as Stephen's speech in general does emphasize God's revelation *outside* of Israel, Jerusalem, and the temple, this does not seem to capture the essence of the Scripture quotation in 7:7. It seems strange that the citation would be used to bring to mind the exodus context and the setting of a "remote desert outpost," when in fact "the mountain" is replaced by "this place" in 7:7. In Stephen's speech, "this place" follows after God's promise of land to Abraham's descendants, and therefore more likely refers to the land. It is consequently better to read Stephen's words from Scripture as a means of authoritatively tying the land to the place of worship. This is further supported by the fact that the last time "this place" was mentioned, the referent of "this place" was the temple (6:14; cf. 6:13), which is located in the land. There is thus a relationship between the temple accusation and God's words to Abraham about future worship.[21] In short, whereas Stephen throughout his speech speaks of God's revelations *outside* of the land promised to Abraham, he also initially suggests that "this place," i.e., this land, is intended as a place of worship. Taken together, these two observations appear to be pointing in the direction that Stephen is not *rejecting* the temple. This is further supported by the observation that the "geographical movement" in the speech is towards the land and the building of the temple.[22] However, we will return to discuss Stephen's relation to the temple and Acts 7:46–50 below (sec. 4.2.4).

4.2.2 God and Joseph: God Acting as Savior in Egypt (7:9–16)

The story of Joseph continues to emphasize God's actions beyond the land. The account of Joseph's life moves the plot into Egypt, and provides a transition to Moses. Little is explicitly said about God here. However, the brief line, "God was with him [Joseph]" (ὁ θεὸς μετ' αὐτοῦ, 7:9), is followed by a sentence which expresses that God saved him from "all his afflictions" and allowed him to gain Pharaoh's favor. The qualification of "all" suggests that it is not only the troubles Joseph faced when he was sold into slavery in Egypt that God saved him from, but also the afflictions that followed later in his life. This sentence about God's favor thus comes to stand as a headline of Joseph's entire life, including how God saves him and his entire family from

---

20. Cf. Conzelmann, *Acts*, 386; Schneider, *Die Apostelgeschichte 1,1—8,40*, 455; Barrett, *Acts I–XIV*, 345; Sleeman, *Geography and the Ascension Narrative*, 145–46. More specifically, Barrett (*Acts I–XIV*, 345) suggests that "τόπος must be taken to refer if not to the Temple itself at least to the Temple site."

21. Tannehill, *Narrative Unity of Luke-Acts*, 2:93.

22. Larsson, "Temple-Criticism," 388.

famine. God is thus portrayed both as Joseph's savior and benefactor—once again acting in a country outside of Israel.

4.2.3 God and Moses (7:17–43)

4.2.3.1 The Revelatory Descent of the Holy God

The theme of God's revelation continues as Stephen's speech reaches the time of Moses. This time is temporally located to when ἤγγιζεν ὁ χρόνος τῆς ἐπαγγελίας ἧς ὡμολόγησεν ὁ θεὸς τῷ Ἀβραάμ ("the time of the promise that God had made to Abraham drew near," 7:17).[23] Thus God's promise, and the fulfillment thereof, set the agenda for the shift in time and characters, from Joseph to Moses; God's plan is being carried out.[24] But even though God is mentioned both in the description of Moses as "beautiful before God" (7:20) and in the depiction of Moses's own belief that "God through him was rescuing them (his kinsfolk)"[25] (7:25), the first *action* of God's that Stephen refers to, is God's revelation to Moses.

The theophany on Mount Sinai is both a "theophany" and an "angelophany"; it is the sight of the angel in the burning bush that draws Moses closer, but the voice of the Lord that he hears. The verb ὤφθη is used of the angel's appearance here, just as it was about God's appearance to Abraham in 7:2 (cf. ch. 4, n. 13). Although angels are also referred to as "Lord" in Acts (cf. 10:4), here the voice identifies itself as "the God of your ancestors, the God of Abraham, Isaac, and Jacob" (7:32).[26] The identification emphasizes the continuity between this revelation and God's revelation in the past.[27] It is relational; through it, God is revealed as the one worshipped by Moses's ancestors, which in turn implies that this is the God whose promises and covenant bind them together. While 7:30 indicates that it is the angel that speaks, Stephen does not make any attempt to differentiate between the angel and God.[28] In this sense, the presentation of God in the account of the burning bush differs from the rest of the narrative in Acts. Here, "the angel

---

23. My translation.

24. Kilgallen, *Stephen Speech*, 44.

25. Stephen's words here could also be seen to point to God's future action in Jesus, cf. 4:12.

26. Note that Stephen changes Exodus's order of events: In Exodus, God orders Moses to remove his sandals prior to God's identification of godself (Exod 3:1–6).

27. Jervell, *Die Apostelgeschichte*, 239.

28. This interchangeability between the angel of the Lord and God is a common feature of passages from the Pentateuch, e.g., in Gen 31:13 (the angel says: "I am the God of Bethel") and Exod 14. See Weaver, *Plots of Epiphany*, 97.

of the Lord" acts as God's representative in releasing the apostles from prison (5:19–20; 12:7–11), directs Philip to Gaza (8:26), and strikes Herod dead (12:23). In these other accounts, the interchangeability between God and his angel is not so apparent. Nonetheless, the angel's role is the same: It is a functionary whose only function is as a representative of God. Its role in the story-time of Acts is therefore the same as in the rest of Israel's Scriptures, where it "appears almost always to help either Israel or an individual"[29] (see e.g., Gen 16:7–14; 22:10–18; Exod 3:1–22; Num 20:14–16; 22:22—23:12; Judg 2:1–5; 6:11–24; 2 Kgs 1:1–18). In sum, then, the interchangeability between the angel and God in Stephen's words (in 7:35) make God's self-revelation more immediate; God seems "nearer" than in the other accounts featuring the angel of the Lord in Acts.

God, having identified godself, identifies the place on which Moses is standing as holy by ordering him to remove his sandals (7:33). Once again, God is revealed in a holy place that is not the temple: This "may be important for Luke's overall argument in the speech . . . . 'Holy' . . . is where the presence of God is."[30] In one way, this recourse to the Moses story functions to negate Stephen's accusers claim that he was speaking against "this holy place" (6:13), because the premises for "holy place" are defined to not exclusively refer to the temple. The theophany characterizes God *godself* as holy:[31] God is holy, for the ground on which Moses stands is made holy by God's very presence. Moreover, through God's revelation to Moses, God is characterized as someone who masters and relates to nature in a way contrary to human expectations: The bush is burning, but it is not consumed. The vision of the angel marks the presence of God, but God does not appear in any other form. Instead, God is revealed by fire and God's own words, which create a reality of holy ground and divine presence.

Stephen continues to reference God's direct speech. "The voice claims that God both sees and hears,"[32] and through these verbs of seeing and hearing (εἶδον, ἤκουσα), God is indirectly characterized as attentive to his people's needs. As a result of God's observations, God has "come down" (κατέβην, 7:34) to free them. These words create the visual impression of a vertical descent; God, whom Acts also elsewhere locates in heaven (cf. 7:55–56), moves from heaven to earth to come to the rescue. In this sense, too, Stephen's speech reminds the narrative audience (i.e., the audience in

29. Bietenhard, "ἄγγελος," 101. Only one exception to the angel's appearance to help is listed: 2 Sam 24:16f.

30. Johnson, *Acts,* 128n33.

31. Note Acts 3:14, where Jesus is also spoken of as holy (ἅγιος), i.e., his character is described with yet another characteristic which God is also characterized with in Acts.

32. Wilson, "Hearing the Word," 465.

the narrative) of how—and where—God has been encountered throughout Israel's history.

4.2.3.2 God Liberates and Gives the Law

The section in 7:35–43 portrays God as the liberator of the Israelites. God responds to the groaning of the people in Egypt, whom God calls "mine" (ὁ λαός μου, 7:34) by sending Moses as both "ruler and liberator" (7:35).[33] Thus God is characterized as a god who cares for his people; and it is this care and the people's rejection which build to a tension in the following. First, we may note that by introducing Moses as God's agent (7:35–38), Stephen's words demonstrate the unfoundedness of the accusation that he has spoken blasphemous words against him.[34] On the whole, the account of how Moses led his people out of Egypt and through the desert follows the same structure as the same accounts in Exodus do. Nevertheless, Stephen's particular emphases contain a few subtle possibilities for provocation. Second, we may note that even though Stephen in his speech does not explicitly mention Jesus (as the righteous one, ὁ δίκαιος) until 7:52, Stephen's Moses indirectly does: "This is the Moses who said to the children of Israel, 'God will raise up for you a prophet like me from your siblings'" (7:37).[35] Whether it is apparent to the court that he is speaking of Jesus is not said; the reader, however, will recognize Stephen's shrewd introduction of him in line with Peter's earlier speech (3:12–26). In this way, Stephen subtly authorizes Jesus's ministry through the very same Moses whose commandments Stephen's accusers said Jesus would change! Stephen's theological point is clear: God stands behind Jesus, just as God stands behind the commandments.[36]

Stephen refers to the commandments given to Moses as "living oracles" (7:38). This term suggests reverence rather than degradation of them.[37]

---

33. Moses is here characterized in a manner similar to Stephen (and Jesus), as someone who performed wonders and signs (τέρατα καὶ σημεῖα, 7:36).

34. Cf., e.g., Holladay, *Acts*, 161.

35. My translation.

36. Although Jesus can hardly be said to be *explicitly* mentioned in the speech except in 7:52, Stephen's accounts of Joseph and Moses, leaders who are rejected by Israel, foreshadow his accusation in 7:51–53 and imply that the wrongful rejection of Jesus can be read as an implicit theme in the foregoing speech. See e.g., Kilgallen, "Function of Stephen's Speech," 185–87. See also E. Jane Via, who suggests that 7:35–37 is part of "Luke's effort to portray Jesus in the pattern of Israel's great saviors" ("Interpretation of Acts 7:35–37," 206).

37. Note that Stephen has already positively referenced and cited from the Torah (in 7:2–45), which further suggests that he cannot have a completely negative view of the law. Cf. Witherington, *Acts*, 262.

What is challenged by Stephen's speech is therefore not the commandments, but the ancestors' unwillingness to accept them (7:39–43).[38] By emphasizing their reluctance, their rejection of Moses, creation of an idol to worship instead of the one God, and God's turning away from them (7:35–43), Stephen's words repeat what Odil Hannes Steck proposes is a characteristic of the Israelites in pre-exilic, monarchic times according to Deuteronomy.[39] This "Deuteronomistic view" of Israel's history follows a pattern where "(1) repeatedly disobedient Israelites (2) are admonished by God's prophets, (3) whose words are rejected, (4) bringing judgment on the disobedient Israelites."[40] We shall later see how this pattern prefigures Stephen's own accusations against the court in 7:51–53. Here, however, we may note how the pattern is exemplified by God's reaction when the people break off their relation to God: God turns away from them.

No motive or feeling suggests why God reacts in this way, but God's turning away nevertheless reveals a god who does not put up with everything. This action is the divine response to a people who have turned away from their god first, and who have rejected Moses (cf. 7:39–41). Paraphrasing a citation from Amos 5:25–27 (Acts 7:42b–43),[41] Stephen suggests that the Babylonian exile was a result of the people's turning away from God, "so that the consequences of the rejection of Moses reach all the way to the exile."[42] The exile is in Israel's history seen as punishment for the people's sins, and so God's rejection may be seen as God passing sentence on the people. God is thus ultimately characterized as their judge.[43]

4.2.4 God Transcends the Temple (7:44–50)

The conflict with the ancestors forms the background for the part of Stephen's speech that introduces the temple. After three sections which deal

---

38. "The emphasis on God's great promise to Israel in the first part of the speech contributes to a sense of tragic loss when the fulfillment encounters rejection" (Tannehill, *Narrative Unity of Luke-Acts*, 2:89).

39. Steck, *Geschick der Propheten*, 68.

40. Witherington, standing on the shoulders of Steck, writes: "This pattern is seen in 2 Kings 17:7-20; Neh. 9:26 (the prophets were killed); and 2 Chron. 36:14–16" (Witherington, *Acts*, 262). Cf. also Moessner, "'Christ Must Suffer,'" 225–26; Tannehill, *Narrative Unity of Luke-Acts*, 2:87. Conzelmann also observes the same pattern (*Die Apostelgeschichte*, 57).

41. The Amos text refers to the capture of the Northern Kingdom by Assyria in the sixth century BCE, and sounds "beyond Damascus" rather than "beyond Babylon."

42. Gaventa, *Acts*, 127.

43. Cf. the pattern identified by Steck.

with important men in Israel's past, the fourth section deals with a place.[44] The "tent of Moloch" (ἡ σκηνὴ τοῦ Μόλοχ, 7:43), a place of idolatrous worship, provides a contrast and catchword for introducing the "tent of testimony" (ἡ σκηνὴ τοῦ μαρτυρίου), which God ordered Moses to build in the wilderness (7:44). According to Exodus, this tent, or tabernacle, was commanded by God to be built as a dwelling place for God (Exod 25:8), and traveled with the people through the wilderness. It therefore functions as yet another example of God's presence with the people outside of Israel; even after their turning away from him.

God remains at center stage in Stephen's account of the people's entry into the land. Here, God's promise to Abraham (cf. 7:3–7) is finally realized as God drives out the nations before them (7:45). In this way, God is indirectly characterized as faithful through the realization of God's promise. But there is a flipside to this faithfulness: It is *partial* to the Israelites. Although it does demonstrate God's faithfulness towards them, it also depicts God as ruthless towards the nations that are driven out.

The tent remains in the land until the time of David, who is positively portrayed as one "who found favor with God" (7:46). This conditions the impression of his request to build a dwelling place (σκήνωμα, 7:46) as positive, but for whom is this dwelling place intended? The earliest manuscripts suggest that David asks to build a dwelling place for the "*house* of Jacob," whereas later ones have the "*God* of Jacob."[45] The question is if these variant readings influence our reading of how God is portrayed in the text. To this, our reply must be put in the negative. The narrative context suggests that both should be taken as a reference to the temple: A dwelling place for the "house of Jacob" in the sense of an abode does not make sense in light of 2 Sam 7. But a dwelling place for the "house of Jacob" might refer to a place where the house of Jacob may come and worship.[46] This would function as a natural introduction to Solomon's building of the temple (7:47). In this sense, "house of Jacob" does not necessarily differ from the second variant, i.e., a dwelling place for the "God of Jacob." It is not so much the difference or similarity between the two variants which lead us to question how God is characterized in this verse, however, but the fact that David's request goes by

---

44. Gaventa, *Acts*, 128

45. "House of Jacob" is attested by e.g., 𝔓[75], Codex Sinaiticus, and "God of Jacob" is attested by e.g., the second corrector to Codex Sinaiticus, and Codex Alexandrinus. The second variant could be understood as a clarification made by later witnesses, and used to explain that the "him" referred to in 7:47 is in fact God.

46. Cf. Witherington, *Acts*, 272–73; Gaventa, *Acts*, 129, following Barrett, *Acts I–XIV*, 372.

unanswered in Stephen's speech. This silence with regards to God's response makes it unclear how the request should be perceived.

We now reach a point in Stephen's speech which has caused much debate. Immediately following Solomon's building of the "house" (οἶκος), i.e., the temple, Stephen declares that, "the Most High does not dwell in houses made with human hands." This verse, together with Stephen's subsequent citation from Isaiah 66:1–2a (7:49–50), raises a question we have anticipated through our earlier treatment of the speech: How does God relate to the temple, and what does this, in turn, allow us to observe about the characterization of God?[47] While this is the form this question takes in the present study, the scholarly discussion has focused on how *Stephen* relates to the temple.[48] Dennis D. Sylva summarizes this debate by pointing out three theses: Stephen either wishes to (1) replace the temple, (2) he rejects the temple, or (3) he affirms God's transcendence of it.[49] We will look at each claim in turn.

When it comes to (1), the replacement thesis, e.g., F. F. Bruce suggests that "It was in Christ too, they believed, that the promise of a new house, built for the name of God, was truly fulfilled."[50] This proposal is based on a canonical reading of the speech, where Bruce uses Luke, Mark, John and Ephesians to support his interpretation.[51] In Acts, however, there is little evidence to support such a thesis.[52] Simply put, there is no language of replacement in Stephen's speech, nor any suggestions as to what the temple would be replaced by.

In favor of (2), Stephen's rejection of the temple, the arguments are somewhat stronger and more diverse. Penner, for instance, reads David's request to build a σκήνωμα (7:46) as something different from Solomon's building of an οἶκος.[53] Penner's argument is partly made on the basis of the conjunction δέ (7:47) and the view that the σκήνωμα was intended as a *tent* for the ark rather than a *temple*. This, however, ignores the LXX

---

47. As Kilgallen puts it, a wrong understanding of the temple "really reveals a wrong appreciation of God's very being" (Kilgallen, "Function of Stephen's Speech," 180).

Cheng asserts that "God in heaven corroborates Stephen's contention of his transcendency (7:48–50)" without substantiating this claim or relating it to God's revelations throughout the speech (*Characterisation of God*, 169).

48. It should be mentioned, however, that Kilgallen suggests that Stephen's opposition to the temple concerns the concept of God: "The first reason for Stephen's opposition to the Temple is that the Temple as *oikos* betrays the real meaning of God" (Kilgallen, *Stephen Speech*, 91, cf. 93).

49. Sylva, "Meaning and Function of Acts 7:46–50," 261–62.

50. Bruce, *Book of the Acts*, 148.

51. Bruce, *Book of the Acts*, 148–49.

52. Sylva, "Meaning and Function of Acts 7:46–50," 262.

53. For this view, see Penner, *In Praise of Christian Origins*, 313–14.

background where σκήνωμα is used synonymously with the temple,[54] traditions that speak of David's intent to build the temple (2 Sam 6:1–19; 1 Chr 15:1–16:43),[55] and lends too much weight to a conjunction (δέ) which by no means necessarily signifies any contrast between David and Solomon.[56] Penner's reading is stronger, however, in its broader argument that Stephen's speech functions to characterize his opponents and provides an invective against them.[57] In emphasizing the Israelites' disobedience throughout the speech, Stephen's ultimate alignment of his accusers with their ancestors (7:51–53) does not come as a surprise. When Solomon does build the temple, and Stephen comments upon its building with a quote stating God's transcendence of it (7:59–60, see below), this could indeed suggest a critique against Solomon's building of the temple.

There are also other arguments in favor of (2) Stephen's rejection of the temple. In his article, "Stephen's Speech (Acts 7:2–53): Is it as 'Anti-Temple' as is Frequently Alleged?," James P. Sweeney suggests that there are generally two grounds on which Stephen's speech is perceived as anti-temple: a) "Solomon's building of a permanent structure (οἶκος) instead of the supposed ideal tent (σκήνωμα) based on an allegedly wrong-headed attempt to localize (and hence confine) the divine presence in vv. 44–50."[58] b) The temple is made with human hands (χειροποίητος, 7:48), a word with allegedly "idolatrous associations" in the LXX.[59] Sweeney has carefully, and for the most part convincingly, reviewed and rebuffed both of these arguments. Here we will, therefore, only rehearse some of his more important points and add some observations of our own.

The problem with (a) is that it presupposes that Stephen's audience is in fact trying to confine God's presence. However, Acts never reveals which views of the temple are held by Stephen's opponents, so this argument relies upon an interpretation for which there is no textual support.[60] A further, related argument against perceiving Stephen's speech as anti-temple is found in the citation from Isa 66:1–2a in Acts 7:49–50: The text from Isaiah expresses a similar view to the one found in 1 Kgs 8:27, in Solomon's prayer

54. Sylva here references 3 Kgdms 2:28; 8:4 LXX; Pss 14:1; 45:4; 73:7.

55. Sylva, "Meaning and Function of Acts 7:46–50," 264.

56. Sylva, "Meaning and Function of Acts 7:46–50," 265. Cf. Walton, "Tale of Two Perspectives?," 140.

57. Penner, *In Praise of Christian Origins*, 316.

58. Sweeney, "Stephen's Speech," 199.

59. Sweeney, "Stephen's Speech," 199.

60. Arguing against Longenecker, Sweeney seems to suggest that there is little *historical* basis for the view that Stephen was anti-temple. See Sweeney, "Stephen's Speech," 199.

of dedication: "This prayer of dedication surely indicates that the temple was not viewed as somehow *localizing* (and thereby *confining*) the divine presence."[61] In other words, neither Isaiah nor 1 Kings suggests that the temple confines God's presence.

Why is Isaiah quoted rather than 1 Kings, which tells the story of the building of the temple? To this, Sweeney responds that "Isaiah 66 stresses more appropriately the issue at hand in the speech, namely, the disobedience of Israel in its rejection of the divine word, despite the prerogative of the temple."[62] While Sweeney is correct in noting that Israel's disobedience is a theme in Isa 66, he fails to mention the verses that follow immediately after Isa 66:1–2 (the verses quoted by Stephen). Isaiah 66:3–4 could easily be taken as criticism of the temple cult, and by extension of the temple. On their own, these verses could therefore be used against Sweeney as an argument that supports the anti-temple perspective. However, the temple itself does not seem to be in view in Isaiah 66:3–4. Immediately after the cult critique, God's voice is heard *from the temple* on a note of retribution (Isa 66:6). Then why, after all, is Isaiah cited in Acts 7:49–50? I would suggest that it is not only Sweeney's observations about Israel's disobedience that makes Isaiah preferable to 1 Kings. This may be illustrated by the following words from Isa 66:5:

> Hear the word of the Lord,
>   you who tremble at his word:
> Your own people who hate you
>   and reject you for my name's sake
> have said, "Let the Lord be glorified,
>   so that we may see your joy";
>   but it is they who shall be put to shame.

I cite this verse in full for two reasons. First, because it substantiates Sweeney's argument that the quote from Isaiah stands in a context where the disobedience of Israel is emphasized, and this theme is also central to Stephen's speech. But in addition to this, it is interesting to observe that Isa 66:5 also mentions rejection for the sake of "my name" and the glorification of the Lord. As we shall see later in this book, the apostles in Acts are persecuted for the sake of *Jesus's* name. This theme seems to be inscribed into the LXX tradition of people suffering for *God's* name (see chapter 5). These verses from Isaiah therefore have the potential to suggest that Stephen, immediately following his speech, suffers death for the sake of God or Jesus's

---

61. Sweeney, "Stephen's Speech," 200.
62. Sweeney, "Stephen's Speech," 200.

name. Furthermore, it is difficult not to notice that Isaiah includes a phrase that speaks of the glorification of the Lord, when it is the God of glory/God's glory which frames both Stephen's speech and vision. In Isaiah, it is the rejecters who call for the Lord's glorification; but in Stephen's speech it is Stephen, accused of speaking against God, who both speaks of and sees God's glory. This study therefore furthers a thesis which to the best of my knowledge has not been proposed before: Even though it may be difficult to decide whether all of Isaiah 66 should be conceptualized as part of the "cultural encyclopedia" evoked by the text, together, the themes of persecution, rejection, and glorification have the potential to help explain why Isaiah provides a better context for understanding Stephen's words than 1 Kings does.

Stephen's use of Isa 66:1–2 leads us to b), and the argument that the emphasis on the temple as created by human hands (χειροποίητος, 7:48) suggests that it should be understood as idolatrous. This argument could be supported in two ways in particular: First, by the immediate context, where τὰ ἔργα τῶν χειρῶν αὐτῶν ("the works of their hands," 7:41) refers the the Israelites' idolatry of the golden calf, and could be seen to condition the reading of 7:48. If one follows this reading, it is possible to understand Stephen's accusers as being accused of an idolatrous attitude towards the temple.[63] There is a difference between an idolatrous attitude towards the temple and complete rejection of the temple itself, however, and the latter does not seem to be in view here—even though a critique is clearly implied (see below).[64]

Secondly, it could be argued that the temple is presented as idolatrous through reference to Acts 17:24, where χειροποίητος is used to express the sentiment that God "does not live in shrines made by human hands." In Acts 17, however, the setting is Athens, which is full of pagan shrines. This suggests a connection between what is human-made and idolatry. Negatively put, the God of Israel is not the same as the pagan gods who can be found in the many, idolatrous temples of Athens; the God of Israel is the creator, Lord of heaven and earth (17:24–25). In Acts 7:48, however, there is no such implicit comparison with pagan gods. I therefore follow Sweeney, who looks at the use of χειροποίητος more broadly: He rebuffs the argument that χειροποίητος is associated with idolatry in 7:48 by demonstrating that it is the contexts in which χειροποίητος appear in the LXX, rather than the semantic meaning of the word itself, which associate it with idolatry. Further references to Josephus and Philo substantiate this. Here χειροποίητος is used

---

63. Dunn, *Acts*, 90–91.
64. Cf. Krodel, *Acts*, 150–51.

in a more mundane sense, of things humans make with their hands.[65] The contrast between what is God-made (7:50) and what is human-made (7:48) should not be downplayed. However, in the context of Stephen's speech this contrast does not imply that the human-made temple is *idolatrous*. However, it does indicate that God, as the Most High, the one who has created everything, cannot be confined by a house created by humans.

In the above, we have offered critical remarks on two common arguments in favor of the view that Stephen rejects the temple. We should not, however, lose sight of the fact that Stephen's speech does critique the temple. When we now turn to (3), the transcendence thesis, we should make clear that God's transcendence of the temple is in principle not necessarily mutually exclusive with the rejection of it. Even so, it is our contention that the arguments presented against rejection above—including the movement in the speech towards the fulfillment of God's promise to Abraham of worship in "this place"—do not imply complete rejection of the temple.[66] As we shall see in the following, however, the transcendence thesis does imply *critique* of the temple.

God's transcendence of the temple is supported not only by our previous interpretation of Stephen's speech as detailing God's agency outside of the land, but by 7:48–50 as well. We may begin by observing that for the first time in the speech, which has until now always referred to God as θεός, God is here called ὁ ὕψιστος, "the Most High." The designation "Most High" is a common circumscription for God in Jewish tradition (cf. e.g., Gen 14:20; Deut 32:8, 2 Sam 22:14; Ps 18:13, etc.), but it is also a designation used of Zeus.[67] In this sense, the text evokes both a "Jewish" and a "hellenistic" cultural encyclopedia from a world where different gods received devotion: In conversation with this cultural context, the title signals that Israel's God is the highest (and therefore "the best"). In the context of Stephen's speech, it indicates God's exaltation above humans, and the citation from Isaiah that follows also suggests that the title links God to God's presence in heaven:

> "Heaven is my throne,
>   and the earth is my footstool.
> What kind of house will you build for me, says the Lord,
>   or what is the place of my rest?
> Did not my hand make all these things?" (7:49–50)

---

65. Sweeney, "Stephen's Speech," 202–3n267; Philo, *Moses* 2.88; Josephus, *J.W.* 1.419–20; 4.614; 7.175–77; 7.294; *Ant.* 4.55–56; 15.324.

66. Contra Matthews, *Perfect Martyr*, 69.

67. Fitzmyer mentions Pindar, *Nem.* 1.90; 11.2 and Aeschylus, *Eum.* 28, as examples. See Fitzmyer, *Acts*, 384. See also Bertram, "ὕψιστος," 615.

As creator, God's seat is in heaven (as expressed through the general cosmology in Acts, cf. 7:55), but also reaches earth (as expressed through God's ability to interact with creation). Through the citation from Isaiah, then, God is here characterized as the creator of heaven and earth, exalted above all as ὁ ὕψιστος. Furthermore, "heaven and earth" could be read as a merism, which would indicate that God is present everywhere. The citation does, moreover, make clear that God's presence transcends the temple.[68] Rather than locating God's presence to a house made by human hands, the quote from Isaiah presents God's dwelling place as creation. This goes hand in hand with a careful reading of 7:48, which "underlines this point, for neither 'tent' (*skēnōma*) nor 'house' (*oikon*) are mentioned in this verse: it is simply that the Most High does not dwell in hand-made *things*—a principle with which any right-thinking first-century Jew would agree."[69]

The foregoing allows us to see that Acts 7:48–50 does contain critique of the temple, not as idolatrous or a place of God's presence—for God is present everywhere—but as a critique of the temple's ability to adequately house God. This critique characterizes God as exalted creator, rather than the temple as a god-forsaken place. If this is to speak "against this place," then perhaps Stephen's accusers are right on this point.[70]

4.2.5 Stephen's Accusation (7:51–53)

Stephen's speech culminates here, with the citation about the temple. It ends, however, when he turns his accusations back against his accusers: They are like their ancestors, who opposed the Holy Spirit; they are the ones who murdered God's Righteous One; they are the ones who have not kept the law (7:51–53). In this alignment of his accusers with their ancestors, Stephen changes his rhetoric: What has been "our ancestors" throughout the entire speech (7:38, 39, 44, 45), now becomes "your ancestors" (7:51–52). Stephen's charges against them mirror the failures of the ancestors in the past: Betrayal of one of their own (Joseph in 7:9, cf. the betrayal of Jesus in 7:52) and idolatry (7:39–41).[71] Importantly, his accusations against his accusers function as an

---

68. Cf. Sylva, "Meaning and Function of Acts 7:46–50," 267.

69. Walton, "Two Perspectives?," 142.

70. One of the questions we have not touched upon in the above reading is an historical one: Would knowledge of the fall of the temple in 70 CE have intensified the understanding of Stephen's temple critique as temple rejection, and perhaps even prophetic judgment? Or would this knowledge rather provide comfort that even without a temple, God's true house is creation? These are questions we can ask, but not answer within the scope of this study.

71. Cf. Parsons, *Acts*, 108: "The *synkrisis* Stephen develops in Acts 7 aligns Stephen

CHAPTER 4: THE GOD OF GLORY AND HEAVEN (ACTS 6:8–7:60) 113

implicit response to their charges: It is they, not he, who have blasphemed against God and Moses and broken the customs.[72] In voicing these concerns, Stephen breaks all the conventions of a defense,[73] as he himself becomes the accuser and drives the situation to a breaking point.

Stephen's shift from "our" to "your" ancestors, introduces a polemic with potentially problematic implications. As Shelly Matthews observes, the Stephen story could be read to reflect a binary between violent Jews and persecuted "Christians."[74] She uses 7:51-52 as an example, with Acts "offering Stephen up as the embodiment of the persecuted prophet, while aligning his murderers with ancestors he does not share."[75] Read from this perspective of identity formation, the Stephen story tells "a story of Christian origins that is problematically framed and ethically troubling."[76] The results are particularly ominous when this non-believing Jew/"Christian" binary is re-inscribed into modern scholarship, cementing "the assertion that the first killers of 'Christians' were 'Jews' is one of the fundaments of the master narrative of Christian origins."[77] Matthews does, however, also note that it is "not the text *itself*, apart from its readers,"[78] which promulgates this anti-Jewish agenda.

I write this, first of all, to acknowledge the very real concerns that Matthews raises about how the rhetoric of the Stephen episode has given rise to ethically problematic readings. I also agree with her observation that it is the text together with its reader, rather than the text in isolation (if one can speak of such a thing), which results in this kind of understanding. My own reading functions as a case-in-point, if nothing else, because of its choice of perspective: It differs from Matthews' interpretation in that it centers more on the character of God and on the characters in the narrative than on the destructive attitudes the rhetoric of Stephen's martyrdom might give rise to. Nor do I agree with all of Matthews' arguments. As I have shown above, I consider Stephen's speech to center on temple critique rather than temple

---

and the church with Abraham, Joseph, the prophets, and Jesus. His opponents are aligned with the Egyptians, Joseph's brothers, the rebellious in the wilderness who disobeyed Moses, and the ancestors who killed the prophets. For Luke, rather than rejecting God's house or God's law, the church is in line with the faithful in Jewish history who have sought to keep covenant with God."

72. Cf. Keener, *Acts: 3:1—14:28*, 1329.
73. Keener, *Acts 3:1—14:28*, 1420.
74. Matthews, *Perfect Martyr,* 9–10.
75. Matthews, *Perfect Martyr,* 72.
76. Matthews, *Perfect Martyr,* 8.
77. Matthews, *Perfect Martyr,* 9.
78. Matthews, *Perfect Martyr,* 28.

rejection,[79] to highlight the initial emphasis on the common ancestry of Stephen and his accusers,[80] and to frequently observe how the character of God is portrayed as constant in Israel's past and the narrative present. This focus on commonality and continuity, especially considering the fact that Stephen himself was a Jew, offers an interpretation that diminishes the texts potentially anti-Jewish slant. Thus I agree with Penner that, "the arguments articulated by Luke look more like intracommunal conflict over self-identity than outright rejection or anti-Jewish sentiment."[81] It is, however, sadly beyond the scope of this study to consider how the characterization of the God of Israel takes part in the formation of a history of Christian origins. This question could nevertheless be profitably asked elsewhere.

4.3 Stephen's Vision: The Glory of God Revealed (7:54–60)

Faced with the council's anger and contempt (7:54), Stephen raises his eyes to heaven (7:55). Stephen, who has spoken of the God of glory and God's revelations, now becomes an internal focalizer through whom the reader is directed towards a revelation of God's glory.[82] In the LXX "*doxa* is applied to the honor and reputation not just of persons, but supremely of God and God's presence."[83] When this insight is applied to Stephen's vision, "glory" denotes God's presence (cf. e.g., Exod 16:10; 24:16–18; Lev 9:23–24; Isa 4:5; Ps 26:8).[84] But we should also observe that in the context of Stephen's speech, the glory of the God Stephen sees has become associated with all the actions that the "God of glory" has worked throughout Israel's history (cf. 7:2). Stephen's vision thus vindicates the words which he has spoken, for the God he has spoken of, is also the God he sees.[85]

Furthermore, following upon a speech that has emphasized God's transcendence of the temple and ability to be universally present, it is also significant that Stephen's vision locates God in *heaven*. This is the throne of God, whose reach extends to all places of the world, and from which God

---

79. Contra Matthews, *Perfect Martyr*, 69.
80. In contrast to Matthews, *Perfect Martyr*, 71.
81. Penner, *In Praise of Christian Origins*, 330.
82. In this way, Stephen is also shown to share "the privilege of prophets and visionaries, and not least that of Moses himself, in that he sees the glory of God (e.g., Ex. 33.18-22; Isa 6.1-4; Ezek 1.28), the glory that appeared also to Abraham (7.2)" (Dunn, *Acts*, 99).
83. See Dennis, "Glory," 313.
84. See Dennis, "Glory," 313–15.
85. Cheng, *Characterisation of God*, 170.

CHAPTER 4: THE GOD OF GLORY AND HEAVEN (ACTS 6:8–7:60)

has been revealed throughout Israel's history (cf. 7:34). In this way, the vision "confirms the primary theological theme of Stephen's defense speech . . . God has never been and will never be confined to a particular place, such as a temple (Acts 7:48)."[86] Stephen's vision also reveals that the God he has spoken of has Jesus standing at his right hand side (cf. Luke 22:69), in the place of honor.[87] Thus the disciples' vision in 1:8 is confirmed: Jesus has been taken up into heaven, and he has been exalted to the right hand of God (cf. 2:34). But more importantly, to see the glory of God is now to see Jesus at the same time.[88]

Because Stephen's words in 7:56 closely echo the words of Jesus in Luke 22:69, scholars frequently read these verses in light of each other and ask why Jesus is standing in Acts, rather than sitting, as in Luke. Talbert offers a summary of some of the theories that abound:

> (a) the standing one is the vindicated righteous man, after death, in the presence of God who protects him with His right hand (Wis 5:1 in the context of 4:16–5:16; (b) the standing one is the living one, the one who will not die (Rev 5:6; Ps-Clementine, *Homilies* 2.22; *Recognitions* 3.47); (c) the standing one is part of the heavenly court, an angel not God (1 Kgs 22:19; Rev 8:2; 3 Enoch 16:3–5); (d) the standing one is the heavenly judge (Isa 3:13; 2:19, 21; Amos 9:1; *Assumption of Moses* 10:3); (e) the standing one is he who offers assistance to martyrs (*Martyrdom of Polycarp* (2:2–3).[89]

Further theories include Jesus's standing as having a priestly function, as standing in welcome or personal aid of Stephen, or as standing in anticipation of his parousia.[90]

---

86. Skinner, *Intrusive God*, 45.

87. Roloff, *Die Apostelgeschichte*, 127.

88. Jesus is referred to as "son of man" by Stephen (7:56), with the exception of a few manuscripts which have "son of God" instead.
Stephen's vision makes it difficult to subscribe to Buckwalter's view that Jesus exemplifies "invisiblity" as one of the "essential characteristics describing the nature of Yahweh's divine presence in the OT" (Buckwalter, *Character and Purpose of Luke's Christology*, 279).

89. Talbert, *Reading Acts*, 64–65. Chibici-Revneanu suggests that Jesus *standing* in heaven implies that he is portrayed as a martyr. But even though there may be other texts which suggest that martyrs stand in heaven like Chibici-Revneanu demonstrates, Acts' own emphasis on Jesus's location in heaven is never on Jesus as the one who has suffered, but rather on the one who has been exalted. *Pace* Chibici-Revneanu, "Ein himmlischer Stehplatz," 477–88.

90. Smith, *Faith of the Jerusalem Temple*, 179–80. Smith himself emphasizes that Jesus is referred to as Son of Man by Stephen, and reads Acts 7:55–56 against the

Among the abovementioned theories, I would argue that (d), Jesus as judge, seems to have the most support within the narrative context. Before explicating this, however, I must hasten to add that there is not necessarily any contradiction between a) and d): Judgment is not inevitably negative, but can also include vindication. Thus, I would suggest that Jesus as judge here has a twofold function: Jesus is vindicating Stephen as well as judging his accusers.[91] In terms of his positive judgment, we have already suggested that Stephen's vision vindicates his words; the God of glory whom he has spoken of, is also the God whose glory he sees.[92] This observation can here be tied more closely to Jesus's standing before Stephen as a judge. In terms of negative judgment, however, I would suggest that this interpretation follows from the narrative context: Stephen's speech has thoroughly emphasized Israel's disobedience against God and their rejection of the prophets, not to mention that Stephen's final charge is that his accusers have killed God's righteous one. We have already observed the pattern in Israel's history where God judges the people who turn against God. Stephen's speech accuses the people of having turned against God's righteous one: Judgment, according to the pattern we have seen, is what follows next. That Jesus is God's judge is further supported by Peter's speech to Cornelius's household, and by Paul's speech in Athens (Acts 10:42; 17:31). Thus, unlike the previous revelations that Stephen has described throughout Israel's history, God is no longer revealed alone. Jesus is revealed *with* God('s glory), standing in God's presence as God's judge. The intimate links between the revelation of God and the revelation of Jesus will, as we shall see, come to characterize God throughout the remainder of Acts.

Our reading of Stephen's words to Jesus further supports this interpretation of Jesus's stance as implying his role as judge. When Stephen relates his vision to the court, they react with murder.[93] Even as the stones are

---

backdrop of Luke 21:27, which "supplements Lk. 22.69 by describing a scenario which explains the standing posture of the SM" (Smith, *Faith of the Jerusalem Temple*, 184). While I acknowledge that the mention of the Son of Man and apocalyptic imagery in both Luke 21:27 and Acts 7:55–56 makes it fruitful to read these texts in light of each other, I am not convinced that the former explains Jesus's standing pose any better than the standing pose of a judge, which, as will be argued below, seems to be a reasonable explanation given the immediate narrative context of Stephen's speech.

91. Roloff (*Die Apostelgeschichte*, 127) suggests that Stephen's prayer for the forgiveness of his enemies speaks against the portrayal of Jesus as judge; I would rather suggest that this prayer of forgiveness relies upon Jesus's mandate to forgive—as a judge.

92. "The vision also implies the vindication of Stephen and his message because he sees the exalted Jesus" (Smith, *Faith of the Jerusalem Temple*, 181).

93. In his social-scientific study of the functions of the temple versus the household in Luke-Acts, J. H. Elliott argues that Stephen's "death is the result of his verdict

falling, he prays to heaven: "Lord Jesus, receive my Spirit." Stephen's words here echo the words of Jesus in Luke 23:46 (which in turn echo Ps 31:5), where Jesus submits his spirit to God. When he speaks again, Jesus seems to remain the object of his address:[94] "Lord, do not hold this sin against them." (cf. Luke 23:34)[95] This prayer implies no less than three functions that Jesus's character takes on, which are usually credited to God: First, the contrast to Luke makes it clear that Jesus is here given God's role in receiving the dead. Secondly, and equally important, is the fact that Jesus is here given God's role as the addressee of prayer. Thirdly, implicit in Stephen's words is also a perception of Jesus as judge; if he were not perceived of as such, Stephen's petition that he not let his executioners' sin count against them would be unfounded (cf. 7:60). We have previously seen that Jesus has been spoken of as God's judge (cf. chapter 3); Stephen's words might imply that this also entails that Jesus is someone who can offer forgiveness. Finally, we may note that these observations—together with the way Stephen's prayer is phrased, i.e., with the verb ἐπικαλέω—allow a re-reading of Acts 2:20–21 where the Lord's judgment is also in view. Just as Peter states that everyone who calls upon (ἐπικαλέσηται, 2:21) the Lord will be saved, Stephen is said to be calling (ἐπικαλούμενον) upon the Lord Jesus to receive his Spirit and not hold his executioners' sin against them (7:59–60). Jesus, then, has truly moved into God's sphere.

4.4 Concluding Observations

The characterization of God in Stephen's speech and vision is closely tied together with two larger strands, God's glory and God's revelation. These are in turn interlaced with smaller strands that come together into a picture of God. *God's glory* frames Stephen's speech and vision. From the outset, God is directly characterized as "glorious" through the designation "God of

---

on the Temple as the house of Solomon but not the dwelling place of God and on its functionaries as the murderers of the Righteous One (7:46–58)" (Elliott, "Temple Versus Household," 93–94). While Elliott's article raises a number of important issues and observations about the role of the temple in Luke-Acts, his analysis of Stephen's rejection of the temple lacks thorough substantiation. As is evident from the arguments presented in our analysis, we are therefore only able to agree with the second part of his claim.

94. Contra Pesch (*Apg 1–12*, 265), who suggests that one should rather understand God as the addressee of "Lord" here. This interpretation makes little sense based on the immediate narrative context.

95. Cf. Luke 23:34. Verse 34 is lacking in some ancient manuscripts, but the variance suggests that Jesus's and Stephen's deaths were perceived as parallels from a very early point in history.

glory." God also continues to be indirectly characterized as such through his deeds in Israel's past: When God's glory is revealed, it is revealed through actions that demonstrate God's faithfulness to his promises to Abraham, through God's care for Joseph, and through his delivery of his people from Egypt. God, however, does not put up with anything: When the people reject Moses and turn to idolatry, God turns away from them in judgment for a time. God's glory could therefore also be seen to be maintained through God's role as the people's judge.

The characterization of God in Stephen's speech is closely tied to an emphasis on *God's revelations* throughout Israel's history: God's first action is to be revealed to Abraham (7:1-8), God reveals godself again to Moses (7:30-38), and finally also to Stephen (7:55-56). As we have observed in this chapter, these revelations—with the exception of the revelation to Stephen—take place outside of the land promised to Abraham. Thus God's universal presence in Israel's past is emphasized, and paves the way for Stephen's statement of God's transcendence of the temple. God, referred to as "the Most High" by Stephen, is the creator and cannot be contained by anything made by human hands: God's proper throne is therefore in heaven, from which God reaches all of earth. This way of characterizing God's ability to be present everywhere also suggests that Stephen is not completely rejecting the temple. His words may de-emphasize and critique the role of the temple, but are equally significant in terms of the point he is making about the character of God.

The focus on God's proper throne as heaven paves the way for Stephen's vision in the story-time. When Stephen raises his eyes to heaven, the themes of glory and revelation unite as Stephen sees God's glory. Unlike the rest of Stephen's speech, which mentions Jesus only in passing, Stephen's vision emphasizes that God's glory includes Jesus's presence. Jesus is now standing at the right hand of God, and Stephen's prayer to Jesus suggests that Jesus here takes on God's role as judge. As we shall see, from this point onwards in Acts, the characterization of God is irrevocably tied to Jesus.

Chapter 5: "Who are you, Lord?" (Acts 9:1–19; 22:1–21; 26:1–23)

5.0 Introduction

The appearance of the risen Lord Jesus to Paul on the Damascus road is a major turning point in the story of Acts. The revelation and Paul's[1] subsequent encounter with the Lord's words through Ananias legitimate Paul as an apostle, and pave the way for his missionary activity from Acts 13 onwards. The significance of these events is emphasized by their being recounted thrice, first by the narrator (Acts 9), and then twice by Paul (Acts 22, 26). If we ask the question of whether—or how—God is characterized through actions in these accounts, however, the answer is not straightforward. The first account of Paul and Ananias's visions does not mention God at all. It is only in the account in Acts 22 that God's agency is brought to the fore: There, in his speech to the people of Jerusalem, Paul reports that Ananias said it was "The God of our fathers" who chose Paul to see and hear Jesus (τὸν δίκαιον, 22:14), and to be his witness. In this way, Paul's work is credited to God, and accredited by God's will. Then, in 26:1–23, Paul interprets his entire mission in the light of God's promise to Israel. Thus, in the three accounts of the origins of Paul's mission, it is possible to observe a movement from no mention of God at all (9:1–19), to seeing God as the one who sent the Lord and chose Paul to be a witness (22:1–21), to finally understanding Paul's entire mission in the light of God's promise to Israel (26:1–23). In viewing these texts together, we see that God is given an active role by the implied author in Paul's becoming a follower of the Way.

This book has previously addressed the question of how God is characterized in relation to Jesus (cf. sec. 2.2.1.2). The present chapter provides an opportunity for looking more closely at how this question is worked out in the narrative. We first turn to 9:1–19. Because God is not mentioned in this text, I here look at how Jesus is described to appear to Paul and Ananias, with the purpose of highlighting how this text creates ambiguous associations to

---

1. Saul is not called Paul until 13:9. I therefore try to follow the narrative sequence in terms of how I refer to his character, but use "Paul" in sections that provide overviews or summaries with references beyond Acts 9.

God. In short, what is the consequence of the fact that Paul's encounter on the road to Damascus resembles a theophany, but turns out not to be one? I will then look at how this ambiguity is maintained or developed by looking at the relation between Jesus's and God's agency when Paul's defense speech to the people of Jerusalem reframes and interprets the first account of his encounter (22:1-21). This will also lead us to observe how God is described in relation to Paul's commission. Finally, I will look at how Paul interprets his entire mission in light of God's actions with Israel (26:1-23). In sum, then, the following chapter will focus on the characterization of God in 9:1-19, 22:1-21, and 26:1-23 by asking the following questions: How is God characterized in relation to Jesus? And how is God characterized through God's work in Israel, and through Paul's life and mission?

5.1 "Who are you, Lord?" (Acts 9:1-19)

Acts 9:1-19 not only contains the first of three accounts of Saul's experiences on the road to and in Damascus; it is the first of two sections in Acts that recounts "double visions" with bearings on the initiation of the gentile mission (cf. 10:1-16). Prior to this point, the gentile mission has not begun in earnest, although it is possible to interpret Philip's baptism of the Ethiopian eunuch as the first gentile baptism.[2] Saul has entered the narrative as an enemy of the church: He is said to have agreed with the stoning of

---

2. It is debatable whether the gentile mission has already been initiated by Philip's proclamation to and baptism of the Ethiopian eunuch (Acts 8:26-40). The question relates to whether the eunuch is to be considered a diaspora Jew or a gentile proselyte or god-fearer. The text does not clearly identify him as either, but demonstrates his piety through his intentions to worship in Jerusalem and his reading of Scripture. Although I find Keener's argument (*Acts 3:1—14:28*, 1568) that Judaism "is not attested in Meroë in this period" (Meroë is the Ethiopian capital) to point in the direction of the eunuch being a gentile, the ambiguity with regards to his Jewish/gentile identity fails to make the eunuch's baptism an obvious part of the emergence of the explicit gentile mission. Moreover, with Philip's abrupt disappearance from the scene and the eunuch's return home without ever being mentioned in the narrative again, his baptism does not generate the same potential challenges with regards to how Jesus-believing Jews should relate to Jesus-believing gentiles as the story of Peter and Cornelius does.

The Ethiopian eunuch's baptism nevertheless serves an important function in the mission at large. As Haenchen (*Die Apostelgeschichte,* 264) notes: "Der Leser hat das Gefühl, dass die christliche Mission mit diesem neuen Gläubigen einen weiteren Schritt tut über die Juden- und Samaritanerbekehrung hinaus." This feeling is strengthened by the step taken towards gentile mission in the Lord's words to Ananias (9:15). However, "the full theological discussion of the gentile mission does not follow until the Cornelius story in Acts 10-11. It is this story that plays the decisive role in Luke's narrative structure of mission from Jerusalem to Rome" (Kartzow and Moxnes, "Complex Identities," 186-87).

Stephen (8:1), and to have persecuted the Jesus movement (8:3; 9:1–2). This, then, is the backdrop against which 9:1–19 must be read.

On the road to persecute the followers of the Way in Damascus, a light suddenly flashes from heaven and Saul falls to the ground.[3] Here, he is addressed by a voice from heaven (9:4). The scene is staged as a contrast between Saul on the ground and whoever speaks high above; thus, the reader's attention is drawn both to the persecutor who is brought down low and to the high authority of the one who speaks. Heaven is often depicted as the place of God in Israel's Scriptures (see e.g., Exod 20:22; Deut 4:36; 26:15; 2 Sam 22:14; 1 Kgs 8:30–49; 2 Kgs 2:1; Ezek 1:1), and the presence of God—or a representative of God's—and is on a number of occasions accompanied by flashing light or lightning (cf., e.g., Exod 19:16; 2 Sam 22:15; Pss 18:14; 77:18–19; 97:4; 144:6; Ezek 1:4, 7, 13). In Acts, however, heaven is a setting God shares with Jesus (cf. 1:1–2, 9–10; 2:2; 7:56). This in itself creates narrative ambiguity for the reader in terms of the light and voice from heaven: Who is speaking, is it God, or is it Jesus?

This question is not answered by the narrative framework. In many ways, Acts 9:1–9 resembles what George Savran has identified as a "theophanic type scene," a narrative pattern of theophanic encounters in Israel's Scriptures. It is possible that "epiphany" would have been a more suitable designation, as it is not only God, but sometimes also God's intermediaries who appear in these encounters.[4] Nevertheless, Savran's work is helpful, for it allows us to observe how the implied author inscribes Paul's encounter with Jesus into a pattern of encounters between human and divine actors throughout Israel's Scriptures. It does, moreover, pave the way for some important observations regarding the relation between God and Jesus. In Savran's article, "Theophany as Type Scene" (2003), part of his later book, *Encountering the Divine* (2005),[5] he suggests that five elements belong to each type scene: 1) the setting of the scene, which separates the protagonist from his or her family or societal sphere;[6] 2) the appearance and speech of the deity, which may also happen through a divine emissary;[7] 3) human response to the divine presence, usually marked by humility or

---

3. For the suddenness of such experiences, see chapter 3.1.
4. "Epiphany" is the designation used by Churchill, who further classifies the epiphany as one of divine initiative. See Churchill, *Divine Initiative*, 41.
5. Savran, *Encountering the Divine*.
6. Savran, "Theophany as Type Scene," 126–28.
7. Savran, "Theophany as Type Scene," 128–30.

fear;[8] 4) expressions of doubt or anxiety;[9] 5) externalization, i.e., the human's return, after having been transformed, back to the public sphere after the divine encounter.[10] Additionally, Savran introduces two helpful terms, borrowed from Robert Alter: Identity and difference: "identity in the basic plot sequence which is described, and difference in the deployment of certain motifs in varying fashion."[11] These terms open up a way of describing the literary similarities between different theophanic scenes, in spite of differences.

It is easy to spot the "identity" or similarities between Paul's vision/audition and the theophanic type scene. First, he is separated from the societal sphere, for he is "in-between" places, journeying, on the road to Damascus (9:3).[12] Paul is also separated from his fellow travelers in his encounter, for even though they hear the voice, they do not see anything (9:7). Secondly, there is the appearance and speech of the divine emissary, in this case Jesus, who is accompanied by a flashing light (9:3-6). Third, there is the human response; Saul has fallen to the ground (9:4), and he queries the identity of the speaker (9:5). The expression of doubt or anxiety is lacking; here, there is "difference" between what we observe in Acts and in other theophany narratives. But Saul's return to the world is a gradual process where he must go through blindness and fasting (9:8-19) before he begins a different life; he is, in every sense, transformed from persecutor (9:1) to proclaimer of Jesus as the Son of God (9:20). In short, in a number of ways, Saul's encounter resembles the theophany narratives, wherein a person encounters either God godself or God's intermediary (cf. e.g., Gen 28:10-22; Exod 3:2—4:17; 33:12-23; Num 22:2-35; Judg 13:2-25, Isa 6:1-13, Ezek 1:1—3:14, etc.). These similarities also allow us to point out some expectations with which the reader approaches Acts 9:1-9: The voice and flashing light from heaven signal a theophany, and so we expect either God or God's representative to appear. The brief ambiguity in terms of whether God, God's representative, or Jesus is speaking,[13] after Paul's question has just been uttered and before Jesus replies, is not solved by the narrative type-scene pattern.

This ambiguity is given a voice through Saul's question, "Who are you, Lord?" (τίς εἶ, κύριε; 9:5). At this point it is helpful to distinguish between

8. Savran, "Theophany as Type Scene," 130-32.

9. Savran, "Theophany as Type Scene," 132-34.

10. Savran, "Theophany as Type Scene," 134-36.

11. Savran, "Theophany as Type Scene," 125.

12. For the emphasis on the in-betweenness or liminality underlined by this setting, see also Spencer, *Journeying through Acts*, 107.

13. Jesus is, of course, also God's representative here, but I single him out for the sake of the discussion.

how the *reader* may understand Saul's question, and how the reader may understand *Saul* to understand this question.[14] To address the latter first: Saul's question seems to be prompted by the fact that his eyes are closed (9:8). We have already noted that within the interpretive framework of theophanic type scenes in Israel's Scriptures, the voice may be identified with either God godself, or God's messenger. Saul may therefore be seeking the voice to identify as either of these, or even as a complete stranger; either way, "the recognition of superior power is also implied in the address."[15] For the reader, however, the question creates dramatic irony. The designation κύριος has, as we have observed, been ambiguous ever since 2:25–36.[16] It may be understood to refer to either God or Jesus, depending on the context. But here, "Luke and the reader know that this is indeed the *kyrios* mentioned in v. 1, i.e., the Lord."[17] Any residual ambiguity evaporates for the moment through the answer, "I am Jesus, whom you are persecuting" (9:5).

God is thus not characterized in this scene; Jesus is. It is a christophany rather than a theophany (cf. 9:17);[18] God is not even mentioned. With Matthew Sleeman's words, "Acts 9:3–6 is best read as combining theophanic elements within a Christological presentation for theological effect."[19] Because the question is raised about the identity of the voice, the scene demonstrates how Jesus's and God's characteristics bleed into each other: The light from heaven and the designation "Lord" blur the lines between God and Jesus's agency. We will observe this again, when we look at Paul's own account of what transpired in 22:6–16. As we shall see, this impacts the general understanding of the characterization of God in Acts, and is the reason why it is important to note how the ambiguity arises not only through the use of "Lord," but also through the "narrative appearance" of Jesus as accompanied by theophanic signs from heaven.

14. This distinction between the reader and Saul's understanding of the voice's origins is also made by e.g., Jervell and Churchill. See Jervell, *Die Apostelgeschichte*, 280; Churchill, *Divine Initiative*, 241–42.

15. Krodel, *Acts*, 176. In light of 9:27, where Barnabas suggests that Paul "saw" (εἶδεν) the Lord, it is possible that Paul should be understood to have seen a man or manlike being; see Pesch, *Die Apostelgeschichte* 1:303.

16. The way is paved for this ambiguity as early as in 1:6, where Jesus is addressed as κύριος. However, it is when David refers to both God and Jesus as κύριος in 2:25–36 that this ambiguity becomes explicit.

17. Hamm, "Paul's Blindness," 64.

18. See e.g., Haenchen, *Die Apostelgeschichte*, 611; Jervell, *Die Apostelgeschichte*, 280; Witherington, *Acts*, 316; Fitzmyer, *Acts*, 420; Spencer, *Journeying through Acts*, 107; Bock, *Acts*, 356; Sleeman, *Geography and the Ascension Narrative*, 199–200. Calling this a theophany, like e.g., Keener does (*Acts 3:1—14:28*, 1630–38), lacks nuance.

19. Sleeman, *Geography and the Ascension Narrative*, 201.

A further ambiguity arises in terms of Saul's blindness. Should this blindness, in addition to its physical reality, be interpreted symbolically, or even as punitive? For obvious reasons, the answer to this question impacts how the reader perceives of God in Acts. It is interesting, but perhaps not surprising, that scholarship to a large extent has explained Saul/Paul's blindness according to "natural causes," i.e., the brightness of the light,[20] rather than treating his blindness together with the other accounts of divine infliction in Acts.[21] Not only do Paul's own words in 22:11 open up for this interpretation; the historical significance of and respect for Paul in the church may have made it more difficult to compare him to others who suffer divine punishment in Acts (cf. 1:16–25; 5:1–11; 12:21–23; 13:4–12). There is, however, good reason to see Paul's blindness as concrete, symbolic, and punitive.[22] The first reason is presented by Dennis Hamm in his article, "Paul's Blindness and Its Healing: Clues to Symbolic Intent." In reference to Acts 9, Hamm largely bases his argument on 9:8 (ἀνεῳγμένων δὲ τῶν ὀφθαλμῶν αὐτοῦ οὐδὲν ἔβλεπεν). Noting that, grammatically, "*aneōgmenōn* can be understood either as middle voice ('when he opened his eyes') or passive voice ('when his eyes were opened'),"[23] Hamm maintains that the irony already present through the use of the term *kyrios* invites both readings. From this it follows that ἀνεῳγμένων may also be understood as a divine passive.[24] This argument is strengthened by the following observation from Brittany Wilson:

> When Saul is finally healed, the detail that 'something like scales [ὡς λεπίδες] fell from his eyes' (v. 18) cements the impression that Saul's blindness is the result of divine infliction. Scalelike objects, after all, are outside obstructions that do not normally appear from gazing too long at a light.[25]

Moreover, that Paul's blindness also has a symbolic dimension becomes apparent later on, when Barnabas suggests that Paul has "seen" (εἶδεν) the Lord (9:27),[26] and then in Paul's own declaration that he was

---

20. See e.g., Pesch, *Die Apostelgeschichte*, 304; Bruce, *Book of the Acts*, 185; Larsson, *Apostlagärningarna 1–12*, 206; Marshall, *Acts*, 356.

21. See the helpful survey of scholarship on divine infliction in Luke-Acts in Gen, "Phenomena of Miracles and Divine Infliction," 8–16.

22. Pace Larsson (*Apostlagärningarna 1–12*, 206), who writes that there is nothing to suggest that Paul's blindness is a punishment.

23. Hamm, "Paul's Blindness," 64.

24. Hamm, "Paul's Blindness," 64.

25. Wilson, "Blinding of Paul," 373; Wilson, *Unmanly Men*, 160.

26. Hamm, "Paul's Blindness," 64.

CHAPTER 5: "WHO ARE YOU, LORD?" (ACTS 9:1–19; 22:1–21; 26:1–23) 125

chosen by God "to see" (ἰδεῖν) Jesus (22:14),[27] even though the account in Acts 9 stresses his blindness.

The nature of Paul's encounter as a *christophany* requires us to understand Paul's blindness as Jesus's act. Here, too, then, Jesus performs one of God's functions in Israel's Scriptures; Jesus takes on God's role as the one to offer blindness and sight (cf. Exod 4:11). But whereas Paul's blindness may be understood as a punishment for persecution, or as symbolic of his inability to see, the development of the plot reveals this blindness as a means to an end: It is a necessary part of Paul's way to having his eyes opened. In this sense, while Jesus may be acting as Paul's judge, he is here acting *both* in judgment and salvation of Paul (cf. chapter 9 in this book).

The revelation to Paul that Jesus is "the Lord" who speaks to him (cf. 9:17), conditions the reader's understanding of whom "the Lord" who appears to Ananias in 9:10 is. This assumption is confirmed as Ananias speaks of his vision to Paul in 9:17: "the Lord Jesus . . . has sent me." In this account of Saul's encounter, it is Jesus who chooses Saul to bring his "name before gentiles and kings and before the people of Israel; I myself will show him how much he must suffer for the sake of my name." (9:15–16).[28] Again, Jesus is presented as the sole agent behind Saul's assignment. Later, we shall see how this presentation is negotiated in 22:14–16. At this point, however, it is worth noting that Saul regains his sight when Ananias lays his hands upon him. The healing of his blindness is followed by his proclamation of Jesus as Son of God and Messiah (9:20–22), which may further indicate that the restoration of his sight should be interpreted symbolically: He now "sees" who Jesus is.

Jesus's intentions for the task Paul is set has universal implications: "Go, for he is an instrument whom I have chosen [σκεῦος ἐκλογῆς] to bring my name before gentiles and kings and before the people of Israel; I myself will show him how much he must suffer for the sake of my name." (9:15–16).[29] While the gentile mission has been foreshadowed since Jesus's words to the apostles in 1:8, it is only at this point that the will to include gentiles as recipients of the believers' testimony is made explicit. As such, this is an important turning point in the narrative: The commission given

---

27. Sight and blindness is a more significant theme in Luke-Acts as a whole than we are able to go into here. Note, however, how the gospel begins with Jesus's proclamation of his ministry as bringing "sight to the blind" (Luke 4:18), and the end of Acts, where Luke returns to the theme of blindness in his judgment of the Jews who do not receive Paul's message in Rome (Acts 28:26–27). For general observations about the theme, see Røsæg, "Blinding of Paul," 159–85.

28. Note the necessity (δεῖ, 9:16) of this suffering.

29. Literally "this one is for me a chosen vessel" (9:15).

to Paul introduces the plotline for the second half of Acts (Acts 13–28), which focuses on Paul as a proclaimer of the gospel. It does, moreover, pave the way for the double vision and baptism of Cornelius's household to follow (10:1—11:18). Last, but not least: The commission, when read in light of 22:14–15, later allows the reader to see God as a god who reaches out beyond the borders of Israel, a god who is not only "the God of our ancestors," but the God of the world.

Jesus's words to Ananias yield a second observation related to the significance of Jesus's *name*. While Paul has been the persecutor of everyone who invoked Jesus's name (see 9:14), he is now chosen to bring his name "before gentiles and kings and before the people of Israel; I myself will show him how much he must suffer for the sake of my name." (9:15–16). Earlier, we have observed that "the name of the Lord" in 2:21 appeared to point to *God* for a first-time reader (see chapter 3). However, as the narrative progresses, "the name of the Lord" appears with a second meaning: 9:16 specifically points to *Jesus's* name, and 4:12 has further prepared the reader to accept that there can be no salvation except by *Jesus's* name. This last statement, however, illustrates just how deeply Jesus in Acts is written into the name-theology of God found in Israel's Scriptures. Karl Olav Sandnes observes that "this theology refers primarily to the first commandment and to texts on the exclusivity and incomparability of Yahve, such as *Shema* and polemic texts in Deutero-Isaiah" (cf. e.g., Joel 2:32/3:5 LXX; Hos 13:4; Jer 3:23; Isa 42:8, 43:10–11, 21–22).[30] God is not incomparable or exclusive in the same way in Acts, however. As Sandnes rightly suggests, much of the plot in Acts is built up around God's taking a people for *God's* name (cf. 15:14); but this is "being implemented by means of Christ's name."[31] We may say that it is largely the proclamation and signs and wonders that take place in the name of *Jesus* that drives the plot forward.

If we interpret 2:21, 4:12 and 9:16 in light of each other, it becomes apparent that Jesus once more comes to share God's characteristics. This observation is strengthened by a look at Israel's Scriptures, where "God says he will do this or that for the sake of his name (e.g., Isa 48,9; Ezek 20,44; Ps 31,4; 79,9)."[32] References to suffering for the sake of God, or God's name (Isa 66:5; Ps 44:22),[33] further undergird the observation that "Jesus's name overall takes the place that God's name was supposed to have

30. Sandnes, "Beyond 'Love Language,'" 52.
31. Sandnes, "Beyond 'Love Language,'" 51.
32. Aalen, "Jesu kristologiske selvbevissthet," 273. The above is my translation of the following: "Gud sier at han vil gjøre det ene eller det andre for sitt navns skyld (f.eks. Jes 48, 9; Esek. 20, 44; Ps 31, 4; 79, 9)."
33. See Aalen, "Jesu kristologiske selvbevissthet," 273–74. .

according to the OT."³⁴ Once more then, the narrator presents a Jesus who has been given the characteristics of God. It is nevertheless important to observe that when Paul later proclaims Jesus, it is as *Son of God* and *Messiah* (9:20, 22). In spite of the melding of the two characters, Paul never claims that Jesus has *become* God.

A second element worth noting in Ananias's words to Paul is his description of Paul as Jesus's "chosen instrument" (σκεῦος ἐκλογῆς) (v. 15). There is accordingly also a motif of election involved in Paul's encounter with, and directions from, the risen Lord. When we read this within the context of both the theophany-like encounter *and* the commission Paul receives, it is difficult not to be reminded of the call narratives of Israel's Scriptures (see esp. Exod 3:1-6; Isa 6; Ezek 2-3). Although Paul's encounter does not follow the same formula as most call narratives (e.g., his vision³⁵ and commission are separated in time, and he never objects to the directive given), the common elements of theophany, election, commission, and promise of hardships ahead are enough to inscribe Paul into a longer tradition of prophets and others in Israel's story who have been called and suffered for God (e.g., Jeremiah, cf. Jer 1:7-8). This makes it all the more interesting to note that Paul is here said to be *Jesus's* chosen instrument rather than God's. Jesus is once more given a role that the reader would expect to be God's.

So far, we have observed that the appearance of Jesus to Paul, the "christophany," resembles the theophanies of Israel's Scriptures, and that Jesus's appearance is thus accompanied by some of the same characteristics as God. In this context, we have also noted that Paul's blindness can be understood as Jesus's action. We have further observed how God and Jesus are both addressed as κύριος, that Jesus appears in "God's" setting of heaven, and that he is inscribed into the name theology of Israel's Scriptures. Finally, we have seen that Jesus appears "onstage," whereas God does not intervene directly in the narrative. In short, the foregoing has demonstrated both the "correlation" and "difference" between God and Jesus's characters, which we initially pointed out in chapter 2 of this book.

So far, our interpretation of Jesus's appearance has been made based on an overarching focus on the characterization of God. This focus, however, runs the risk of overlooking the fact that Jesus's initial encounter with Paul is not only comparable to *God's* encounters with humans. Rather, as we have indicated earlier, Jesus's characterization may be interpreted within two different, but overlapping frameworks: That of God, and that of God's

---

34. Aalen, "Jesu kristologiske selvbevissthet," 285.
35. Paul sees the light before he is blinded.

exalted intermediaries. This, in turn, has christological implications: Is Jesus here (1) presented as "simply" yet another exalted intermediary figure,[36] or (2) is Jesus here characterized like the God of Israel?[37] What kind of answers one offers obviously has implications for the portrayal of God in Acts. In posing these questions, however, the methodological limitations of what I am asking bear repeating: I am not inquiring into what the actual author's intention was in presenting Jesus the way (s)he does. Nor am I attempting to posit any historical hypothesis as to why this kind of presentation of Jesus was possible in the late first century CE. I am, however, suggesting that the narrative framework of the Damascus Road encounter in Acts 9 evokes the reader's associations to other theophanic type scenes that include God or divine intermediaries in ancient Jewish literature. Thus, I am making a narrative claim, which is dependent upon *how* the implied author presents Paul's encounter.[38] It is a narrative claim that presupposes a "cultural encyclopaedia" that includes knowledge of the aforementioned theophanies. But this narrative claim can neither confirm nor deny any historical hypotheses as to "why" Jesus is or came to be presented the way he is.[39]

36. That Jesus is merely presented as an intermediary figure seems to be implied by Jervell, who considers Jesus's exaltation as enthronement and reception of the Davidic promises, and as a gift of his proper status (33). Although Jervell notes that "Luke in some sense regarded Jesus as on a level with God," he also argues that "Jesus is not divine, not pre-existent, not incarnated, not the creator or tool of creation, not the universal reconciler, not the *imago dei* etc." (Jervell, *Theology*, 29, 30).

37. In Lukan studies, Jesus's characterization like the God of Israel has been argued by, e.g., Buckwalter, *Character and Purpose of Luke's Christology*, esp. 173–92, 275–84; Turner, "Spirit of Christ and 'Divine' Christology," 413–36; Henrichs-Tarasenkova, *Luke's Christology*.

A mediating perspective between the two views above is, most notably, offered in two groundbreaking works by Hurtado, namely *One God, One Lord: Early Christian Devotion and Ancient Jewish Monotheism* (1988) and *Lord Jesus Christ: Devotion to Jesus in Earliest Christianity* (2003). Hurtado considers that part of the conceptual background for the development of early high Christology were the various divine/chief agent figures in ancient Jewish traditions. He does, however, see Jesus as being distinguished from these in a remarkable way because he received worship. On this background, Hurtado traces what he calls a binitarian form of monotheism, where "there are two distinguishable figures (God and Jesus), but they are posited in a relation to each other that seems intended to avoid a ditheism of two gods, and the devotional practice shows a similar concern (e.g., prayer characteristically offered to God through/ in the name of Jesus)" (Hurtado, *Lord Jesus Christ*, 53).

38. Like, e.g., Rowe and Henrichs-Tarasenkova. I find it profitable to consider Lukan Christology not as a static identity to be extracted from Luke's books, but as something which is developed throughout the course of the narrative in relation to its other constitutive elements, such as its plot and other characters. See Rowe, *Early Narrative Christology*, 9–23; Henrichs-Tarasenkova, *Luke's Christology*, 26–55.

39. Because we are making narrative rather than historical observations, this study

In order to preserve the nuances inherent in Acts' narrative, I propose a twofold answer to both of the above questions relating to how Jesus is characterized. These observations correlate with what we have earlier described as correlation and difference. (1) Jesus is presented as an intermediary figure insofar as his appearance is accompanied by characteristics (i.e., from heaven, light/fire/lightning) that overlap with other intermediaries who appear in ancient writings of Jewish epiphanies (cf. e.g., Ezek 1:26; Dan 7:13–14; Jos.Asen. 14.4–14, etc.).[40] Jesus is also described as an intermediary figure insofar as the functions he shares with God may be viewed as a mediation of God's character, where Jesus is onstage and God offstage.[41] *However*, the cumulative effect of Jesus's character being written into the name theology of Israel's Scriptures, his sharing the designation *kyrios* with God, and being credited with the same actions as God's character, suggests that Jesus's characterization also goes beyond that of simply another intermediary figure. His character simply has too much in common with what a reader would expect of the God of Israel.[42] The immediately preceding observations also suggest

---

does not look at the question of whether Paul's vision was a *merkabah* vision. This interpretation of Paul's vision was, to the best of my knowledge, first proposed by John Bowker, who considers whether Paul on his way to Damascus was reflecting on the opening vision of Ezekiel, and whether what he saw was the foundation for the reversal of his beliefs; see Bowker, "Merkabah Visions," 171. Acts does not, however, provide any mention of such reflection by Paul, and so this remains at the level of speculation.

Bowker's observations have more recently been taken up and developed by Timo Eskola, whose study considers whether early Jewish merkabah mysticism influenced the development of early Christology. Eskola's study is more convincing in its attempt to prove that early Jewish mysticism underlies the New Testament theology of Jesus's exaltation in his resurrection; see Eskola, *Messiah and the Throne*. That the Damascus Road Encounter is not *presented* as a *merkabah*-like vision in Acts, however, is convincingly argued in Churchill, *Divine Initiative*, 234–38. In short, Churchill observes that what have been claimed to be the characteristics of *merkabah* visions are too general to support the weight of the argument.

40. A pagan reader might also have been able to discern of Jesus's appearance as in some sense divine, for light or radiance is one of the most common hallmarks of divine presence. See Petridou, *Divine Epiphany*, 21.

41. C. F. D. Moule suggests that we in Acts find an "absentee Christology" (Moule, "Christology of Acts," 179–80). It is the phrase he introduces, rather than the actual contents by which he qualifies it (he notes that Jesus is still active through the Spirit, appears in visions, etc.; Moule, "Christology of Acts," 179), which is problematic: Jesus may be located in heaven, but, as e.g., the Damascus vision shows, he is by no means inactive in Acts. An absent-but-active Christology is further developed in Sleeman, *Ascension Narrative*. *Pace* Jervell (*Theology*, 33), who suggests that the exalted Christ is passive; the entire Damascus event suggests that he is not.

42. I must concede that in order to stay on topic, this study does not unpack the characteristics of other intermediaries of God. We *have* observed, however, that other intermediary figures may also—to varying degrees—share characteristics and functions

Jesus is characterized like the God of Israel on a number of occasions. *However*, the fact that Jesus is characterized like God does not suggest that Jesus is presented *as* the God of Israel: There is, as mentioned above, difference in addition to correlation.[43] As we shall see later in this chapter, Jesus is, e.g., also presented as an exalted person whose proclamation is theocentrically turned towards God (26:23), and whose task overlaps with Paul's mission (26:18). These observations do, in short, textually substantiate the initial observations about the correlation and difference between God's and Jesus's characters made in chapter 2.

The interplay between correlation and difference between God and Jesus's characters does, however, also result in ambiguity. This coheres well with what we have observed so far in this chapter: While it is clear that both Saul and Ananias encounter *Jesus* in 9:1–19, these verses nevertheless highlight the narrative ambiguity we have observed since 2:36 in terms of whom "the Lord" is. We shall see that this ambiguity remains at work in the other accounts of Paul's encounters. His question, "Who are you, Lord?," is consequently allowed to echo in the background as we go on to read these texts.

5.2 The God of Our Fathers (Acts 22:1–21)

In Acts 22:1–21, Paul offers an apologetic speech to the Jerusalemites who have just attempted to kill him.[44] By this point in the narrative, Paul has be-

---

with God. Jesus is therefore not unique in this. Earlier in this book, we have, e.g., noted that the angel of the Lord and God are sometimes interchangeable in the LXX (see ch. 4, n. 28). We have also observed how epiphanies of God's representatives resemble theophanies (see this chapter, 5.1). I therefore wish to make absolutely clear that it is the *sum* of the way Jesus is characterized in Acts which I have in mind above, not merely the general observation that Jesus shares some of God's characteristics. It is moreover clear that *within Acts*, Jesus uniquely shares all these characteristics with God. No other intermediary figure in Acts, including the Spirit and the angel of the Lord, share this number of characteristics with God's character.

43. Speaking of Jesus as "either" God's co-regent, "or" subordinated to God in the way Christology is sometimes wont to do, fails to catch the nuances of Acts' own presentation.

44. The contents of the Jerusalemites' accusations against Paul are not entirely clear (see 21:34), but the reader has been given the impression that at least some of them may be connected to the claim that Paul encourages the Jews living among gentiles to forsake their Jewish laws and customs of teaching against the temple and of bringing uncircumcised Greeks into it (see 21:20–22). In this sense, the charges resemble those made against Stephen in 6:13–14. The fact that the narrator specifically mentions that Paul is addressing his audience in Hebrew (22:2), Paul's first words ("I am a Jew"), and his initial emphasis on his strict education according to the law (22:3–5), undergird the nature of Paul's speech as a defense of Paul himself, and more specifically of his Jewish

come the main protagonist. He has been set aside for mission by the Holy Spirit (13:2), performed signs and wonders (e.g., chs. 13–14; 19:11–12), proclaimed Jesus as God's resurrected Son and Messiah (e.g., 13:16–41), suffered stoning and flogging (14:19–20; 16:22–23), and been imprisoned (16:24–40). The reader has thus been given every reason to consider Paul's words truthful and reliable. His speech in Jerusalem has the form of judicial oratory,[45] which above all functions as an argument based on Paul's past to demonstrate that Paul is a faithful Jew.[46] God is first mentioned in 22:3, where Paul emphasizes that both he and his audience have been zealots "for God."[47] Rhetorically, this underscores the common identity of Paul and his narrative audience, and furthers his argument that his own work emerges from a point of departure similar to theirs. While God is mentioned here as the object of their zeal, no action of God's is mentioned until 22:14–16. Here, God is indirectly characterized through Ananias's words, as reported by Paul:

> The God of our fathers has chosen you to know his will, to see the Righteous One and to hear his own voice; for you will be his witness to all the world of what you have seen and heard. And now why do you delay? Get up, be baptized, and have your sins washed away, calling on his name.[48] (22:14–16)

These words name God the agent behind Paul's encounter on the Damascus road. Verses 14–16 will therefore be our point of departure for addressing the questions of God's role and characterization in Paul's commission, and for looking at how God is characterized in relation to Jesus in Paul's speech.

The designation used of God here, "The God *of our fathers*," emphasizes that God is the common God of Paul, Ananias, and his audience. Furthermore, the designation functions as direct characterization of God, which identifies God as the God of Israel's ancestors; God is known by the people who worship him. The account of God's choice legitimates Paul's

---

identity. It is within this framework that the second account of his experiences on the road to and in Damascus should be read.

45. Soards, *Speeches in Acts*, 111.

46. Tannehill, *Narrative Unity of Luke-Acts*, 2:275. Tannehill uses the term "renegade from Judaism."

47. In the present context, being a "zealot" is connected to negative actions, i.e., Paul's persecution of the believers, and the Jews' persecution of Paul outside the temple.

48. I follow the NRSV translation here, but have chosen to translate πατέρων with "fathers" on this occasion rather than with the NRSV's more inclusive "ancestors." I do so because I find that "fathers" more easily evokes what I believe is a point in several of Paul's speeches, namely that God's promises to important men in Israel's past have been fulfilled through Jesus's resurrection.

work, because it shows that Paul's commission is from God godself. As Tannehill notes, the shift from an omniscient narrator in Acts 9 to Paul's perspective in Acts 22 results in shifts in the narrative. Most notable for the present inquiry is the fact that here Paul's commission is not given directly by the Lord to Ananias, but through Ananias's report to Paul.[49] Whereas it was Jesus who said he chose Paul in 9:15 (cf. 20:24), in the present context it is God's agency which is emphasized.[50] Thus Paul's commission may in Acts 22 be understood as the result of a "double agency," where Paul is commissioned by both Jesus and God (cf. 22:21). However, Jesus's choice of Paul is traced back to God's choice. While God and Jesus are therefore both described as agents of the same action, the primary initiative comes from God.[51] On this basis, a certain hierarchy may be observed, in which God is characterized as the principal agent. Furthermore, Ananias's words portray God as the orchestrator of Jesus's and Paul's encounter. But because Jesus is the one who appears "onstage," in the narrative, God's character by implication and contrast appears to act "behind the scenes." God's agency is clear, but only through Jesus's appearance and Ananias's words. God is therefore portrayed as both an active and a hidden God.

Ananias says that God has appointed Paul for a threefold purpose: Paul is to know (γνῶναι) God's will, see (ἰδεῖν) his Righteous One, and hear (ἀκοῦσαι) his voice (22:14). It is not entirely clear what knowing God's will is referring to here. Anything from God's entire plan and purpose of salvation, to Paul's bearing witness to the gentiles, could be in view. However, given that both seeing and hearing God's Righteous One (Jesus, cf. 3:14; 7:52) here seem to denote Paul's encounter with the risen Jesus, it seems likely that knowing God's will refers to that encounter and Paul's commission to be a witness.[52] In this way, Paul's encounter with Jesus is ultimately credited to God's will. God's act of choosing Paul is thus part of the way in which God continues to be indirectly characterized as an orchestrator of events.

The choosing to know, see, and hear, result in Paul's commission as "his witness / witness to him" (μάρτυς αὐτῷ, 22:15). Paul is thus "included within the circle of early disciples who have seen and interacted with the post-Easter Jesus (1:3)."[53] While the indirect object could be read ambiguously to refer to either God or Jesus, there is good reason to understand it

---

49. Tannehill, *Narrative Unity of Luke-Acts*, 2:275–76.

50. Cf. Marguerat, "Saul's Conversion," 197.

51. Bruce, *Book of the Acts*, 417.

52. *Pace* Conzelmann, *Acts*, 187, who suggests that God's entire plan of salvation is in view.

53. Holladay, *Acts*, 425. Cf. Pervo, *Acts*, 632. Note that Paul is called ὑπηρέτης and μάρτυς in 26:16, cf. Luke 1:2.

to refer to Jesus. Not only is Jesus the immediately preceding object (22:14), but bearing witness is in Acts primarily connected to Jesus (cf. 1:8; 1:22; 2:32; 3:15; 5:32, etc.). The same observation may be made about 22:16: Whose name Paul shall call on as he is baptized is not specified. However, the general emphasis on Jesus's rather than God's name in the rest of Acts invites the reader to understand Jesus's name as being implied here too. Thus, assuming the reader's familiarity with the Jewish practice of calling on God's name, the text may here be read as a renegotiation of this practice to include the invocation of Jesus's name. It might even be possible to take this reading one step further, and suggest that *within* Acts, the invocation of Jesus's name *replaces* the invocation of God's name, as the narrative never mentions the latter. This impacts the portrayal of God, because God and Jesus are once more shown to share the same "territory." Furthermore, in the present text, turning to God also involves a turn to Jesus during baptism. Baptism is here described as a cleansing of sins, but the subject of the "cleansing" (ἀπόλουσαι) is not entirely clear. Again, there is ambiguity in terms of whether God or Jesus is the referent.[54]

God commissions Paul to be a witness "to all the world of what you have seen and heard" (22:15). When this is read in the light of Paul's previous and future mission in Acts, it is clear that "the world" includes both Jews and gentiles (cf. 22:21 and 9:15). Again, God's will to include the gentiles as recipients of the believers' testimony is made explicit, and God is indirectly characterized as "God of all."

The final part of Paul's speech relates a second vision, which takes place in the temple (22:17-21).[55] As the Jews' cultic center, it is little wonder that the temple is the context of the prayer that precedes Paul's vision. In Acts as a whole, the temple setting is ambivalent:[56] It is mainly a setting for the proclamation of Jesus as the Messiah (5:21-42), but its importance as the house of God is deemphasized in Stephen's speech (7:47-50). There, we have already seen that even though Stephen does not reject the temple, creation as a whole is highlighted as God's dwelling place. The temple is also, as J. H. Elliott points out, a setting of conflict, both in earlier texts (3:1-4:22; 5:12-42), and in the context leading up to the present speech, where Paul is

---

54. Cf. Witherington, *Acts*, 672.

55. Historically speaking, Paul is most likely praying in the court of Israel; it is emphasized in Acts 21:26 that Paul has completed the days of purification required to enter here. As Spencer suggests, Paul's emphasis on his praying in the temple effectively counters the temple charge from 21:28: "he came to this place to pray, not stir up trouble" (Spencer, *Journeying through Acts*, 220).

56. See e.g., Walton, "Tale of Two Perspectives?," 135–49.

seized in the temple and dragged out (21:30).⁵⁷ In the vision referred to in Paul's speech, however, the temple is simply the setting for a scene of worship; Paul reports to his audience that he was praying there when he fell into a trance and received the vision (22:17–18).

Paul's second vision further inscribes Jesus into a setting commonly associated with God, i.e., a setting of worship and temple. Paul initially says that his vision was of "him" (22:18), so neither Jesus nor God is mentioned by name. The interpretation of whom this refers to therefore partly depends on how one interprets "*his* witness" in 22:15—I have already made a case for understanding this as Jesus. This reading also makes sense in light of 22:8 and 22:19: In 22:8, Jesus identifies himself as the one whom Paul is persecuting, whereas 22:19 speaks of Paul's persecution against those "who believed in you." It is therefore likely that Paul's second vision is also of Jesus. Paul addresses him as "Lord." While this designation may simply mean "sir," the title, when invoked in a temple setting, is also theologically loaded: "Jesus, whom Paul's interlocutors have rejected, is polemically asserted as the Lord of the Temple, under characteristic traits that assimilate him to God."⁵⁸ Jesus's orders to Paul are similar to those assigned to God in 22:15, which allows us to observe a "double agency" at work once more. Unlike Cheng, I would highlight that there is more at stake here for the portrayal of God than simply God expressing a new revelation through Jesus.⁵⁹ Rather, Paul's vision could be said to characterize Jesus in ways that resemble God: Through the same action, and in the same setting. The result of this inscription of Jesus into "God's territory" is that God's will is expressed through Jesus; but because God's presence is mediated through someone else, God is also removed further from the scene. The vision of Jesus consequently brings God both closer and further away.

---

57. Elliott, "Temple Versus Household," 97.

58. Marguerat, "Saul's Conversion," 150. This provocation in naming Jesus "Lord" in the temple is also noted by Churchill, who reads it as a threefold provocation in response to the accusation that Paul had brought Greeks into the temple (21:28): "First, Paul claims that Jesus appeared to him in the temple, thereby placing Jesus at the very seat of Yahweh, in the temple. Second, Paul claims that Jesus sent him from the temple, reversing the direction of the crowd's accusation. Finally, Paul replaces the offense of a single Gentile with a call to all the Gentiles, by Jesus, from the temple" (Churchill, *Divine Initiative*, 209).

59. Contra Cheng, *Characterisation of God*, 126–27. I do agree, however, when Cheng summarizes her analyses of Paul's speeches by noting that, "For the interest of Paul's personal affairs, God is moved to the background as Jesus is moved to the foreground" (Cheng, *Characterisation of God*, 133).

5.3 The God of Life (Acts 26:1–23)

In Acts 26:1–23, Paul's defense speech before king Agrippa draws up a narrative of God's works which grounds Paul's commission and proclamation in God's promise and the hope of Israel. The speech is in itself a fulfillment of Paul's commission to go to gentiles and *kings* and the people of Israel in 9:15; making Paul's bearing witness one function of his trial in Acts.[60] Paul first addresses the king (26:2–3), goes on to speak about the grounds for the trial (26:4–8), and then recounts his own background from the time he persecuted the Jesus movement (26:9–11), to his encounter on the road to Damascus (26:12–18), and finally to the proclamation resulting from this encounter (26:19–23). It is thus primarily the way Paul presents God's actions in relation to his own life that characterizes God in this speech.

Paul understands himself to be on trial because of his hope in God's promise (26:6, cf. 23:6; 24:15; 25:19). The theme of promise draws a connecting line between Paul's first and last speech in Acts:[61] In his first speech in Pisidian Antioch, Paul focused on the promise as realized in the coming of Jesus as a savior of Davidic descent to Israel (13:23), and on his resurrection from the dead (13:32–33). In the present context, before Agrippa, Paul does not take an explicit point of departure in Jesus, but in Israel's hope in God's promise of the resurrection. That it is the resurrection which is in view, is indicated by Paul's question in 26:8: "Why is it thought incredible by any of you that God raises the dead?"[62] The dead, νεκρούς, is written in the plural, and the verb, ἐγείρει, is written in the present tense. This indicates that Paul is both referring to Jesus's resurrection, a present reality, but also to a more general resurrection. Paul's question is framed "in terms suggesting that to deny the possibility of resurrection is to place limits on divine power."[63] It is clear that Paul's character understands no such limits to pertain to God: Through his question, God is indirectly characterized as someone with power over death; God is the God of life.[64]

---

60. Cf. Neagoe, who understands the purpose of Paul's trials—as it comes to expression in 9:15–16—to be "that witness will be borne to Jesus' name" (*Trial of the Gospel*, 187).

61. Keener, *Acts*, 4:3500.

62. Paul's question is timely, for among the Jews the resurrection was a contested issue: The Pharisees believed in the resurrection, but the Sadducees did not (see 23:8).

63. Pervo, *Acts*, 629.

64. For a sketch of "the conceptual background against which the Lukan conception of resurrection may be interpreted," see Anderson, *"But God Raised Him,"* 48–91, 48. Anderson concludes: "the resurrection of the dead is a key aspect of Israel's hope for restoration as the covenant people of God" (91).

The third and final account of Paul's encounter on the road to Damascus (26:12-18) is slightly different from the first two. For the present inquiry, it is worth noting that Ananias does not appear at all. Instead, Paul is commissioned directly by Jesus. This brings the scene closer to the form of a call scene/commission narrative, because the vision and commission are not separated.[65] The order to stand on his feet (26:16) echoes the order to Ezekiel (Ezek 2:1 LXX), and thus echoes another call scene.[66] Here, Paul may also be understood to present some form of objection to the call, so frequently associated with call narratives, through his former way of life: Jesus says he is kicking against the goads (26:14), which are "sharp, pointed sticks used to move cattle in the desired direction."[67] Paul is, in short, futilely "resisting a greater power."[68] This instruction may also be read in light of 26:16, where Jesus says Paul has been "pre-determined" (προχειρίσασθαι) to serve and bear witness. Paul's appointment may thus be seen as part of a greater plan. In Acts 26:16-18 it is once more Jesus who commissions Paul. While this coheres with both 9:15-16 and 22:21 where Jesus is also the agent, God is in contrast to 22:14 not mentioned at all. By this point, however, the reader has been invited to see that God stands behind Paul's encounter with Jesus.

While the first two accounts focused on Paul's commission to witness to what Paul *has* seen and heard (ἑώρακας καὶ ἤκουσας), a future horizon is included in 26:16: Paul is to testify not only about the things in which he has seen Jesus, but also about the things in which Jesus will reveal himself to him in the future (ὀφθήσομαί σοι).[69] These verbs of sight, revelation,

---

65. Cf. e.g., Bock, *Acts*, 716-18.

66. Recently, Dale C. Allison has argued that "there was a tradition of assimilating visions and commissioning stories to Ezek 1-2," most notably in 1 Enoch 14:8—16:4, and Joseph and Aseneth; see Allison, "Paul and Ezekiel," 817-18. This makes it more plausible that Ezekiel can be considered evoked as part of the cultural encyclopedia of the reader. Allison traces a number of other parallels between Acts 9, 22, 26 and Ezekiel as well, but seems to admit that these allusions are too scattered between the three accounts for the reader to necessarily pick up on them. See Allison, "Acts 9:1-9," 823.

67. Talbert, *Reading Acts*, 207.

68. Gaventa, *From Darkness to Light*, 83; cf., e.g., Keener, *Acts*, 4:3515; Fitzmyer, *Acts*, 758-59.

69. The Greek in 26:16 is difficult: The manuscripts are divided in terms of whether με is included as a direct object of Paul's seeing or not, but both with and without this direct object, the sentence seems to express something along the lines that Paul shall be a witness both to his encounter with Jesus, but also to future things where Jesus will appear to him. Cf. Witherington, *Acts*, 744.

and seeing are further connected to the purpose of Paul's mission to the gentiles and Jews:[70]

> I am sending you to *open their eyes* so that they may turn from darkness to light and from the power of Satan to God, so that they may receive forgiveness of sins and a place among those who are sanctified by faith in me. (26:17–18, my emphasis).

This third account of Paul's encounter does not mention his own blindness, a theme included in the first two accounts. Instead, it is now those he proclaims to that are characterized as unseeing, possibly echoing Isa 42:6–7.[71] This further supports the observation that blindness is here used metaphorically[72] about those who are not able to perceive the will of God. Turning towards light is equated with turning towards God.

Grammatically, it is not entirely clear whether it is Paul who is set to turn the people, or the people who are to turn: Because ἀνοῖξαι (26:18) refers to Paul's action, it could be argued that it is more likely that the next infinitive, ἐπιστρέψαι, has the same subject, i.e., Paul. In light of Acts as a whole, however, this argument is problematic, because, "In Acts, those who respond positively to Christian preaching do so by 'turning' to God. It seems probable, then, that 'to turn from darkness to light' refers to the action of those who hear rather than to Paul's action" [73] (cf. 3:19; 9:35; 11:21; 14:15; 15:19; 26:20; 28:27). Nevertheless, their turning is still a result of Paul's work. Paul's entire mission is here essentially theocentrically summarized: "the light that Paul experienced . . . became the light that he mediated to others,"[74] and which resulted in the opening of their eyes. Significantly, in 26:23, this is also "identified as the work of the risen Lord 'proclaiming light' in fulfillment of prophecy."[75] Light thus becomes a catchword that binds together both Paul and Jesus's work (cf. also Luke 2:32). This yields some important observations. First, that turning towards the light is to turn towards God (cf. 26:18). Jesus is also to proclaim light (cf. 26:23), which effectively depicts him as God's mouthpiece and witness.[76] Thus, both Paul's and Jesus's work are correlated, and may be seen as directed towards

---

70. The universal mission is mentioned here, but negatively: Paul will be rescued *from* both gentiles and his people to whom he is sent.
71. Cf. Gaventa, *From Darkness to Light,* 85; Witherington, *Acts,* 745; Holladay, *Acts,* 476; Marshall, *Acts,* 396.
72. Hamm, "Paul's Blindness," 67.
73. Gaventa, *From Darkness to Light*, 86.
74. Hamm, "Paul's Blindness," 67.
75. Hamm, "Paul's Blindness," 67.
76. Gaventa, *Acts,* 346.

God. This means that even if Jesus on numerous occasions takes on the characteristics of God, God is characterized as the one for whom Jesus proclaims light. Secondly, light is the opposite of darkness, it is the opposite of Satan's power, and connotes something that brings life.[77] In short, Paul's and Jesus's work are ultimately theocentric, and the metaphor of light associates God with the powers of life.

If we retain the focus on how God is characterized in relation to Jesus, it is worth noting that Jesus's words in 26:18 condition the reception of a place among the holy on faith in Jesus. But what does faith in Jesus entail? Is Jesus elevated to the level of God? In one sense, the fact that the believers' faith now has to be directed towards Jesus in addition to towards God, means that Jesus comes to be presented in yet another way similar to how God is presented. However, I would propose that "faith in Jesus" here first and foremost entails hope in God. This makes sense in the light of Paul's speech in general: Here Paul's basic argument is that God's promises to Israel in the past may be seen to cohere with Paul's proclamation of the resurrection in the present. He mentions this hope no less than three times in 26:6–7:

> And now I stand here on trial on account of my hope (ἐπ' ἐλπίδι) in the promise made by God to our ancestors, a promise that our twelve tribes hope (ἐλπίζει) to attain, as they earnestly worship day and night. It is for this hope (ἧς ἐλπίδος), your Excellency, that I am accused by Jews!

This undergirds the argument that faith in Jesus must entail hope in Jesus's resurrection as a sign that God raises and will raise the dead (cf. 26:8, 23), and thereby hope in the fulfillment of Israel's hope and God's promise. To have faith in Jesus thus implies faith in God's faithfulness.

God's faithfulness is also brought to expression through Paul's focus on the continuity between past and present in 26:22–23.[78] Here, Paul emphasizes that God has helped him up till this point, which to the reader recalls all the times in the narrative so far when Paul has escaped or been aided in the face of opposition (cf. e.g., Acts 9:23–25, 29–30; 14:19–20; 16:25–40; 17:13–14; 18:9–10).[79] His words here function as a theological interpretation of these events in retrospect. But Paul also declares that everything he has proclaimed—including Jesus's suffering—is fulfillment of the words from the prophets and Moses. Marguerat's observation is apt: Together with 26:6–8,

---

77. Note that one of the results of this turning is the offer of forgiveness of sins (cf. 2:38; 5:31; 10:43; 13:38), whose implications for the characterization of God are mentioned elsewhere in this study (see ch. 3).

78. Cf. Fitzmyer, *Acts,* 761; Holladay, *Acts,* 478.

79. Cf. Kilgallen, "Paul before Agrippa," 182.

CHAPTER 5: "WHO ARE YOU, LORD?" (ACTS 9:1–19; 22:1–21; 26:1–23)   139

verses 22–23 form an *inclusio* where Jesus's resurrection (26:22–23) realizes Israel's hope of resurrection (26:6–8), which means that "the whole speech is governed rhetorically by the promise–fulfilment scheme."[80] In this way, God's action in aiding Paul in the present also reveals God's faithfulness, for it is part of bringing to pass what has already been foretold through Scripture.

The result of Paul's experience on the road to Damascus can be described through Acts' own words as a kind of *turning*.[81] This is the expression used in 15:3 about the gentiles who come to faith, τὴν ἐπιστροφὴν τῶν ἐθνῶν. The same language is found in 26:18 about Paul's commission as the Lord's witness to both Jews and gentiles, with the goal that they will turn from darkness to light, τοῦ ἐπιστρέψαι ἀπὸ σκότους εἰς φῶς.[82] We have seen that this turning is further connected to the opening of eyes, and is a turn from Satan to God. While both 15:3 and 26:18 refer to Paul's own mission, they reflect Paul's own experience through the interconnections created by the cluster of

---

80. Marguerat, "Saul's Conversion," 153.

81. Scholarship continues to debate whether Paul receives a "call" or if what happens is a "conversion." The two traditional positions may be represented by Krister Stendahl and Alan Segal. Noting the similarities between the prophetic calls of Ezekiel, Isaiah, and Jeremiah, Stendahl observes that "Paul's experience is also that of a call – to a specific vocation . . . .. The mission is the point" (Stendahl, *Paul among Jews and Gentiles*, 10). Segal, while granting that, "From the viewpoint of mission, Paul is commissioned," nevertheless argues that "from the viewpoint of religious experience Paul is a convert" (Segal, *Paul the Convert*, 6). For Segal, "To call Paul's experience a conversion not only has the effect of authenticating it with great emotional power and mystery, but it also clarifies Paul's call to Christianity as a call to join and later define a new community" (Segal, *Paul the Convert*, 11).

These two positions illustrate that although there is some agreement about whether Paul's experience can be viewed as a "call," this is a category that is not necessarily considered to adequately capture or interpret everything that happens to Paul as he turns from being a prosecutor to someone who is prosecuted. Later in Acts, Paul continues to proclaim "the God of our fathers" (e.g., 22:14), but also argues against those who claim circumcision as necessary for salvation (15:1). In effect, he is declaring that one of the key Jewish identity markers is no longer necessary for gentiles in order to believe in Israel's God and Jesus as his Messiah. In short, there seems to be more at stake here than "merely" a call.

One of the main challenges with the call/conversion debate, is that "conversion" is defined in such different ways. In a sense, the definition comes to define what you see. Today "conversion" has become a social scientific term for a phenomenon variously defined, ranging from a change in religion to an inner psychological experience. For examples, see Gaventa, *From Darkness to Light*, 4–16. The definitions listed here may be some decades old, but Gaventa's book nevertheless offers insight into how differently conversion as a phenomenon has been perceived. A more recent work of scholarship addressing "conversion" in Luke-Acts is made in Green, *Conversion in Luke-Acts*. Here Green explores "conversion" in Luke-Acts using a cognitive approach.

82. In Acts, turning is both theocentric and connected to repentance, as witnessed in Peter's speech in 3:19, cf. 14:15; 26:20. See Green, *Conversion in Luke-Acts*, 2.

light, eyes, seeing, and turning towards God: In Acts 9:8, 18, Paul's own eyes *were opened* and his sight restored after his encounter with the light and Lord on the road. This opening of eyes also entails recognition of Jesus as Lord, Messiah and Son of God, as evidenced by Paul's proclamation throughout Acts (see 13:32-39; 17:1-3; 18:5, etc.), and, notably, immediately after his eyes are opened in Damascus (9:19-22). Understood within the framework of Acts as a whole, the Damascus event involves a redirection towards God that brings God to new light for Paul: Jesus is God's son, and by implication, this means that God is Jesus's father, the one who raised him from the dead and made him Lord and Messiah. Paul's vision of God has changed to include the fulfillment of God's promises through Jesus.

Based on the above, we may observe that the speech that contains the third and final account of Paul's experience draws together the lines of a meta-narrative[83] that Paul can be understood to be a part of: God has given a promise of resurrection to the ancestors, and has made this promise come true through the resurrection of Jesus Christ. God has chosen Paul to see Jesus, whom he addresses as "Lord," and who together with God commissions Paul as a witness to both Jews and gentiles. God has, moreover, helped Paul in his work till this very day (26:22); and Paul continues to hope for God's resurrection of the dead in the future. In drawing up the lines of this meta-narrative that Paul sees himself to be a part of, it becomes clear that God is characterized as ever present: The story begins and ends with God's promise. God is the faithful God, whose story includes resurrection. God's faithfulness is therefore also seen in his power over death in giving life.

5.4 Concluding Observations

Together, the three accounts of Paul's encounter with the risen Jesus show how God's faithfulness to this promise has been revealed in the resurrection of the Messiah. In this sense, God's faithfulness bridges Israel's past and the narrative present. Yet as the risen and ascended Messiah, Jesus's character comes to take on characteristics that belong to God: He appears from heaven, in the temple, and is addressed as Lord. When one character receives the characteristics of another, it engenders the question of what happens to the character to whom these characteristics are usually assigned. The question in the context of this study consequently becomes what happens to God's character when Jesus takes on some of God's characteristics

---

83. By "meta-narrative" I mean an overarching account (which includes God's promises to Israel), which provides an interpretive framework within which Paul's presentation of his own life and experiences is placed.

post-ascension. I would suggest the answer is that God becomes further removed from the scene. The same actions are assigned to God and Jesus, meaning there is a "double agency" at work, but God is the "first agent" or "initiator." The difference between God and Jesus is that Jesus is the one who appears in the narrative, who is seen and heard, and who is acting on God's behalf. The result is that God remains active, but through Jesus; God's presence is invisible, save through someone else.

Through Paul's commission and proclamation, 9:1–19; 22:1–21; and 26:1–23 emphasize that God's promise realized through Jesus's resurrection must be proclaimed to Israel, kings, and gentiles (9:15). God's actions in revealing his Righteous One to Paul (22:14), and through this the appointment of Paul to testify (9:15; 22:15; 26:16), are part of a greater movement to make the fulfillment of God's promises through the resurrection of Jesus available to the world. This allows us to see that all the actions of God mentioned in Acts 9, 22, and 26, and Paul's commission in particular, are bound together by the same meta-narrative, not as random occurrences, but as intrinsically woven parts relating to God's promise, fulfillment, and the proclamation thereof. In this way, God is portrayed as the ultimate orchestrator of events, a universal sovereign with care for the entire world, and finally, the faithful keeper of promises.

Chapter 6: God's Impartiality
(Acts 10:1—11:18; 15:1-21)

6.0 Introduction

Together Acts 10:1—11:18 and 15:1-21 represent the narrative initiation of and consent to the gentile mission. The present chapter looks at how these passages, step by step, construct a portrayal of God as savior of the gentiles. The gentile mission has been foreshadowed since the beginning of Acts (see, e.g., 1:8; 2:17-21; 9:15), and has been steadily prepared for in a narrative build-up that encompasses the scattering of the Jesus believers into Judea and Samaria (8:1), the baptism of the Ethiopian eunuch (8:26-39), and Saul's commission by the risen Lord (9:1-19). This build-up reaches its climax in Acts 10:1—11:18. Here the visions and encounter of Cornelius and Peter culminate in the descent of the Spirit on Cornelius and his household and their subsequent baptism (10:1-48). This story marks a significant turning point in Acts, indicated both by its central location in the narrative and the space devoted to it.[1] Furthermore, the events are recounted twice: first by Peter to the believers in Jerusalem (11:1-18), and then at the Jerusalem meeting of apostles and elders, where the manner in which the gentiles will be saved is contended (15:1-21). Peter's words in 15:6-9 may be read as the final interpretation of what transpired in 10:1—11:18: In giving the gentiles the Holy Spirit, God has testified to them and cleansed their hearts by faith, and thereby made no distinction between gentiles and Jews (15:8-9).

Peter's explicit affirmation of God's involvement points to what we shall see may be understood as God's main action in 10:1—11:18 and 15:1-21: God's gift of salvation to the gentiles (cf. 11:14, 18; 15:11). The "action" of "God's gift of salvation" is above all represented by the descent of the Holy Spirit on Cornelius and his household. This action provokes the question fundamentally at stake in the three chapters we are looking at:

---

1. 10:1—11:18 is the high point in a series of scenes running from Acts 8 that culminate in the gentiles' reception of the Holy Spirit and their baptism. After this turning point, the gentile mission moves into focus and the emphasis shifts from Peter to Paul, with Peter's words in 15:7-11 being his final ones in Acts.

CHAPTER 6: GOD'S IMPARTIALITY (ACTS 10:1—11:18; 15:1-21)

What shall the Jesus believers do with the gentiles who have also received the gift of the Spirit? While this is the presenting issue in the three accounts viewed under one, our own focus remains on the characterization of God through actions. The portrayal of God in these chapters involves a narrative movement from enigmatic visions to explicit affirmations of God's impartiality, which is narratively substantiated by the descent of the Spirit (10:44), the affirmation of the Jerusalem believers (11:18), and by the apostles and elders in Jerusalem (15:6-21).

In the following, we begin by looking at Cornelius's and Peter's visions, and how they characterize God through actions in the story-time (10:1-23a). We then go on to look at how God is characterized by Peter through the theological insights he reaches upon his encounter with Cornelius and his household (10:23b-48). Two things in particular will be of interest to our survey here: First, Peter's speech to the gentiles takes its point of departure in his new understanding of God's impartiality, and the apostle spells out the implications of this impartiality as it comes to expression in the story of Jesus's life, and after his resurrection. As we shall see, this speech has implications for the portrayal of God through the way Peter depicts Jesus both pre- and post-ascension. Second, we look at how the descent of the Spirit upon the gentiles, understood as an act of God, represents something new in comparison with what God has done before in Israel's past. After this, we go on to look at how God is presented as Peter defends his dealings with the gentiles to the believers in Jerusalem (11:1-18). Finally, we will see how God is characterized through the theological debate at the apostle meeting in Jerusalem (15:1-21). This will then allow us to offer some concluding observations about how God is portrayed—and portrayed as savior—in relation to the initiation of the gentile mission.

6.1 Cornelius and Peter (10:1—11:18)

The story about Cornelius and Peter begins in Caesarea, where the new setting and change in protagonist from Peter to Cornelius signals a shift in the narrative. The entire story so far has foreshadowed and built up to the events that now unfold:[2] Jesus's words that the apostles will be witnesses to the ends of the earth (1:8); the descent of the Spirit on "all flesh" (2:17, cf. 2:21, 39); the movement of the mission beyond Jerusalem (Acts 8); and the Lord's words to Ananias that Paul shall bear his name "before gentiles and kings and before

---

2. These events have also been foreshadowed since the beginning of the Gospel of Luke (1-2), see especially Luke 2:29-32.

the people of Israel" (9:15), are all steps along the way.³ Peter's encounter with Cornelius may therefore be seen as the culmination of a larger narrative build-up that prepares for their meeting.

The word *salvation* (σωτηρία) itself is absent from 10:1—11:18, except in its verbal form: An angel has told Cornelius that he and his household will be given a message by which they will be *saved* (σωθήσῃ, 11:14). Instead, in the rest of the story about Cornelius and Peter, the concept of God's salvation to the gentiles is more closely connected to the expression of God's impartiality (cf. 10:34). We will see that in the context of 10:1—11:18, this characteristic is concretized through God's lack of differentiation in dealing with Jews and gentiles. This may be observed through the two visions and whom they are given to, through Peter's universalization of the gospel message, the vindicating descent of the Holy Spirit upon Cornelius and his household, and the gentiles' subsequent baptism. Salvation, then, may here be seen to be expressed by the ways in which God visits the gentiles and includes them among his people and purpose, through an extension of his gifts and promises to them. The characterization of God in the story of Cornelius and Peter takes place gradually and develops as the visions are acted upon, reinterpreted, and acted upon again. To this we now turn.

6.1.1 Two Visions: God's Enigmatic Orchestration (10:1–23a)

The two visions in 10:3-16 present God in the story-time through representation and mediation by an angel (10:3-6) and a voice (10:10-16). In themselves, the visions are incomplete: It is not until each character acts upon his vision and the two of them encounter each other that God's purpose is more fully comprehended.⁴ Visions such as these were not uncommon in writings in antiquity,⁵ and frequently served as validation of a specific course of action.⁶ In Acts, however, "the complementary visions go beyond this simple confirmatory function, and in fact are key to the furthering of the

3. Joel B. Green suggests that Peter, in the passages leading up to Cornelius's introduction, is moving geographically away from Jerusalem, but also that he is crossing boundaries by moving among the sick, acquiring corpse impurity, and staying with a tanner who would be considered perpetually impure (Green, *Conversion in Luke-Acts*, 97). However, Green does not substantiate that a lame man would be considered unclean according to the law; Peter touches Tabitha only after she has returned to life, and the status of the tanner's impurity is disputed; see Oliver, "Simon Peter Meets Simon," 50-60.

4. Cf. Tannehill, *Narrative Unity of Luke-Acts*, 2:128-32.

5. Wikenhauser, "Doppelträume," 100-11; Talbert, *Reading Acts*, 94-95; Miller, *Convinced*, 21-63.

6. Humphrey, "Collision of Modes?," 72.

story."[7] Because these visions are given by God, God's action here becomes crucial for the development of the plot. In the following, we shall see how *whom* God speaks to, *when* God speaks to them, *how* God speaks to them, and the points of view from which all of this is narrated inform the characterization of God in 10:1–11:18.[8]

The first vision is given to Cornelius the gentile, not to Peter. This serves a narrative function: It allows the vision to foreshadow God's impartiality in terms of whom God communicates to and includes in God's plans. Thus God is initially brought into the narrative, not through a description of God's actions, but through the narrator's characterization of Cornelius. In addition to being a centurion of the Italian cohort (10:1) and a gentile (10:28), Cornelius is characterized in terms of Jewish piety:[9] He and his household are god-fearing, and Cornelius is said to pray constantly and give alms (10:2).[10] In sum, Cornelius is characterized both by his allegiance to the Romans and by his allegiance to the God of Israel. This introduction of Cornelius paves the way for the following events, which come to focus not so much on how god-fearing gentiles relate to God, as on how God relates to god-fearing gentiles.

Cornelius's vision (10:3–6) is narrated in the third person by the omniscient narrator. This lends a sense of objectivity to the scene. The current setting seems to be one of prayer. This is made explicit in 10:30, and is indicated in 10:2–5: Cornelius is described as praying διὰ παντός, the angel

---

7. Humphrey, "Collision of Modes?," 72. Cf. also Miller, "Symbolic Dream-Visions," 446. Here Miller suggests that symbolic dream-visions "serve the purpose of directing or redirecting the plot of a narrative."

8. It would also have been possible to focus more on the significance of the geographic settings of the story of Cornelius and Peter. As Wilson ("Geographic Movement," 81–96) diligently demonstrates, geography is key to both the development of the plot and the suspense of the story (93). When I have chosen not to focus on geography in the current chapter, it is primarily a matter of delimitation. Furthermore, the characterization of God in these chapters is more closely linked to the interaction with Peter and Cornelius through the angel and the vision. That is not to say, however, that the geographic movement does not underscore the universality of the God of Acts; both in terms of where and with whom this God acts.

9. Spencer, *Journeying through Acts*, 119.

10. Cornelius's character touches upon the debate of whether gentile god-fearers, referred to in Acts as either φοβούμενος τὸν θεόν or σεβομένη/ος τὸν θεόν, are to be considered a separate "class" of adherents to Judaism in antiquity. It has been contended that Acts does not serve as evidence that "god-fearers" ever existed; see Kraabel, "Disappearance of the 'God-Fearers,'" 113–26, esp. 120. However, it seems more likely that the terms we translate with "god-fearers" referred to people with different ties to Judaism. Shaye J. D. Cohen makes clear just how broad the scope of the terms may be in "Crossing the Boundary," 13–33. For a broader survey of this discussion, see e.g., Witherington, *Acts*, 341–44; Hengel and Schwemer, *Paul between Damascus and Antioch*, 61–70.

mentions that God has received his prayers (10:5), and the time (the ninth hour) has earlier been introduced as a time of prayer (3:1). Finally, the setting for Cornelius's vision is his own home, into which the angel is said to enter. God's representative is consequently the first in this narrative to cross a social boundary by entering the home of the gentile.[11]

Cornelius's vision negotiates a tension between God's immediate presence and remoteness. The angel who comes to Cornelius is unnamed, and therefore given a role through its designation as an angel *of God* (ἄγγελος τοῦ θεοῦ, 10:3). Again, we are dealing with the figure of the "angel of the Lord" (cf. chapter 4), respectfully addressed by Cornelius as κύριε (10:4). Just as in 5:19-21 and 8:26, the angel functions as God's representative. This role is further suggested by the angel's words: "Your prayers and your alms have ascended (ἀνέβησαν) as a memorial (μνημόσυνον) before God." (10:4) The verb ἀναβαίνω locates God somewhere "above," i.e., in heaven.[12] We have already observed that in the narrative cosmology of Acts, heaven is the realm from which God interacts and interferes with the earthly realm. In some sense, however, the heavenly realm is removed from the earthly one, locating God at a distance from Cornelius. Two elements mediate the distance: Firstly, Cornelius's *prayers* have ascended to God as a memorial offering. According to Luke Timothy Johnson, the memorial offering (μνημόσυνον) combines the notion of "cereal offerings made to God (Lev 2:2, 9, 16; 5:12), and whose odor (in an anthropomorphic image) rises to the presence of the Lord, so that he 'remembers' the person making the sacrifice (Lev 6:15; Sir 38:11; 45:16)," with the notion of prayer as a spiritual sacrifice.[13] Significantly, then, God accepts this gentile's "sacrifice." Secondly, the *angel* mediates the distance by representing God. In this way, the narrator indicates both God's presence (through the angel) and distance (above) at the same time.

Cornelius's vision is enigmatic. It tells the gentile *what* God wants him to do, but not *why* God wants him to do it.[14] Importantly, through the vision God is shown to interact with and interfere in the life of the godfearing gentile. This does, as previously indicated, foreshadow the insight reached later in the story, namely, that God does not differentiate between Jews and gentiles (10:34). So far, however, this is only *shown*, not made explicit. God's intentions are not revealed. It is up to Cornelius to do or

---

11. Cf. Humphrey, "Collision of Modes?," 77.

12. Movement to heaven is movement upwards, cf. e.g., Acts 1:9-11; 10:16; 11:10. See Walton, "'Heavens Opened,'" 61-62.

13. Johnson, *Acts*, 183.

14. Wilson, "Geographic Movement," 91.

CHAPTER 6: GOD'S IMPARTIALITY (ACTS 10:1—11:18; 15:1–21)

not do what he is told, and it is only in his fulfillment of God's will that God's will becomes apparent.

Peter, like Cornelius, receives his vision in a setting of prayer (cf. 11:5).[15] Prayer in these scenes (and in the rest of Acts, e.g., 4:23–37, 16:25–27) is linked with divine interference in a way that makes it part of the way Acts characterizes God: God may be petitioned, and responds to prayer. This coheres with Holmås's discoveries in his study on prayer in Luke-Acts: "Vitally important is also the infallible consistency with which Luke presents divine affirmation as attending diligent and persistent prayer, which indicates a concern with the faithfulness of God in responding graciously to the needs and hopes of a godly people undergoing tribulations."[16] Thus the fact that God responds to prayer may be seen as an aspect of God's faithfulness. Importantly, this faithfulness is here extended both to Cornelius the gentile and to Peter the Jew.

Unlike Cornelius's vision, where God is represented by the angel, Peter's vision is of a four-cornered sheet filled with four-footed animals, reptiles, and birds. Peter is the internal focalizer here; the reader is invited to see through his eyes. The vision is accompanied by a voice. As its origins are not mentioned, it is not clear whom it belongs to. F. Scott Spencer suggests that because Peter addresses the speaker as "Lord" and does not seem confused by its command, it could belong to Jesus.[17] This does, Spencer argues, cohere with the Lukan image of Jesus as someone concerned with different aspects of table fellowship.[18] This proposal would, moreover, tie in well with the last time a voice spoke whose owner was not seen: Saul, on the Damascus road, was addressed by Jesus (9:5). The notion that a reader is likely to interpret a situation based on what precedes it therefore strengthens Spencer's claim. However, κύριε might be addressed to any lord, as can be seen from Cornelius' address of the angel (10:4). Jesus is not mentioned. Spencer's hypothesis is plausible. However, the text itself does not invite a specific interpretation, and the origins of the voice remain unclear. Given this lack of specificity, it must suffice to note that the voice derives its function from speaking on behalf of God. Unlike the way God is presented in Israel's past in Acts (see sec. 4.2.1.1), God is not presented as speaking directly.

Peter's vision challenges the reader's perception of God by challenging the perception of what makes a Jew pious. The voice tells Peter to rise,

---

15. That Peter is praying is only indicated in Acts 10, but it is confirmed in 11:5.

16. Holmås, *Prayer and Vindication*, 263. Cf. Plymale (*Prayer Texts of Luke-Acts*, 113), who suggests that "Luke consistently reports that the prayers of the faithful, seeking involvement in the plan of salvation, are answered positively and immediately."

17. Cf. also Sleeman, *Geography and the Ascension Narrative*, 226.

18. Spencer, *Journeying through Acts*, 120–21.

slaughter, and eat (10:13). However, purity regulations forbade Jews from eating some of the kinds of meat on the sheet (cf. Lev 11).[19] When Peter refuses to eat, this creates a gap in the text that must be filled by the reader in order to make sense of his reaction. It may be possible to suggest that Peter, being hungry, perceives of the command as a kind of test.[20] Peter refuses to do the voice's bidding, not only once, but thrice (10:16).[21] In doing so, he may initially be understood as a pious Jew, unwilling to give up his ancestral traditions and customs which had at the time become an identifying mark of Judaism.[22] His unwillingness to eat, however, is put into question when the voice claims to speak on God's behalf: "What God has made clean, you must not call profane" (10:15). As the voice comes from heaven (implying divine revelation, cf. 7:55–56),[23] and seems to be connected to Cornelius' vision of the angel, there is no reason to put its reliability into doubt. Through its command, the implied author indicates that Peter's reaction is misguided, and that the voice's words do indeed represent God's point of view.

The voice's statement in 10:15 indicates three things: First, God has the power to cleanse. Second, God has cleansed something that used to be unclean. Third, God's authority trumps human, and in this case Peter's, authority. Thus God's action must not be contradicted. These observations point towards God's impartiality: The appearance of unclean and clean meat together reveals that God no longer distinguishes between the two; both are clean. The question is, however, whether Peter's vision should be read as a signal that Jewish dietary regulations are to be abandoned, or whether its application is figurative and should be applied to the gentiles. Chris A. Miller summarizes what is at stake in the following way:

> Many would say that Gentiles are allowed entrance to God's people *only* because the barrier of the Law (as symbolized by food laws) was first abolished. This interpretation is often supported *externally* by reading the vision in light of later Epistles or even earlier pronouncements of purity by Jesus and *internally* by the alleged meaning of Peter's vision itself. Others argue that

---

19. See Gaventa, *From Darkness to Light*, 113–14.
20. Talbert, *Reading Acts*, 95.
21. It is possible that Peter's refusal to eat may be read upon the background of stories of the time: "The heroes and heroines of Israel's popular tales of the period demonstrated their loyalty to their people and religion by refusing to eat the food of Gentiles. (e.g., Dan. 1.8–16; Tobit 1.10–13; Additions to Esther 14.17)" (Dunn, *Acts*, 137). If we apply this as an interpretive frame of reference to our own reading, Peter's reaction would seem heroic at first; and the voice's bidding all the more surprising.
22. Dunn, *Acts*, 137.
23. See also Gaventa, *Acts*, 166.

the Jewish (Torah-observant) messianic movement did not first drop its nationalistic identity in the Law but instead moved simply to embrace Gentiles.[24]

Miller's summary allows us to reframe our question according to the topic of God's actions: Does Peter's vision suggest that God abolishes Jewish dietary regulations in order for the gentiles to be allowed entry into God's people? Or does Peter's vision primarily refer to the cleansing of the gentiles,[25] suggesting that God's action *precedes* the question of food laws? We would argue the latter, asserting that the view that Peter's vision in reality abolishes Jewish dietary regulations and *thus* removes the barrier for the gentiles is not tenable in light of a narrative reading of Acts as a whole. The reasons for this may be argued as follows: 1. The voice from heaven refers to "the things God has cleansed" (ἃ ὁ θεὸς ἐκαθάρισεν, 10:15), which does not specify exactly what God has cleansed.[26] Even though the voice's words clearly do encourage Peter's eating at the moment in question, it is later demonstrated that God's cleansing refers to something other than the meat (cf. 15:8–9). By implication, what is at stake according to Acts is not primarily the cleansing of food, but the cleansing of the gentiles. 2. Peter does not immediately understand his vision; he is puzzled (10:17). In other words, Peter's reaction does not show him to be considering the option that dietary laws are overturned.[27] In this way the narrator shows that the vision's true significance has not yet been revealed. 3. Peter does not allow unclean food to *enter* his mouth, but an angel *enters* Cornelius's house (10:3), Peter *enters* Cornelius's house (10:25, 27); Peter is accused of *entering* the house of uncircumcised men (11:3); Peter speaks again of his refusal to let unclean food *enter* his mouth (11:8), and refers to how he *entered* Cornelius's house (11:12). In all these cases, εἰσέρχομαι is used.[28] In short, the problem of entry is developed to pertain to crossing thresholds rather than food crossing into Peter's mouth. 4. Finally, and most significantly, the interpretation of the vision in Acts itself is clear: Peter interprets it to pertain to people rather than food laws (10:28).

All these observations combine to show that what is at stake in Peter's vision is primarily the cleansing of the gentiles. That is not to say, however, that it is insignificant that the vision is of meat: Because the possibility of defilement was an obstacle to table fellowship between Jews and gentiles,

24. Miller, "Men or the Menu?," 302.
25. Thus, e.g., Jervell, *Die Apostelgeschichte*, 305.
26. Woods, "Interpreting Peter's Vision," 178.
27. Miller, "Dream-Visions," 453.
28. Miller, "Men or the Menu?," 311–13.

the cleansed meat is also symbolic of fellowship made possible. However, it is not entirely clear from Acts itself whether the gentiles' new status should also be understood to result in the abrogation of food laws.[29] The accusation that Peter has eaten with gentiles (11:3) could be interpreted along these lines. Not everyone would agree with this observation, however, and Miller argues that "Simply eating with Gentiles was a significant charge in itself and does not necessitate that Peter ate unclean food."[30] This distinction could be useful; but it is not made by the implied author in Acts. Of more weight, then, is the fact that the apostolic decree (15:19–21) seems to imply that dietary regulations are still in place for the Jewish believers. The question of food arises as a consequence of the gentiles' acceptance of the word of God, and in James's speech, it becomes clear that God's choice of the gentiles is prior to the question of food (see chapter 6.3). Our argument therefore stands: Together, the above observations suggest that even though Peter's vision is of food, it does not signify the abandonment of food laws *in order to* allow the gentiles entrance into God's people. God's action of including the gentiles precedes the question of food in Acts. Accordingly, God's action in Peter's speech should primarily be interpreted to concern God's changing of the gentiles' status. The implications of this—including the implications for God's character—are unpacked as the story unfolds.

Peter and Cornelius's visions are both enigmatic, but in different ways. Cornelius is given a directive and follows it without any hint of God's purpose behind it. Peter is similarly given an order, but with a partial explanation: He may slaughter and eat because God has cleansed what used to be unclean. Why God has done so and with what consequences are not immediately revealed. This creates suspense in the narrative. Both visions function as "divine promptings,"[31] or even initiatory revelations that spark Cornelius to action and invite the reader's puzzlement as well as Peter's (cf. 10:17). In short, while the visions to Cornelius and Peter suggest certain things about God's character and will, i.e., God's impartiality and power to cleanse, the full implications of this are only made clear as the story progresses. At this point, God's impartiality may have been *shown* to the reader, but God's character remains otherwise veiled.

---

29. Contra, e.g., Marshall, *Acts*, 185–86; Pervo, *Acts*, 269, who consider the purity regulations to be cancelled for the Jesus believers here. Or, to be more specific, Pervo states that a "major portion of the purity code has been abolished."

30. Miller, "Men or the Menu?," 309. Miller further notes that Acts does not make clear whether or not Cornelius himself was following Jewish food laws; given his favorable standing among the Jews, he might have followed these (309–10).

31. Tannehill, *Narrative Unity of Luke-Acts*, 2:128.

CHAPTER 6: GOD'S IMPARTIALITY (ACTS 10:1—11:18; 15:1-21)

Peter's puzzlement meets with the beginning of a "solution" when Cornelius' men arrive in Joppa. Their timely arrival just as Peter ponders his vision indicates that God's orchestration of events is coming to fruition, and this is confirmed when the Spirit's voice breaks into the story: "Now get up, go down, and go with them without hesitation; for *I* have sent them" (10:20, my emphasis, reflecting the emphatic Greek ἐγώ). When Cornelius's men arrive, however, they say that their master was "directed by a holy angel" (10:22). The Spirit's words thus blend together divine and human agency in terms of who is bringing Peter and Cornelius together. It also raises the question of whether it is possible to distinguish between God and the Spirit when it comes to who directed Cornelius to send for Peter, when the text itself does not make this distinction. The Spirit's words therefore influence the presentation of God: They show that God is the true orchestrator of Cornelius's and Peter's meeting, and that it is in the cooperation of divine and human action—God's vision and Cornelius's obedience—that God's will is eventually revealed.

In stating this, however, we touch upon a debated issue in scholarship on Acts: the relationship between divine and human agency. Is, as Haenchen suggests, God simply portrayed as a puppeteer, making his human marionettes dance by means of compelling divine interventions?[32] Or is God portrayed as dependent upon the cooperation of humans? The question is difficult to answer, mainly because Acts is unified by the controlling theme of God's plan and purpose—and hence the main plot unfolds according to this purpose. I would suggest, however, that even if God's plan of salvation is coming to fruition with a certain necessity, this does not exclude the importance of human agency. God may orchestrate events in Acts, including Cornelius's and Peter's meeting, but we should not forget how God was first presented in setting up their encounter: In the depiction of Cornelius, the angel appears to him in response to his prayers (10:4). This alone is enough to suggest that even if God is portrayed as the great orchestrator of events, God is also responsive to humans.[33]

32. Haenchen, *Die Apostelgeschichte*, 307–8.

33. The relation between divine and human agency in Acts merits a study on its own, as the topic raises far more questions than we can go into here. Such a study would have to define the notion of agency more closely, and look at different models for understanding the relationship between human and divine agency. This is done in a different context in Barclay and Gathercole, *Divine and Human Agency* (2006). With the proviso that we have not made a thorough study of how divine and human agency relate to each other in Acts, we would nevertheless tentatively suggest that the third model for human and divine agency proposed by John M. G. Barclay may be at work in Acts. This model "presents divine agency in terms of *non-contrastive transcendence*. Here divine agency is certainly not in principle exclusive of human agency: transcendence is not viewed in

In addition to emphasizing God's direction of events, there are two things to note about the second account of Cornelius's vision (10:22). First, it is recounted from the perspective of Cornelius's men. The initial account (10:3–6) and characterization of the centurion (10:2) are thus corroborated from men that serve Cornelius, and therefore strengthen what has already been said about him. Less detail is given to Cornelius's piety than before,[34] but enough to present him to Peter as a righteous man with the favor of both God and the Jewish nation. Secondly, the words of Cornelius's men function as a reply to Peter's inquiry about their coming. This allows the point of the vision to move more clearly to the fore: The men are sent because Cornelius wants to hear Peter's words.[35] Although this is not directly relevant to the characterization of God, it shows that God's purpose in getting Peter and Cornelius together is related to what Peter has to tell Cornelius.

6.1.2 Peter in Cornelius's House: Interpreting God's Directions (10:23b–48)

6.1.2.1 Peter and Cornelius (10:23b–33)

Prior to his encounter with Cornelius, Peter is puzzled (ἐν ἑαυτῷ διηπόρει, 10:17) about what his vision means. The encounter between Peter and Cornelius, however, results in a new understanding of God's message: "You yourselves know that it is unlawful for a Jew to associate with or to visit a Gentile; but *God* has shown me that I should not call anyone (μηδένα [. . .] ἄνθρωπον) profane or unclean" (10:28, my emphasis). These words are an interpretation of what Peter has seen and heard. He now explicitly states that his vision has been given by God, and construes its message to relate to humans rather than animals: He should not call *anyone* profane or unclean. The message is generalized, and God's activity made more explicit. God's

---

contrastive terms. God's sovereignty does not limit or reduce human freedom, but is precisely what grounds and enables it. The two agencies thus stand in direct, and not inverse proportion: the more the human agent is operative, the more (not the less) may be attributed to God" (Barclay and Gathercole, *Divine and Human Agency*, 7; emphasis original). In this model, God is not a puppeteer, and divine and human agency are not identical, but human agency may nevertheless be effected by God. This would explain why so many actions in Acts are also attributed to God.

34. While the repetition of the angel's words *show* Cornelius's piety, he is not directly characterized as devout, god-fearing, generous, or constantly praying like he was in 10:2.

35. "The emphasis of the vision is more explicitly on Peter's forthcoming testimony"; Witherup, "Cornelius Over and Over," 55.

revelation is, moreover, recognized by Peter as trumping Jewish concerns about associating with gentiles (cf. 10:28).[36]

Peter's interpretation is part of the movement in 10:1—11:18 through which God's character comes more clearly into view. Peter's new understanding of God's message paves the way for the recognition of God's impartiality in 10:34-35. This interpretive movement is facilitated by what God has "shown" Peter. But Peter's vision alone has not caused his understanding; he has also been "shown" its meaning through his encounter with Cornelius and his household.[37] Consequently, the text characterizes God as someone who also uses experience—in this case Peter's encounter with Cornelius's men—to give insight into God's will.

The third account of Cornelius's vision is given in response to Peter's question about why he has been summoned. Having previously been recounted by an objective narrator (10:3-6) and Cornelius's men (10:22), Cornelius's own account of the vision now somewhat redundantly substantiates his piety and recognition by God. Herein lies, as we have previously seen, the grounds for an emerging depiction of God's impartiality. Cornelius links God to the turn of events and Peter's coming: "So now all of us are here in the presence of God to listen to all that the Lord has commanded you to say" (10:33). As Cornelius has not yet heard of Jesus, "Lord" should here be understood as synonymous with God. The gentile's words evoke a theological setting ("the presence of God") for the speech that follows.[38] Through Cornelius's invitation for Peter to speak, the two visions have served their initial function in bringing the two men together in God's presence, and by paving the way for Peter's words.

6.1.2.2 Peter's Speech and the Descent of the Spirit (10:23b–48)

The narrative movement from initially enigmatic visions to a direct statement about God's impartiality reaches its climax once Peter and Cornelius have each related his vision to the other. Then Peter exclaims: "I truly understand that God shows no partiality (οὐκ ἔστιν προσωπολήμπτης ὁ θεός), but in every nation anyone who fears him and does what is right is acceptable to him" (10:34-35). This is a theological statement, and the first

---

36. The historical background for the concept of gentile impurity is not entirely clear. Most likely, different positions existed on the matter, and were acted upon in different ways. See Wahlen, "Peter's Vision," 507–8.

37. Cf. Tannehill, *Narrative Unity of Luke-Acts*, 2:130.

38. Cornelius's words also "communicate in spatial terms the very lesson about divine impartiality" (Wilson, "Jew-Gentile Relations," 94) which Peter next utters in response to Cornelius's invitation to speak.

explicit characterization of God in 10:1—11:18.³⁹ Recourse to the cultural encyclopedia and the literary context in Acts may help us understand it better: First, the concept of divine impartiality is rooted in ancient Jewish thought, and comes to expression in different ways in Jewish literature. In her study of divine impartiality, Jouette M. Bassler makes a number of observations, some of which have implications for our study: First, God's impartiality is a concept with judicial overtones, suggesting "a righteous or honest courtroom judgment, whether temporal or divine, in which the wicked are properly punished and the righteous adequately rewarded" (cf. 2 Chr 19:6-7).⁴⁰ Interestingly, in Exod 23 and Lev 19:15, impartiality is specified to entail a transcensdence of social distinctions.⁴¹ In Deut 10, however, the concept is more closely related to covenantal theology. God's impartial justice here finds its expression in care for the widows, orphans, and "sojourners" / "strangers." While Bassler never understands impartiality to *blur* the distinction between Jews and gentiles,⁴² "by including the resident *aliens* the possibility is opened for a new understanding of impartiality that not only breaks out of the courtroom setting but also cuts across ethnic boundaries."⁴³

If we bring Bassler's observations with us to Acts 10, we may note two things in particular: First, it is not new to Jewish tradition that God's impartiality concerns God's relationship with gentiles. Secondly, the concept points to God's just judgment and thus belongs to the characterization of God as a judge. In the context of 10:1—11:18, God's impartiality is linked to the characterization of Cornelius.⁴⁴ Cornelius is acceptable (δεκτός) to God because of his fear of God and his righteous deeds. Peter draws general

---

39. The expression (προσωπολήμπτης) stems from a context of greeting: To lift the face of a man one is greeted by, and who has turned his face away from you in a gesture of respect, was an oriental expression of recognition and esteem. See Lohse, "προσωπολημψία, προσωπολήμπτης, προσωπολημπτέω, ἀπροσωπολήμπτως," 779. When Peter describes God as οὐκ ἔστιν προσωπολήμπτης, he is therefore suggesting that God does not differentiate between Jews and gentiles.

40. Bassler, *Divine Impartiality*, 8.

41. Bassler, *Divine Impartiality*, 9.

42. Bassler, *Divine Impartiality*, 44.

43. Bassler, *Divine Impartiality*, 13. See also 32–44, where Bassler looks at texts in which God's impartiality comes to expression as a way of relating to both Israel and the nations. The texts in question are difficult to date, however, which is why I do not include them in the discussion above. However, cumulatively, together with Bassler's observations about Jews and gentiles above, these texts may suggest that God's impartiality contains the possibility of being significant in terms not only of God's relationship to the Jews, but to the nations too.

44. I am grateful to the article by Bassler, "Luke and Paul on Impartiality," 546–52, for this insight.

CHAPTER 6: GOD'S IMPARTIALITY (ACTS 10:1—11:18; 15:1-21)

consequences from this specific case: God's impartiality encompasses *anyone* who is acceptable to him in this way. This explicit characterization of God therefore sums up the meaning of Peter's vision as Peter has come to understand it: "God does not favour one ethnic group over another."[45] This will, as we shall see, also be key to understanding what follows in and after Peter's speech, as the declaration of God's impartiality foreshadows the descent of the Spirit and the inclusion of the gentiles into the community of Jesus believers through baptism.

The declaration of God's impartiality leads into Peter's last missionary speech in Acts. Here God is indirectly characterized through God's actions in Israel's history through Jesus, both in Jesus's life and after his ascension. But the speech also works out the implications of the impartiality of God that Peter has just declared, in a tension between Jesus's particular sending to the people of Israel, and the universal status of Jesus as "Lord of all" (10:36). God, Peter says, sent a message of peace, εἰρήνη (10:36), to the children of Israel through Jesus. At first, God is thus portrayed as the particular God of Israel. The relation between God and Jesus is stated through a list of, for Acts by now nearly standard, verbs: God anointed (ἔχρισεν) him with the Holy Spirit and power, God was with him (ἦν μετ' αὐτοῦ), God raised (ἤγειρεν) him, and allowed him to appear (ἔδωκεν αὐτὸν ἐμφανῆ γενέσθαι) after his resurrection (10:38-41). Peter's aside, however, which presents Jesus as "Lord of all" (10:36), reflects back on his declaration of God's impartiality: The description of Jesus as "Lord of all," "reflects a biblical description of God as 'Lord over all the earth' (Josh 3:11, 13; Ps 97:5, Zech 4:14), revealing God's sovereignty to judge (Mic 4:13) and rule (Zech 6:5) all nations."[46] This reading is strengthened by Peter's introduction of Jesus as God's judge later on (10:42). In calling Jesus "Lord of all," Peter is closely connecting Jesus's identity to God's, perhaps even suggesting that God has "shared his Lordship with Jesus Christ."[47] In spite of the fact that Peter says God's message of peace was proclaimed to "the people of Israel," his speech here opens towards the gentiles as they may be understood to be included among the "all."[48] Altogether, the ways in which Peter speaks of the relationship between God and Jesus demonstrates that

---

45. Holladay, *Acts*, 237.
46. Keener, *Acts*, 2:1800.
47. Dunn, *Acts*, 142.
48. Matthew L. Skinner also notes that Jesus healed *all* who were oppressed (10:38) and that release from sins is given to *everyone* who believes in him (10:43). He considers this Peter's highlighting of "evidence of God's impartiality" (Skinner, *Intrusive God*, 83).

God authorizes and validates Jesus's actions; in turn, Jesus's actions frame the message and character of God.

Jesus's character thus becomes the lens through which God's character is viewed. God's message of peace may be understood to include "reconciliation to God and the withdrawal of the judgments attached to the previous state of enmity,"[49] which presupposes that something has gone wrong in the relationship between God and Israel. This message of reconciliation is here concretized through Jesus's works of doing good and healing the oppressed (10:38). Later, Peter says reconciliation is offered by means of forgiveness to everyone who believes in Jesus's name (10:43). This leads to two observations: First, Acts focuses on reconciliation through Jesus as an expression of God's salvation. But reconciliation is not merely "formal" reconciliation; it is concrete restoration, offered, e.g., through Jesus's actions of doing good and healing the oppressed.[50] Jesus's ministry and the restoration it brings thus become a concrete manifestation of God's saving activity. In short, through Jesus's works, Peter proclaims God as savior and shows how God comes to humanity's aid.

The scope of God's saving actions is not confined to the past, but includes both future judgment and forgiveness (10:42–43). Peter declares that Jesus is God's appointed judge of living and dead (10:42), and that forgiveness is offered through belief in Jesus, to *all who believe in him* (πάντα τὸν πιστεύοντα εἰς αὐτόν, 10:43). These words have at least two implications: First, God's impartiality is here revealed through the judgment and forgiveness offered through *Jesus*. This means that God's own role as judge is moved further to the background because he now acts through someone else. Secondly, as we have seen, Peter's words open up the narrative of God's saving works to include the gentiles who come to faith. Ethnic criteria are here abandoned as a precondition for God's salvation, but Peter's words nevertheless show that the God of Acts is still partial in that God does not accept just anyone—God's impartiality extends to those who fear God and perform righteous deeds (10:34–35). Given these conditions, we may say that God is here presented as a god whose forgiveness (and judgment) show no partiality. In this way, God's salvation and God's impartiality are brought together, making God's impartiality an aspect of how God is portrayed as savior.

---

49. Keener, *Acts*, 2:1798.

50. This ties in with a more holistic understanding of salvation in Luke-Acts, represented by Joel B. Green and Mark Allen Powell, which has been succinctly summarized among newer trends in Lukan soteriology in Reardon, "Recent Trajectories and Themes in Lukan Soteriology," 85–86.

CHAPTER 6: GOD'S IMPARTIALITY (ACTS 10:1—11:18; 15:1–21)

The sudden descent of the Spirit (10:44) functions as a "divine stamp of approval" on Peter's words. Here God's impartiality is once more *shown*, as the gift of the Spirit which was first extended to the Jews at Pentecost is now extended to the gentiles.[51] In many ways, the description of the two events resemble each other: We may, e.g., observe that in reference to the event in both 11:17 and 2:38, the Spirit is spoken of as a gift; the Spirit's descent results in glossolalic praise of God (2:6–11, cf. 10:46),[52] and Peter compares the apostles' experience to that of the gentiles (10:47).[53] However, it is debated whether the Spirit given is in fact a soteriological gift (so, e.g., Dunn[54] and Turner[55]), or merely a "sign of salvation" revealed through the

---

51. That God gives the gift of the Spirit may also be understood within the context of hospitality. In Andrew E. Arterbury's article, "The Ancient Custom of Hospitality, the Greek Novels, and Acts 10:1—11:18," 53–72, Arterbury argues that "the custom of hospitality provides the primary backdrop for an informed reading of this radical event in the life of the early church" (53). Arterbury continues a discussion initiated by Gaventa in *From Darkness to Light* (1986). Gaventa suggests that Cornelius's conversion is closely connected to "the issue of *hospitality*, the sharing of food and shelter between Jews and Gentiles. By means of the issue of *hospitality*, Luke demonstrates that the conversion of the first Gentile required the conversion of the church as well" (Gaventa, *From Darkness to Light*, 109–10). Reading Acts 10:1—11:18 through this lens, Arterbury is able to observe the dynamic between Peter and Cornelius as a series of hospitality scenes. Of primary interest to our study, is Arterbury's observation that the gift of the Holy Spirit "resembles a gift that is given in the course of hospitality (cf. Longus 3.7-11, 4.5-6, Heliod. *Aeth*. 5.15.1)" (Arterbury, "Ancient Custom of Hospitality," 70). Because this gift is made by God, "theologically it may be possible to claim that God has personally extended hospitality to these Gentiles" (71). If this is the case, then God the gift-giver may be understood as God the host, who is now including the gentiles in a relationship with God through the gift of the Spirit. This relationship is "validated" when Peter orders Cornelius and his household to be baptized, thus fully and actually including the gentiles in the Jesus movement.

That hospitality is in fact an issue worth considering in this text is also argued in Karl Olav Sandnes's essay, "Omvendelse og gjestevennskap," 325–46, (trans.: "Conversion and Hospitality"). Noticing that several major conversion scenes in Acts (9:17-19; 10:48—11:3; 16:14-15) end with an extension of hospitality to or by the one who has converted, Sandnes suggests that in Acts 10:48, "Peter is again invited to recognize what God has already recognized. The common table in Cornelius' house initiates and socially confirms the fellowship that God has already made possible through Spirit and baptism" (335, my translation). In short, Cornelius's offer of hospitality is the consequence of God's own extension of hospitality. Original quote: "Peter innbys igjen til å anerkjenne det Gud allerede har anerkjent. Det felles bord i Kornelius' hus innleder og stadfester sosialt det fellesskap som Gud gjennom Ånd og dåp allerede har muliggjort."

52. Cornelius and his household's response to the reception of the Spirit seems to be a matter of speaking in tongues (γλώσσαις), rather than in different languages (ἑτέραις γλώσσαις) like in 2:4. Cf. e.g., Fitzmyer, *Acts*, 239, 467.

53. Turner, *Power from on High*, 380.

54. Dunn, *Baptism in the Holy Spirit*, 80–82.

55. Turner, *Power from on High*, 387.

"prophetic nature of the gift"[56] (so Menzies). Menzies suggests that the gift of the Spirit and the cleansing of the gentiles' hearts (15:8-9) are two different acts: "God's bestowal of the Spirit bears witness (v. 8) to the reality of his act of cleansing (v. 9)."[57] Additionally, he asserts that, "Luke equates the gift of the Spirit granted to Cornelius's household, not with cleansing and forgiveness, but with the Pentecostal gift of prophetic inspiration."[58]

Menzies' argument that 15:8-9 might suggest that the Spirit is the witness to the gentiles' cleansing rather than synonymous with it, may make sense at first glance. However, I share Turner's reading of these verses in light of 11:16. The reason behind this is that in 11:16, the descent of the Spirit is referred to as an act of baptism (ὑμεῖς δὲ βαπτισθήσεσθε ἐν πνεύματι ἁγίῳ.[59] If baptism is understood as a ritual act of cleansing (cf. 22:16), then this provides a case for reading the two parts of 15:8-9 as synonymous after all. When these parts are read together, the part about the gift of the Spirit can be understood as a parallelism to the cleansing of the gentiles' hearts.[60]

For the reader familiar with Israel's Scriptures, this development may seem rather surprising: Here, "The Spirit was a gift promised only for the covenant people (cf., e.g., Isa 42:1; 44:3; Ezek 36:26-27; 37:14, 29; Joel

56. Menzies, *Empowered for Witness*, 215.
57. Menzies, *Empowered for Witness*, 217.
58. Menzies, *Empowered for Witness*, 218.
59. Turner, *Power from on High*, 387.
60. In a recent article, Timothy W. Reardon offers a substantial argument for reading Acts 15:9 as the gentiles' being cleansed "on account of" their faith, rather than by faith. See Reardon, "Cleansing through Almsgiving," 463-82. Reardon suggests that almsgiving, which forms part of the characterization of Cornelius, is the means of his cleansing, and that the narrative presents Cornelius as "clean" before his encounter with Peter (cf. 10:15). Reardon's argument deserves a more thorough engagement than I can offer here, but I must mention two observations which give me pause: 1. The final words referred to in Peter's speech (10:34-43) concern *having faith* and *forgiveness of sins* (10:43). Faith in Jesus is thus presented by Peter as a precondition for forgiveness, and this results in the same status before God as cleansing. The Spirit then descends even as Peter is speaking (10:44). To me, this, together with 11:17, suggests that faith (in Jesus) and forgiveness of sins could be more closely linked to the gentiles' status as cleansed before God than Cornelius's earlier almsgiving. 2. Reardon argues that while the Spirit is a witness to the gentiles' cleansing, it does not cleanse (15:8-9). Interestingly, the only evidence he cites in support of this observation is Turner: "God's gift of the 'Spirit of prophecy' would readily 'bear witness' to the fact that they were 'clean' because it was a widespread Jewish assumption that Israel's sin was the cause of God's removing the Spirit of prophecy from Israel and that the gift would only be returned when God had first restored Israel in obedience" (Reardon, "Cleansing through Almsgiving," 470, citing Turner, *Power from on High*, 383). Reardon, however, fails to note that Turner only reaches his conclusion a few pages later, and there Turner actually suggests that the Spirit *is* the agent of Israel's cleansing, and that it is to be understood as such in 15:8-9. See Turner, *Power from on High*, 387.

2:28–29)."⁶¹ When it is now given to the gentiles, the concept of God's impartiality is negotiated in a manner that allows the gentiles to be seen not only as under God's sovereignty *outside* of God's people, but as *part* of this people: "As the plot develops from the day of Pentecost onwards, *the Spirit also begins to function as verifying certain group-characters (unnamed) as incorporated into God's (eschatological) community.*"⁶² In contrast to the role of the Spirit in Israel's Scriptures, here it does not merely empower certain individuals,⁶³ but validates the gentiles' belonging to the people to whom God's message through Jesus is proclaimed. This belonging is further emphasized when the gentiles are baptized, just as the Jews were on Pentecost. While Acts never ceases to depict the particularity of God as the God *of Israel*, the movement depicted in the Cornelius story is part of the narrativization of how the God of Israel becomes the God of all.⁶⁴ God is doing something new, compared to what God has done in Israel's past. We may say, with Shauf, that "Acts displays divine impartiality in the form of an expanding partiality,"⁶⁵ which now also includes the gentiles. God is thus truly presented as God of all.

6.2 Peter in Jerusalem: God's Gift to the Gentiles (11:1–18)

In Jerusalem, Peter must defend his dealings with the gentiles to the circumcised. Unlike 10:1–16, 30–33, which was largely told from the narrator's and Cornelius's points of view, we here hear of how Peter himself perceives of the events that have transpired. Holmås notes that Peter's account begins with Peter's prayer experience, and "ends with the emphatic declaration that this is unequivocally from God."⁶⁶ If we hold this together with the observation that "Peter's καθεξῆς narration is orderly in the sense that it provides a persuasively arranged narrative which highlights the true meaning of the narrated events,"⁶⁷ we may observe that Peter's account is theologically structured: It is designed to demonstrate both God's initiative and God's purpose of salvation to the gentiles.⁶⁸

---

61. Keener, *Acts*, 2:1809.
62. Hur, *Dynamic Reading*, 276.
63. One exception to the Spirit empowering indviduals is found in Num 11:25, where the spirit is put upon seventy elders.
64. Marguerat, *First Christian Historian*, 36–37.
65. Shauf, *Divine in Acts*, 202.
66. Holmås, *Prayer and Vindication*, 211.
67. Holmås, *Prayer and Vindication*, 211.
68. Cf. Schneider, *Die Apostelgeschichte*, 2:82.

The characterization of God in these verses is indirect and concerns God as savior. In recounting Cornelius's vision, Peter adds: "he will give you a message by which you and your entire household will be saved" (11:14). Neither Cornelius nor the narrator has previously related Cornelius's vision in this way, making this Peter's interpretation: "Memory and recent events interact.... A growing understanding of the breadth of God's purpose and the depth of God's power is the result."[69] And God's purpose, according to Peter, is salvation. God is thus by implication characterized as savior.

While Peter does not repeat his statement about God's impartiality (10:34), the fact that he equates the gift of the Holy Spirit to "us" (on Pentecost) to the gift that was given to "them," i.e., the gentiles (11:17), expresses the same sentiment. The gift of the Spirit to the gentiles *is* the expression of God's impartiality. In 11:16, Peter recalls Jesus's words in 1:5, and applies them to the current situation. One might say that 15:16–17 echo and reframe 1:5–8: The Spirit that was promised is now given to the gentiles too, thus enabling the apostles' witness to the ends of the earth. To Peter, not to take the consequences of the Spirit's gift to the gentiles and include them in the community of the Jesus movement through baptism, is therefore tantamount to opposing God (11:17).

To the Jerusalem church, Peter's argument proves persuasive: They praise God and acknowledge that "God has given even to the gentiles the repentance that leads to life." (11:18). Thus, they too recognize the manner in which God has made salvation possible for the gentiles. In this way, the story of Cornelius and Peter is brought to a close, in a way that suggests that it has consequences reaching beyond the immediate case of Cornelius and his household, and to the entire gentile world. God's actions have revealed God as their savior too.

6.3 The Apostolic Council (15:1–21)

Acts 15 is located close to the heart of Acts, between Paul's first (13:2—14:28) and second (15:30—18:22) missionary journeys. Mission to the gentiles thus remains in focus as the apostles search for common ground for the gentile mission that Paul has embarked upon. Together with 10:1—11:18, Acts 15 marks an important turning point in this mission: While the narrative in Acts 10:1—11:18 began to address the question of whether gentiles could be saved, Acts 15:1–21 continues the discussion of *how* they are able to be saved. Do the gentiles have to be circumcised and follow the

---

69. Tannehill, *Narrative Unity of Luke-Acts,* 2:145.

Mosaic law, as some claim (15:1, 5), or are both Jews and gentiles saved through Jesus's grace (15:11)?

To a certain extent, the answer to these questions has already been provided by the narrative context: When 15:1-21 is read against the backdrop of 14:27, God's saving purpose is evident through Barnabas and Paul's mission among the gentiles. Tension is therefore created, not so much with regards to *which* claim is right, but with regards to *how* the question will be settled. This, in turn, emphasizes the importance of the arguments presented at the apostolic council. In the debate that ensues, the implied author presents God's actions through the disciples, Barnabas, Paul, Peter, and James, who argue that the gentile mission is in line with God's purpose, and that God's works are in evidence in this mission. This, then, is first and foremost a *theological* debate, rooted in different understandings of God's character that are informed by the Jesus movement's experience and the way it leads them to interpret Scripture. In the following, it is the theology of the debate that is in focus. We will look at how God is presented, both through the initial build-up to the meeting (15:1-5), and as part of the arguments laid out by the apostles and elders in Jerusalem (15:6-21).[70]

6.3.1 A Problem and Dispute (15:1-5): Contending Views of God

In 15:1-2, dissension arises over the question of circumcision. At stake here is not only the gentiles' inclusion among God's people, but the understanding of the grounds on which God's salvation operates, and consequently how God is to be understood as savior. The statement "Unless you are circumcised according to the custom of Moses, you cannot be saved" (15:1) is therefore also a theological claim: God does not save the uncircumcised. This claim, however, is negated in several ways. First, by the narrative context: The descent of the Holy Spirit on Cornelius and his household, together with the partial success of Paul and Barnabas's mission, have already shown the reader that the gentiles are included in God's purpose of salvation. This is further evidenced by the current setting, Antioch, which is a city first introduced to the reader as a place where the gospel was successfully proclaimed to the gentiles (11:19-24). When the contentious claim is introduced in 15:1, the narrator uses the favorable and partial term "brothers" about its addressees, which must here refer to the gentile believers. This

---

70. Alex T. M. Cheung has presented some convincing arguments for why the narrative could be seen to start in 14:27, but I have chosen to focus on the debate proper (beginning with the contentious statement) and therefore begin in 15:1. See Cheung, "Narrative Analysis," 137-54.

"reveals Luke's disposition on the matter, a disposition that is never in question throughout the story."[71]

The disposition of the implied author is further shown by way of how the opposing parties are presented: The men who come down to Antioch are unnamed, functioning solely as agents of their message. By way of contrast, Paul and Barnabas have previously been favorably characterized as people doing the work of God (cf., e.g., 13:2–3, 46–47). When they voice their disagreement with the men from Judea, it is therefore clear that their opinion is concomitant with that of the implied author and an expression of God's purpose. The point of view of the implied author is further indicated by the report of the joy the news of the gentiles' conversion brings to *all* the believers/"brothers" (πᾶσιν τοῖς ἀδελφοῖς, 15:3), as Paul and Barnabas journey to Jerusalem to debate the issue with the apostles and elders.

Jerusalem retains some significant functions in Acts. It is the city in which Jesus ordered his disciples to remain and wait after his resurrection (1:4). It is also the city in which the Holy Spirit was given, from which the mission sprang (1:8; 2:1–47), and in which Peter's account of Cornelius's conversion has previously received acclaim (11:1–18).[72] In short, the fact that the issue is to be debated in this setting signals both the weight of the matter, and the fact that the debate there will—like much that has previously taken place in the city—have consequences for the entire mission:

> The authorization of the Gentile mission must come from Jerusalem and nowhere else because it is to the Jerusalem apostles that the commission and power for the mission "in Jerusalem, in all Judea and Samaria, and even to the end of the world" is originally given by the risen Christ prior to his Ascension (1:4–8). The unity between the Jewish and Gentile churches is undergirded by the fact that they both have their source in Jerusalem.[73]

God's actions are the first thing recounted when Paul and Barnabas reach Jerusalem: Upon their arrival, they report "all that God had done with them" (15:4). In essence, this summarizes their signs, wonders, and proclamation, not to mention their favorable reception by a number of gentiles earlier in the narrative (Acts 13–14). Barnabas and Paul's report of God's actions stands in contrast to the Pharisees' statement that "It is necessary (δεῖ) for them [the gentiles] to be circumcised and ordered to keep the law of Moses" (15:5). This second statement is more extensive

71. Gaventa, *Acts*, 213.
72. I owe this last insight to Talbert, *Reading Acts*, 127–28.
73. Cheung, "Narrative Analysis," 145.

now than the first time it was uttered (15:1), in that it now includes not only a demand to be circumcised, but to keep the entire Mosaic Law as well.[74] Whereas Paul and Barnabas's words present God as the one who has authorized and made their mission possible, the believers from the Pharisees seem to possess a different understanding of God. The verb δεῖ does, as we have previously seen, frequently function as a watchword for divine necessity in Acts, and is "a typical Lukan vehicle for describing that God's plan, as expressed in Scripture, be fulfilled."[75] It may also be understood as such here; as a consequence, the believers from the Pharisees can be understood to be arguing that it is God who demands circumcision and obedience to the law. Interpreted as such,[76] it becomes clear that both sides of the debate invoke God as the authority behind their beliefs. Tension thus arises concerning their two ways of understanding God's will.

6.3.2 The Council at Jerusalem (15:6–21)

God's will—and by implication, God's character—is debated as the elders and apostles in Jerusalem meet to discuss the issue of the gentiles' inclusion (15:6). Only four characters and their points of view are named: Peter (15:7–11), Barnabas and Paul (15:12), and James (15:13–21). Peter and James's words are referenced in direct speech, whereas Paul and Barnabas's experiences are only recounted in a summary. Together, the different accounts present only one side of the debate, i.e., the views in favor of gentile inclusion without circumcision. Thus, they mutually reinforce each other and reveal the theological bias of the implied author in terms of how God is presented.

6.3.2.1 Peter's Speech (15:7–11): God's Testimony to the Gentiles

Peter's brief speech is theological and grounded in his own experience.[77] Together verses 7–9 serve as an interpretation of the events surrounding his encounter with Cornelius and his household (10:1–48). In Peter's interpretive account, God is portrayed as the unequivocal initiator of the gentile mission. A series of verbs identify God's role: God *chose* (ἐξελέξατο, 15:7) Peter to proclaim the gospel to the gentiles; God *testified* (ἐμαρτύρησεν, 15:8) to the

---

74. Gaventa, *Acts*, 214.
75. Cosgrove, "Divine Dei," 174.
76. This is also done in Gaventa, *Acts*, 214.
77. The theological nature of Peter's speech, and/or its focus on God has been recognized by a number of scholars. See, e.g., Gaventa, *Acts*, 215 and Parsons, *Acts*, 211, both taking their cue from Tannehill, *Narrative Unity of Luke-Acts*, 2:184.

gentiles by *giving* (δούς, 15:8) them the Spirit; God *made no distinction* (οὐθὲν διέκρινεν, 15:9) between the gentiles and Jews by *cleansing* (καθαρίσας, 15:9) their hearts through faith. These observations thus elaborate on the manner of the gentiles' salvation. Because topics previously touched upon in 10:1–48, namely God's lack of distinction, God's cleansing of the gentiles, and the gift of the Spirit are repeated here, they reinforce the close association between these elements and the portrayal of God as savior.

Peter presents the intention behind God's selection of him as a mouthpiece[78] as twofold: That the gentiles hear (ἀκοῦσαι) the gospel and believe (πιστεῦσαι, 15:7). His reference to God's choice strengthens the reliability of Peter's character, and shows that the gentiles became believers through God's purpose. God's acceptance of the gentiles is tied to the explicit characterization of God as ὁ καρδιογνώστης, "the knower of hearts" (15:8, cf. 1:24). The term indicates God's knowledge of a human's inmost being,[79] a characteristic of God familiar in Jewish thought (see Ps 139; Jer 17:9–10). Because it is used here in conjunction with God's gift of the Spirit, it would seem that the Spirit is given based upon God's insight into the character of the believing gentiles. In a twist of irony, the God to whom the apostles have been given the task of being witness (1:8), now bears witness (ἐμαρτύρησεν) to the gentiles (15:8), disclosing that God's purpose includes them.

The gift of the Holy Spirit reveals God's impartiality: This is indicated by the juxtaposition of αὐτοῖς (gentiles) and ἡμῖν (Jews) as its recipients (15:8). Moreover, Peter explicitly states: "in cleansing their hearts by faith he has made no distinction (οὐθὲν διέκρινεν) between them and us" (15:9). This assertion employs different language for God's impartiality than 10:34 (cf. προσωπολήμπτης), and is here tied to cleansing through faith. Peter's statement has social and soteriological consequences. First, his assertion that the gentiles have now been cleansed has implications in the narrative for whether Jews might socialize with gentiles, and thus has direct bearings on the legitimacy of the Jewish mission to the gentiles. Secondly, read on the background of 10:15, this statement implies that God has done something new with the god-fearing gentiles by cleansing them: Their status before God has been changed. While a new action might arise from a change in the agent's character, the implied author is careful not to present God's character as changing. The foreshadowing and validation of the gentile mission ever since the beginning of Acts (1:8; 2:17–21; 10:1—11:18; 13:47) locates the mission's roots in Jesus's command, experience,

---

78. Literally translated, "God made his choice among you that through my mouth," (15:7), which is also the translation given in the NAB.

79. Behm, "καρδιογνώστης," 613.

and Scripture. God's impartiality has consequently been foreshadowed, and is therefore not something new. What is new, however, is how this impartiality comes to expression through God's actions of giving the Spirit to the gentiles and cleansing their hearts through faith. These actions flesh out what "impartiality" in Acts implies.

We have seen that Peter's argument against the Pharisees is based on experience and is a testimony to God's impartiality. From this, Peter draws the conclusion that circumcision of the gentiles is contrary to God's will; specifically, he equals the demand to put the "yoke" (of circumcision) on the gentiles' shoulders to putting God to the test (15:10). His experience is, in short, used as an argument against the Pharisees' interpretation of the law. Instead, Peter posits that salvation is given "through the grace of the Lord Jesus" (15:11).[80] Grace then, while not directly attributed as a characteristic of God's, nevertheless comes to stand at the heart of salvation and consequently of how God as savior may be observed. This grace is impartial. This is brought more clearly into view as Peter, interestingly, makes the *gentiles* the point of departure for how salvation is brought about: "we will be saved ... in the same manner as they" (15:11). Peter's argument, in short, portrays God as someone who saves believers through grace without making a distinction between them.

6.3.2.2 Barnabas and Paul's Reports (15:11–12): "All That God Had Done With Them"

Paul and Barnabas's report presents God as active in the gentile mission. By referencing "all the signs and wonders (σημεῖα καὶ τέρατα) God had done through them among the gentiles" (15:12), they substantiate Peter's argument: Their experiences are grounded in God's actions. Indirectly, then, Paul and Barnabas's report functions as "proof-from-experience," because God's work through them among the gentiles indicates that their mission is god-willed. Similar summaries of the gentile mission earlier in the narrative (14:27; 15:4b) reinforce this impression. To a large degree, Acts 13–14 also functions as an illustration of the God-willed gentile mission through Paul

---

80. It has been argued (by, e.g., Tannehill, *Narrative Unity of Luke-Acts,* 2:185) that the text's emphasis is on *both* faith and grace as prerequisites of salvation, but the Greek text is more ambiguous: "Rendered somewhat literally, v. 11 reads: 'On the contrary, through the grace of the Lord Jesus we believe to be saved just as also they.' The implication could be that both groups believe *in order to be saved* or that both believe it to be the case *that they will be saved.* ... Yet neither approach is satisfying in this context, where the emphasis appears to lie more on the commonality of salvation by the action of the Lord Jesus than on any human means to that salvation, especially in view of the earlier emphasis on God's intervention" (Gaventa, *Acts,* 217; emphasis original).

and Barnabas's signs, wonders, and proclamation.[81] Moreover, these signs and wonders present Paul and Barnabas's work as in line with Jesus's ministry, for Jesus was attested to by God through "mighty works and wonders and signs (τέρασι καὶ σημείοις)" (2:22).[82] Last, but not least, in Peter's Pentecost speech, τέρατα in heaven and σημεῖα on earth (2:19) were declared to be a mark of the last days leading up to the Day of the Lord. We have previously seen that Peter's words in Acts 2 foreshadow the gentile mission by stating, "then *everyone* who calls on the name of the Lord shall be saved" (2:21, my emphasis). Barnabas and Paul's account of God's signs and wonders through them among the gentiles therefore discloses God's continued work, and the coherence between the actions of God in the past and the present.

6.3.2.3 James's Speech (15:13–21): "A People for His Name"

James's speech offers the debate's third and final perspective on God's role in the question of the gentiles' salvation. James first affirms Peter (here called Simeon)'s claims (15:14–18), supports the gentiles' inclusion by citing Scripture (15:15–18), and ultimately brings the discussion to an end by putting forth a decision (15:19–21). Through this speech, James reinforces what has already been said by adding his own authority to it. More importantly, because Scripture is cited as the final part of James's argument, the experiences of Peter, Paul, and Barnabas come to be bracketed by the Pharisees' and James's different interpretations of God's purpose as expressed through the law and Scripture. By quoting from the prophets, James presents a claim to God's perspective on the gentiles' inclusion in the discussion.

While James's character is never properly introduced, he has been referred to briefly in 12:17, and will be referred to again in 21:18, when Paul goes to see him during his last visit to Jerusalem. In spite of James's lack of introduction, he is "the only character in Acts whose authority no one questions."[83] This could suggest, as Tyson does, that the reader "is expected to know who this person is."[84] We are therefore here in the rare position that it is not the implied author's favorable characterization which

---

81. Barnabas and Paul's words bear semblance to both 14:27 and 15:4b, but with some variation: The latter text mentions "*all* that God had done *with* them" rather than the *signs and wonders* done *through* them. While the focus may be slightly different, the two variations ultimately seem to bear witness to the same thing: God's activity among the gentiles through the missionaries.

82. See also 4:30; 5:12; 14:3. Signs and wonders characterize the Jesus movement's mission from the beginning.

83. Jervell, *Luke and the People of God*, 185–86.

84. Tyson, "Implied Reader," 29.

induces the reader to regard James's character as trustworthy, but the lack of any introduction at all. In the immediate narrative context, however, there are some pointers that allow us to regard James's view as authoritative: He agrees with Peter's view (15:14), refers to and cites Scripture (15:15–18), and commands authority in the decision-making process (15:19).[85] James's voice is therefore the third and final one in the debate that may be said to represent the implied author's point of view on God's role.

In acknowledging Peter's account, James uses words that recall God's role in the history of God's salvific intervention among the Jews. The verbs ἐπεσκέψατο λαβεῖν (15:14) "dramatizes the divine action being reported and adds emphasis to God's action in relation to the Gentiles."[86] The term "visited" is used frequently in the LXX in contexts referring to God's salvific intervention (cf., e.g., Gen 21:1; 50:24; 1 Sam 2:21, etc.),[87] and thus puts God's visitation of the gentiles in Acts in continuity with God's visitation of Israel in earlier times. Consequently, at the same time as James affirms that God has visited the gentiles too, his words conjure a broader associative canvas of God's actions: God is the one who continues to intervene to save throughout history.

God's visitation of the gentiles is described as "a first" (πρῶτον ὁ θεὸς ἐπεσκέψατο, 15:14), and with a specific purpose, λαβεῖν ἐξ ἐθνῶν λαὸν τῷ ὀνόματι αὐτοῦ (15:14). The use of πρῶτον can be interpreted in light of the initiatory significance the Cornelius incident has had in Acts; this descent of the Spirit on the gentiles and the cleansing of their hearts (cf. 15:8–9) has led to the general inclusion of gentiles among the Jesus believers (Acts 13–14). Possibly of more significance, however, is the fact that this is the first time in Acts that the purpose of the gentiles' visitation is stated as God's taking a people for his name. As Dahl suggests, this means that "God has made provision to take a group of people out of the Gentile nations and make them his own."[88] This in itself does not address the issue of the gentiles' soteriological status in relation to the Jews, but it does confirm the gentiles' status as people of God. In this sense, James's words suggest that God is not merely characterized by God's relation to Israel, but also by God's relation to the gentiles.

---

85. It is also clear that James is an "insider" from the way that he assumes familiarity with the other believers, exemplified through his address of them as "my brothers."

86. Soards, *Speeches in Acts*, 93.

87. See also Luke 1:68, 78; 7:16; noted in Bruce, *Acts of the Apostles*, 339.

88. Dahl, "People for His Name," 326.

The final part of James's speech authorizes the gentile mission through a Scripture citation from the "prophets."[89] As we shall see, the citation characterizes God as both faithful to Israel, and as intentionally including the gentiles. God's voice is heard through the first-person singular pronoun (15:16–17). Through a series of alliterative verbs (ἀναστρέψω, ἀνοικοδομήσω, ἀνοικοδομήσω, ἀνορθώσω), it is made clear that God's intentions are to restore what is fallen, i.e., "the dwelling of David" (ἡ σκηνὴ Δαυίδ, 15:16). It is not immediately apparent what this dwelling refers to, which has resulted in a number of different solutions proposed by various scholars. These suggestions include Jesus's resurrection,[90] God's eschatological temple consisting of both Jews and gentiles,[91] the restoration of Israel,[92] and the Davidic dynasty.[93]

It seems unlikely that David's dwelling refers to Jesus's resurrection, partly because, as Gaventa notes, "Acts 15:16 employs the verb *anoikodomēsō*, ('rebuild') rather than the verb *anastēsō* ('raise up') that appears both in LXX Amos 9:11 and in Acts for the resurrection of Jesus (e.g., 2:24, 32; 3:26, 13:33, 34)."[94] The latter two proposals are somewhat stronger. Richard Bauckham's intricate treatment of James's citation as a composite of prophetic texts (Hos 3:5, Amos 9:11–12, Jer 12:15–16, Isa 45:20–22) that mutually interpret each other, concludes by understanding David's dwelling to be the eschatological temple consisting of both Jews and gentiles.[95] This, however, raises the question of why the rebuilding of this dwelling is described as a *precondition* for the gentiles' seeking the Lord. The second to last proposal, which sees David's dwelling as the restoration of Israel, may have some merit in light of the rest

---

89. The citation is a variation of the LXX version of Amos 9:11–12 (the Hebrew version of the text speaks of the possession of the nations rather than the inclusion of them), possibly influenced by Hosea 3:5, Jeremiah 12:15, and Isaiah 45:21; see Bauckham, "James and the Jerusalem Church," 454–55. Acts does not include the last part of Amos 9:11 ("and I will build it up as in the ancient days [καθὼς αἱ ἡμέραι τοῦ αἰῶνος]"), but ends the entire citation with "thus says the Lord who has made these things known from long ago (ἀπ' αἰῶνος)." Whether this ending is influenced by Isaiah 45 or is just a variation of Amos, the result is an emphasis on the fact that the gentiles have been included in God's plan since ancient times.

90. Haenchen, *Die Apostelgeschichte*, 389. Haenchen is also quoted (in support) in Schneider, *Die Apostelgeschichte*, 2:182–83.

91. Bauckham, "James and the Jerusalem Church," 454–57. Cf. also Nägele, *Laubhütte Davids*, 90–93; Ådna, "James' Position," 154–59.

92. Dunn, *Acts*, 204; Jervell, *Die Apostelgeschichte*, 395; Gaventa, *Acts*, 219.

93. Bock, *Acts*, 504; Glenny, "Septuagint and Apostolic Hermeneutics," 3–6, 18–20; Keener, *Acts*, 3:255–56; Holladay, *Acts*, 302. Keener also understands the restoration of the Davidic dynasty to imply the restoration of Israel; see Keener, *Acts*, 3:2257.

94. Gaventa, *Acts*, 219.

95. Bauckham, "James and the Jerusalem Church," 453–62.

CHAPTER 6: GOD'S IMPARTIALITY (ACTS 10:1—11:18; 15:1-21)   169

of Acts. Here this theme is raised by the apostles at the very beginning of the narrative (1:6).[96] But while theirs is an initial concern for the restoration for *Israel*, Peter later speaks of restoration as a *universal*, eschatological event (3:21). His words are illustrative of the rest of the movement in Acts, which goes from foreshadowing to realization of the gentile mission. It would therefore be somewhat surprising if James's quote were to suddenly shift the focus back to the particular restoration of Israel.

In light of Acts as a whole, and the focus on Jesus as the fulfillment of the Davidic promise, the "tent" of David is probably best understood as the restoration of the Davidic dynasty:

> Whatever else the restoration of David's "hut" or "tent" means, it surely implies the restoration of David's "house" or dynasty (for the play on different meanings of David's "house," see 2 Sam 7:6-7, 11-13, 16), so dilapidated by the captivity that it is here called a hut.[97]

This interpretation retains the context of Amos 9, where "'booth of David' looks at the dilapidated state of the kingship from David's line."[98] In the context of Acts, the restoration of the Davidic dynasty refers to Jesus: Throughout the narrative, Jesus has repeatedly been affirmed as the Messiah who fulfills the Davidic covenant (cf. e.g., 2:29-36, 13:22-23).[99] This allows us to see that in terms of the characterization of God, the first part of James's citation (15:16) depicts God as the restorer of the Davidic dynasty, which, implicitly, also portrays God as faithful to God's promises to Israel. However, it is the second part of the citation (15:17-18) which carries the main point about the issue at hand: The restoration has a purpose, indicated by the conjunction ὅπως, namely that people may seek the Lord (κύριον, 15:17).[100] Among these people, the gentiles are specifically mentioned. Their belonging to God is marked by the words "over whom my name has been called"—echoing 15:14. God has made God's claim on the gentiles,[101] and the words from Amos authorize the gentile mission through Scripture. Finally, it is also made clear that the gentiles' inclusion has been a part of God's plan for a long time (vv. 17c-18): The God who is working restoration for Israel's

---

96. See also Luke 1:32-33. Cf. Jervell, *Die Apostelgeschichte*, 395; Gaventa, *Acts*, 219.

97. Keener, *Acts*, 3:2255.

98. Tanner, "James's Quotation of Amos 9," 67.

99. Cf. Luke 1:32-33, 69.

100. The fact that the Lord at the end of the same verse appears to refer to God indicates that the "Lord" the people may seek also refers to God.

101. "To call or to invoke the name of somebody over someone is to express ownership (cf. 2 Sam 12:26-28)" (Ådna, "James' Position," 146).

benefit is also calling the gentiles to be God's own. In short, the citation portrays God as savior in a way that is defined by God's plan for and salvation of the gentiles too. Together, restoration of the Davidic dynasty and salvation of the gentiles point to the universal restoration spoken of by Peter in 3:21, indirectly characterizing God as universal savior.

James's final words are words of decision. The so-called apostolic decree is introduced with the emphatic διὸ ἐγὼ κρίνω (my emphasis) that ties it to the foregoing citation.[102] This decree does not characterize God as such, but shows how Acts portrays some of the consequences of the Jesus believers' new understanding of God's universality. The decree has engendered no little debate with regards to how it should be interpreted: Is it meant to ask the gentiles to turn from idolatry,[103] or to maintain fellowship between Jews and gentiles?[104] Does it have its background in Leviticus 17–18,[105] the Noahic commandments,[106] a broader scope of Jewish scriptural texts,[107] or does it refer to activities engaged in by the pagans in the temple cult?[108] Are its prohibitions to be read as specific ethical prohibitions related to purity (as in, e.g., 𝔓⁷⁴, A, B, ℵ) or as a more general moral code (D)?[109] And finally, how does 15:20 relate to 15:21 and the proclamation of Moses in the synagogues?

To date, there exists no scholarly consensus about most of the answers to the above questions, and the background for the decree remains elusive. However, as Witherington observes, the practices prohibited seem to have had their social setting in "the attending of temple feasts and all that they entail."[110] In this sense, the decree prohibits practices which would be

---

102. The decree is repeated in 15:29 and 21:25, signaling its significance in the mission.

103. "The Gentiles have turned to the living and true God; what they are being asked to turn from is idolatry and the accompanying acts of immorality" (Witherington, *Acts*, 463).

104. Spencer, *Journeying through Acts*, 167.

105. Pesch, *Die Apostelgeschichte*, 2:81; Talbert, *Reading Acts*, 159–60.

106. Parsons finds that the decree echoes both the Noahic commandments *and* Leviticus 17–18; see Parsons, *Acts*, 210–14.

107. Callan, "Background of the Apostolic Decree," 284–97.

108. Witherington, *Acts*, 461–64.

109. 𝔓⁷⁴, A, B, ℵ, etc. read.: "but to write to them to abstain from pollution by idols, and (from) fornication, and strangled [animals] and from blood." (my own translation). D (and with some slightly different versions in other Western texts) read: "but to write to them to abstain from pollution by idols, and from fornication and blood and what they do not wish to be done to themselves not do to others."

110. Witherington, *Acts*, 462, see also 462–65.

tantamount to worshipping other gods.[111] The decree may therefore be understood as a warning and safeguard against idolatry.[112] These observations may be profitably read in light of 15:21, which is connected to the foregoing through the coordinating conjunction γάρ. Pervo, following Tannehill, suggests that the underlying point of James's statement is that the gentile Jesus believers "need to find ways of living with people deeply committed to Mosaic law."[113] However, it is equally possible that it suggests that "The implication is that knowledge and observance of the law was well sustained in diaspora synagogues and not at all threatened by the compromise proposed."[114] Finally, we may observe that the decree does not mention circumcision, and supports Peter's proposal that the "yoke" of the law should not be put on the gentiles too. In short, to phrase it in anachronistic terms: The gentiles do not have to become Jews to become Christians. James's argument therefore negates the Pharisees' initial claim. Accordingly, the requirements placed upon the gentiles serve a sociological function rather than a soteriological one.[115] However, throughout our analysis of the apostolic council, and finally James's speech, we have seen that this solution has its roots in a theological view of God as impartial and someone who has called the gentiles to be God's own.

6.4 Concluding Observations

In this chapter, we have seen that Acts' portrayal of God as savior of the gentiles is inextricably linked to God's impartiality. This impartiality is first foreshadowed through the visions in which God visits both Cornelius the gentile and Peter the Jew, responding to the prayer of both and preparing for their encounter with each other. In addition to foreshadowing what is to come, these visions mediate God's presence and express God's will, if not immediately God's purpose. The visions also balance a tension between

---

111. See also Savelle, who reviews the proposed potential backgrounds for the apostolic decree. Although he suggests that "the commonly suggested origins say more about the ethos that gave rise to the prohibitions" (468), Savelle also concludes that, "concerning the nature of the prohibitions the most likely explanation is that all four were associated to some degree with pagan religious practices" (468). See Savelle, "Reexamination," 449–68.

112. Cf. also Gaventa, *Acts*, 222–23.

113. Pervo, *Acts*, 379, citing Tannehill, *Narrative Unity of Luke-Acts*, 2:190.

114. Dunn, *Acts*, 206. The meaning of the sentence has engendered much debate, but no consensus.

115. Cf. Parsons, *Acts*, 218.

God as present and intervening, and God as present behind the scenes, "in heaven," orchestrating events from afar.

While the visions are enigmatic at first, God's character is revealed more clearly through the interaction of human and divine agency: Cornelius and Peter's encounter could equally be seen as ordered by Cornelius, or by the angel, or by God who sent the angel, or by the Spirit. The visions function as "divine promptings." It is only as these promptings are acted upon by Cornelius and Peter that God's purpose emerges. This purpose is twofold: First, that Peter change the way he perceives of the gentiles' status, and that social interaction between Jews and gentiles is hence made possible; second, that Peter proclaim the good news to the gentiles. These actions may in turn be seen as the human manifestation of God's impartiality, lodged in God's purpose as savior of both Jews and gentiles.

Because divine and human agency are thus intertwined, human experience plays a part in how God's character is portrayed. The encounter between Cornelius and Peter serves as the interpretive key that allows Peter to see that his vision was God's own way of telling him he should not call anyone profane or unclean (10:28). God has done something new, cleansed the gentiles, and thereby overturned traditional customs. In other words, Peter's new experience of God's actions results in a new understanding of what is permitted in the present. Finally, it is by listening to Cornelius's own account and self-presentation that Peter gains new insight into God's character: "I truly understand that God shows no partiality, but in every nation anyone who fears him and does what is right is acceptable to him" (10:34–35). Thus God's impartiality, which was at first merely shown and foreshadowed, here becomes explicit through Peter's direct characterization of God. In other words, through the cooperation of the human and the divine, God's character is revealed to the reader.

The insight into God's impartiality is maintained as Peter proclaims the gospel message to Cornelius's household. In his speech, too, God is portrayed as savior. This portrayal is fleshed out through God's actions with and through Jesus, spanning from Jesus's ministry and into the future through his role as judge of living and dead. The God Peter proclaims to the gentiles is a universal God, who through Jesus works good deeds, and brings reconciliation, judgment, and forgiveness to everyone who believes in him. While Peter's words draw up a narrative of God's saving actions which also opens up towards the gentiles, it is the descent of the Spirit into the story-time that validates Peter's words. Once more, God's impartiality is revealed as the coming of the Spirit brings the gentiles the same gift as the Jews. Thus God does something new, something that has not been done before in Israel's past. The gift of the Spirit by God is shown in 10:44, and then told of when Peter relates what has transpired to the Jesus believers in Jerusalem in 11:17: "If then God gave them the same gift that he gave us when we believed in the Lord Jesus Christ, who was I that I could hinder God?" Peter does, in other words, include the gentiles' salvation in God's purpose.

By the beginning of 15:1–21, the gentiles have become part of the story of the mission (11:19–26; 13:44–49; 14), and the question in 15:1 relates to how they are saved. We have looked at the apostolic council as a theological debate, in which two different understandings of God's salvation contend against each other: Does God save only Jews and gentile proselytes, through circumcision and the Law of Moses? Or, does God save without distinguishing between believing Jews and gentiles, through the grace of Jesus Christ? Phrased with this study's query in mind, how do the answers to these questions affect how we understand God as savior? The perspective of the implied author is here made clear through the use of three mutually reinforcing accounts, bracketed by the Pharisees' interpretation of what God demands through the law, and James's own interpretation of God's will as expressed through the prophets.

In this context of dispute, experience is given a decisive role in how God is depicted by the different characters. In short, what happens in Acts's own story-time is vital to the portrayal of God. In a strongly interpretive retelling of 10:1–48 in 11:4–17, Peter emphasizes his own experience of God's lack of distinction between Jews and gentiles, by highlighting God's testimony to the gentiles through the gift of the Spirit. In this speech, Peter speaks of God as the subject of all that has transpired, ultimately portraying God as someone who saves believers through grace without making a distinction between them. Next, Barnabas and Paul point to all the signs and wonders God has done among the gentiles. Through these words, their own ministry among the gentiles is joined together with that of the apostles, Jesus, and even God in Acts. According to Peter, Paul, and Barnabas's perspectives, God is already working out his salvation among the gentiles, without distinguishing between them and the Jews.

The above-mentioned accounts are finally validated by James's concluding speech. Not only does James interpret Peter's experience as God's action of taking a people for his own among the gentiles, using words that recall God's actions in times past. In citing Scripture, James also brings God's own perspective to the table: God is the returning builder who has restored the Davidic dynasty, with the purpose of including the gentiles among his people. Here Scripture is read in light of the apostles' experience and validates it as being in line with God's purpose. Implicitly, the claims of those who argue that the gentiles must be circumcised and follow the law could initially be considered to be in accordance with Scripture, but these demands oppose the apostles' experience of God's purpose and thus gain no approval at the meeting. Finally, James's words reinterpret Scripture, and suggest that God's choice of the gentiles is foretold through it. Thus, God's character remains the same in Israel's past and in the present: Even though God's actions in the present are new, these actions have been a part of God's plan as expressed through Scripture since ancient times.

Even though none of the speakers mention circumcision directly, God's salvation and impartiality are shown to be independent of circumcision and the law. This, then, is the theological basis of the apostolic decree, which mainly regulates social concerns: Now that Jews and Jesus believing gentiles are both considered part of God's people, their fellowship with each other must be built upon respect of Jewish customs and a lack of idolatry.

Chapter 7: The Faithful God: Paul's Proclamation in Pisidian Antioch (13:13–52)

7.0 Introduction

How does the review of God's actions throughout Israel's history characterize God in Paul's speech in Pisidian Antioch? The proclamation to the synagogue audience in 13:16b–41 is Paul's first missionary speech in Acts, and is delivered at a point in the narrative where Paul is taking over as the main protagonist after Peter (cf. 13:2). In Paul's speech, a choir of voices—Paul's, and through Scripture, God's and the prophets'—speaks of the significance that God's actions for Israel in the past have for Israel in the present. In proclaiming Jesus's resurrection as the fulfillment of God's promises, God's faithfulness becomes an actuality of the narrative present and forgiveness of sins is proclaimed as available through Jesus. The way God is characterized in Israel's past is therefore intimately connected with how God is characterized in the narrative present.

Paul's proclamation meets with a mixed response. When the Jews in Pisidian Antioch reject the word of God, Paul and Barnabas's subsequent turn to the gentiles highlights a tension that runs throughout the remainder of Acts: The word of God is proclaimed but it is not accepted everywhere. Nevertheless, the proclamation continues. This leads me to a claim to be explored in the final section of this chapter, namely, that the implied author's presentation of God also relies on the narrative of how God's word spreads in spite of rejection. In short, I suggest that it is possible to understand not only Paul's speech as revealing God's faithfulness, but to read the continued plot of Acts—including the continued proclamation and variegated reception of the word—as a narrative of how God's faithfulness endures in spite of rejection.

Because Paul's speech about God's faithfulness to God's promises may profitably be read in light of the response these promises are met with, I focus on 13:13–52. In this way, the speech may be read not only as an interpretation of events in Israel's past and promises for the present, but in conversation with the reactions of Paul's audience. After a brief introduction of the occasion and setting for Paul's "word of exhortation" (13:13-16a), we will turn to the speech proper (13:16b-41). We then look at the reactions Paul's proclamation is met with (13:42-52). Here, we will focus particularly on how the narrator presents Paul's mission in light of God's purpose, and how this stands in continuation and contrast with how God is portrayed in the speech.

7.1 Setting the Stage (13:13-16a)

In Pisidian Antioch, Paul's proclamation is the response to the synagogue officials' request for a word of exhortation (λόγος παρακλήσεως, 13:15). Scholars have argued that, from the point of view of rhetorical criticism, the speech should be classified as either epideictic or deliberative.[1] It may consequently be divided it into five parts:[2] 1) the *exordium* (13:16b); 2) the *narratio* (13:17-25); 3) the *propositio* (13:26); 4) the *probatio* (13:27-37); and 5) the *peroratio* (13:38-41).[3] Although I make no claims about the author's rhetorical *intentions* in the speech, these rhetorical categories allow us to observe the *function* of the different parts more clearly than if we were to follow a structure based solely on where the audience is addressed (13:16, 26, 38).[4] I will therefore be using these rhetorical categories throughout my analysis. The present chapter is divided into three sections: I will look at the *exordium* and *narratio* together (13:16-26), followed by the *propositio* and *probatio* (13:27-37), and finally the *peroratio* (13:38-41).

---

1. E.g., George A. Kennedy sees the speech as epideictic: "Despite the call for an exhortation, which implies a deliberative speech, Paul's remarks are epideictic, aiming at belief, not at action" (Kennedy, *New Testament Interpretation*, 124). Ben Witherington, on the other hand, suggests that Acts 13:13-52 is an example of deliberative rhetoric, because it is "meant to urge a change in belief and/or behavior (in this case, both, as the focus on behavior in vv. 40-42 shows)" (Ben Witherington, *New Testament Rhetoric*, 63).

2. I here use the definitions for these five sections found in Witherington, *New Testament Rhetoric*, 16: "The *exordium* is the beginning of the discourse, attempting to make the audience open and well-disposed to what follows. The *narratio* explains the nature of the disputed matter or the facts that are relevant to the discussion.... The *propositio* or thesis statement is crucial and normally follows the *narratio* though sometimes it comes before 'the narration'.... The *probatio* enumerates the arguments for the proposition, supporting the speaker's case.... Finally, the *peroratio* sums up or amplifies some major argument and/or makes a final appeal to the deeper emotions to make sure the argument persuaded."

3. Witherington, *New Testament Rhetoric*, 63.

4. A number of commentators opt to divide the speech into sections starting with a new address of Paul's audience. Cf., e.g., Talbert, *Reading Acts,* 120; Gaventa, *Acts,* 196.

By this point in Acts, Paul's character has been established as reliable: He has been called by the risen Lord, proclaimed the word of God, and faced peril in Damascus and Jerusalem (9:1–31). Moreover, his and Barnabas's present journey has been ordered by the Holy Spirit (13:2b). Now, as Paul stands before a synagogue audience consisting of both Jews and, presumably, god-fearing gentiles (οἱ φοβούμενοι τὸν θεόν, 13:26),[5] the setting allows him to fulfill the role he was foreshadowed to play in 9:15: "he is an instrument whom I have chosen to bring my name before *gentiles* and kings and before *the people of Israel*" (my emphasis). In other words, the speech in its setting is an expression of how God's purpose is being worked out through Paul and his mission.

7.2 Paul's Speech (13:16b–41)

7.2.1 God's Actions in Israel's History (Exordium and Narratio, 13:16b–25)

In the first part of Paul's speech, God is characterized by God's relation to Israel. The *exordium*, or address, to "Men, Israelites, and fearers of God" (13:16b, my translation), invites listeners into his speech and makes clear that his message is intended for Jews and godfearers alike. Its main thrust is towards the Jews, however, for the relationship between God and the audience is established by God's ancient choice of their ancestors (ὁ θεός [. . .] ἐξελέξατο τοὺς πατέρας ἡμῶν). This choice, in turn, results in a number of actions by God throughout their history. In the following verses (16b–25), God is the subject of fourteen actions.[6] One might say, with Gaventa, that this first section of the speech "relentlessly presents Israel's history *as* the history of God's activity."[7] Within this history, which here functions as a *narratio*, are the background facts that become the backdrop for Paul's argument.

Whereas Stephen focused on Moses in his account of the exodus (7:20–43), Paul focuses on the people in his account of the same event. Playing on the verb ὕψωσεν and the adjective ὑψηλοῦ (13:17), Paul speaks of the people whom God *raised* up in Egypt and their exodus thence, led by God's *raised* arm. This image of the raised arm echoes the language used in other accounts of the exodus, which also speak of God's "mighty," or sometimes "raised," arm

---

5. Here, the godfearers in question seem to be proselytes, cf. 13:43.
6. These actions are expressed through fourteen verbs, counting the participles.
7. Gaventa, *Acts*, 198.

(cf. Exod 6:1, 6; Deut 4:34; 5:15; 9:26; Ps 136:11–16).[8] The anthropomorphic image of the raised arm in Acts 13:17 may be understood as symbolic of God's power,[9] creating a subtle connection between the people's prosperity and God's power and care for them in and on their way out of Egypt.

The exodus story sounds in the background of Paul's words, and Acts 13:18 echoes the first part of Deut 1:31 LXX. Interestingly, the textual witnesses to both the Septuagint and to Acts are divided in terms of what kind of action is assigned to God: God either "nourished" (ἐτροφοφόρησεν) or "put up with" (ἐτροποφόρησεν) the people in the wilderness (13:18).[10] Chen, who follows the former reading, observes that through the allusion to Deut 1:31, "Luke may have implied a comparison of God's care for Israel with that of a father for his child."[11] It is certainly conceivable that the father image could be a possible background for understanding this way of describing God's care.[12] In this case, the relationship between God and Israel would here implicitly characterize God as Israel's father. However, given the lack of familial language for God and Israel's relationship throughout the remainder of the speech, the reading is not so strong that we consider it to greatly impact the portrayal of God in Acts 13.

For the competent reader familiar with the Exodus story, neither "nourished" (ἐτροφοφόρησεν) or "put up with" (ἐτροποφόρησεν) seem out of place as verbs describing God's action: In Exodus account of the journey out of Egypt, God both nourished his people *and* put up with them.[13] Given the ambiguity of both the external and internal evidence, the choice of reading mainly becomes a question of emphasis:[14] Is the focus on the people's behavior and God's continued patience and overbearing towards them; or is the focus more on God alone, and on God's acts of kindness

---

8. See e.g., Bruce, *Book of the Acts*, 254, who suggests that the arm emphasizes God's "mighty power." See also, e.g., Ps 76:15 (LXX), which speaks of God's arm in conjunction with the exodus and redemption of Israel; cf. also Pesch, *Apg. 13–28*, 35; Fitzmyer, *Acts*, 510.

9. Johnson, *Acts*, 231.

10. Both versions are supported by some of the oldest witnesses: Ἐτροφοφόρησεν is found in 𝔓[74], A, C*, etc., whereas ἐτροποφόρησεν is supported by ℵ, B, C2, D, L, etc. For this text-critical problem, see Metzger, *Textual Commentary*, 405, or alternatively, the excursus in Parsons, *Acts*, 194.

11. Chen, *God as Father*, 149.

12. Deut 1:31 explicitly employs this father-son imagery, and this, together with the portrayal of God as father elsewhere in Acts, makes this the more likely interpretation. We should not neglect to note, however, that τροφοφορέω is also a verb that can be used to reflect motherhood (see 2 Macc 2:27).

13. Chen, *God as Father*, 149.

14. See ch. 7, n. 10.

towards them? Both readings make sense in light of the present context. As we shall see, as Paul's speech continues, a tension between Israel and God comes to the fore, and this might favor "put up with." However, as the rhetorical function of the *narratio* is to establish God and Israel's relationship as a positive and solid relationship, the latter reading adds more to the speech's rhetorical aim. Nonetheless, as both God's care and indulgence are expressed elsewhere in Paul's speech, neither reading fundamentally adds to or alters its characterization of God.

God's power and care continue to be expressed through God's gift of the land after the defeat of seven nations. The verb for "gave as inheritance" (κατακληρονομέω, 13:19) for this gift underscores the special relationship between God and Israel, and ultimately emphasizes the characterization of God as Israel's powerful and caring God in 13:17–19. This "positive characterization" only relates to Israel, however: God is characterized as partial to Israel, but ruthless to the nations that he destroys for Israel's sake (13:19). Here we encounter a tension between how God is described to relate to the nations (gentiles) in Israel's past, and in the present according to Acts: In our previous chapter, we saw that the encounter between Peter and Cornelius, and the descent of the Spirit upon the latter and his household, show that God's partiality now extends to the gentiles.

The positive characterization of God, expressed through God's relation to Israel, continues in the following verses: Here God continues to act throughout Israel's history through the gift of rulers. However, the sudden subject change from God to Israel in 13:21 when the people asks for a king, disrupts the pattern of God as sole agent, with the effect that Israel's request may implicitly be perceived as negative (cf. 1 Sam 8:7).[15] God's subsequent action demonstrates God's indulgence and control: Israel's request for a king is initially granted, but Saul is later removed (13:21–22).

Paul's review of God's actions throughout Israel's history reaches its culmination in Jesus as the fulfillment of God's promise of a savior to Israel (13:23). Jesus is only briefly mentioned, but two testimonies frame his introduction: God's witness to David, and John the Baptist's witness to Jesus. David, in contrast to Saul, is given the ultimate commendation through God's own testimony: "I have found David, son of Jesse, to be a man after my heart, who will carry out all my wishes" (13:22b). Bearing witness is a significant motif in Acts; it is what the apostles are commanded to be and do by the risen Lord (1:8), and indeed, the very theme from which the plot

---

15. Cf. Parsons, *Acts*, 194. Although God does give the people a king, 1 Sam 8 interprets the people's request as negative insofar as it is seen as a rejection of Yahweh's overlordship (see 1 Sam 8:7). This rejection is interpreted as Israel's sin; see Klein, *1 Samuel*, 75–76.

of Acts derives its movement. The theme of bearing witness, however, seems mostly to be connected to the function of the disciples and the Spirit as witnesses to Jesus.[16] God, on the other hand, is only described twice or thrice as bearing witness; in 13:22, possibly in 14:3, and in 15:8.[17] Neither time is this witness to Jesus. In the context of God's first and last testimonies, the "heart" is mentioned. In 13:22, David pleases God's heart; in 15:8, God testifies to the gentiles by sending the Spirit because of God's knowledge of their hearts. In both contexts, then, God's testimony relates to how God is moved by the character of those whom God speaks of. The matter is slightly different in 14:3, where "the Lord" (here an example of ambiguous god-language) testifies to his word by granting signs and wonders to be made through Barnabas and Paul. Because the witness function bears such significance in Acts in general, there is reason to pay attention to what God is pointing to on the rare occasions that God is the one to testify. In the present context, God's testimony emphasizes David's importance.

God's words about David may be understood as the ultimate approval of David. The testimony is linked to how David perfectly exercises God's will (13:22). Importantly, as David's posterity, the credibility of David transfers to Jesus. John the Baptist's words further confirm Jesus's greatness: "I am not worthy to untie the thong of the sandals on his feet" (13:25). In this way, Jesus is briefly introduced as part of the narration of God's works throughout history, but John's words create an expectation that more will be said about him. Simultaneously, John's words remind the reader of Israel's needs for repentance (13:24). This final section of the *narratio*, then, which introduces Jesus as David's posterity and whispers of Israel's need for repentance, builds up to the rest of the speech where these themes are further developed. Moreover, in presenting Jesus as a savior in fulfillment of God's promise (13:23),[18] God's act of bringing Jesus as a savior to Israel demonstrates both God's faithfulness and God's salvific intentions. Indirectly then, God is characterized as savior. Both God's action of sending Jesus, but also God's faithfulness to Israel prior to this, are fundamental aspects of the *narratio's* function. The *narratio* establishes a common ground between Paul and his audience, and his review of God's faithfulness throughout Israel's

---

16. Cf. Trites, *New Testament Concept of Witness*, 128–53.

17. Parsons (*Acts*, 195) suggests that 10:43 should be included among the references to God giving witness. In 10:43, however, God is only the implicit subject: The verse speaks of witness given through the prophets.

18. 13:23: Some textual witnesses have "salvation" (σωτηρίαν) instead of "a savior, Jesus" (σωτῆρα Ἰησοῦν) here. Neither variant impacts the characterization of God in this speech, however, and both variants suggest that salvation is brought through Jesus because this salvation/savior comes from David's posterity.

history provides the "relevant facts" or basis for Paul's further argument. It is, in short, against the background of the *narratio* that the rest of the speech's portrayal of God must be understood.

7.2.2 God's Message of Salvation (Propositio and Probatio, 13:26–37)

The second part of Paul's speech centers on Jesus's resurrection as the fulfillment of God's promises to Israel. This part begins with the *propositio*, or central thesis statement of the speech, that God's actions in the past are being actualized to the narrative audience in the present: "to *us* the message of this salvation has been sent" (13:26, my emphasis). Kevin L. Anderson notes:

> One can hardly miss the contact between this statement about the arrival of the word of 'salvation' (σωτηρία) and 13:23, which heralded the fact that God has brought to Israel 'a Savior (σωτήρ), Jesus.' The history of God's activity in Israel, climaxing with David and his heir *par excellence*, Jesus, is directly relevant to an understanding of God's present message of salvation to his people.[19]

The *propositio* in 13:26, then, functions as a bridge between the *narratio* and *probatio*, by stating that the history recounted in 13:17–25 is directly relevant to Paul's synagogue audience. The *probatio* (13:27–37) explicates this by arguing how Jesus's resurrection is the fulfillment of God's promises. Thus, "Paul, like Peter, presents the things concerning Jesus in terms of a consistent divine activity."[20] Moreover, in this part of his speech, Paul suggests that Jesus's death and resurrection are firmly lodged in God's purpose (13:27–31): While holding the residents and leaders of Jerusalem accountable for Jesus's death, he simultaneously states that they fulfilled Scripture ("everything that was written," 13:29). In this way, they unwittingly become part of God's plan.[21] While the actions of the residents of Jerusalem and their leaders may be seen as part of this plan, however, Paul's negative characterization of them through their ignorance and demand to have Jesus killed without cause for sentence, allows their actions to be seen both as necessary and to run counter to God's own character. Thus, although Jesus's death is fulfillment, it is significant that God is not the subject of Jesus's death. God is the one who *raised* Jesus (13:30). In contrast to the residents and leaders of Jerusalem who bring death, God is characterized as the one who gives life.

---

19. Anderson, *"But God Raised Him,"* 242.
20. Squires, *Plan of God*, 70.
21. Note the fulfillment language in 13:27, 29, and 33; cf. Johnson, *Acts*, 234.

Paul declares that Jesus's resurrection[22] is the fulfillment of God's promise (13:32–33). His citation from Ps 2:7 in Acts 13:33 is connected to Jesus's resurrection through the subordinating conjunction ὡς. It therefore seems that Ps 2 is here used as an argument for or proof of Jesus's resurrection from Scripture. But what promise does Jesus's resurrection fulfill? The speech itself does not make it clear, leaving a gap to be filled by the reader. This gap may, as Anderson plausibly argues, be filled by turning to Acts 2:30–31.[23] Here, Peter links Jesus's resurrection to the fulfillment of the Davidic covenant: "he knew that God had sworn with an oath to him that he would put one of his descendants on his throne" (2:30). He identifies the descendant as the Messiah (2:31), and more specifically Jesus (2:32), who was raised up and exalted at God's right hand (2:32–33). Acts 2:29–36 demonstrates that it is not the dead-and-buried David (2:29, 34), but the risen Jesus that fulfills God's promise to David.[24] Thus, if one keeps 2:30–31 in mind when reading 13:32–33, the former verses allow the reader to understand that it is the same promise that is referred to in 13:32–33: Jesus's resurrection is the fulfillment of God's promise to David that he would put his descendants on his throne.[25] This reading is further strengthened by the speech's focus on Jesus as David's descendant; indeed, that Jesus is of David's posterity is no less than the culmination of the *narratio* in 13:17–25. The fact that Jesus is the fulfillment of God's promise does not only reveal a faithfulness that stands in continuity with the way Paul presented God's relationship to Israel in the first part of the speech, but also portrays God as a father to "his son" through the citation from Ps 2:7 (cf. 13:33b).[26] It is as

---

22. There has been some debate as to whether ἀναστήσας in 13:33 refers more generally to Jesus's appearance and ministry, or to Jesus's resurrection. For a survey of the central arguments of the discussion, see Anderson, *"But God Raised Him,"* 244–46. Ultimately, I agree with Anderson that the structure of the speech, where the death and resurrection of Jesus immediately precede 13:33, and the fact that Jesus's resurrection is interpreted as the fulfillment of God's promise in 2:30–31, are solid reasons to read ἀναστήσας as a reference to Jesus's resurrection.

23. Anderson, *"But God Raised Him,"* 246.

24. If the quotation of Ps 2:7 in Acts 13:33b is read in light of 2:30–36, Jesus emerges as the enthroned Messiah even though Paul does not name him by this title.

25. Cf. Tannehill, *Narrative Unity of Luke-Acts*, 2:170. See also Goldsmith, "Acts 13:33–37," 321–24, who argues that Acts 13:33–37 is a *pesher* on 2 Sam 7; Schneider, *Die Apostelgeschichte*, 2:133; Kilgallen, "Acts 13:38–39," 490. Alternatively, the Nathan promise could be presumed to be known to the reader as part of his/her cultural encyclopedia.

26. It is possible that in the present context, "his son" can be considered a messianic reference: "God is said to have begotten Jesus, just as it was said of old that God had begotten the historical unnamed king of the Davidic dynasty at his enthronement" (Fitzmyer, *Acts*, 517). Acts 13:33b, which connects Jesus's resurrection with his sonship,

the Father of Jesus, the descendant of David, that God fulfills God's promise to both David and to Israel.[27]

The two citations to follow in 13:34–35 further link the fulfillment of God's promises to Israel to the resurrection of Jesus. The first citation, from Isa 55:3, states that the holy things (τὰ ὅσια) made to David will be given to (a plural) *you* (ὑμῖν, 13:34). The second citation, from Psalm 16:10, makes it clear that God's holy one (ὁ ὅσιος) will not see corruption (13:35). The "catchwords" *holy/holy* and the repetition of the verb *give* (δίδωμι) invite a reading of these verses where they mutually interpret each other.[28] As Barrett notes, the citation from Isa 55:3 is abbreviated to omit the explicit reference to the covenant.[29] The meaning of τὰ ὅσια can, however, be inferred from the immediate narrative context in the speech, which suggests that God's promises to David are in view.[30] While the plural object in the first citation makes it unlikely that these promises are given to any one person, and therefore likely signifies Israel,[31] the second citation is directly related to Jesus's incorruptibility. Here I disagree with Gaventa's suggestion that the promises in 13:34 are given to Jesus;[32] the plural recipient of the gifts makes Israel a more likely recipient. This also makes sense in light of the *propositio* in 13:26, where Paul states that the message of salvation is sent *"to us."* When these citations are understood to mutually interpret each other, it seems the best reading is as follows: The holy promises to Israel are the ones fulfilled in the resurrection of God's holy one.[33]

Briefly summarized then, in the *probatio* (13:27–37), Paul provides arguments in support of his declaration (the *propositio*) that salvation has been sent to Paul's audience (cf. 13:26). These arguments are based in Scripture and the citations therefrom reveal that this salvation has been sent through Jesus. His resurrection is presented as the realization of God's promise to

---

could therefore be understood to echo 2:36, where Peter presents Jesus's resurrection as his enthronement as the Messiah. With Dunn, we might say that the language reflects "the enthusiastic re-evaluation of Jesus' status as an immediate consequence of the stunning event of his resurrection (see also on 2.36)" (Dunn, *Acts*, 180).

27. Chen, *God as Father*, 157.

28. deSilva, "Paul's Sermon," 43; Bock, *Acts*, 457.

29. Δώσω replaces Isaiah's διαθήσομαι ὑμῖν διαθήκην αἰώνιον (Isa 55:3); Barrett, *Acts I-XIV*, 647.

30. Cf. e.g., Jervell, *Die Apostelgeschichte*, 360. There seems to be no real difference between the covenant to David and God's promises to David, however.

31. Tannehill, *Narrative Unity of Luke-Acts*, 2:171.

32. Gaventa, *Acts*, 200.

33. Bruce (*Book of the Acts*, 260) sees the resurrection of Jesus as the fulfillment of one of these promised blessings; see also Fitzmyer, *Acts*, 517.

David, and hence undergirds God's faithfulness—a faithfulness that is in direct line with God's actions throughout Israel's history.

7.2.3 Forgiveness and Warning (Peroratio, 13:38–41)

The final section, the *peroratio*, of Paul's speech actualizes God's actions in the past—from promise to fulfillment—through the offer of forgiveness of sins through Jesus to the synagogue audience. This forgiveness is played out against the Law of Moses (13:39). As Gaventa observes, "It is unclear whether Paul refers to some particular sins for which the law is ineffective or whether he intends a reference to the general impotence of the law; the Greek can be read either way."[34] The question that arises here is whether God—by way of the Law's impotence—is here characterized differently in the past from in the narrative present. If we read Acts 13:39 in light of 7:38, we see that the law given to Moses is designated "living oracles" (7:38). As such, we may say that the gift of the law by God is in itself not negatively portrayed by the implied author of Acts—for Stephen, like Paul, is a reliable character narrator. However, Paul's words in 13:39 do contain Torah-criticism to the extent that the Law is not considered effective against all sins. Why it is not effective remains unclear, but it is also evident in later passages that the Law is a "yoke" the people have not been able to bear (15:10–11). We may therefore say that even if God's *act* of giving the law is not negatively portrayed, the law itself comes under critique in Acts. This does not in itself greatly impact the characterization of God, however, for God is still depicted as the redeemer of Israel: The offer of forgiveness in 13:38–39 construes a relationship between God and Paul's audience, both Jews and god-fearing gentiles, in which there is both need for such forgiveness, and in which God offers it. In terms of how God emerges in this speech, therefore, God may be seen to work for Israel's redemption through Jesus, and is thus portrayed as their redeemer.

This also fits the picture painted in Luke-Acts as a whole, where a connecting line is drawn between Israel's restoration, repentance, and the forgiveness of sins (cf. Luke 1:68–79; Acts 2:37–40). In raising Jesus, God has fulfilled the Davidic promise, demonstrating God's faithfulness. However, fulfillment comes with an offer that must be accepted or rejected: The *peroratio* functions as an appeal to Paul's audience. Thus, Paul's "word of exhortation" also ends as an exhortation in the form of a note of warning.[35] The citation from Hab

---

34. Gaventa, *Acts*, 201.

35. See also Kilgallen ("Acts 13:38–39," 482), who suggests that "Verses 38–39, which speak of forgiveness and an otherwise impossible justification, seem to be the

1:5 in 13:41 underlines that God is at work in the present ("in your days I am doing a work [ἔργον]"). The narrative context and the thrust of the quote suggest that it refers to "the missionary proclamation of the Christ-event to Jews and Gentiles."[36] This is supported both by the fact that Paul and Barnabas have been called to "a work" (τὸ ἔργον, 13:2), and by the warning thrust of the quote, which foreshadows the disbelief their work will be met with later. For the purposes of our study, this means that the apostles' proclamation is here presented as God's "work" or "action."

7.3 In the Face of Opposition (13:42–52): Continued Proclamation

While Paul's proclamation is initially favorably received by both the Jews and proselytes in the synagogue, the narrator reports that "the Jews" reject their message on the following Sabbath. Thus, the scene ends, as Tannehill observes, "with unresolved tension between their rejection of the word of salvation and God's commitment to bring salvation to Israel, as presented in the speech."[37] Paul and Barnabas's subsequent declaration that they will go to the gentiles (13:46–47) does not in itself point to an action by God, neither explicitly nor implicitly. When I nevertheless now turn to look briefly at the reactions of the Jews and the consequent declaration of a forthcoming gentile mission, I do so because the narrative responses to the speech open up interpretive questions about how the speech may be understood within the context of Acts as a whole. In Acts 13:42–50, the response from the Jews and gentiles point to the tension Tannehill identifies, namely, how may the faithfulness of God, illustrated in Paul's speech, be interpreted in light of the responses to his proclamation?

---

fitting response to the synagogue leaders' request."

36. So Fitzmyer, *Acts*, 519. Contra, e.g., Barrett, *Acts I-XIV*, 652, who views "the work" as referring more narrowly to what God "has done in Christ," and Jervell, who suggests that the gentiles' partaking in Israel's salvation is in view; Jervell, *Die Apostelgeschichte*, 361.

37. Tannehill, *Narrative Unity of Luke-Acts*, 2:168–69. It is worth noting van de Sandt's observation that the citation from Isa 55:3 (Acts 13:34b) and the citation from Hab 1:5 (Acts 13:41), if read in their LXX contexts, offer two very different illustrations of Israel's fate: "He [Luke] therefore remonstrates with Israel upon two clearly distinct scenarios: either forgiveness of sins and justification (vv. 38–39 = Isa 55,6–11 and 45,23–25) or disappearance for the sake of the Gentile nations (vv. 40–41 = Hab 1,5–11)" (van de Sandt, "Quotations," 55). Van de Sandt does, however, hold that the Isaianic vision prevails in Acts, seeing as Jesus is David's descendant, and that "the 'sure blessings of David' (13,34), was made to Israel (cf. also Acts 3,25–26)" (56). See van de Sandt, "Quotations in Acts 13:32–52," 55–57.

To ask this question is to step into what has been one of the most contentious debates in scholarship on Acts, i.e., how the mission to the Jews and gentiles should be understood in light of Jewish rejection. For our purposes, the question may be rephrased as follows: How may Acts' God be understood to relate to Jews and gentiles in light of some of the Jews' rejection of God's word? Three decades ago, this debate was framed in terms of whether the gentile mission replaced, supplemented, or completed the mission to Israel.[38] While the proponents of these three views use different texts in support of their arguments, the words of Paul at the end of Acts (28:24–28) have often been given a central place in the discussion: Do Paul's final words signal a rejection of the Jews? And if so, do they signal a rejection of *all* Jews, or the end of the Jewish mission? Over the last years, however, scholarship has come to highlight the fact that the first Jesus-believers were Jews. Important in this respect is the fact that the implied author highlights Paul's Jewish ethnicity (22:3–4; 26:4–7) and proclamation to Jews (e.g., 14:1; 22:1).[39] The message is proclaimed by Jews, to Jews. Thus the first view in the old debate, represented by Haenchen's famous dictum that "Luke has written the Jews off"[40] (based on Acts 13:46; 18:6; and 28:28), becomes untenable.

A narrative reading of Acts further substantiates this claim. The problem is that Haenchen's abovementioned dictum takes Paul (and Barnabas)'s statements that they will turn to the gentiles in 13:46, 18:6 and 28:28 at face value, and understands this to the exclusion of mission to the Jews. However, this perspective fails to take into account the fact that Paul keeps returning to the synagogues throughout Acts.[41] In fact, right after Acts 13, instead of portraying Paul as an apostle to only gentiles from this time onwards, the implied author immediately locates Paul in a synagogue in Iconium (Acts 14). Although some Jews reject the word of God there, too (14:2), a number of *both* Jews *and* gentiles nevertheless become believers (14:1).[42] Thus, while Paul's words in 13:46 may sound definitive, the further course of events makes such an interpretation difficult.

38. Powell, *What Are They Saying?*, 67–72. I say three decades ago, but the different points of view still provide a point of reference for modern discussions; see e.g., Chen, who identifies the two ends of the spectrum as failure of the mission to the Jews, and continued hope for (some of) Israel. See Chen, *God as Father*, 234–36.

39. Cf. e.g., Keener, *Acts*, 2:2098.

40. Haenchen, "Acts as Source Material," 278. Jack T. Sanders proposes an even more radical reading: "Both in the opening scene of Jesus' ministry and in the closing scene of Paul's the scripture is cited in order to show that God's salvation was *never* intended for the Jews" (Sanders, *Jews in Luke-Acts*, 82).

41. See e.g., Meek, *Gentile Mission*, 135; Keener, *Acts*, 2:2097.

42. Robert Maddox is also a representative of this first view. See Maddox, *Purpose of Luke-Acts*, esp. 42–65.

As a consequence of the scholarly turn away from Jewish rejection, the connection between the gentile mission and Jewish opposition is de-emphasized. Thus Keener argues that the gentile mission is *prior* to Israel's hardness,[43] and James A. Meek notes that this mission receives its justification in the citation from Isa 49:6 (Acts 13:47) rather than in Jewish opposition.[44] Both may be seen as newer representatives of the second view, that mission to the gentiles supplements mission to the Jews. We should note, however, that this view has traditionally included both hope and pessimism with regards to the Jews' salvation. Tannehill takes the more pessimistic view. He reads Luke-Acts as a tragedy, in which "the central focus of Jewish hope, the main object of earnest intercession, is rejected by Jews as they reject Paul and his message."[45] However, salvation for the Jews is, according to Tannehill, not beyond reach, in spite of the fact that Jewish rejection "dominates the final scene in Acts."[46] David L. Tiede, while conceding that it might be plausible to read Luke-Acts as a tragic tale,[47] sees Simeon's oracle in the Gospel of Luke as determinative for the rest of the narrative as it both announces "Israel's hope as God's will in no uncertain terms, but he also alerts the reader that Jesus will provoke a crisis in Israel."[48] Tiede reads Acts 28 in light of Simeon's words, and concludes that "God is determined that this salvation and reign of Jesus be for the light to the Gentiles and unto the glory of Israel, but for the present the hearts of many in Israel have been disclosed to be hardened against the understanding and healing which God intends for Israel."[49] Thus both Tannehill and Tiede, with different emphases, highlight the hardening of Israel at the end of Acts, but still hold out hope for the Jews' salvation. Both scholars read Luke-Acts as a single narrative, and although the present study focuses on the latter book, we shall soon see that there are good reasons to agree with the main lines of their argument.

It is difficult to find any scholar today who promotes the third view, that mission to the Jews has reached a successful completion.[50] I would argue

---

43. Keener, *Acts*, 2:2097.
44. Meek, *Gentile Mission*, 135.
45. Tannehill, "Israel in Luke-Acts," 78.
46. Tannehill, "Israel in Luke-Acts," 85.
47. Tiede, "Glory to Thy People Israel," 25.
48. Tiede, "Glory to Thy People Israel," 26.
49. Tiede, "Glory to Thy People Israel," 29.
50. The prime proponent of this view is Jacob Jervell. Jervell furthers the argument that salvation reaches the gentiles *through* the repentant Israel. He suggests that at the end of Acts, the mission to the Jews is complete, the mission to the gentiles continues. See Jervell, *People of God*, 68–69.

that Paul's declaration in 28:25–28 bears the marks of prophetic critique/indictment and warning, not of completion of the Jewish mission. Moreover, Paul's warning appears right after 28:24, where the Jews are divided in their conviction of Paul's words. Contra Maddox, who understands Paul's words to refer to *all* Jews here,[51] I believe Tyson adds an important nuance: "although Luke feels that any positive response from individual Jews should be noted and celebrated, that response is not sufficient, since what is intended is the conversion of the people as a whole and that, since this wholesale conversion has not occurred, the Pauline mission will hereafter be directed toward Gentiles."[52] I do not, however, follow Tyson in the conclusion he draws from this: "The passage leaves no hint that there will be a return to the Jewish mission, and it gives every indication that the previous mission to the Jews . . . has been a failure."[53] While I concede that the Jewish mission is not without failure in Acts, I disagree that Paul's final words show that there will be no return to the Jewish mission. Although 13:46 and 18:6 have been taken by others to build up to a final rejection in Acts 28,[54] it is equally possible to observe the pattern established by Paul's repeated return to the Jews as a guide for how the end of Acts should be read: Many do not listen, but some do. Paul's proclamation nevertheless continues. Furthermore, 28:30–31 does not specify whom Paul keeps proclaiming the word to in Rome, but they are "all" (πάντας) welcomed by him. In other words, the reader is not informed of whether his audience from this point on includes Jews, or gentiles, or both. In this sense the end of Acts is open; the Jewish mission is not definitively closed.[55]

If we return to Acts 13:46 and read Paul and Barnabas's words about their audience's rejection in light of Paul's speech, then this rejection stands

51. Maddox, *Purpose of Luke-Acts*, 43.
52. Tyson, "Jewish Rejection," 126–27.
53. Tiede, "Glory to Thy People Israel," 127.
54. Cf. Maddox, *Purpose of Luke-Acts*, 43–44.

55. These reasons for why the ending of Acts does not necessarily signify the end of the Jewish mission are basically the same ones as those offered in Troftgruben, *Conclusion Unhindered*. Importantly, Troftgruben also observes that "Acts 28:25b–28 may be largely a rebuke aimed at bringing about the repentance of the hearers" (127). Not only does this stand in the Jewish tradition of prophetic indictment of God's people; it also follows the pattern of some of the speeches in Acts which encourage repentance as a response, such as, e.g., Peter's Pentecost speech in Acts 2. See Troftgruben, *Conclusion Unhindered*, 127–29.

In terms of the question of whether Acts' ending is open or closed, Troftgruben argues that "the ending of Acts is a complex mixture of features that conveys a sense of completion to the narrative, a lack of resolution to some important matters, and an expectation that God's witness continues beyond the narrative's ending" (Troftgruben, *Conclusion Unhindered*, 186).

out in sharp contrast to the faithfulness of God that is at the heart of the entire speech. It is, moreover, this faithfulness that seems to lie behind Paul and Barnabas's statement that it was necessary to proclaim the word of God to the Jews first (13:46). As Paul's continued reappearance in synagogues makes clear, this necessity continues to permeate his mission: God's faithfulness stands. I therefore agree with the second view, and Tiede who states, "Deuteronomy and the prophets and the intertestamental traditions expressed all kinds of divine threats toward Israel and saw God's blessing of the Gentiles as a reproach toward Israel, but they never entertained the idea that God would ever be faithless, even to a faithless people."[56] Indeed, it would seem strange for a narrative like Acts, which emphasizes salvation to the Jews (e.g., 15:8–11) and the continuation of the story of the Septuagint to the extent it does, to purport to tell the *end* of the story of God's faithfulness to Israel. In Acts, some Jews may reject the word of God, but God's action is not one of rejection in turn: The word of God continues to be proclaimed to Jews throughout the narrative. This being said, however, God's warning to the Jews about their ignorance, as the discussion above has shown, runs from 13:41 till the very end of Acts (28:26–28). The tension between God's salvation and the Jews' rejection of it is therefore never fully resolved in the course of Acts.

How, then, should Paul and Barnabas's declaration that they will now turn to the gentiles (13:46) be interpreted? In stating their purpose, they cite Isa 49:6 as a commandment given to them by "the Lord" (13:47). Whom does the "Lord" refer to? Jesus's command for the apostles to be witnesses to the "ends of the earth" in 1:8, which foreshadows the gentile mission, makes it possible to read Jesus as the subject in 13:47. This could also be substantiated by Jesus's words to Ananias about Paul's task in 9:15. The immediate narrative context makes this reading slightly difficult, however, especially if we ask who the Lord in the rest of the speech is. The only occurrence of κύριος appears in 13:44, as "the word of the Lord" (τὸν λογόν τοῦ κυρίου).[57] On its own, this phrase could be understood as

---

56. Tiede, "Glory to Thy People Israel," 33.

57. It has been suggested by David W. Pao that "the word" in Acts is "an independent reality that possesses an active will" (Pao, *Acts and the Isaianic New Exodus*, 160). In favor of this argument, Pao points to the word's "growth" in Acts 6:7, 12:24, and 19:20, suggesting that in Luke's writings, only living things grow, such as John the Baptist (1:80) and Jesus (2:40). He offers another argument with reference to 13:48, where the gentiles "praise" (ἐδόξαζον) the word – a verb which elsewhere in Luke-Acts only takes God or Jesus as its object. Finally, Pao uses Acts 20:32 as an example of how the word has the ability to "build up and to give the inheritance" (161–62). It is difficult to fault Pao's observations, but it is equally difficult to be convinced by them. Pao's comparisons between other independent beings and "the word" are not in themselves

"the word about the Lord, *i.e.*, Jesus." However, two verses later the "word of God" appears (13:46) in what appears to be a synonymous expression. In the close context of 13:47, "Lord" therefore seems to refer to God. Secondly, the citations in 13:33b and 13:34b are both presented as *God's* words. Although this alone does not suggest that the command in 13:47 is from God, it adds cumulative force to the argument. The consequence of this reading is that it makes it possible to see God's character as speaking on the matter of the gentile mission. Not only does this lodge the gentile mission in God's plan, but it shows God's impartiality (cf. 10:34) in God's desire to bring the mission to the ends of the earth.

Finally, the turn to the gentiles does not, as argued above, suggest a turn away from the Jews. When Barnabas and Paul cite Isaiah to speak of their task, Scripture itself becomes an argument in maintaining the continuity between how God is presented in Israel's past (through Scripture) and in the present (through the apostles' proclamation). The turn to the gentiles thus demonstrates that in spite of Jewish rejection, the fulfillment of God's promises reaches beyond the Jewish people, and seeks fulfillment through continued proclamation. God's faithfulness does, in other words, not rely on acceptance or rejection. It endures through the continued spread of the word. In short, the Jews' rejection and Paul and Barnabas's response to it demonstrate more fully what God's faithfulness entails: It is a faithfulness that is lived out as the message of God's salvation is proclaimed to the ends of the world.[58]

---

enough to prove that the word is also an independent being. Moreover, Pao's arguments fail to account for all the other times in Luke-Acts where "the word" (ὁ λόγος) is not personified, but simply refers to that which is spoken or heard (e.g., 4:4; 4:31; 5:5, etc.). If we look beyond Luke-Acts, praise of God's word is not a foreign concept, although we do not necessarily see the same word for "praise" as in Acts 13:48 (cf. Ps 55:5 LXX). Moreover, Pao does not discuss why hypostatization is a better explanation for how "the word" is depicted in Acts than the literary categories of personification and metonymy. In the present study, I view the (relatively few) occasions on which the word is described as an independent being as instances of personification, and where the contexts suggest so, I take it metonymically to refer to the contents of the apostles' proclamation (cf. e.g., 2:22; 4:4; 6:2), as essentially a λόγος τῆς σωτηρίας (13:26).

58. It is worth noting that "the word of God" is a theme both in the sections leading up to Paul's speech *and* after, cf. 12:24; 13:5, 48–49. In other words, it continues to spread even after Paul and Barnabas's rejection. Cf. Morgan-Wynne, *Paul's Pisidian Antioch Speech*, 139–40.

7.4 Concluding Observations

In this chapter, we have seen that Paul's speech to the synagogue audience in Pisidian Antioch characterizes God through God's faithfulness to Israel both in the past and in the narrative present. The *narratio* (13:17–25) of the speech establishes (and characterizes) God as Israel's God through God's election of and actions *for* Israel, culminating in the savior from David's posterity, Jesus. In this way, God is portrayed as savior in initiating salvation for Israel, and the *propositio* (13:26) of the speech actualizes the message of salvation for the synagogue audience. Through a number of Scripture citations, the speech's *probatio* (13:27–37) reveals that God's faithfulness is based in Scripture and that the fulfillment of God's promise is fundamentally fulfillment of the Davidic covenant. God's faithfulness may be seen in the resurrection of Jesus, implicitly understood as the Messiah. Jesus's death and resurrection are, furthermore, lodged in God's plan, which depicts God as the master of history. Finally, the *peroratio* (13:38–41) reveals that God through Jesus is also reaching out with forgiveness—though a dire warning foreshadows the Jewish rejection to come.[59]

God's faithfulness may be observed against the backdrop of the variegated reactions Paul's speech is met with. When it is, the necessity of proclaiming the word of God to the Jews first, may be seen as an expression of this faithfulness and favor. Paul and Barnabas's turn to the gentiles and the following narrative reveal that God's faithfulness also encompasses the gentiles, reaching towards the ends of the earth. Nevertheless, the implied author continues to give glimpses of Paul's proclamation in synagogues, and thus shows that God's faithfulness to the Jews is not a foregone matter. It continues to be proclaimed to those who will listen.

---

59. Morgan-Wynne also emphasizes the above aspects of God in the speech: God as the faithful God of promises, the electing God, the God of salvation, and the God of history. See Morgan-Wynne, *Paul's Pisidian Antioch Speech*, 141–43.

Chapter 8: **God as Savior at Sea (27:1–44)**

8.0 Introduction

In this chapter, we turn to look at how the narrative in 27:1–44 depicts God's rescue of Paul and those with him from a storm (27:1–44). This "mini-narrative" depicts a decisive moment in Acts' larger story: The necessity of Paul's going to Rome has already been stated (19:21; 23:11), but the storm-tossed seas put this end in danger. Acts 27:1–44 illustrates how God comes to the rescue in the story-time of Acts, acting for Paul and the ship's crew's salvation. Acts 27:1–44 is structured like a small narrative within Acts' larger narrative: The problem is introduced and a warning issued (27:1–12); the problem emerges (27:13–20); Paul foreshadows its resolution with a message from God (27:21–26); suspense continues to build (27:27–32); a meal is eaten (27:33–38); final complications arise, and the plot reaches its resolution (27:39–44).

Because the section is shaped like a mini-narrative, it differs from many of the texts we have looked at so far. While the speeches in particular explicitly name God and God's actions, the narrative of the storm depicts God's actions as revealed and mediated through a messenger who comes to Paul in the night, and through Paul's words and deeds onboard the ship. In this sense, the characterization of God in Acts 27:1–44 is implicit, and emerges through a close reading of this story in the context of Acts as a whole. As we shall see, God is here, first and foremost, presented as the master of God's own plan, as one whose presence encompasses the deeps of the sea, whose deliverance is physical and concrete, and whose salvation can triumph in even the most hopeless of situations.

8.1 Setting the Scene: A Problem and a Warning (27:1–12)

That Paul's journey to Rome is willed by God has been made clear earlier in Acts: Paul himself has stated that it is necessary (δεῖ, 19:21), and Jesus has appeared to Paul and likewise spoken of the necessity of his witness there (δεῖ, 23:11).[1] At first, it seems clear how this will come to pass: Paul, towards the end of his stay in Cæsarea, comes under the charge of the centurion Julius, and continues his journey as a prisoner to Rome by sea. In Fair Havens, however, the matter of the journey is complicated: It is past the Fast, or Day of Atonement, and the reader familiar with crossings of the Mediterranean in antiquity would know that this signalled the *mare clausum,* the cessation of all navigation until (the month we now call) March.[2] A conflict therefore arises concerning the question of whether or not to continue the journey: the ship has already lost time due to heavy winds (cf. 27:4–8); the ship captain's advice to press on (27:11); and Fair Havens is unsuitable for winter harboring (27:12). However, the crew is faced with perilous waters (27:9), and Paul warns them against the dangers of continuing the journey (27:10).

The warning sounded by Paul involves a twofold threat against ship and cargo and the lives of everyone onboard. The reader has learned to perceive of Paul as a reliable character (see chs. 5 and 7), and his utterance could be understood nearly as a prophetic warning of impending doom. For the first-time reader, Paul's words could, however, also be understood to carry a subtext involving reluctance to reach Rome in spite of the necessity of his going there. This slight uncertainty also makes it difficult for the reader to discern whether Paul here speaks on God's behalf or merely his own: Would God wish Paul to brave the crossing in wintertime, and hence reach his fated destination soon, or are God's intentions different?

8.2 The Journey: Hope is Lost (27:13–20)

The answer to the above question does not immediately present itself. While the sailors' initial hope is raised by a mild southern wind (27:13), suspense arises with a violent northeaster so forceful that numerous attempts are made to save the ship (27:14–20). This northeastern wind is also called a "typhoon wind" (ἄνεμος τυφωνικός, 27:14), which could evoke associations of the Greek god Typhon. Although clearly intended as a reference to the wind in Acts, its name may nevertheless bring the Greek god to the reader's mind. If it does, then the story's outcome opens up for an interpretation that allows it to be read as an account that emphasizes the supreme and saving power of *Israel's* God (see sec. 8.4 below).[3] At the moment, however, there is no salva-

---

1. Squires, *Plan of God,* 174–77. For the use of δεῖ in Acts, see sec. 1.1.2 in this book.
2. See Philo, *Embassy* 3.15; Roloff, *Die Apostelgeschichte,* 361.
3. See also ch. 10 in this book for more on how Acts presents Israel's god as the "strongest" God. Typhon is e.g., described by Hesiod as "violent" (δεινός), "insolent" (ὕβριστος), and "lawless" (ἄνομος) (Hesiod, *Theog.* 306–7).

tion in sight. The increasing loss of control and the hopelessness of the situation finally reach a climax through the description of the utter darkness that envelopes the travelers at night, as they drift under a starless sky: "all hope of our being saved (σῴζεσθαι) was at last abandoned" (27:20).

Two things in particular are worth noting here. First, for reasons long debated and never finally settled, the implied author here (27:1—28:16) writes himself into the story (cf. also 16:10-17; 20:5-15; 21:1-18).[4] The question of whether the author has made use of different sources[5] or was actually present at the scene goes beyond the scope of this study. While it was asserted for a long time that the use of the first-person plural belonged to the genre of seafaring stories in antiquity,[6] this has long since been disproved.[7] For present purposes, we may nevertheless ask about the effect of this kind of narration upon the reader. Whether or not the author was actually present at the scene, the *narrator* does present himself as having taken part in the events described. In this way, the hopelessness and direness of the situation give the impression of having been experienced "from the inside," and thus increase the suspense. At the same time, the fact that the narrator obviously lives to tell the tale offers hope of a solution to the very same situation. In this sense, the narrator's presence among the "we" potentially increases the curiosity of the reader, not with regards to *whether* the crisis will be resolved, but with regards to *how* it will be resolved.

Secondly, the climax of despair is equal to the abandonment of hope of "our being saved" (σῴζεσθαι ἡμᾶς, 27:20). While salvation is a common term for rescue in antiquity, in Acts it is used almost exclusively of God's work of salvation of those who turn to the Lord and become believers (cf. 2:21, 40; 4:12 cf. 4:9; 11:14; 15:11; 16:30–31), and of the healing of those who are sick (4:9; 14:9). In the context of Acts, therefore, the loss of hope of salvation does, especially because the narrator counts himself among

---

4. It varies whether scholars count three, four, or five "we-passages" in Acts: Those who suggest three divide them into 16:10-17; 20:5—21:18; 27:1—28:16; those who suggest four draw the lines between 16:10-17; 20:5-15; 21:1-18; 27:1—28:16; those who favor five make yet a final distinction, i.e., 16:10-17; 20:5-15; 21:1-18; 27:1-29; 28:1-6. See Campbell, *We Passages*, 1.

5. E.g., Dibelius suggests Luke may have used an "itinerary source" behind Paul's journeys, and Werner Kümmel asserts the Lukan account is based on a source which is a travel narrative. See Dibelius, "Style Criticism," 5, 7–8; Kümmel, *Introduction to the New Testament*, 184–85. See also Haenchen, *Die Apostelgeschichte*, 636; Barrett, *Acts XV–XXVIII*, 1179.

6. See Plümacher, "Wirklichkeitserfahrung und Geschichtsschreibung," 2–22; Robbins, "By Land and Sea," 215–42.

7. See e.g., Hemer, "First Person Narrative," 81–86; Praeder, "Problem of First Person Narration," 206–14; Witherington, *Acts*, 483.

the "we," signify a situation so dire that even God is not believed to be able to fix it. For the time being, it also solidifies the impression that this journey was *not* willed by God, that Paul was right, and possibly even that Paul is now abandoned by God.

At this point, it is worth pausing to note how replete the story is with both nautical terminology and terminology related to sea voyages, e.g., πέλαγος (open sea), 27:5; λιμήν (harbor), 27:8; κυβερνήτης (shipmaster), ναύκληρος (ship captain), 27:11; νότος (south wind), 27:13; ἄνεμος τυφωνικός (typhoon), εὐρακύλων (northeaster), 27:14; πρύμνα (stern), 27:29; ναύτης (sailor), πλοῖον (ship), σκάφη (small boat), θάλασσα (sea), πρῷρα (prow), ἄγκυρα (anchor), 27:30; πηδάλιον (rudder), 27:40. It is little wonder, then, that a number of scholars, including Charles Talbert, J. H. Hayes, Richard I. Pervo, and Dennis R. MacDonald, have observed that the story falls into the literary category of "sea voyage" or "shipwreck story" in antiquity.[8] As Talbert and Hayes have noted, these sea voyages perform different theological functions, and sometimes the storm is even caused by the divine. In the case of the present story, however, they rightly argue that the narrator highlights the natural causes of the storm—in my opinion most notably through the emphasis on the time of year (27:9–10, 12).[9] In this way, God is excluded as the initiator of the storm: "the storm is due to natural causes, the outcome is due to the divine will."[10]

That it is finally God's will to save Paul and the ship's crew comes close to the conclusion of MacDonald, which follows upon his argument that "Luke seems to have intended his audience to contrast the shipwrecks of Odysseus and Paul."[11] MacDonald's perspective in this citation is author-oriented, but it is quite possible that a competent reader would be able to contrast the two

---

8. See Pervo, *Profit with Delight*, 51–52; MacDonald, "Shipwrecks of Odysseus and Paul," 88–107; Talbert and Hayes, "Theology of Sea Storms," 267–83. Talbert and Hayes provide an impressive list of comparative material relating to "type-scenes" involving storm and shipwreck in antiquity. See esp. 268–69 in their essay.

9. Talbert and Hayes, "Theology of Sea Storms," 271–72. Talbert and Hayes also mention the implied greed of the pilot and owner of the ship in wanting to sail on (27:11), and the fact that other ships have wintered in a safe harbor (28:11).

10. Talbert and Hayes, "Theology of Sea Storms," 271. The impression that this is not a story of divine retribution is solidified by way of its contrast or perhaps even reversal of the Jonah story: Whereas Jonah must be thrown overboard before the sea stops raging (Jonah 1:1–17), in Acts, rescue comes through Paul's god, who "grants" Paul the lives of everyone with him (27:24), and is conditioned on everyone staying on-board the ship (27:31).

11. MacDonald, "Shipwrecks of Odysseus and Paul," 93. Echoes from the *Odyssey* are also spotted in, e.g., Bruce, *Acts of the Apostles*, 523, 527; Dunn, *Acts*, 334; Witherington, *Acts*, 764. Dunn, however, is not explicit in terms of where in Homer these echoes come from.

shipwrecks: The Odyssey may be considered part of the cultural encyclopedia of the reader, for in Greco-Roman *paideia*, the Odyssey was read in Greek and Roman elementary education.[12] Even if we cannot review MacDonald's entire analysis here, his conclusion is directly relevant to our study: He concludes by noting that whereas the storm in Odysseus's case is sent by Zeus, the God of Israel is the deliverer from the storm in Acts. Moreover, unlike Zeus, who drowns Odysseus's crew, Paul's god saves everyone onboard the ship.[13] This conclusion, in turn, anticipates our own evaluation of how God is portrayed as savior in Acts 27:1-44.

8.3 God in the Deep (27:21-26)

So far, questions have arisen for the reader about God's will, but God has remained conspicuously absent. This changes, however, when Paul receives a visit in the night. This is related by Paul, not the narrator, in line with the shift in narration where the narrator is included among those onboard. Paul has, in short, been visited by an angel from God (27:23) in the night.[14] Whether this visit took place in a dream, or while Paul was awake, is not clear.[15] Of course, this is not the first time an angel steps into a time of crisis in Acts (cf. 5:17-21; 12:1-19). This time, the temporal setting emphasizes that God's messenger steps into the story while it is utterly dark. Through the angel's appearance, on a ship, in the middle of the ocean, during a storm, in the night, God is indirectly characterized as one whose presence extends everywhere, even unto the chaotic ocean and complete dark: God does not abandon those onboard the ship who have lost hope of being saved (cf. 27:20).

Paul's fellow travelers appear to consist mainly of gentiles, for he refers to the angel not merely as "an angel of God," but as "an angel of the God to whom I belong and whom I worship." (27:23).[16] This introduction of God does, moreover, emphatically indicate "that whatever follows by way of sustenance and rescue comes from God rather than from Paul."[17] God is the

---

12. Sandnes, *Challenge of Homer*, esp. 40-58; Hezser, "Torah Versus Homer," 10.

13. MacDonald, "Shipwrecks of Odysseus and Paul," 106-7.

14. Krodel (*Acts*, 476) suggests that "a knowledgeable reader would understand this as a reference to an 'angel-Christology.'" He offers no reasons for this, however, and Luke-Acts does not give us any reason to understand this as Jesus rather than the same kind of "angel of the Lord" who has appeared as early as in Luke 1 and Acts 5.

15. Keener, *Acts*, 4:3660. Contra Parsons who claims it is a dream (Parsons, *Acts*, 356).

16. Cf. Bock, *Acts*, 737.

17. Gaventa, *Acts*, 353.

savior here, and Paul's emphasis on the fact that it is the God *to whom he belongs* who has sent the angel, strengthens the story's portrayal of God as one who does not abandon his own. Finally, in a context where Paul's god is not necessarily known by all, and where the other passengers and crew may have worshipped other gods, Paul's words also provide a context for interpreting from which god salvation comes (cf. 4:12).

The angel's message vindicates Paul's earlier warning (27:10) as at least partially true: The ship will be lost, but no lives. The necessity of Paul's arrival in Rome (see above) is reemphasized by the angel's declaration of the need for Paul to stand before the emperor (δεῖ, 27:24). In short, God's plan remains unaltered.[18] Moreover, the angel tells Paul that "God has granted (κεχάρισται) safety to all those who are sailing with you." It has been proposed that the verb χαρίζομαι suggests that Paul has prayed for the safety of everyone onboard,[19] and that it is therefore due to Paul's intervention that they will now be saved. This may be to read too much into the text, however. Nevertheless, the fact that "God has 'granted' Paul the lives of those aboard means, at the very least, that God has altered the natural expectation of the situation."[20] The message the angel delivers has consequences not only for Paul, but for his fellow gentile travelers. In this way, the narrative continues to affirm that although God is Paul's god, God is also a god whose care extends not only to Jews, but to gentiles as well.

Finally, the angel's words reaffirm Paul's destination as Rome, confirming the Lord's words to him in Jerusalem (23:11), and revealing that God's purpose will not be thwarted by a storm. In contrast to the hopelessness just described (27:20), Paul responds to this message with faith, and encourages a courageous response in everyone else (20:25).

8.4 Complications (27:27–32)

Paul's words foreshadow salvation and relief, but suspense continues to build as some of the sailors make to abandon the ship. Paul, however, who through the visit from the angel is revealed to the reader as a reliable interpreter of events, takes charge and tells the centurion and soldiers that salvation is dependent on the continued presence of everyone onboard:

---

18. Cf. e.g., Fitzmyer, *Acts*, 777; Jervell, *Die Apostelgeschichte*, 611: "Gott handelt mit Paulus, und nichts kann ihn hindern."

19. So Marshall, *Acts*, 410; Tannehill, *Narrative Unity of Luke-Acts*, 2:332, following G. Schneider, *Die Apostelgeschichte*, 2:393n76.

20. Keener, *Acts*, 4:3662.

"The ship can carry all, and the divine plan is that all should be saved."[21] The soldiers, who respond by cutting the ropes so none of the crew may abandon them, thus act in faith in Paul's authority, and by extension in his insight into God's plan.

8.5 Food (27:33–38)

The meal scene that follows is somewhat anticlimactic, almost an interlude in the suspense of the narrative. Yet for this very reason, the space devoted to it signals that it is somehow significant. Overall, scholars seem to claim one of three things about the meal: Either, that this (1) is merely a "typical Jewish meal," or, that the scene in some sense (2) alludes to or (3) represents what is anachronistically known as "the Eucharist." Before we enter this debate, we must pause to note the significance of the meal as Paul presents it: Everyone onboard must eat, τοῦτο γὰρ πρὸς τῆς ὑμετέρας σωτηρίας ὑπάρχει (27:34). Salvation is conditioned on eating.[22] Why it is so, is not said; nor is this condition referred to again, after the travelers have been saved. But precisely *because* they are saved, Paul's words are presented as true: Salvation and eating are intrinsically linked. It is, moreover, worth noting the temporal setting; daybreak is approaching (27:33). This also underlines the significance of the meal as part of a turning point before salvation and the return of light.

Already with this observation, we can note that the narrative invites the reader to see this as more than an ordinary Jewish meal,[23] if by ordinary, we mean that it primarily concerns bodily sustenance.[24] That is not to say, however, that scholars are not right to note that it contains elements typical of Jewish meal practice (taking bread, giving thanks to God, eating).[25] But in addition to these elements, the meal's setting in the midst of a storm and the typical Lukan motif of meal fellowship, suggest that the meal is not simply "a meal." It signifies something more. As we shall see, the understanding of

---

21. Tannehill, *Narrative Unity of Luke-Acts*, 2:333.

22. Schneider also notes this connection between the meal and "salvation" in 27:34. To him, this indicates that the meal at sea and the Eucharist point to the same thing: "Die Mahlzeit hat eine ähnliche Transparenz auf die Eucharistie hin, wie das Stichwort σωτηρία in V 34b auf die Bedeutung 'Heil' hin offen ist" (Schneider, *Die Apostelgeschichte*, 2:397).

23. Contra Marshall, *Acts*, 414.

24. This is not to say that a meal is not also a social event.

25. Cf., e.g., Marshall, *Acts*, 413–14; Johnson, *Acts*, 455. Note also that the Western text, which adds ἐπιδίδους καὶ ἡμῖν (v. 35), does, as e.g., Johnson (*Acts*, 455) and Fitzmyer (*Acts*, 779) suggest, make the allusion to the Eucharist stronger.

the meal has implications for how God is portrayed as savior in this story. We will therefore look further into its significance.

Does the meal's significance arise purely from its setting in the storm, or is it somehow bound together with the meal's (possible) relation to Jesus's last supper with his disciples? And, if we speak of the meal's relation to Jesus's last supper, are we talking about textual allusions to the last supper in Luke 22, or historical allusions to the ritualization of this meal in the form of a eucharistic meal? One of the problems in entering this debate is that the latter questions are often melded together. A number of scholars assert that we in Acts 27 find either a eucharistic meal or an allusion thereto.[26] The problem is that these links are difficult to establish, and often biased by what the scholars in question consider a eucharistic meal to be in the first place.

Keener, for instance, following Witherington, argues that this is not a eucharistic meal. He suggests that it cannot be so, because the eucharistic meal is not a dominant theme in Luke-Acts, the words used to describe the scene are typical of every Jewish meal, there is no wine or interpretation of the elements, Paul does not distribute the food, the bread satisfies hunger, the pagans remain pagan, and there is a focus on Paul's heroism rather than on ecclesiology.[27] These arguments, however, seem to rely not only on a very specific understanding of what "the Eucharist" is, but also on what it therefore has to signify in the narrative context in Acts (the pagans would have to become believers; the meal's function is ecclesiological and would constitute a church; the Eucharist is not first and foremost meant to satisfy hunger, etc.). We might call this a sacramental understanding of the Eucharist. However, if all the elements of a sacramental view of the Eucharist become the point of departure for the comparison between the meal at sea in Acts and Jesus's last meal with his disciples in, e.g., Luke, then the meal at sea will inevitably fail to meet the standards raised and created by the later doctrine of the church.

---

26. Cf. e.g., Conzelmann, *Die Apostelgeschichte*, 155. If one considers Paul's last meal to be an echo of Jesus's last supper, it could be argued that the scene is part of the presentation of Paul's character as echoing Jesus's on his way to the cross. If there is any validity to the latter suggestion, then it is connected to Paul and Jesus's eating a meal together with their present companions before they are brought to trial; beyond this, however, there is little resemblance between the meals (though rather more parallels between their respective paths to trial!). See, e.g., Parsons, *Acts*, 360 for shipwrecks as a common metaphor for death, and salvation as symbolic of resurrection. For parallels between Paul and Jesus, see e.g., Radl, *Paulus und Jesus*; Moessner, *Lord of the Banquet*, 296–307.

27. Witherington, *Acts*, 773; Keener, *Acts*, 4:3642–43.

A better way of phrasing the question may therefore be to ask if, and if so what, aspects of the meal would be able to evoke associations of a eucharistic meal. In this context, it is worth noting Praeder's observations:

> Luke-Acts lacks references to blessings or thanksgivings at ordinary meals. Taking bread, blessing or thanksgiving, breaking bread, and distributing of bread are reported only at the extraordinary meals of the feeding of the five thousand, the last supper, and the evening meal at Emmaus (Luke 9:16; 22:19; 24:30). All three meals are supposed to be seen in relation to Christian eucharistic meals.[28]

Praeder's observations are based on Luke-Acts as a whole. In our introduction, we established the Gospel of Luke as part of the cultural encyclopedia of the reader, and Acts 27 is one of the places where the text in Luke may help us better read the text in Acts. The similarities Praeder points out between Luke 9:16; 22:19; 24:30; and Acts 27:35 are difficult to overlook. While the claim that all of the meals are *supposed* to be seen in relation to "Christian eucharistic meals" is difficult to substantiate, it is possible to argue that these meals all evoke *connotations* to such eucharistic meals. In support of this, one need only look at the discussion among scholars, who in some way or another seem more or less bound to argue in favor of or against a representation of the Eucharist in Acts 27. This would not have been necessary, had the connotations created by the text not been understood to be forceful by so many. These connotations may be summed up by the words λαμβάνω, εὐχαριστέω, κλάω, used both during Jesus's last meal in the Gospel of Luke (22:19) and in the description of the meal at sea in Acts. It may, of course, be argued that these connotations are a result of these very words having been taken up by the church's use of them in the liturgy of the Eucharist, and that the ecclesial praxis thus generates the associations. While this may be the case, it is impossible to say whether it is the praxis or the text that primarily evoke the connotations. Either way, the associations are *also* rooted in the text. Like Praeder notes, the words of taking, thanking, and breaking weaves the meal at sea into a web of Lukan texts recounting special, specific meals, among which we find Jesus's last supper with his disciples. Thus, textually speaking, it may be argued that Acts 27:33–38 at the very least has *potential* to allude to the meal scene in Luke 22; and, historically speaking, to later "eucharistic," or ritualized, forms of Jesus's last supper.

Is this meal the same kind as the one shared between Jesus and his disciples in Luke 22:14–23? The short answer is that the description of the scene in Acts is so frugal that it is difficult to decide one way or another. Any answer

---

28. Praeder, "Acts 27:1—28:16," 699.

would depend on what one sees as the determining factors of the meal Jesus shared with his disciples in the first place. Is it the fellowship of believers? The sharing of bread and wine? The specific remembrance of Jesus? If so, neither of these factors are present in Acts 27.[29] This becomes particularly clear in comparison with the meal scene in Acts 20. On historical grounds, the meal shared here is commonly understood as a eucharistic meal.[30] Several factors lead to this conclusion, including the gathering of believers on the first day of the week with the specific purpose of breaking bread together, and Paul's proclamation as part of their gathering. This setting differs widely from the one at sea, where the bread is neither shared among believers, nor on the first day of the week, nor in the context of proclamation. In short, none of the factors of the former meal is constitutive of the latter, and therefore cannot help us beyond the possibility of the meal as an *allusion* to Jesus's last meal. This discussion therefore does not get us any further in terms of how the meal scene helps the reader perceive of God.

Of more significance, however, is the following: In the meal scene in Acts 27, the gentiles are not described as believers, but by eating the same bread, they share in meal fellowship with Paul. This may be seen as "an act of faith in what God is accomplishing,"[31] by which the travelers are included in God's promise that they will all be saved. There is thus in this scene a clear connection between promise, salvation, and meal. Just as the travelers share in the bread for which Paul gives thanks to his God before all, so the whole group will be saved by the very same God. Consequently, the meal scene gathers together those whom God will save. It points to God as savior, who works salvation through bodily nourishment as well as the foreshadowed escape from the sea.

8.6 Firm Ground (27:39–44)

As the ship runs aground on a reef, a final obstacle is presented when the soldiers plan to kill the prisoners. This time, however, the centurion intercedes. In this way, he becomes an instrument of God's plan,

---

29. "Acts has earlier referred to believers sharing bread (2:46), but has not shown an explicit fulfillment of Jesus' instructions in Luke 22:14–20, making an exegetical judgment here difficult" (Gaventa, *Acts*, 355).

30. The meal scene in Acts 20 does, at the very least, share a number of the characteristics of the Eucharist recorded by Justin Martyr in his *First Apology*, 67: It takes place on the first day of the week, there is a breaking of bread, and instruction by the president. Justin also mentions readings from "the memoirs of the apostles or the writings of the prophets" before the instruction.

31. Keener, *Acts*, 4:3648.

and demonstrates that in spite of many attempts to thwart God's plan to get Paul to Rome, God remains in charge of the journey. Thus, "all were brought safely (διασωθῆναι) to land" (27:44). God is consequently characterized as the ultimate ruler of events; as one whose arm extends even into the darkest night and ocean's deep. In this context, we also do well to note Loveday C. A. Alexander's observation that the sea was considered "Greek" territory.[32] This, together with the aforementioned observations about this story's resemblance to other shipwreck stories, including the Odyssey, and the allusion to the Greek god Typhon, suggests that the implied author is "laying claim to a cultural territory which many readers, both Greek and Judeo-Christian, would perceive as inherently 'Greek.'"[33] It is, moreover, under Roman power.[34] In terms of the portrayal of the God of Israel, the shipwreck story in Acts implicitly suggests who the true god and ruler of the sea is—for it is this God who ensures Paul's safe crossing. Through this rescue, God stands faithful to God's promise. God's salvation is in this way made manifest as something entirely concrete: rescue from storm and chaos. Significantly, as the rescue concerns not only Paul, but the gentiles with him, God continues to be presented as god of all.[35]

8.7 Concluding Observations

Acts 27:1–44 depicts God's intervention in the story-time of Acts, but the characterization of God is implicit: God is primarily revealed through the appearance of the angel and in the fulfillment of God's plan to get Paul to Rome. The reader knows Paul will reach Rome, but not how. When the storm arises, a reader familiar with other shipwreck stories might ask if this is a story of divine retribution. The narrator of Acts, however, stresses the natural causes of the wind, and even though tension continues to build in terms of how Paul will be rescued, it is his and the ship's crew's salvation that are emphasized. This is made clear both when the angel appears with a

---

32. Alexander, "'In Journeyings Often,'" 83–84.
33. Alexander, "'In Journeyings Often,'" 85.
34. Carter, "Aquatic Display," 92.

35. A shipwreck might, in light of Hellenistic beliefs, be viewed as divine retribution. But the opposite could also be true: The escape of Paul and everyone with him can be read as a statement of Paul's innocence. See Miles and Trompf, "Luke and Antiphon," 259–67. See also Talbert, *Reading Acts,* 216. Note, however, that David Ladouceur partly criticizes, partly expands upon Miles's and Trompf's argument. Reviewing more ancient sources and looking at Acts' shipwreck story together with the Maltese incident and Paul's continued journey to Rome, Ladouceur argues that we here find a chain of arguments that together demonstrate Paul's innocence (Ladouceur, "Hellenistic Preconceptions," 435–49).

message that God remains faithful to God's word that Paul will reach Rome, and in the intrinsic link between the meal at sea and salvation. In the rescue of Paul and the ship's crew, God is once more implicitly characterized as faithful to God's words and the divine plan to get Paul to Rome. The God of Israel is further revealed as the true ruler of the Greek sea, able to transcend the waters, and able and willing to reach into the deepest dark and across the tallest waves. Finally, God is once more demonstrated as god and savior "of all," for not only Paul, but everyone with him, are saved.[36]

---

36. So also Gaventa, *Acts*, 356.

Chapter 9: The God of Power and Wonder

9.0 Introduction

From its very beginning, the narrator of Acts invites the reader into a world full of "strange acts."[1] Here we read about a man who has risen from the dead and is taken up into heaven; the apostles start speaking in different tongues; angels appear in unforeseen places; Philip is moved by the Holy Spirit over a great geographical distance; people are healed and blinded and demons exorcised; the apostles are freed from prison in amazing ways; visions and dreams are given; some characters suddenly drop dead, and others are brought back to life. In short, here are many astonishing acts. In the foregoing chapters, we have looked at actions of God's that are either narrated by the narrator or recounted in characters' speeches at important turning points of the narrative. The "strange acts" just mentioned,[2] however, though by no means insignificant, occur less frequently at major turning points.[3] There are a few exceptions: The ascension, for instance, is a necessary precursor to Jesus's pouring out the Spirit at Pentecost, and the blinding of Paul in 9:8–18 is part of the larger turning point through which Paul becomes a follower of the Way. Generally speaking, however, these actions do not represent turning points in and of themselves,[4] but are scattered throughout the

---

1. Cf. the title of Rick Strelan's book; Strelan, *Strange Acts: Studies in the Cultural World of the Acts of the Apostles* (2004).

2. I try to be careful not to use the term "miracle" here, because it is so dependent on worldview. Twelftree puts it well: "Perhaps, then, a miracle can only be perceived (or not) and interpreted against an existing world view – faith, religion or community – and its set of perceptions. In other words, perhaps a miracle is no more than my way of seeing as extraordinary what another sees as ordinary" (Twelftree, "Introduction," 12).

3. That is not to say that these acts do not have some important functions. To mention just a few: Through them, the implied author parallels the lives of Paul and Peter (and Stephen) with that of Jesus, hence authorizing their mission by way of continuity with Jesus's own ministry. In this way, it is also made clear that the signs and wonders performed by the apostles are closely connected to their work of bearing witness to the ends of the earth (cf. 1:8), so that they are witnesses both through action and proclamation. Moreover, the signs and wonders performed by the apostles spark proclamation, cf. e.g., 3:1—4:22.

4. Some of these strange acts do, however, perform an important plot function in

narrative, with a particular density in the first fourteen chapters. Many of them are, as we shall see, also acts of God. Thus, they too force the question: How do these actions add to the portrayal of God?

On a general level, this is the question asked in the following chapter. However, because it is not possible to cover this topic in its entirety within the scope of this study, the clue as to how it will be answered lies in the word "add." Some of the abovementioned actions, such as Jesus's ascension, the theophany at Pentecost, visions and dreams, and the visit of an angel to Cornelius, have been treated elsewhere. To speak of them here would therefore not add much new beyond what we have already observed in previous chapters. Among the remaining material, however, a number of actions occur with some frequency within the story-time and do add something to the portrayal of God that has not yet been covered. These actions can be loosely grouped together into two groups. The first is the signs and wonders performed by the apostles throughout Acts, and their miraculous releases from prison chains—hereafter called "acts of restoration." Restoration here signifies that through the act, something is restored which a person has lost, e.g., health or freedom. The second group concerns the deaths of Judas (1:16–25), Ananias and Sapphira (5:1–11), and Herod (12:21–23), and the blindings of Paul (9:1–19) and Elymas (13:4–12), which we will here call "acts of infliction." Infliction here signifies something unpleasant to be endured.[5] In what sense God may be understood to perform either of the actions in question will be discussed in the following chapter. Finally, the reader should note that the choice of distinguishing between these two groups of actions is pragmatic—a way of entering the texts and approaching the subjects at hand—rather than any attempt to say that they are two essentially different "classes" of action.[6]

The present chapter is divided into two main parts according to the themes above. The first part will summarily point to some of the aspects of

---

e.g., leading up to some of Peter's major speeches (see 2:1–36; 3:1–26). I owe this observation to Cheng, *Characterisation of God*, 91–92.

5. Cf. "inflict," 2b, *Merriam-Webster.com*, 2017, https://www.merriam-webster.com.

6. It is quite possible that, e.g., the blinding of Elymas could be classified as a "deed of power," "sign," or "wonder" (cf. 19:11), even if I do not treat it under that headline.

The names of the two groups of actions are interpretive in that they signify what happens through these actions, but we will also see that the dichotomy between the two can be questioned: Paul's blindness may be seen as part of his path to restoration, which may suggest that God is here revealed as savior just as much as judge. Until we reach the point where a case may actually be made for this, however, the categories should simply be taken to signify how a person is affected by what takes place (i.e., restored, inflicted), but should not be taken as interpretive regarding the *ends* or purpose for which the actions are performed.

the acts of restoration that are of significance to the characterization of God in Acts. This part does not add anything new to research on these acts, but suggests how their frequency and significance are constructive elements of the portrayal of God, and how they relate to our previous discoveries. The second part will deal with an aspect of God that has largely been neglected in the previous chapters. How is God characterized when people are blinded and struck dead? If this question were to go by unanswered, a significant aspect of the portrayal of God in Acts would remain in the dark.

9.1 Acts of Restoration

God's acts of restoration are performed through the apostles, worked directly, or take place through the mediation of the angel of the Lord. Through these actions, people's health or lives are restored, whether through release from death, illness, evil spirits, or escapes from prison chains. In Acts itself, there is no single terminology that encompasses all of these events at once. With the exception of the apostles' releases from prison or prison chains (5:17–21; 12:6–10; 16:25–34), however, the restorative acts performed by the apostles belong to what the narrator calls "signs" (σημεῖα), "wonders" (τέρατα), and "deeds of power" (δυνάμεις). We therefore begin this chapter by establishing the perspective from which the "signs," "wonders," and "deeds of power" worked by the apostles may also be viewed as God's actions. We then present an overview of the signs and wonders in Acts, and begin to approach the question of how they characterize God. In doing so, we touch both upon the question of God's power, and also look at how the signs and wonders add color to the picture Acts draws of God as savior. Finally, we offer some observations on how the apostles' miraculous escapes from prison and chains tie in with the theme of God's plan and how God is portrayed as the master of history throughout Acts.

9.1.1 Signs, Wonders, and Deeds of Power

In Acts, "signs and wonders" (σημεῖα καὶ τέρατα) are signs of the eschatological age (see ch. 3),[7] and connected to the apostles' healing of the sick and their exorcism of those with unclean spirits (4:22; 5:12). These actions are worked by or through the apostles, but on a number of occasions credited to God. This is most immediately illustrated by what happens when the lame man by the Beautiful Gate is healed by Peter.[8] Rather than thanking

---

7. Cf. O'Reilly, *Word and Sign*, 187–89.
8. This healing is called a sign (σημεῖον) by the council in 4:16.

Peter, the man leaps to his feet and praises *God* (3:8, cf. 4:21). The man is here demonstrating what is affirmed elsewhere in Acts: The signs (σημεῖα), wonders (τέρατα), and deeds of power (δυνάμεις) worked by Jesus and the apostles are from God. Peter's words are illustrative of this: "Jesus of Nazareth, a man attested to you by God with deeds of power, wonders, and signs that God did through him among you" (2:22, cf. 10:38; 19:11). This, then, is the interpretive lens provided by the implied author, which allows the reader to understand the signs, wonders, and deeds of power as mediated (and implicit) acts of God, even where God is not directly mentioned.

Through the mention of signs and wonders, Acts once more proves to stand in the tradition, and continue the story, of the LXX, where "signs and wonders" (σημεῖα καὶ τέρατα)[9] are presented as part of God's agency, either as God works signs and wonders directly (e.g., Exod 7:3; 11:9–10; Deut 4:34; 6:22; 7:19; Ps 77:43 LXX, etc.), or through intermediaries (e.g., Exod 7:9; 11:10; Ps 104:26–27 LXX). To mention some examples, in the LXX signs and wonders are directly connected to the work Moses and Aaron do on behalf of God (e.g., Exod 4:1–9; 7:8–11; 11:10; Deut 34:10–12).[10] Moreover, even if the words "signs and wonders" are not present in the stories of Elijah and Elisha, some of the work they do, such as the revival of the widow's son in Zarephath (1 Kgs 17:17–24), the healing of Naaman (2 Kgs 5:1–14), and the blinding and opening of the Arameans' eyes (2 Kgs 6:18–23), closely resemble what falls under this category in Acts.[11] That God acts through intermediaries in this way is therefore firmly rooted in the biblical tradition. In light of this, it is worth noting that in Acts, the apostles take on a role that only God, God's great prophets, and Israel's leaders have in Israel's Scriptures: Thus, the narrative leaves no doubt as to whether the apostolic mission is divinely sanctioned as a place of God's works.

In addition to the speeches we considered earlier, which accord signs and wonders to God (2:19, 22), Jesus (2:22), and Moses (7:36), accounts abound of signs and wonders that take place in the story-time of Acts.

---

9. Hebrew: ומפתים אותת.

10. The prominence of the theme of God's signs and wonders in the exodus tradition is also expressed through the tradition which looks back on "the 'signs and wonders' which God performed *in the past* to free his people from slavery in Egypt. These texts are found in Israel's legal, prophetic, and poetic traditions" (Jos 24:5; Jer 32:20; Ps(s) 78:43, 135:8–12; Neh 9:6–15; Sir 45:3; Bar 2:16) (Kee, *Miracle*, 149).

11. I owe the observation that most of the signs and wonders that occur throughout the Hebrew Bible are predominantly found in the Moses (Exodus and Numbers), Elijah, and Elisha narratives (1 Kgs 17—2 Kgs 13) to Moberly, "Miracles in the Hebrew Bible," 62.

Focusing on those that we here call "acts of restoration,"[12] we find mention of some in narrated form, while others are mentioned in summaries:

- Summary: Many signs and wonders are done by the apostles (2:43).
- Peter (and John?) heal a crippled beggar by the Beautiful Gate (3:1–10).
- Summary: Signs and wonders are done through the apostles' hands; people are healed when Peter's shadow falls on them (5:12–16).
- Summary: Stephen performs great signs and wonders among the people (6:8).
- Summary: Philip performs signs and miracles (8:6–7, 13).
- Peter heals Aeneas (9:32–35).
- Peter raises Tabitha from the dead (9:36–42).
- Summary: Signs and wonders are done through Paul and Barnabas (14:3).
- Paul heals a crippled man (14:8–18).
- Paul casts out an evil spirit (16:16–18).
- Summary: God does deeds of power through Paul's hands (19:11–12).
- Eutychus lives (20:7–12).
- Paul shakes off the viper and lives (28:1–6).
- Paul heals the father of Publius (28:7–8).
- Summary: Paul heals many others on Malta (28:9).[13]

Presented in such an overview, it becomes apparent how integral to the narrative weave of Acts these signs and wonders are: They appear throughout the entire story, from beginning until end. Not only are they specifically mentioned in the first summary of the apostles' work (2:42–47); the healing of the lame man (3:1–21) introduces the first "mini-narrative" about what the apostles do after Pentecost. Thus it would seem that the apostles' work of bearing witness (cf. 1:8) cannot only be narrowed down to proclamatory witness, but must include bearing witness *through* signs and wonders as well. This is not so strange, given both that the preface

---

12. It is possible that some of the "acts of infliction" should be numbered here if this list were to reflect all the "signs and wonders" in Acts. Debating whether these can be seen as signs and wonders or not, however, falls outside the scope of this chapter.

13. Even though the expression "signs and wonders" is not used in 28:9, we are talking about the same kind of work which Paul has performed previously in Acts, and which has been referred to as signs and wonders.

ad Theophilum summarizes that the author's first book was about "all that Jesus *did* and taught" (1:1, my emphasis), and that Peter and John declares they "cannot keep from speaking about what we have *seen* and heard" (4:20, my emphasis).[14] While the latter verse could, e.g., also refer to the apostles' encounter with the resurrected Jesus, when it is read in light of 1:1, the apostles' witness can be understood as testimony to Jesus's works as well. It follows from this that the apostles are not only proclaiming what they have seen Jesus do, but are themselves *doing* what Jesus has done by exorcising and healing the sick.[15] The oft-noted Jesus–Peter/Paul(/Stephen)–parallels in Acts[16] are further testament to this as a narrative strategy of the implied author: The apostles' ministry mirrors Jesus's. Both their and Jesus's ministry are ultimately testimony to God.

The apostles' work through signs and wonders is continued throughout Acts. However, it is frequently observed that the majority of them are found in the first half of Acts.[17] Nevertheless, we should not overlook the fact that even though the narrative accounts cease towards the end, they do not disappear. Mention of signs and wonders continues throughout Acts' final chapter. It may therefore be more accurate to say that the first half of Acts establishes signs and wonders as an inherent part of the apostles' activity, and even though narration of them decreases as the story goes on, the summary mention of signs and wonders performed later on (19:11–12; 28:9) demonstrate that they remain an integral part of the apostles' mission.

While Acts thus clearly does credit the signs and wonders to God through the summaries mentioned above, explicit mention of God as an agent is conspicuously absent from the healing and exorcism narratives themselves. There is possibly one occasion on which signs and wonders (see below) is performed in the context of prayer (28:8), which could *imply* that God acts in response.[18] However, God's agency is only made *explicit* through the apostles' speeches (2:22; 10:38), and once by the narrator (19:11). It is therefore the apostles' and narrator's guiding voices that aid

---

14. I owe this observation to McConnell, *Topos of Divine Testimony*, 1.

15. Cf. Twelftree, *In the Name of Jesus*, 130–31.

16. The parallels between Jesus and Peter/Paul were noted as early as by Bruno Bauer in 1850. See particularly the following pages in the survey of research on miracle stories in Acts in Neirynck, "Miracle Stories," 182–88. See also Moessner, "'Christ Must Suffer,'" 220-56. Moessner, however, does not focus on signs and wonders in his treatment of the parallels between the characters in question.

17. Source criticism often used to explain the density of the signs and wonders in the first half of Acts by considering the "miracles" in Acts 1–12 as belonging to a "Petrine source" (Neirynck, "Miracle Stories," 188–95).

18. Cf., e.g., Talbert, *Reading Acts*, 218.

the reader's discernment of God as the power behind what takes place.[19] Here Acts is in many ways similar to the LXX, where signs and wonders are also primarily part of the intradiegetic discourse of God's actions, or are mentioned in non-historiographical texts, like the psalms. This further substantiates the argument we made in our second chapter (2.1.4), that Luke is employing biblical history as a genre.

If God's name is absent from the narration of the signs and wonders, however, Jesus's name is not: Peter heals "in the name of Jesus Christ of Nazareth" (3:6), and goes as far as telling Aeneas that "Jesus Christ heals you" (9:34). The believers pray for healing, signs, and wonders to be done through the name of Jesus (4:29–30); Paul commands the prophetic spirit to leave the slave girl in the name of Jesus (16:16–18), and the seven sons of Sceva attempt to take up the same practice of exorcising in the name of Jesus (19:13–15).[20] It seems that, in Acts, "the name of Jesus refers to the power and authority by which the healings are done."[21] In other words, the narrative focus is on Jesus rather than on God, as the signs and wonders seem to point to the risen Jesus's power and legitimacy as God's agent (cf. 2:22). Therefore,

---

19. Cf. Marguerat, *First Christian Historian*, 91.

20. While Jesus's name is used in all these contexts, it is clear that the disciples' work is positively affirmed by the implied author, whereas the sons of Sceva's attempt to exorcise in the name of Jesus is not. Although the word is not used, the latter activity could be understood as an attempt at "magic" (cf. 8:9–24). For more on this discussion, see Reimer, *Miracle and Magic* (2002). Here Reimer argues that scholarship must move beyond the old distinction between miracle and magic as supplicative versus manipulative. Instead, it must move to the sociological view of the two as fundamentally similar practices, but where magic is perceived negatively in inter-group polemics (3–14). Based on a study of *Acts* and the *Life of Apollonius of Tyana*, Reimer concludes that something can be understood as magic "if it is performed for the personal advantage of the intermediary, it is carried out in such a way as to suggest a manipulation of divine beings, it is overtly undermining acceptable social and political structures within a given community and/or is understood to be an act of religious deviance" (250). By way of contrast, a "miracle" seems to be an expression of mediated divine power that is not used for personal advantage, and "is not overtly undermining the acceptable social and political structures of a given community, and/or it can be understood to occur within an established religious framework" (250). If we read Acts 19:11–20 within this context, we see that the sons of Sceva are invoking Jesus's name as something foreign to them, as "the Jesus whom *Paul* proclaims" (my emphasis). This makes it difficult to see the sons of Sceva as mediators of Christ's power, and easier to see them as attempting to use it for their own purposes. Perhaps this is how we should understand the question of the evil spirit: It asks for the seven sons' identity (19:15) because it does not recognize them as true representatives of Jesus's name.

21. Henriksen and Sandnes, *Jesus as Healer*, 87. See also Bietenhard, "ὄνομα, ὀνομάζω, ἐπονομάζω, ψευδώνυμος," 277. Note, moreover, that demons are exorcised and healing and anointing take place "in the name of Jesus" in other New Testament books as well. See Matt 7:22; Mark 9:38; 16:17; Luke 10:17; Jas 5:14.

CHAPTER 9: THE GOD OF POWER AND WONDER

Keith Warrington can write of the healing in Acts 3 that it is a "Christological sign" and "Christocentric miracle."[22] In this way, Acts signifies a shift in comparison with the biblical tradition, where "the role of Yahweh is decisive and nonnegotiable: 'I am the LORD who heals you' (Exod. 15:26 CEB; cf. 2 Kings 5:7–15; Isa. 57:19)."[23] While God's role in Acts remains decisive, God's role as the only one whose name is used in healing *is* negotiated to also include Jesus: God's power is now visible in him.[24] This is exactly what we have observed in previous chapters, when we asked the question of "What happens to the characterization of God when Jesus goes to heaven?" We may say, with Sandnes's words, that "God's power to heal and to do extraordinary things is manifested in the power of the name of Jesus."[25] God is no longer characterized directly, but through Jesus.

"Power" is a key term when it comes to the signs and wonders in at least two respects: First, the signs and wonders are closely linked to "deeds of power" (δυνάμεις, 2:22), and secondly, to the question of whose power (δύναμις) and name the signs and wonders are done by (ἐν ποίᾳ δυνάμει ἢ ἐν ποίῳ ὀνόματι ἐποιήσατε τοῦτο ὑμεῖς; 4:7, cf. 4:16, 22).[26] The question just cited, which is asked of Peter and John by the religious leaders after the healing of the crippled man, could perhaps relate both to the healing and to the preaching of the two apostles, but the verb ποιέω favors the former. The leaders' question seems to inquire about whose authority the apostles represent: In the Greco-Roman world, deeds of power could signify the powers, or manifestation of the power a divine being,[27] and the leaders may be attempting to find out "whose men" the apostles are.[28] Read together with 14:8–18, where Paul and Barnabas are mistaken for gods (Zeus and Hermes) after Paul has healed a man, and 28:1–6, where Paul is taken for a god because he survives a viper's bite, it seems clear that underlying the signs and wonders performed by the apostles are contrasting world views in which the ability to work signs and wonders are a matter of whose

---

22. Warrington, "Acts and the Healing Narratives," 205, 206.

23. Green, "Healing and Healthcare," 332.

24. "Der Apostel ist so etwas wie der Mittler der Macht Jesu, die im Namen gegenwärtig ist" (Horn, "Entsetzen an der Schönen Pforte," 138).

25. Sandnes, "Beyond 'Love Language,'" 51.

26. Δύναμις is, in other words, used both of the power itself, and the deeds acted out through the power in question.

27. "δύναμις" in *LSJ*, paras. VI–VII. Grundmann, referencing P.Oxy., XI, 1381, 206ff, suggests that "These miracles of Aesculapius and similar gods are called δυνάμεις, acts of power. (Grundmann, "δύναμαι, δυνατός, δυνατέω," 289).

28. Cf. also Garrett, *Demise of the Devil*, 66. Garrett suggests the officials' question could be based on a supposition that a demonic or diabolical agent is at work.

power, i.e., god, one represents—or is. At stake in the working of signs and wonders is therefore not only the legitimation of the apostles as men of God, but through the signs and wonders, "The power of the Christian god is made to look greater than that of others."[29] In a world with many gods available for worship, Acts demonstrates that the God proclaimed by the apostles is the greater.[30] In this sense, the signs and wonders are "communicative and meaningful acts"[31] that communicate God's power; portraying God as a great and powerful God.

With these words, we return to the question of characterization. Having established signs and wonders as acts and expressions of God's power, we can start looking at how God is characterized through these actions. We have already suggested that God is portrayed as powerful, but powerful in what sense? Looking at the signs and wonders, we see that it is God's power over *bodies* and *spirits*, *life* and *death*, that is revealed: Crippled and paralyzed people walk again (3:6-8; 8:6-7; 9:33-34; 14:8-10), sick are healed (5:12-16; 19:11-12; 28:9), unclean spirits and a spirit of divination depart from bodies (5:16; 8:6-7; 16:16-18; 19:11-12), a dead woman and boy are returned to life (9:40-41; 20:9-12), Paul survives a viper's bite (28:3-5), and a sick man is healed from fever and dysentery (28:7-8). God is thus characterized as all-powerful, for God has power over both the physical and the spiritual.

These signs and wonders further reveal God as an active god: The God of Israel did not only act in the near and distant past, but is also at work in the narrative present. One important aspect of this activity is that it points to God as healer, and in Acts, healing is an aspect of salvation. Put differently, through healing, God is characterized as savior. To assert

---

29. Strelan, *Strange Acts*, 13.

30. Cf. Acts 19, where Paul's proclamation that "gods made with hands are not gods" (19:26) is met with the insistent cry from the Ephesians: Μεγάλη ἡ Ἄρτεμις Ἐφεσίων (19:28, cf. 19:34). This further illustrates that which god is great(er) is a topic of some concern in Acts. I do, moreover, find this emphasis on Israel's God as the "greater god" to be a more convincing interpretation of the Lystra passage in 14:8-20 than the one offered by Conrad Gempf in "Mission and Misunderstanding," 56-69. Gempf suggests that the purpose of the passage lies in its historical setting, which he finds to be concerned with questions about what Christianity (sic.) is, whether it is a Jewish sect, and if so, why there are so many gentiles in it; in addition to questions that are asked about Paul's role: "The Lystra story would fit such a setting well and contribute in a small way toward answering such questions—Christianity integrates into paganism no better and no more easily than it integrates into Judaism" (Gempf, "Mission and Misunderstanding," 68). Not only is the distinction Gempf makes between Judaism and "Christianity" somewhat (contentious and) outdated; but it looks to questions asked outside the text which do not seem to be at stake in the actual narration of the Lystra episode in Acts.

31. Rydryck, "Miracles of Judgment," 25.

that healing is a feature of salvation, however, is not without its difficulties. "Salvation" (σωτηρία) is a loaded term, both in theology in general and in Lukan studies more specifically. To consider healing as an aspect of salvation has not consistently been a perspective taken by Lukan scholars. Hans Conzelmann, who initiated the modern debate on salvation in Luke-Acts by presenting his thesis on the delay of the parousia and Luke's attempt to deal with this through a tripartite salvation historical scheme, views salvation after the time of Jesus primarily as a matter of the future:

> The truth is that in the life of Jesus in the centre of the story of salvation a picture is given of the future time of salvation—a picture that is now the ground of our hope: his life is an event which procures for us forgiveness and the Spirit, and thereby entrance into a future salvation.[32]

Conzelmann, however, is vague in terms of what salvation actually *entails*. He seems to suggest both that salvation includes Satan's absence[33] and that it is concerned with *life*: "For Luke the content of salvation is ζωή, or σωτηρία, and the basis of it is forgiveness, which in turn is conditional upon repentance (Acts ii, 38; v, 31; viii, 22; Luke xxiv, 47)."[34] Because salvation is here relegated to the future and somewhat vague, it excludes healing in Acts' story-time as part of salvation. Marshall, however, in contrast to Conzelmann's salvation historical scheme, extends the time of salvation to include the time of the church. He suggests that, "Salvation is not a thing of the past, belonging to the ministry of Jesus. It takes its start from then; the 'today' of fulfilment continues right through into the time of the church."[35] While Marshall does argue that "for Luke 'now' is the era of salvation and the associated blessings, the reversal of conditions for the rich and the poor is associated with the future,"[36] he also suggests that "the healing ministry of Jesus is definitely seen as a part of His broader power to save."[37] In other words, even though he asserts a view of salvation which partly emphasizes the future, Marshall's extension of the era of salvation to the "now," and his view of Jesus's healing ministry as part of his power to save, do open up for understanding the signs and wonders in Acts as part of salvation.[38]

32. Conzelmann, *Theology of St. Luke*, 36–37.
33. "When Jesus was alive, was the time of salvation; Satan was far away, it was a time without temptation" (Conzelmann, *Theology of St. Luke*, 16).
34. Conzelmann, *Theology of St. Luke*, 228–29.
35. Marshall, *Luke*, 121.
36. Marshall, *Luke*, 144.
37. Marshall, *Luke*, 96.
38. I am having difficulties understanding the basis for Reardon's claim that

Later research on Acts makes the connection between signs and wonders and salvation more explicit. As Timothy Reardon's article, "Recent Trajectories and Themes in Lukan Soteriology" (2013), demonstrates, Lukan scholarship seems to have moved from Conzelmann's future view of salvation, to what Reardon coins more "holistic" conceptions of salvation. This is exemplified by Mark Allen Powell and Joel B. Green.[39] For Powell, salvation entails participation in the reign of God, and "may involve either the introduction of positive features (peace, blessing, eternal life) or the removal of negative ones (disease, demons, sin)."[40] In other words, healing is here explicitly understood as part of salvation. For Green, salvation is also holistic in the sense that it "embraces the totality of embodied life, including its social, economic, and political concerns."[41] In a sentence leading up to this statement, Green asserts that salvation "embraces life in the present, restoring the integrity of human life."[42] Because healing may be viewed precisely as restoring the integrity of human life, by restoring a person to his or her communities, to e.g., work, participation in cultic life, etc., Green's definition also allows for healing to be understood as an aspect of salvation.[43]

The best arguments for viewing healing as an aspect of salvation, are found in Acts' own narrative. This may be observed through a return to the healing of the lame man in 3:1–10. We have previously noted that the healed man's immediate reaction is to praise God. When Peter later addresses the astonished onlookers, he declares that it is faith in Jesus's name that has made the man strong (3:16, cf. 4:7–10). Later, when confronted by the council, Peter speaks of what has taken place by stating that the man "has been *saved*" (σέσωται, 4:9).[44] Although English translations frequently favor other words here, e.g., "made well" (NASB), "been healed" (NRSV), and "made whole" (KJV), the literary context provides a stronger argument

---

"Marshall offers a presupposed spiritualized salvation" (Reardon, "Lukan Soteriology," 81). Reardon seems to build this on Marshall's statement that "The movement in Scripture is from the more physical aspects towards moral and spiritual deliverance" (Marshall, *Luke*, 94). While it is true that Marshall does see a shift in perspective from the salvation from enemies in the Hebrew Bible to the deliverance from sins in the NT, it seems to me that he is more nuanced than simply offering a presupposed spiritual view of salvation in Luke-Acts.

39. Reardon, "Lukan Soteriology," 84–86.

40. Powell, "Salvation in Luke-Acts," 6.

41. Green, *Gospel of Luke*, 25.

42. Green, *Gospel of Luke*, 24.

43. Witherington also argues that "Luke's concept has social, physical, and spiritual dimensions" (Witherington, *Acts*, 144, see also 821–43).

44. Note also the fourfold "Your faith has saved you" (ἡ πίστις σου σέσωκέν σε) in Luke in accounts of healings (Luke 7:50; 8:48; 17:19; 18:42).

CHAPTER 9: THE GOD OF POWER AND WONDER

for translating σέσωται with "has been saved." This may be illustrated by what Peter says when he follows up the statement in 4:9 by developing what he has already asserted in 3:16:

> "This Jesus is 'the stone that was rejected by you, the builders; it has become the cornerstone.' There is salvation (ἡ σωτηρία) in no one else, for there is no other name under heaven given among mortals by which we must be saved (δεῖ σωθῆναι ἡμᾶς)."[45] (4:11-12)

Peter's words in 4:11-12 suggest a broader framework within which the healing of the lame man may be understood, i.e., that of salvation. The phrases ὑπὸ τὸν οὐρανόν ("under heaven") and ἐν ἀνθρώποις ("among people") imply a universal perspective,[46] which is also suggested by the rest of the mission in Acts. Not only are the words used for salvation here the same ones as in 4:9; the man's healing is closely connected to Jesus's name (3:16; 4:7-10), just as salvation is in 4:11-12 and 2:21: "Since, as told by Luke, the healing of the temple beggar is a matter of someone being 'saved' through the invocation of the name of the Lord Jesus, it would seem that we are to understand the healing in the light of the Joel quote"[47] (i.e., Acts 2:21).[48] In other words, the healing of the lame man should be understood as an act of the salvation proclaimed in Acts.

This interpretation is supported by the uses of σῴζω and σωτηρία in the rest of Acts, which include both concrete present and future eschatological perspectives: Σωτηρία appears to include both a concept of eschatological salvation and salvation as expressed through more concrete acts of saving (4:12; 7:25; 13:26, 47; 16:17; 27:34). Σῴζω seems to have the same function, in that saving and being saved are used both as a more general reference to God's act of salvation (2:21, 40, 47; 4:12; 11:14; 15:1, 11; 16:30, 31), and is also tied to more specific acts of saving (4:9; 14:9-10; 27:31-44). The variegated use of σωτηρία and σῴζω is the reason why I speak of healing only as an aspect of salvation in Acts: Healing cannot be fully equated with salvation; nor can salvation be fully equated with healing.[49] Unfortunately, however, exploring the exact relationship between the two is beyond the scope of this study. For now we may note that because the healing of the lame

---

45. Ἡ σωτηρία and ἐν (before ἀνθρώποις, 4:12) are, in contrast to the other consistently cited witnesses, not there in Codex Bezae. The sentence nevertheless ends with ἐν ᾧ δεῖ σωθῆναι ἡμᾶς, and so salvation through Jesus's name is still in focus.

46. Cf. Sandnes, "Beyond 'Love Language,'" 47.

47. Hamm, "This Sign of Healing," 152.

48. Note that σῴζω is also used of healing in 14:9-10.

49. Witherington, "Salvation and Health," 151.

man is the first of the healing accounts in Acts, it also has a paradigmatic function in that it conditions our understanding of the later healings. In this sense, speaking of this healing as "salvation" means that it is possible to view all the healings in Acts under this purview.

To understand healing as an aspect of salvation, and God as savior through healing, also finds support in the cultural encyclopedia of antiquity. As Ben Witherington observes, in pagan, cultic contexts, one of the things σωτηρία amounted to was the restoration of good health.[50] Moreover, Joel B. Green suggests that, in the wider Greco-Roman world, "salvation" seems to have been understood more broadly, and as a "semantic cousin of benefaction":

> As such, salvation had to do with the exercise of beneficent power for the provision of a variety of blessings, 'a general manifestation of generous concern for the well-being of others, with the denotation of rescue from perilous circumstances.' This might include the health of the state, including its internal safety and the security of its borders; being rescued from a disaster at sea; the healing of physical malady; and more.[51]

For an ancient reader, then, it would not be strange to find healing under the linguistic domain of salvation in Acts.

In conclusion, we may say that when healing is understood as an aspect of salvation, then this provides content to *how* God should be understood as savior. Put differently, a savior who saves a person from enemies is different from a savior who heals; the God of Acts does both, and in articulating both, the image of God as savior is broadened. To view God as someone whose saving power is only a matter of future, "spiritual" salvation paints a very different picture of God than one in which God's saving power is also made visible in the signs and wonders that heal. When healing is viewed as part of Acts' presentation of salvation, then restoration of health is part of God's saving action: God as savior cares for the present, not merely the past and the future; God cares for bodies and communal restoration; God the savior is also God the healer.

---

50. Witherington, "Salvation and Health," 148. Specifically, Witherington connects the above observation to the cults of Isis, Asklepius, and the Dionysiac mysteries (148–49).

51. Green, "Salvation," 87. Green's citation is from Danker, *Benefactor*, 324. For more on salvation, see also Foerster and Fohrer, "σῴζω, σωτηρία, σωτήρ, σωτήριος," 965–1024.

9.1.2 Release from Prison

God releases followers of the Way from prison on three occasions: Twice, an angel of the Lord rescues the apostles (5:17–21a; 12:6–11), and once an earthquake unfastens their chains (16:23–40). To see these releases as acts of God requires familiarity with the biblical tradition. We have already noted that in Israel's Scriptures, the "angel of the lord" (ἄγγελος κυρίου) "appears almost always to help either Israel or an individual"[52] (see Gen 16:7–14; 22:10–18; Exod 3:1–22; Num 20:14–16; 22:22—23:12; Judg 6:11–24; 2 Kgs 1:1–18, etc.). In our treatment of Acts 7, we observed that in Stephen's recounting of Exod 3, the angel of the Lord who appeared to Moses was more or less indistinguishable from God. In the prison escape accounts, however, the angel is more clearly distinguished from God (12:11).[53] Nevertheless, the angel has no individual features, but fills the sole function as God's agent. In the final prison account, there is no angel, but the prison chains of Paul and Silas are unfastened after an earthquake. Here, too, the shaking earth is a sign of divine epiphany: The last time the earth was shaking in Acts, was in a context of God's response to prayer (4:31); similarly, earthquakes signal God's (coming) presence in Israel's Scriptures (cf. e.g., Num 16:31–32; Exod 19:18; 1 Kgs 19:11). While all three accounts are in a sense stories of release, their narrative contexts and content differ and therefore express slightly different things about God. Here, we offer no full analysis of these accounts, but point out some observations of relevance to our inquiry.

The first prison escape account (5:17–21a) is set in a narrative context where tension and conflict between the apostles and the Jewish leadership in Jerusalem is steadily increasing, and eventually culminates with the stoning of Stephen in 7:58–60. Peter and John have already been to prison once (4:3); this time, the narrator suggests that all the apostles are put behind lock and key (5:17–21a). When the angel of the Lord opens the prison doors, it is the middle of the night. The temporal setting therefore indicates darkness, which neither concretely nor symbolically proves to be an obstacle to divine intervention. The angel of the Lord brings the apostles out (ἐξάγω, 5:19). The use of this verb for the angel's action could possibly be taken as an allusion to the Exodus account, where the angel of the Lord also plays a central role

---

52. Bietenhard, "ἄγγελος," 101. Only one exception is listed: 2 Sam 24:16f.

53. This coheres well with the picture drawn by Darrell D. Hannah, who suggests that whereas the angel of the Lord more or less indicated an extension of Yahweh or Yahweh's presence in pre-monarchical times, the angel was later distinguished from Yahweh. See Hannah, *Michael and Christ*, 19–22. Cf. also John B. Weaver: "The distinction between God and the angel is more sharply defined as the biblical tradition grows. The angel becomes more clearly identified as a messenger and envoy of the deity" (Weaver, *Plots of Epiphany*, 98).

in the liberation of the Israelites from Egypt (cf. Exod 3:2; 14:19; 23:20, 23; 32:34).[54] While the verb is not directly connected to the angel in these accounts, it *is* used explicitly of God's deliverance of the Israelites (cf. e.g., Exod 3:8, 6:6–7; 7:4–5; 12:17, 42, 51; 13:3, 9, 14, 16; 16:6, 32; 18:1; 20:2; 29:46; 32:11). Read from this perspective, the prison break scene functions as a small mirror of God's liberating activity in the history of Israel; reflecting and connecting the lines between past and present.

It is the angel's message to the apostles that claims the central focus of the scene: "Go, stand in the temple and tell the people the whole message about this life (τῆς ζωῆς ταύτης)" (5:20).[55] The demonstrative pronoun αὕτη could refer to the life to which the apostles are liberated; in light of what the apostles are actually portrayed to proclaim, however, it is perhaps more relevant to observe that "every other mention of ἡ ζωή in Acts 1–8 occurs as a reference to the resurrected life of the Messiah"[56] (cf. 2:28: 3:15; 8:33). Thus, the release by the angel both allows and commands the apostles to continue the ministry of witness foretold by Jesus in 1:8. This work of bearing witness is, as we have seen throughout this study, presented as part of God's purpose. Hence, the angel's orders function to ensure the continuation of God's plan. Although God is not directly mentioned, God is indirectly characterized as the savior of the apostles and the director of history, through the work of the angel.

In 12:3–11, Peter is imprisoned by Herod. In the build-up to the apostle's incarceration, Herod is introduced to the narrative for the first time (12:1). The antagonism between him and the followers of the Way reaches its peak in his execution of James (12:2). Peter's imprisonment therefore signals no small peril to his life. His release from prison by an angel of the Lord should be read as a contrast story to the death of Herod by the same angel; both are smitten by the angel (πατάσσω is used in both 12:7 and 12:23).[57] In Peter's case, however, the angel's visit means release and life; for Herod, the result is death.

The account of Peter's escape is framed by the believers' fervent prayer to God on his behalf (12:5), and ends with Peter's interpretation of the event as God's work (12:11, cf. 12:17). In this sense, the event characterizes God as responsive to the needs of the apostle and the believers.[58] The release begins with the angel's appearance (ἐπέστη, 12:7) and ends with its disappearance

---

54. Weaver, *Plots of Epiphany*, 101–2.
55. "The temple" (τὸ ἱερόν) is omitted in 𝔓[74].
56. Weaver, *Plots of Epiphany*, 112.
57. Miller, *Convinced that God Had Called Us*, 217.
58. Cf. Weaver, *Plots of Epiphany*, 284.

(ἀπέστη, 12:10). In between, the release is structured around the angel's orders (ἀνάστα, 12:7; ζῶσαι; ὑπόδησαι; περιβαλοῦ; ἀκολούθει, 12:8), which in each case is followed by a mention of Peter's compliance. Looking back at the event, Peter credits his escape to God:[59] "Now I am sure that the Lord has sent his angel and rescued me from the hands of Herod and from all that the Jewish people were expecting" (12:11). Similarly, when he is reunited with the other believers, he explains that "the Lord had brought (ἐξήγαγεν) him out of prison" (12:17). The same verb, ἐξάγω, is used in both 12:17 and 5:19, connecting the two events, and possibly alluding to the exodus here too. In pointing to God as the one who has sent his angel, where God becomes the liberator "behind the scenes," Peter's words make God's power over the ruler Herod visible. Moreover, when Peter's release is read in contrast to the death of Herod (12:20-23), it is apparent that God is the God who brings life as well as death. Through this contrast between those to whom he brings life and those to whom he brings death, God is characterized as partial to the followers of the Way.

In the final prison account, 16:23-40, Paul and Silas are imprisoned in Philippi when an earthquake unfastens their chains. While the first two accounts result in prison breaks, however, in this one Paul and Silas do not immediately leave their cell. As Matthew L. Skinner observes, Paul's refusal to leave the prison shows that the purpose of the account is not the prisoners' release.[60] Instead, the scene "serves as a demonstration of divine power over serious attempts to control the proclamation of the gospel."[61] We observe this through the conversation about salvation which follows after the earthquake: The jailor, ready to fall on his sword because he believes he has failed his duty (15:27), is alerted to the prisoners' presence, and asks: τί με δεῖ ποιεῖν ἵνα σωθῶ; (16:30). The irony of the situation is obvious: Paul and Silas have already been saved, but save the jailor's life when they alert him to their presence. Furthermore, when the jailor next asks how to be saved, his question can be understood on two levels: The narrative context suggests that the jailor does not know about Paul and Silas's proclamation of Jesus, and that his question therefore refers to what he must do in order to keep the prisoners inside so that he will not be dishonored. For the reader, however, the verb σῴζω is intimately connected with God's salvation, and so on a second level, the question refers not to the concrete situation in prison, but rather to the apostles' proclamation of salvation through Jesus. This second level of

---

59. It is unlikely that "Lord" refers to Jesus here, as he does not perform any similar actions in Acts.

60. Skinner, *Locating Paul*, 92–93.

61. Skinner, *Locating Paul*, 93.

meaning is affirmed by Paul and Silas's reply to the jailor: "Believe in the Lord Jesus, and you will be saved, you and your household." (12:31). In this brief scene, then, the reader's expectations of what will happen to the prisoners is turned upside down when it turns out that this is an account not of their salvation, but of their jailor's. In this sense, God is revealed as a God of power and surprises; a savior who saves in unexpected ways.

9.2 Acts of Infliction

At least six people in Acts suffer either death or blindness: Judas's belly bursts open as he falls headlong into a field (1:16–25); Ananias and Sapphira fall down dead after having lied to the Holy Spirit, God, and Peter (5:1–11); Paul is blinded on his way to Damascus (9:1–19); Herod is struck by an angel and eaten by worms (12:21–23), and Elymas is blinded (13:4–12). Is God behind this? As this chapter argues, the response to this question is "yes." But if the answer is in the affirmative, then how is God characterized through these acts of infliction? The following will attempt to answer these questions, first by looking at the deaths of Judas, Ananias, Sapphira, and Herod, and then at the blindings of Paul and Elymas.

9.2.1 Death as Divine Judgment

What is God's involvement in the deaths of Judas, Ananias, Sapphira, and Herod, and how does this involvement characterize God? While it is common to see the deaths of the latter three characters as some form of divine judgment, surprisingly, Judas is hardly ever mentioned in most scholars' lists of "punishment/punitive/retributive miracles" in Acts.[62] This silence, however, is not without exceptions: In his study of how Acts 1:15–26 can be understood within its historical context, Arie Zwiep notes that Judas "is in fact the first person in the plot of Acts to suffer *divine punishment*" (my emphasis).[63] Michael Rydryck also treats Judas's death as a "judgment miracle."[64] O. Wesley Allen similarly sees it as retribution,[65] and David R.

---

62. See e.g., Gen, "Phenomena of Miracles." Gen goes through an impressive amount of research on "divine infliction" in Luke-Acts, but not one of the scholars he mentions speak of Judas. This is consonant with the impression I have from my own research; Judas's death is frequently left out when speaking about God's infliction/retribution/judgment.

63. Zwiep, *Judas*, 176.

64. Rydryck, "Miracles of Judgment," 30–31.

65. Allen, *Death of Herod*, 120–24.

McCabe also interprets it as such.[66] As we shall see, because Judas's death is the first one in Acts, the interpretation of his demise has implications for how the further sudden deaths in Acts should be read, and therefore merits some attention.

It is possible that Judas's death has not always been interpreted as divine judgment because of the account's lack of mention of explicit divine interference. Unlike Herod's end in 12:20–23, there is no angel to strike Judas dead. But there are at least three reasons why Judas's death may be viewed as more than a timely demise: First, Judas is negatively characterized as "a guide for those who arrested Jesus" (1:16), and his action is explicitly denounced as "injustice" (ἀδικία) by Peter (1:18). In other words, there is a "motive" for regarding his death as punitive. Secondly, Judas's death is, according to Peter, foretold by the Holy Spirit through Scripture, i.e., Psalms 68:26 LXX and 108:8 LXX:

> The two Scriptures . . . which Luke assembles in verse 20 function as *ex eventu* proof and *ante eventum* divine imperative, respectively. The church then proceeds to fulfill (obey) the divine directive of the latter. This is the context of the δεῖ in verse 21 relative to the appointment of a successor for Judas.[67]

In framing Judas's death both as foretold, and as something whose consequences the disciples are now to act upon (1:24–26), the implied author suggests that Judas's death is part of God's plan. Third, this connection between Judas's death and God's will is made stronger by the fact that death as divine retribution is a common theme in antiquity.[68] One example will suffice to illustrate this point: In his treatment of Catullus's death, Josephus describes how his bowels fell out, and explicitly interprets this as proof of God's punishment (*J.W.* 7.451–453). Although I am not claiming any dependence between these two texts, Josephus's account does demonstrate how a grotesque death could be explicitly interpreted as a result of the divine will by an ancient historian.

While there is accordingly good reason to read Judas's death as divine punishment, there is more focus on the inevitability of his death than on God as the agent behind it. God is here characterized "behind the scenes," hidden, with no feeling or motive attributed to God's character. God's character is therefore only revealed through God's plan. Consequently, it is up

---

66. McCabe, *How to Kill*, 200–8.
67. Cosgrove, "Divine Dei," 174.
68. See e.g., Nestle, *Griechische Studien*, 567–96; van der Horst, "Hellenistic Parallels," 24; Klauck, *Judas*, 116–21; Speyer, "Gottesfeind," 996–1043; Allen, *Death of Herod*, 35–69; Zwiep, *Judas*, 63–68.

to the reader to fill in the gap that allows the former disciple's death to show and implicitly characterize God as a righteous judge, acting in retribution, taking a life for a life.

In reading the death of Judas as God's retribution for his treachery, the reality and possibility of God's punishment of evil deeds is introduced to the narrative. With this expectation, the reader approaches the story of Ananias and Sapphira in 5:1-11. Read within its narrative context, it is clear that the couple's mistake presents a breach of the fellowship ethic of having all possessions in common (4:32). This ethic is embodied in the immediately preceding presentation of Barnabas's character, who is said to have "sold a field that belonged to him, then brought the money, and laid it at the apostles' feet" (4:37). Ananias and Sapphira are also introduced as having sold land; by way of contrast, they, however, hold back from their proceeds and then lie about it. The couple's deception is judged severely by Peter, whose words characterize Ananias as being in league with the devil: "Ananias, why has Satan filled your heart to lie to the Holy Spirit and to keep back part of the proceeds of the land?" (5:3). The contrast between the believers' hearts, which are filled with the Holy Spirit (4:31), and Ananias's, filled by Satan, is palpable.[69] In a twist of irony, Ananias thus becomes the opponent of the Spirit: According to Peter, Ananias's lie is not primarily directed towards the believers, but towards the Holy Spirit (5:3), and indeed, God (5:4).

Following Peter's declaration of Ananias's crime, Ananias dies. Sapphira, his wife, shares her husband's fate and drops dead immediately after Peter has pronounced her fate (5:10). Like Herod's misdeed (see below), their crime is theologically presented: Herod does not give God the glory; Ananias lies to God/the Holy Spirit.[70] Accordingly, both acts represent injustice done towards God. It is therefore plausible to see the deaths of Ananias and Sapphira as God's judgment of their deeds,[71] just as in the cases of first Judas, and later, Herod. This observation is substantiated by further similarities between the three death-as-divine-judgment accounts: The immediacy (παραχρῆμα, 5:10) of Sapphira's death resembles the angel's immediate (παραχρῆμα) and fatal blow against Herod in 12:23, and their manner of dying is similarly described with the verb ἐκψύχω (5:10; 12:23). Both accounts are, furthermore,

---

69. Thomas, "Acts of the Apostles," 235; Spencer, "Scared to Death," 69.

70. Although not entirely comparable because it concerns *blasphemy* against the Holy Spirit, Mark 3:29 offers an example of how severely offenses against the Holy Spirit could be considered: ὃς δ' ἂν βλασφημήσῃ εἰς τὸ πνεῦμα τὸ ἅγιον, οὐκ ἔχει ἄφεσιν εἰς τὸν αἰῶνα, ἀλλὰ ἔνοχός ἐστιν αἰωνίου ἁμαρτήματος ("... whoever blasphemes against the Holy Spirit can never have forgiveness, but is guilty of an eternal sin.").

71. See also Dormeyer, "Ein plötzlicher Tod," 147, where Ananias's sudden death is understood as the punishment ("Strafe") of God.

"followed by claims concerning the growth of the community (5:12–16; 12:24)."[72] If the reader, moreover, recalls Judas's treachery in the Gospel of Luke as initiated by Satan (22:3), there is a further connection to Peter's judgment of Ananias: Judas acted on Satan's orders, and bought land; Ananias withholds proceeds from a land sale, and is also described as being in league with Satan.[73] Together, all these similarities suggest that the account of Ananias and Sapphira bears enough semblance to the deaths of Judas and Herod to understand divine judgment as their cause of death too.[74] God is, in other words, indirectly presented as their judge.

To view Ananias's and Sapphira's deaths as an implicit act of God is not an uncontentious statement, and it must be made with one important disclaimer: The account of Ananias and Sapphira is not primarily *about* God. In fact, the purpose of 5:1–11 seems to be to instil fear in the believers, both the characters inside the text (5:11) and the actual readers of it.[75] God's explicit presence is completely absent, except as the object of wrongdoing. God can, in short, only be *interpreted* as the couple's judge. However, not everyone would agree that God is at work here. To offer one example, F. Scott Spencer argues that "No one, divine or human, lifts a lethal finger. Ananias and Sapphira literally die of shame."[76] Spencer, who reads the story through the lens of an ancient concept of shame,[77] also offers an interpretation that can only be *implicitly* derived from the story. In the narrative context of Acts, however, Spencer's claim lacks the strong narrative precedent and literary connections observed above in support of the interpretation of the couple's deaths as divine judgment.

That God is behind Ananias's and Sapphira's demise is further supported by David R. McCabe's published doctoral dissertation, *How to Kill Things with Words* (2011). In this study, McCabe convincingly argues that Peter's words to the couple are those of an "apostolic-prophetic speech

---

72. Allen, *Death of Herod*, 125.

73. Spencer, *Journeying through Acts*, 67.

74. *Pace* Spencer. In Spencer, "Scared to Death," 67n20, Spencer retracts his previous description of the deaths of Ananias and Sapphira as their being "suddenly struck dead by the hand of God" (cf. Spencer, *Journeying through Acts*, 67). While I agree with Spencer that God's presence in the account of Ananias and Sapphira is entirely passive, I find the arguments presented in the text above convincing in terms of pointing to the couple's deaths as an *implicit* act of God.

75. In this, I agree with Spencer that the fear seizing the congregation could be directed towards fear of shame and death. See Spencer, "Scared to Death," 74.

76. Spencer, "Scared to Death," 73.

77. Spencer's primary dialogue partner here is Aristotle.

act of divine judgment."⁷⁸ Among the observations made by McCabe, it is particularly worth noting his treatment of how Peter's character has been built up throughout (Luke-)Acts to perform this apostolic-prophetic function,⁷⁹ and that the form of the apostle's accusing questions resemble those of prophetic figures in Israel's Scriptures in their confrontations with individuals.⁸⁰ Just like these prophetic figures, Peter relays divine judgment. In a summary statement, McCabe notes that, "Peter's encounter with each of the couple results in actions of indictment and execution *as a result of divine judgement relayed through the venue of Peter's condemnatory accusations*. The evidence is their immediate death."⁸¹ Thus McCabe's observations support and expand upon our own interpretation of the couple's death as God's act, as he understands it to be conveyed through Peter. Moreover, McCabe's work points our attention to the fact that God's act does not merely portray God as Ananias's and Sapphira's judge. Looking at the narrative context where the ethos of the believing community is in focus (4:32–37), we may observe that "God has defended and guaranteed the sanctity of the communal ethos of generosity and unity."⁸² Thus another side to the portrayal of God as judge in 5:1–11, is also the portrayal of God as the protector of the Jesus believers' way of community.

Our final scene, the death of Herod (12:20–23), is the only death-as-retribution scene in Acts where there is an explicit divine agent and motive behind the death: The angel of the Lord *immediately* strikes Herod (παραχρῆμα, cf. 5:10) when he fails to deflect the people's praise and give God the glory when he himself is hailed as a god (12:22–23).⁸³ In this way, Herod exemplifies what happens to a political leader who attempts to take the place of God. Herod, as a result of the angel's blow, is eaten by worms and dies (12:23). Accordingly, the Herod of Acts meets his end in a fashion similar to other figures whose demise are in some sense connected to worms: Antiochus IV Epiphanes (2 Macc 9:5–12), Queen Pheretime (Herodotus, *Hist.* 4.205), Herod the Great (Josephus, *Ant.* 17.168–169; *J.W.* 1.656), Alexander the False Prophet (Lucian, *Alex.* 59), and Sulla (Plutarch, *Sull.* 36.2–3). While it is true that "one variant feature of these accounts is whether the authors

---

78. McCabe, *How to Kill*, 208.
79. McCabe, *How to Kill*, 183–99.
80. McCabe, *How to Kill*, 214, cf. 125–27.
81. McCabe, *How to Kill*, 217.
82. McCabe, *How to Kill*, 216.
83. Cf. Josephus, *Ant.* 19.343–52, where Herod's death also follows upon his being hailed as divine.

make reference to any ultimate causality (e.g., God, the gods, or Justice),"[84] the angel's blow in Acts leaves no doubt as to whether Herod's death should here be understood as divine judgment.[85]

Where does this leave us in terms of characterization of God? As we begin to answer this question, we note O. Wesley Allen's perceptive observation that, "In its immediate context, the failure refers to Herod's silence in response to the crowd's acclamation. But read within the context of the chapter as a whole, the comment refers to the tyrant's failure to recognize the divine power that has countered his persecution."[86] Herod, whose cruel design has already been overturned by God in Peter's prison release, has put to death sixteen guards (12:19, cf. 12:4), but failed to overturn God's purpose. That this is one of the main points of the story, is clear from the notice made by the narrator immediately following Herod's death: "But the word of God continued to advance and gain adherents" (12:24).[87] In this sense, Herod's death is not only presented as a contrast to Peter's release to life (see above); Herod the ruler is also indirectly contrasted to God the ruler by way of their opposing purposes. Through the narrator's statement that Herod's death is due to his failure to give God the glory, God is by way of contrast to be understood as the real sovereign deserving of glory.[88] Moreover, through Herod's death, God emerges as a retributive judge.

9.2.2 The Blindings of Paul and Elymas

In chapter 5 our reading of Acts 9:1–19 led us to conclude that God was acting towards Paul's later change through temporary blindness. While the blinding of Paul may thus be seen as an act of infliction, Paul's blindness was also part of the process on his way to being healed and seeing again. Rather than repeating our previous argument here, we pause to make one reflection: In Acts Paul's blindness and his healing lead to his salvation, as he is included in the community of believers through baptism (9:18) and turn his life around, proclaiming Jesus as the Son of God (9:19–22). He is thus given a chance at a new life. While Paul's blindness does seem

---

84. Amundsen and Ferngren, "Disease and Disease Causality," 2955.

85. See also Mead, "Dressing up Divine Reversal," 230, following Allen, *Death of Herod*, 71–74.

86. Allen, *Death of Herod*, 107.

87. Cf. Dicken, *Herod as a Composite Character*, 151–52.

88. It could be asked whether the death of Herod should be read as a critique of the Roman Empire, or merely of rulers in the tradition of Antiochus Epiphanes, who do not give credit where credit is due.

to carry an element of retribution in it, a penalty for past persecution (cf. 9:1–4), it is up to the reader to make this connection by filling in the gaps the narrator leaves untold. In Paul's case, however, infliction leads to salvation, and can thus also be considered an act of salvation. God—through the ascended Jesus's action—is thus indirectly characterized as both the judge and merciful savior of Paul.

The second account of blinding in Acts lacks the salvific element found in the first. Paul and Barnabas have embarked on their first journey together, and have reached Salamis, where their proclamation is an initial success. Here, the blinding of Elymas (13:6–12) takes place after the magician has tried to turn a proconsul, Sergius Paulus, away from his newly gained faith. Through Paul's direct characterization of him as "son of the devil," "full of deceit and villainy," and someone who makes the Lord's straight ways crooked (13:10), it is apparent to the reader that Elymas is evil and working against God's purpose. Paul, by contrast, is characterized as "filled with the Holy Spirit" (13:9) when he pronounces a temporary blindness upon Elymas: "the hand of the Lord is against you, and you will be blind for a while, unable to see the sun" (13:11).[89] Earlier in this book, we observed that blindness in Acts carries both a symbolic and concrete dimension. The concrete darkness that immediately (παραχρῆμα, 13:11) comes over Elymas at Paul's words, is established by the narrator in 13:11. Elymas's blindness is, moreover, also symbolic of his inability to see the truth of Paul and Barnabas's proclamation. It could be that Susan Garrett is right in noting that "The consignment of Bar Jesus to 'mist and darkness' is a consignment to the authority of his master, Satan (cf. Acts 26:18; Luke 22:53)."[90] If so, this would tie in well with Paul's characterization of Elymas (13:10).

Through Paul, full of the Spirit, "the agent of God confronts and overpowers the agent of Satan (cf. 5:3; 8:22–23)."[91] That Paul acts as God's agent throughout Acts has become obvious through our previous chapters. What is not so obvious, however, is whether it is God or Jesus whom Paul refers to as "Lord" here. The ambiguity is strengthened by the repetition of a non-specified κύριος in 13:10–12. This ambiguity is not resolved, for reasons may be put forward in favor of seeing either God or Jesus as the agent here. To mention just two such arguments, we may note that the God of Israel is always the subject of the "hand of the Lord" in the LXX. One of the expression's uses there, is in the context of God's disfavor and judgment (Exod

---

89. For a reading of Paul's words as a curse, see Kent, "Curses in Acts," 412–40.

90. Garrett, *Demise of the Devil*, 83. This fits well with Paul's description of Elymas as being in league with the devil (13:10).

91. Gaventa, *Acts*, 193.

9:3; Judg 2:15; Ruth 1:13; 1 Sam 5:6, 9; 7:13; 12:15). On this background, understanding "Lord" as the God of Israel is more appropriate. But a second observation complicates the matter. Peter mentions the "paths of the Lord," which is an allusion to a passage in Isaiah (40:3–5). In the Isaianic context, the referent is God, but the same passage is also cited in Luke 3:4: Here, John the Baptist proclaims the coming of the Lord, and it becomes obvious throughout the course of the Gospel that he is referring to Jesus. Depending on one's judgment of the allusion as primarily Lukan or Isaianic, one could understand the referent as either God or Jesus.

The above examples are illustrative of why the ambiguity of Paul's statement cannot be completely resolved. They also suggest why we can just as easily say that "God" is behind the blinding of Elymas as "Jesus." God and Jesus's characters are therefore nearly completely blurred together here, and they can therefore both be said to act—and be characterized—as the judge of the magician's symbolic blindness. Because this judgment also tells the truth of Elymas's character (he is "blind"), we can also say that truth is revealed through judgment. This means that the characterization of God and Jesus as judge is as someone who utters truth through judgment.

9.3 Concluding Observations

In this chapter, we have observed a general tendency for God to be indirectly characterized as savior and judge through acts of restoration and infliction. After having looked at these acts, "savior" and "judge" have become more than generic terms: As *savior*, God is not only the savior who brings life in the future. Instead, we have seen that healing in Acts should be understood as an aspect of salvation. Accordingly, God is presented as savior in the story-time's present, restoring life and bodies. Furthermore, God is also characterized as *judge*. The accounts of the acts of infliction in particular are revelatory of what this entails: As judge, God is master of life and death, and able to deal immediate judgment. This judgment may lead to sudden death, as in the case of Herod, or to salvation, as in the case of Paul. In the case of the former, God is revealed as the true sovereign in the encounter with the earthly king; with the power to fulfill his purpose in spite of opposition. God is, however, not shown to punish every ill deed performed in the narrative. Stephen's executioners, for instance, simply disappear from the story. Thus Acts does not depict any fixed or inevitable causality between misdeeds and God's judgment.

In Acts some of the actions we have touched upon are explicitly called "signs," "wonders," and "deeds of power." As we have seen, these reveal continuity with actions performed by God in Israel's past. In Acts' narrative present, however, these actions are initially introduced as a herald of the last days on the way to the Day of the Lord (2:17–21). It is perhaps not so strange, then, that within this temporal setting, the actions which we have dealt with characterize God both as savior and judge. Moreover, we have also observed that God is characterized as powerful through the apostles' work. As the apostles travel through a world where multiple gods are worshipped, their practical act of bearing witness reveals the power of the God of Israel above everyone else's.

The sheer abundance of acts of restoration and infliction in the story-time of Acts characterizes God as active. It is therefore ironic that this activity simultaneously reveals and conceals God. In the healing accounts, for instance, God's power is primarily manifest in Jesus, and it is Jesus's name, rather than God's, which is mentioned. Similarly, the roles of God and Jesus are blended in the accounts of Paul and Elymas's blindings, thus making it ambiguous how God is characterized—save in tandem with Jesus. In this context, it is curious to note that neither Jesus nor his name feature in the death-as-punishment scenes. In other words, here it is less ambiguous that God is the one who deals death in judgment. Without overstating the evidence, this may suggest that this is one of the areas where God and Jesus's characters are not blended in Acts:[92] God remains the master of life and death.

---

92. Note, however, the contrast to the Gospel of Luke, where Jesus raises the widow's son in Nain (Luke 7:11–17).

Chapter 10: The Portrayal of God in Acts

10.0 Introduction

How is God characterized through actions—in Acts? Throughout this study, we have observed how the portrayal of God is constructed in relation to three "temporal frames." The first one is defined by the story-time events of the narrative itself, which is delimited by its beginning in Jerusalem and end in Rome. Secondly, there is Peter's interpretation of what takes place in the story-time as part of the "last days" (2:17), which begin after Jesus's ascension and the election of a twelfth apostle, covers the entire narrative of Acts, and points to the day of the Lord's judgment and salvation. Thirdly, there is the history of Israel as expressed through Scripture. The different characters repeatedly interpret their present situation (in the story-time) on the background of this past. In short, when the portrayal of God is drawn, it is within the boundaries of a narrative, where the plot is interpreted as part of "the last days" by an intradiegetic narrator, and constantly presented on the background of Israel's Scriptures. The image of God comes into being through the interplay between these elements and the reader.

The very first question asked by the disciples in Acts is when Jesus will restore the kingdom to Israel (1:6). The story ends, however, with a word of warning and judgment against the unrepentant Israel, and a statement that God's salvation has been sent to the gentiles (28:26–28). Between these two poles spans a narrative which develops this movement from hope to warning through the spread, rejection, and reception of the word of God from Jerusalem, to Samaria, and onwards to Rome. In this book, we have observed God's presence behind every step of this movement. I say "observed," but in Acts God's actions are nearly always performed through others. It is therefore the narrator, different characters, and information from the reader's cultural encyclopedia that make observation of God's character possible. The main body of texts we have analyzed function as greater or smaller turning points in the narrative, while in our last chapter, "The God of Power and Wonder," we have looked more broadly at a number of texts that suggest how God's character is at work in the story-time of Acts. In sum, we have looked at where and how God can be seen to be at work, and on this basis suggested how God's actions characterize God in Acts.

In this final chapter, we take a step back from individual texts and return to the narrative of Acts as a whole. On the basis of the observations we have made so far, we now look at last at the sum of the characterization of God, asking what kind of portrayal of God is drawn in Acts through God's actions. In doing so, we synthesize our findings and offer summative observations about how God is characterized in Acts as a whole. We do so by returning to the questions originally asked in our introduction: What is the portrayal of God through actions in Acts? In what ways do the actions and characterization of God in the story-time relate to the actions of God spoken of in Jesus's life and ministry, and in Israel's more distant past? How does Jesus's ascension into heaven impact the characterization of God? These last two questions are, this chapter argues, the key to the distinctive portrayal of God in Acts.[1]

10.1 God of the Past, Present, and Future

The implied author of Acts is concerned with the past, present, and future. We have seen this particularly in the speeches, where God's actions in Israel's past are frequently summarized. Although the speeches focus on different moments in Israel's past, the history they speak of is more or less a history of God's actions. The move from past to story-time present is, to a large degree, facilitated by the realization of God's promises in Jesus, and the resulting offer of forgiveness of sins and salvation. But throughout this study we have observed that, precisely as the implied author moves between Israel's distant past, the time of Jesus, and finally the story-time of Acts, something happens to the portrayal of God. The referent of "the Lord" becomes ambiguous, and whether God is the one to perform certain actions becomes so too.

Through our reading of Acts, we have identified a moment in time which is crucial to the way God is portrayed in this narrative: The ascension of Jesus. The impact of Jesus's ascension first becomes apparent when the descent of the Spirit is initially interpreted by Peter as God's promised action (2:17), but is then presented by him as Jesus's act of pouring out the Spirit

---

1. The first of these last two questions is temporal: It concerns the relationship between how God is depicted in the past and in the narrative present. The last question is more "relational," in the sense that it asks how the characterization of Jesus impacts the characterization of God post-ascension. Nevertheless, as the ascension can also be defined as a moment in the story-time, it will be evident from the observations made in this concluding chapter that the answers to each question are sometimes linked to each other and to some extent overlap with each other.

(2:33). In other words, Jesus's character comes to "take over" one of God's actions. From this time onwards, God's characteristics come to characterize Jesus more and more. It is the central contribution and claim of this study that this also influences the way *God* is presented. Moreover, as gentiles are included in the people of God through the reception of the Spirit, the portrayal of God as savior shifts from the way Acts depicts it in Israel's past, to how God as savior is presented in the story-time and its future. There is nothing new in claiming that Acts narratively depicts how God becomes the God of all, but in the following I will demonstrate that there are subtle ways in which Acts portrays God differently in Israel's past than in the narrative present and future. Thus, we may say that in Acts, the distinctive portrayal of God emerges in a dynamic between past, present, and future. We will explore this in the following pages.

10.1.1 A Changing God, or Changing Perceptions?

In our introduction, we classified Acts as biblical history. As such, it is perhaps not surprising that God is presented in Acts in much the same way as God is presented in the Septuagint: God acts through others, through visions, dreams, theophanies, and the angel of the Lord. Moreover, the signs and wonders that signal the eschatological age bind together the works of God (2:19), Moses (7:36), Jesus (2:22), the apostles (2:43; 5:12; 14:3; 15:12), and Stephen (6:8). This means that even as the last days are introduced, this way in which God acts through others does not change; the signs and wonders are a feature both of the past and the present. God remains recognizable as a "God of power and wonder." At the same time, however, it should be noted that "signs and wonders" feature more frequently in Acts than they do in the accounts of Israel's past. There, "signs and wonders" cluster more frequently around particular events, i.e., the exodus, the stories of Elijah and Elisha, and the promise of eschatological signs and wonders.[2]

In Israel's past, God is not characterized in entirely the same way as in the story-time, however: We have already noted that after Jesus's ascension, Jesus's character comes to take on a number of God's characteristics. This moves God further away from the narrative scene, characterizing God as more distant, and making it ambiguous when God acts. We will explore this further below. For now, however, we may note that the God of Acts is always mediated: Unlike the scriptural stories recounted by Peter and Stephen (3:25; 7:3, 7), the narrator does not present God as speaking directly in the

---

2. I owe thanks to Steve Walton for reminding me to include this observation in this chapter.

story-time. This does not mean that God's speech is not mediated. Direct speech is credited to e.g., the *Spirit* (4:25; 8:29; 13:2), which is a functionary of God's, but it is only when referring to the past that speech is *directly* attributed to God. The manner in which God is characterized in the past therefore differs slightly from Acts' present.

The God of the past is described as the "God of the fathers," and continues to be described as such in the story-time. But the God whose partiality to Israel is revealed through this relationship with Israel's fathers, is nevertheless presented as "the God of all" in Acts. God is portrayed as impartial, but this is a particular kind of impartiality. As Shauf observes, "Acts displays divine impartiality in the form of an expanding partiality tied to a strong particularity."[3] Put differently, God is no longer portrayed as partial to Israel alone, but God is still the God of Israel in particular. This is largely expressed through God's promises, which we shall soon see are made to Israel, but nevertheless have universal consequences.

Does this make the God of the past different from the God of the future? In reading Acts, it would seem that it is the characters' perceptions of God, rather than God, that change. We have seen this in Peter's declaration of God's impartiality after his encounter with Cornelius—now he understands what God's impartiality entails (10:34–35). On the surface, this declaration offers nothing new in terms of how God is presented, for God is called impartial in Israel's Scriptures too. However, through the angel and Peter's encounter with Cornelius, this conception of God gains a content that specifically relates to how gentiles are to be perceived in relation to God. We have also seen that the experiences of the Jesus movement lead to an interpretation of Scripture which is based on Jesus as the fulfillment of the restoration of the Davidic dynasty: As James speaks at the apostolic council, he grounds the inclusion of the gentiles into the people of God in this restoration (15:16–18). In this sense, the Scripture written in the past speaks truth about God's actions in the present; but what God does now is nothing that is not already there to be read about in Scripture.

10.1.2 God as Faithful, Judge, and Savior

Three aspects in particular dominate the characterization of God in Acts: God is, above all, presented as *faithful*, *judge*, and *savior*. The prominence of these features is readily discernible already from the beginning of Acts, most particularly from the description and interpretation of the events at Pentecost: Here, God is revealed as *faithful* to his promise of sending the Spirit

---

3. Shauf, *Divine in Acts*, 202.

(1:4–5). Even as this promise is realized, however, Peter interprets the events with words from the Scriptures, signaling the beginning of the last days which end with the Day of the Lord and a promise of salvation for everyone who calls on the name of the Lord (2:20–21). As the Day of the Lord must be recognized as the day of God's judgment, the timeline projected by Peter's speech ends with the judgment and salvation of God. Thus, we may say that God's *faithfulness* bridges past and present, and is the foundation based on which the story of Acts unfolds towards the time of salvation and judgment beyond the present of the story-time. God's characteristics as faithful, judge, and savior are in other words intimately connected, and each feature could easily be subordinated to the other(s); when I treat them separately, it is because it allows us to concentrate more specifically on each aspect of God's character. In the following, we turn to look more closely at what it *means* that God is depicted as faithful, judge, and savior in Acts.

10.1.2.1 God as Faithful

To ask what it means that God is faithful, entails asking to whom God is faithful, concerning what God is faithful, and when God is faithful. We have just observed that initially in Acts, God's faithfulness is revealed through the realization of God's promise of sending the Spirit. This is, in fact, the main way through which God's faithfulness is revealed throughout the story: God keeps what God promises. In the texts that we have looked at, four promises stand out: The promise of the gift of the Spirit (1:4), the promise of land to Abraham (7:5), the promise to David of putting one of his descendants on his throne (2:30; 13:22–23, 32–33), and the promise to the fathers of resurrection from the dead (26:6–8). These promises are all made in the past, to significant people in the history of Israel. Initially they also seem to primarily concern Israel; the Spirit is poured out in Jerusalem on Jews during a Jewish festival, and it is only through the course of the narrative that the reader learns to understand Jesus's words in 1:8 and Peter's declaration that the Spirit will be poured out on "all flesh" (2:17) to be applicable to gentiles too. In other words, when God is portrayed as faithful, it is first and foremost a God who is faithful to *Israel* that we see.

Even if God's faithfulness is observed through God's relationship with one people, however, in the narrative present this faithfulness comes to have universal consequences. The pouring out of the Spirit is repeated when God acts through orchestration of the encounter between Peter and Cornelius, after which it is made quite clear that the gentiles have also received the Spirit (10:44–47). One might ask if this does not change

God's course of action as perceived by the apostles in 1:6, whose primary concern is with the restoration of Israel. However, after the gift of the Spirit to the gentiles, the apostolic leaders return to Scripture and read it anew: Significantly, at the apostolic council James interprets the gentiles' inclusion into the community of believers through a quote from Scripture (15:16–18). His interpretation suggests that God's faithfulness in the past has not changed in aim or purpose with the gentiles' reception of the Spirit in the present. On the contrary, it suggests that God's salvation of the gentiles is foreseen in Scripture too. In this sense, God's faithfulness may also be seen as an expression of the constancy of God's character; God does not change, even though the way—or which parts of—Scripture is read is changed by the believers' experience of God.

God's faithfulness is also demonstrated through the realization of God's promise of land to Abraham's descendants. Here God's partiality to Israel readily comes to the fore, for other nations are driven out before them (7:45). God, in his faithfulness to one nation, is consequently also portrayed as ruthless towards other nations in the past.

God's faithfulness to Israel is also realized through Jesus, in at least two ways. First, Jesus represents the realization of God's promise to put David's offspring on his throne. Secondly, Jesus's resurrection is also an initial realization of the promise to the fathers and the hope of Israel (26:6–8) that the dead will be resurrected. We will look more closely at the impact of Jesus's character on the portrayal of God in the subchapter about God as savior. Here, however, we may note that through the course of the narrative, Jesus comes to be perceived by the reader as the Lord whose name everyone who calls upon shall be saved (cf. 2:21). As "everyone" also includes the gentiles, God's faithfulness to Israel also comes to expression through God's gift of salvation and life to everyone in the world who accepts the word of God.

Finally, we have observed God's faithfulness beyond God's promises on at least two occasions in the story-time of Acts: First of all, in our analysis of Acts 13, we argued that God's faithfulness also comes to expression through the continued proclamation to the Jews in spite of rejection. This faithfulness is expressed when Paul and Silas, who upon meeting with mixed responses warn they will turn to the gentiles instead of the Jews, but nevertheless continue to proclaim the word of God in synagogues. While this faithfulness cannot be directly ascribed to any action of God's in the story, it is nevertheless closely connected to the realization of God's promises to Israel: It is through the proclamation that the Jews hear of Jesus, and are promised forgiveness of sins and the gift of the Spirit. Secondly, when God releases the followers of the Way from prison, God's faithfulness comes to expression through God's aid of the Jesus movement.

10.1.2.2 God as Judge

God is portrayed as judge in Acts. Based on the texts we have looked at, we might say that this image of God arises from four different strands: 1. God's judgment in the future, on the Day of the Lord (2:20). 2. God's judgment in the past, both of the nations that Israel serve (7:7), and of Israel's idolatry (7:42). 3. God's ordaining of Jesus as judge of the living and the dead (10:42, cf. 17:31). 4. God's judgment of individuals in the story-time through acts of infliction that cause either blindness or death (1:16–25; 5:1–11; 12:21–23; 9:1–19; 13:4–12). I wish to make one disclaimer, however: Our text selection has not covered events in Acts in which God could be implicitly understood as the judge of *good* deeds and lives.[4] It is therefore possible to consider more aspects of God as judge than what we have done here. In short, however, the selection we have looked at shows us that God's role as a judge is depicted as a constant aspect of God in both the past, present, and future of the story-time.

Because the timeline Peter projects leads to the Day of the Lord, one might say that judgment is on the horizon throughout the entire narrative. Interestingly, in Stephen's speech, we see that even though God is primarily portrayed as Israel's God, God is not only the judge of Israel, but of the nations too (7:7). God is therefore presented as judge of the gentiles in Israel's past too. This feature is further developed as Peter comes to understand God's impartiality to concern a lack of distinction between Jews and righteous gentiles (10:34). "Impartiality" does, as we have seen, originally belong to a judicial context. This may be viewed in light of what happens when the Jews in Jerusalem hear the story of Peter's encounter with Cornelius. They then conclude that the gentiles have received the repentance that leads to life (11:18). If repentance is a condition for God's judgment, then God's impartiality and gift of salvation to the gentiles can also be seen as aspects of God as their judge.

In Israel's past, God is depicted as judge. In the story-time of Acts, however, it is made clear that God has set *Jesus* to be the judge of the living and the dead (10:42). In this way, Jesus's character takes on one of God's functions, which makes it difficult to see, in e.g., the blindings of Elymas and Paul, whether it is Jesus's mediated judgment or God's direct judgment that takes effect. However, while there are other aspects of the characterization of Jesus that blur the distinction between his character and God's in the narrative, Jesus's becoming God's judge is stated clearly as God's own action (10:42, cf. 17:31). Thus, it is clear from whom Jesus gains this authority

---

4. Shauf suggests that, e.g., the raising of Tabitha can be understood as an act of (positive) retribution. See Shauf, *Divine in Acts*, 240–43.

and on whose behalf he acts. In this sense, we may say Jesus acts as God's representative,[5] but that God is the ultimate judge.

What kind of judge is God? In our analyses, we have looked more at God's judgment of ill deeds than reward of good ones, and here we therefore limit ourselves to comments about the former. Even so, the portrayal that emerges is multifaceted. First of all, God's judgment is connected to people's repentance and God's forgiveness throughout the narrative. If people repent and are baptized, their sins will be forgiven. This is what Peter tells those who ask what their course of action should be after having heard his Pentecost speech (2:37–38). The pattern of repentance, often connected with forgiveness (3:19; 8:22; 17:30; 26:20), continues to be proclaimed throughout Acts, and is in 17:31 explicitly connected to judgment. Because forgiveness is depicted as a real possibility, God is portrayed as a forgiving judge.

In the story-time of Acts, God's judgment goes two ways: God is the one who offers *salvation* through God's judgment, as in the case of Paul, and God is the one who deals *death* or *blindness* in judgment, as in the cases of Judas, Ananias, Sapphira, Herod, and Elymas. We have observed that to a large extent, God is concealed as judge by the implied author. Only in the case of Herod is it explicitly an angel of the Lord who strikes the ruler dead, which indicates whence judgment comes. In the cases of Judas, Ananias and Sapphira, God is not mentioned at all; though in the case of Judas, Peter suggests his death is foretold by Scripture, and by implication, part of the plan of God. The lack of mention of God, however, means that it is the characters' deeds that stand out as the causes of the different characters' deaths. The competent reader is nevertheless able to discern God as their judge, not least because of the *topos* of divine retribution in literature from antiquity. Finally, in the case of Paul, his blindness leads to a change in life and perspective as he himself becomes a follower of the Way. In his case, God's judgment seems merciful rather than harsh; a means of salvation rather than retribution.

10.1.2.3 *God as Savior*

To ask how God is depicted as savior, includes asking whom God saves, in what ways God saves, and when God saves. Similar to the image of God as a judge, the portrayal of God as savior is drawn on a timeline that stretches from Israel's past into the future and Day of the Lord. While the story of Acts

---

5. This is not a strange observation in light of the rest of the biblical tradition, cf. eg. 1 Cor 15:24–28 and John 5:22. There are plenty of differences between these texts and Acts, but Jesus is given power of judgment in all of them.

begins with the disciples' question of when the kingdom will be restored *to Israel* (1:6), it is foreshadowed from the start that God's salvation will be for "*everyone* who calls on the name of the Lord" (2:21, my emphasis). Thus, the image of God as savior exists in the tension between "old" expectations of Israel's restoration, and the movement of Acts, which takes the apostles, the Jesus movement, and the reader far beyond the borders of Israel.

That God is savior not only *in* Israel, is particularly emphasized in Stephen's speech. Stephen highlights all of creation as the place of God. In drawing up the history of Israel from the time of Abraham and onwards, he locates God's revelation beyond the borders of the land, implicitly suggesting that God is not bound by the land. When persecution of the Jesus movement in Jerusalem breaks out immediately afterwards, the way to proclamation beyond the city has been theologically prepared through recourse to God's revelations in Israel's past. As the gospel crosses geographical boundaries, the signs, wonders, and deeds of power performed by the apostles depict God's power. In a world where a number of gods is worshipped, the power of the God of Israel is depicted as greater than any of the others'—not only because God is the only god at work in the narrative, but because God does powerful deeds.

That God is not only savior for Israel, but for the gentiles too, is depicted in multiple ways. God as universal savior is foreshadowed by Jesus's words about the spread of the gospel (1:8), and implied by the citation from Joel which states that God's spirit will fall on all flesh (2:17), and that salvation is for everyone who calls upon the name of the Lord (2:21). But in the story-time of Acts, the most explicit affirmation of God as savior to the gentiles takes place first when Paul is commissioned as a "light for the gentiles" (13:47), and then through the descent of the Spirit upon Cornelius and his household (10:44–47). As the gentiles receive the Spirit, it is clear once and for all that God is also savior of all—at least all those who receive the word of God, repent, and are baptized (2:38).

God is not only savior in the narrative present or future. In accounts of Israel's past, God is also depicted as savior. God is Joseph's savior in Egypt (7:9–10), and God saves Israel from Egypt (7:25, 35–36). In contrast to the time after Jesus's ascension, God is never once mentioned as saving a gentile, but God's saving activity is focused around one people.[6] This may, to some degree, be due to the fact that the narrative audience of the speeches largely consists of Jews and god-fearing gentiles.[7] However, it is conspicuous that Paul's mention of God's actions in the past

---

6. Note, however, the widow of Sarephath and Naaman the Syrian in Luke 4:25–27.
7. Narrative audience = audience in the narrative.

when he speaks to the Athenians in 17:22-31 primarily concerns creation (17:24-27). While we have not analyzed this text in the present study, it nevertheless fits the overall picture in Acts: It is only with the descent of the Spirit that God's salvific agency is depicted to cross first ethnic boundaries, and then the geographical boundaries of the land. Thus, even though God is depicted as creator of both Israel and the nations, and this aspect of how God is portrayed does not *change*, there is a tension between how God is *depicted* in the past and the story-time: It is only in the present (and future) that God is depicted as savior of *all*.

God is also depicted as savior through actions in the story-time of Acts. This happens through concrete acts of salvation, which take place through e.g., healing (4:9; 14:9), and rescue from a storm at sea (27:13-44). Thus, the picture drawn of God as savior is not merely colored by future expectations, but from concrete events that demonstrate God's care for both the lives and health of people in the present. God as savior is, perhaps most importantly, also the one who gives life. God may be the judge of the living and the dead, but God is also the savior of the living and the dead: God saves the apostles from prison, resurrects dead members of the church, and most importantly, has proven true to Israel's hope that the dead will be resurrected through the resurrection of Jesus. Thus God the savior is first and foremost the God of life.

10.2 God and Jesus

The change in how God is portrayed in the past compared to the narrative present, happens through a key event in the story-time of Acts: Jesus's ascension. We have seen that in Acts, heaven is the place in which God is located and from which God operates (7:49; 7:55). The interaction of the heavenly with the earthly sphere can be observed in a number of places throughout the narrative: Jesus is taken up into heaven (1:2, 10-11, 22), the appearance of the Spirit at Pentecost is accompanied by a sound from heaven (2:2), Paul sees light flash from heaven (9:3; 22:6; 26:13), and Peter's vision contains a sheet that descends from heaven (10:11-16). Heaven thus signals the intervention of the divine.[8] However, through the ascension, when Jesus and God's characters go from being located in different settings (earth and heaven) to operating from the same place (heaven, 7:56), it becomes more difficult to separate their activity, and hence also their characters.[9] The first example of

---

8. Walton, "'Heavens Opened,'" 62.
9. Henrichs-Tarasenkova, *Luke's Christology*, 190.

this is when Jesus pours out the Spirit on behalf of his father (2:33). As Steve Walton suggests, this has bearings on the portrayal of God:

> In Luke's story, both heaven and earth are transformed through Jesus and by the Spirit. This process of transformation affects even how God is to be seen and understood, for there is now a human being in heaven at God's right hand – and he pours out the Spirit upon God's people to equip them to reclaim creation for its Creator.[10]

Now that heaven is a setting that encompasses both Jesus and God, it is difficult for the reader to "peek in," as it were, and see whose interference is detected on earth. God is, in other words, no longer the only actor behind the scenes, and Jesus and God have become nearly inseparable. Thus, it is ambiguous whether the "theophany" at Pentecost is in fact a revelation of God's presence (if Jesus is the one pouring out the Spirit), and the "christophany" Paul encounters on the road to Damascus resembles a theophany. As Stephen's vision suggests (7:55), to see God's glory in heaven now also involves seeing Jesus as the risen and ascended Lord.

We have also noted that the challenge of distinguishing between God and Jesus's characters is augmented by the fact that both God and Jesus are referred to as ὁ κύριος / κύριος. Sometimes the context makes it clear whom the designation refers to, either because it is directly or contextually linked to either (ὁ) θεός or (ὁ) Ἰησοῦς. For instance, we see the disciples use this term to address Jesus in 1:6, and κύριος appears together with his name in 1:21. In 17:24, on the other hand, Paul speaks of ὁ θεός as κύριος over heaven and earth. A number of times, however, the context is of no help; the referential ambiguity that then arises is part of what I in this study have named the "ambiguous discourse of God" in Acts (see sec. 2.1.1). This ambiguity is present in the disciples' prayer to the "Lord" in 1:24 (see ch. 1, n. 97), and as the narrative continues, the ambiguity is made explicit when both God and Jesus are referred to as κύριος in 2:34 and Jesus is proclaimed God's exalted κύριος in 2:36. From a *christ*ological perspective, this means that Jesus in some ways comes to be characterized as God.[11] From a *theo*logical perspective, this means that Jesus in some ways comes to characterize God. In addition to the ambiguous discourse of God, this "two-way characterization" in which Jesus and God's characters come to characterize each other, is perhaps most clearly expressed through the roles and purpose shared by God and Jesus. Both share the same purpose of salvation (see above and

---

10. Walton, "'Heavens Opened,'" 60.
11. Cf. Henrichs-Tarasenkova, *Luke's Christology*, 172–90.

below). As the savior sent to Israel, Jesus reveals *God* as savior. As the judge appointed by God, Jesus enacts *God's* judgment.

Another feature of the correlation between God and Jesus's characters is expressed through their salvific roles and purpose. The exact nature of salvation is a debated theme in Lukan studies, ranging from a focus on Jesus's atonement on the cross to more holistic understandings of salvation.[12] Few, however, would disagree that in Acts, salvation originates with God, and is available through the ascended Jesus: "God exalted him at his right hand as Leader and Savior that he might give repentance to Israel and forgiveness of sins" (5:31, cf. e.g., 4:12; 15:11). Throughout this book, we have observed that as this happens, Jesus is inscribed into a name-theology of God's name: While Peter declares early on that "everyone who calls on the name of the Lord shall be saved" (2:21), and the reader initially takes this to refer to God, Peter's later statement in 4:12 suggests that it is Jesus's name to which salvation is linked. Salvation is, in other words, insolubly linked to both God *and* Jesus. Perhaps this may, at least partially, explain why Jesus and God are credited with some of the same actions throughout Acts. While it is God in Peter's citation from Joel who pours out the Spirit (2:17–18), in 2:33 Peter says it is Jesus who has poured out the Spirit. In a similar vein, Paul says it was "the God of our ancestors" (22:14) who chose to reveal Jesus to him and be his witness, whereas the narrator says that *Jesus* chose Paul to be a witness to the gentiles in 9:15. The correspondence between these actions blurs the distinction between God and Jesus.

At the same time, there are also numerous actions in Acts, which are credited to God and not Jesus. In our chapter on "The God of Power and Wonder," we particularly noted that whereas Jesus is involved in some acts of infliction, Jesus is not mentioned where the matter is life or death (1:16–20; 5:1–11; 9:36–41; 12:20–23; 20:9–12). Thus God, in contrast to Jesus, is portrayed as the giver of life and death. Closely connected to this is the characterization of God as creator and the one who resurrected Jesus. These actions are God's alone in Acts, not Jesus's. The overlap between actions therefore largely goes one way, in that it is Jesus's actions which are credited to God, or originate with God, and not the other way around. In short, the characterization of God in Acts simultaneously depends both on God's correlation with and distinction from Jesus; it is partially in the tension between these, and the narrative ambiguity that arises from it, that the portrayal of God in Acts emerges. In terms of the portrayal of God, the appearance of Jesus from heaven with God's functions and characteristics means that God's character

---

12. For a survey of the debate, see Reardon, "Lukan Soteriology." See also chapter 9.1.1.

is more strongly mediated, but also further removed from the scene because someone else is now there in God's stead.

10.3 Outlook

In this final section, we suggest some avenues for further research and briefly address one of the conversations this study has only tangentially touched upon. First of all, it must be reemphasized that the portrayal of God which we have presented above is limited by the focus and material of this study. We would maintain that our summary does justice to the main lines of the characterization of God in Acts. At the same time, we also recognize that had our focus on the characterization of God moved beyond actions, the portrayal of God in Acts might, metaphorically speaking, have been painted in more colors. It does, moreover, remain an open question to what extent our discoveries would have been different in content or emphasis had we also considered the characterization of God in the Gospel of Luke. Future research might consider the characterization of God in this Gospel, either in conjunction or comparison with Acts. Such a project would then also face the challenge of looking at how God is characterized in Jesus's parables.

As a narrative study, one of the questions considered in this project has been how the characterization of Jesus post-ascension impacts the characterization of God. The answers I have presented to this above have both christological and theological implications. In order to better illustrate what this study does and does not say, I will briefly present some reflections in conversation with the following citation from Richard Bauckham:

> If Jesus reveals who God is, if God's identity is as God crucified, how does this revelation relate to the identity of the God of Israel? Is this the same God? Is his identity in Jesus consistent with his identity in the Old Testament revelation? Is the revelation of his identity in Jesus only the universal revelation, to the world, of the divine identity already fully known to Israel? Or is his identity more fully known in Jesus?[13]

First, let me say that Bauckham's argument follows from his outlook on New Testament Christology as presented in *God Crucified*. Unlike the present project, it is not limited to one biblical book. Bauckham's concerns are, moreover, based on considerations about the historical development of Christology. Nevertheless, Bauckham's questions in the above come intriguingly close to the ones we have asked in this study. This is the case

---

13. Bauckham, *Jesus and the God of Israel*, 51.

particularly as these questions relate to how the characterization of Jesus influences the characterization of God, and to how the depiction of God as presented in the story-time relates to how God is presented in Israel's past—or, to use Bauckham's words, in the Old Testament revelation. Like Bauckham, we have observed that Jesus reveals who God is: First, through God's actions with Jesus, most notably in raising him from the dead and making him Lord, judge, savior, and Messiah. Secondly, Jesus reveals who God is by mediating God's presence and actions through his active interference in the plot. The outpouring of the Spirit, and his commission of Paul are two examples of this. Thirdly, Jesus reveals who God is by working for the same purpose of salvation.

Based on Acts alone, however, it is difficult to claim that God's identity is properly expressed through the phrase "God crucified." When Jesus's death is described in Acts, it is God's sovereign plan, and later God as the giver of life and exalter of Jesus that are emphasized; not God's identification with Jesus on the cross. Thus, Acts emphasizes Jesus's exaltation rather than his suffering. However, suffering is a pregnant motif in Acts. Jesus believers are persecuted, imprisoned, flogged, and killed. In this way, the experience of these believers reflects the experience of Jesus. In his encounter with Paul, Jesus identifies with the suffering persecuted ("Saul, Saul, why do you persecute me?" 9:4). Whether, or how, this suffering impacts the portrayal of God in Acts, is a conversation that points beyond the scope and limits of this study.

Bauckham's claim about God's identity attempts to find a way "beyond the standard distinction between 'functional' and 'ontic' Christology,"[14] and argues that "the so-called divine functions which Jesus exercises are intrinsic to who God is."[15] I would not argue against the content of this claim; as we have seen, Jesus and God share many of the same functions, and Jesus is identified *with* God. However, our reading distinguishes between God's and Jesus's characters, and maintains the importance of highlighting the dynamics and differences between them. As such, our study has not resulted in the claim that Jesus is identified *as* God.

Bauckham asks about the relation between God's identity as presented in Israel's Scriptures and God as revealed in Jesus. To this, we have offered an answer that highlights the continuity and consistency of God's character. Most importantly, we have noted that God's actions in Acts provoke a reading of Scripture wherein God's faithfulness to God's promises bridges Israel's

---

14. Bauckham, *Jesus and the God of Israel*, x.
15. Bauckham, *Jesus and the God of Israel*, x.

past and present to reveal the constancy of God's character (see 10.1.1).[16] However, Bauckham's subsequent question of whether God is more *fully* known in Jesus cannot be answered on the basis of the present study. To do so would require a study of not only the death and exaltation, but life, of Jesus. What we have claimed, however, is that God according to Acts cannot be known *apart* from Jesus, "for there is no other name under heaven given among mortals by which we must be saved" (4:12).

---

16. Cf. also Bauckham, *Jesus and the God of Israel*, 53.

Bibliography

Aalen, Sverre. "Jesu kristologiske selvbevissthet. Et utkast til 'jahvistisk kristologi.'" In *Guds sønn og Guds rike*, edited by Sverre Aalen, 271–88. Nytestamentlige Studier. Oslo: Universitetsforlaget, 1973.

Abrams, Meyer Howard. *A Glossary of Literary Terms*. 6th ed. New York: Harcourt Brace Jovanovich, 1993.

Adams, Sean A. *The Genre of Acts and Collected Biography*. SNTSMS 156. Cambridge: Cambridge University Press, 2013.

Ådna, Jostein. "James' Position at the Summit Meeting of the Apostles and the Elders." In *The Mission of the Early Church to Jews and Gentiles*, edited by Jostein Ådna and Hans Kvalbein, 125–61. WUNT 127. Tübingen: Mohr/Siebeck, 2000.

Alexander, Loveday C. A. *Acts in its Ancient Literary Context: A Classicist Looks at the Acts of the Apostles*. LNTS 289. London: T. & T. Clark, 2005.

———. "'In Journeyings Often': Voyaging in the Acts of the Apostles and in Greek Romance." In *Acts in its Ancient Literary Context: A Classicist Looks at the Acts of the Apostles*, 69–96. LNTS 289. London: T. & T. Clark, 2005.

———. *The Preface to Luke's Gospel: Literary Convention and Social Context in Luke 1.1–4 and Acts 1.1*. SNTSMS 78. Cambridge: Cambridge University Press, 1993.

Allen, O. Wesley. *The Death of Herod: The Narrative and Theological Function of Retribution in Luke-Acts*. SBLDS 158. Atlanta: Scholars, 1997.

Allison, Dale C. "Acts 9:1–9, 22:6–11, 26:12–18: Paul and Ezekiel." *JBL* 135 (2016) 807–26.

Amit, Yairah. *Reading Biblical Narratives: Literary Criticism and the Hebrew Bible*. Minneapolis: Fortress, 2001.

Amundsen, Darrel W., and Gary B. Ferngren. "The Perception of Disease and Disease Causality in the New Testament." In *ANRW* 37.3:2934–2956. Part 2, *Principat*, 37:3. Edited by Hildegard Temporini and Wolfgang Haase. Berlin: de Gruyter, 1996.

Anderson, Kevin L. *"But God Raised Him from the Dead": The Theology of Jesus' Resurrection in Luke-Acts*. PBM. 2006. Reprint, Eugene, OR: Wipf & Stock, 2007.

Aristotle. *The "Art" of Rhetoric*. Translated by John Henry Freese. LCL. London: Heinemann, 1926.

———. *Poetics*. Translated by Stephen Halliwell. 2nd ed. LCL. Cambridge: Harvard University Press, 1995.

Arnold, Bill T. "Luke's Characterizing Use of the Old Testament in the Book of Acts." In *History, Literature, and Society in the Book of Acts*, edited by Ben Witherington III and Jacob Jervell, 300–323. Cambridge: Cambridge University Press, 1996.

Arterbury, Andrew E. "The Ancient Custom of Hospitality, the Greek Novels, and Acts 10:1–11:18." *PRSt* 29 (2002) 53–72.

Aune, David E. *The New Testament in its Literary Environment*. LEC 8. Cambridge: Clarke & Co., 1987.
Bal, Mieke. *Narratology: Introduction to the Theory of Narrative*. 3rd ed. Toronto: University of Toronto Press, 2009.
Bal, Mieke, and Jane E. Lewin. "The Narrating and the Focalizing: A Theory of the Agents in Narrative." *Style* 17 (1983) 234–69.
Barclay, John M. G., and Simon J. Gathercole, eds. *Divine and Human Agency in Paul and His Cultural Environment*. LNTS 335. London: T. & T. Clark, 2006.
Barreto, Eric D. "A Gospel on the Move: Practice, Proclamation, and Place in Luke-Acts." *Int* 72 (2018) 175–87.
Barrett, C. K. *A Critical and Exegetical Commentary on the Acts of the Apostles: Introduction and Commentary on Acts XV–XXVIII*. Vol 2. ICC. Edinburgh: T. & T. Clark, 1998.
———. *A Critical and Exegetical Commentary on the Acts of the Apostles: Preliminary Introduction and Commentary on Acts I–XIV*. Vol 1. ICC. Edinburgh: T. & T. Clark, 1994.
Bassler, Jouette M. *Divine Impartiality: Paul and a Theological Axiom*. SBLDS 59. Chico, CA: Scholars, 1982.
———. "Luke and Paul on Impartiality." *Bib* 66 (1985) 546–52.
Bauckham, Richard. "James and the Jerusalem Church." In *The Book of Acts in its Palestinian Setting*, edited by Richard Bauckham, 415–80. The Book of Acts in its First Century Setting 4. Grand Rapids: Eerdmans, 1995.
———. *Jesus and the God of Israel: God Crucified and Other Studies on the New Testament's Christology of Divine Identity*. Milton Keynes: Paternoster, 2008.
Bede. *The Venerable Bede: Commentary on the Acts of the Apostles*. Translated by Lawrence T. Martin. Cistercian Studies Series. Kalamazoo, MI: Cistercian, 1989.
Behm, Johannes. "καρδιογνώστης." In *TDNT* 3:613.
Bennema, Cornelis. *A Theory of Character in New Testament Narrative*. Minneapolis: Fortress, 2014.
Bennett, Andrew, and Nicholas Royle. *An Introduction to Literature, Criticism and Theory*. 5th ed. New York: Routledge, 2016.
Berlin, Adele. *Poetics and Interpretation of Biblical Narrative*. BLS. Sheffield: Almond, 1983.
Bertram, Georg. "ὕψιστος." In *TDNT* 8:614–20.
Bibb, C. Wade. "The Characterization of God in the Opening Scenes of Luke and Acts." *Proceedings* 13 (1993) 275–92.
Bietenhard, Hans. "ἄγγελος." In *NIDNTT* 1:101–3.
———. "ὄνομα, ὀνομάζω, ἐπονομάζω, ψευδώνυμος." In *TDNT* 5:242–81.
Bock, Darrell L. *Acts*. BECNT. Grand Rapids: Baker Academic, 2007.
———. *Proclamation from Prophecy and Pattern: Lucan Old Testament Christology*. JSNTSup 12. Sheffield: JSOT, 1987.
Bockmuehl, Markus. "Why Not Let Acts Be Acts? In Conversation with C. Kavin Rowe." *JSNT* 28 (2005) 163–66.
Bonz, Marianne Palmer. *The Past as Legacy: Luke-Acts and Ancient Epic*. Minneapolis: Fortress, 2000.
Bovon, François. "Le Dieu de Luc." *RSR* 69 (1981) 279–300.
———. *Luke the Theologian: Fifty-Five Years of Research (1950–2005)*. Translated by Ken McKinney. 2nd rev. ed. Waco, TX: Baylor University Press, 2006.

Bowker, John. "Merkabah Visions and the Visions of Paul." *JSS* 16 (1971) 157–73.
Brawley, Robert L. *Centering on God: Method and Message in Luke-Acts*. Literary Currents in Biblical Interpretation. Louisville: Westminster John Knox, 1990.
Brox, Norbert, ed. *Irenaeus: Gegen die Heresien III*. Fontes Christiani 8.3. Freiburg, Germany: Herder, 1995.
Bruce, Frederick Fyvie. *The Acts of the Apostles: The Greek Text with Introduction and Commentary*. 3rd ed. Grand Rapids: Eerdmans, 1990.
———. *The Book of the Acts*. NICNT. Rev. ed. Grand Rapids: Eerdmans, 1988.
Buckwalter, Douglas. *The Character and Purpose of Luke's Christology*. SNTSMS 89. Cambridge: Cambridge University Press, 1996.
Burchard, Christoph. "Joseph und Aseneth." In *Unterweisung in erzählender Form*, edited by Werner Georg Kümmel, 579–733. JSHRZ. Vol 2. Lieferung 1–6. Gütersloh, Germany: Gütersloher Verlagshaus, 1999.
Burnett, Fred W. "Characterization and Reader Construction of Characters in the Gospels." *Semeia* 63 (1993) 3–78.
Burridge, Richard A. "The Genre of Acts—Revisited." In *Reading Acts Today: Essays in Honour of Loveday C.A. Alexander*, edited by Steve Walton, 3–28. LNTS 427. London: T. & T. Clark, 2011.
Callan, Terrance. "The Background of the Apostolic Decree (Acts 15:20, 29; 21:25)." *CBQ* 55 (1993) 284–97.
Campbell, William S. "The Narrator as 'He,' 'Me,' and 'We': Grammatical Person in Ancient Histories and in the Acts of the Apostles." *JBL* 129 (2010) 385–407.
———. *We Passages in the Acts of the Apostles: The Narrator as Narrative Character*. StBibLit 14. Atlanta: Society of Biblical Literature, 2007.
Carter, Warren. "Aquatic Display: Navigating the Roman Imperial World in Acts 27." *NTS* 62 (2016) 79–96.
———. *God in the New Testament*. Nashville: Abingdon, 2016.
Charlesworth, James H. "From Messianology to Christology: Problems and Prospects." In *The Messiah: Developments in Earliest Judaism and Christianity*, edited by James H. Charlesworth, 3–35. Minneapolis: Fortress, 1992.
Chatman, Seymour B. *Story and Discourse: Narrative Structure in Fiction and Film*. Ithaca, NY: Cornell University Press, 1980.
Chen, Diane G. *God as Father in Luke-Acts*. Edited by Hemchand Gossai. StBibLit 92. New York: Lang, 2006.
Cheng, Ling. *The Characterisation of God in Acts: The Indirect Portrayal of an Invisible Character*. PBM. Milton Keynes: Paternoster, 2011.
Chester, Andrew. "High Christology—Whence, When and Why?" *Early Christianity* 2 (2011) 22–50.
Cheung, Alex T. M. "A Narrative Analysis of Acts 14:27—15:35: Literary Shaping in Luke's Account of the Jerusalem Council." *WTJ* 55 (1993) 137–54.
Chibici-Revneanu, Nicole. "Ein himmlischer Stehplatz: Die Haltung Jesu in der Stephanusvision (Apg 7.55–56) und ihre Bedeutung." *NTS* 53 (2007) 459–88.
Churchill, Timothy W. R. *Divine Initiative and the Christology of the Damascus Road Encounter*. Eugene, OR: Pickwick, 2010.
Cohen, Shaye J. D. "Crossing the Boundary and Becoming a Jew." *HTR* 82 (1989) 13–33.
Conzelmann, Hans. *Acts of the Apostles: A Commentary on the Acts of the Apostles*. Translated by James Limburg, et al. Hermeneia. Philadelphia: Fortress, 1987.
———. *Die Apostelgeschichte*. Tübingen: Mohr/Siebeck, 1972.

———. *Die Mitte der Zeit.* 7th ed. BHT. Tübingen: Mohr/Siebeck, 1993.

———. *The Theology of St. Luke.* Translated by Geoffrey Buswell. New York: Harper & Row, 1961.

Cosgrove, Charles H. "The Divine Dei in Luke-Acts: Investigations into the Lukan Understanding of God's Providence." *NovT* 26 (1984) 168–90.

Culpepper, R. Alan. *Anatomy of the Fourth Gospel: A Study in Literary Design.* Philadelphia: Fortress, 1983.

Cyril of Jerusalem. *The Works of Saint Cyril of Jerusalem.* Vol 2. Translated by Leo P. McCauley SJ, and Anthony A. Stephenson. FC 64. Washington, DC: Catholic University of America Press, 1970.

Dahl, Nils Alstrup. "The Neglected Factor in New Testament Theology." In *Jesus the Christ: The Historical Origins of Christological Doctrine*, edited by Donald H. Juel, 153–63. Minneapolis: Fortress, 1991.

———. "A People for His Name." *NTS* 4 (1958) 319–27.

Danker, Frederick W. *Benefactor: Epigraphic Study of a Graeco-Roman and New Testament Semantic Field.* St. Louis: Clayton, 1982.

Darr, John A. *Herod the Fox: Audience Criticism and Lukan Characterization.* Sheffield: Sheffield Academic, 1998.

———. *On Character Building: The Reader and the Rhetoric of Characterization in Luke-Acts.* Literary Currents in Biblical Interpretation. Louisville: Westminster John Knox, 1992.

Davies, John G. "Pentecost and Glossolalia." *JTS* 3 (1952) 228–31.

Dennis, John A. "Glory." In *DJG*, 313–15.

deSilva, David A. "Paul's Sermon in Antioch of Pisidia." *BSac* 151 (1994) 32–49.

Dibelius, Martin. "The Speeches in Acts and Ancient Historiography." In *Studies in the Acts of the Apostles,* edited by Heinrich Greeven, translated by Mary Ling, 138–85. Mifflintown, PA: Sigler, 1999.

———. "Style Criticism of the Book of Acts." In *Studies in the Acts of the Apostles,* edited by Heinrich Greeven, translated by Mary Ling, 1–25. Mifflintown, PA: Sigler, 1999.

Dicken, Frank. *Herod as a Composite Character in Luke-Acts.* WUNT II 375. Tübingen: Mohr/Siebeck, 2014.

Dicken, Frank, and Julia A. Snyder, eds. *Characters and Characterization in Luke-Acts.* LNTS 548. London: Bloomsbury T. & T. Clark, 2016.

Donahue, John R. "A Neglected Factor in the Theology of Mark." *JBL* 101 (1982) 563–94.

Dormeyer, Detlev. "Ein plötzlicher Tod als Warnung (Der Betrug des Hananias und der Sapphira).—Apg 5,1–11." In *Kompendium der frühchristlichen Wundererzählungen,* edited by Ruben Zimmermann et. al., 145–57. Band 2: Die Wunder der Apostel. Gütersloh, Germany: Gütersloher Verlagshaus, 2017.

Downs, David J., and Matthew L. Skinner, eds. *The Unrelenting God: God's Action in Scripture. Essays in Honor of Beverly Roberts Gaventa.* Grand Rapids: Eerdmans, 2013.

Dunn, James D. G. *The Acts of the Apostles.* EpC. Peterborough, UK: Epworth, 1996.

———. *Baptism in the Holy Spirit: A Re-Examination of the New Testament Teaching on the Gift of the Spirit in Relation to Pentecostalism Today.* SBT II 15. London: SCM, 1970.

———. "Κυριος in Acts." In *The Christ and the Spirit: Collected Essays of James D.G. Dunn,* 241–53. Grand Rapids: Eerdmans, 1998.

Eco, Umberto. *The Role of the Reader: Explorations in the Semiotics of Texts.* Advances in Semiotics. Bloomington: Indiana University Press, 1994.

Elliott, John H. "Temple Versus Household in Luke-Acts: A Contrast in Social Institutions." *HTS Teologiese Studies* 47 (1991) 88–120.

Eskola, Timo. *Messiah and the Throne: Jewish Merkabah Mysticism and Early Christian Exaltation Discourse.* WUNT II 142. Tübingen: Mohr/Siebeck, 2001.

Falls, Thomas B. *Writings of Justin Martyr: A New Translation.* FC 6. New York: Christian Heritage, 1948.

Filtvedt, Ole Jakob. *The Identity of God's People and the Paradox of Hebrews.* WUNT II 400. Tübingen: Mohr/Siebeck, 2015.

Fitzmyer, Joseph A. *The Acts of the Apostles: A New Translation with Introduction and Commentary.* AB. New York: Doubleday, 1998.

Fletcher-Louis, Crispin H. T. *Luke-Acts: Angels, Christology and Soteriology.* WUNT II 94. Tübingen: Mohr/Siebeck, 1997.

Foakes-Jackson, Frederick John. "Stephen's Speech in Acts." *JBL* 49 (1930) 283–86.

Foerster, Werner, and Georg Fohrer. "σώζω, σωτηρία, σωτήρ, σωτήριος." In *TDNT* 7:965–1024.

Fotis, Jannidis. "Character." In *The Living Handbook of Narratology,* edited by Peter Hühn et al, rev. ed. Hamburg: Hamburg University. http://www.lhn.uni-hamburg.de/article/character.

Freedman, Amelia D. *God as an Absent Character in Biblical Hebrew Narrative: A Literary-Theoretical Study.* StBibLit 82. New York: Lang, 2005.

Freedman, David Noel, ed. *The Anchor Bible Dictionary.* 6 vols. New York: Doubleday, 1992.

Frøvig, Daniel Andreas. *Kommentar til Apostlenes gjerninger.* Oslo: Aschehoug, 1944.

Garrett, Susan R. *The Demise of the Devil: Magic and the Demonic in Luke's Writings.* Minneapolis: Fortress, 1989.

Gaventa, Beverly R. *The Acts of the Apostles.* ANTC. Nashville: Abingdon, 2003.

———. *From Darkness to Light: Aspects of Conversion in the New Testament.* Philadelphia: Fortress, 1986.

Gempf, Conrad. "Mission and Misunderstanding: Paul and Barnabas in Lystra (Acts 14:8–20)." In *Mission and Meaning: Essays Presented to Peter Cotterell,* edited by Antony Billingtone et al., 56–69. Carlile: Paternoster, 1995.

Gen, Raymond M. "The Phenomena of Miracles and Divine Infliction in Luke-Acts: Their Theological Significance." *Pneuma* 11 (1989) 3–19.

Genette, Gérard. *Narrative Discourse: An Essay in Method.* Translated by Jane E. Lewin. Ithaca, NY: Cornell University Press, 1980.

Glenny, W. Edward. "The Septuagint and Apostolic Hermeneutics: Amos 9 in Acts 15." *BBR* 22 (2012) 1–25.

Goldsmith, Dale. "Acts 13:33–37: A Pesher on 2 Samuel 7." *JBL* 87 (1968) 321–24.

Green, Joel B. *Conversion in Luke-Acts: Divine Action, Human Cognition, and the People of God.* Grand Rapids: Baker Academic, 2015.

———. "'God My Savior': The Purpose of God in Luke's Gospel." In *The Theology of the Gospel of Luke,* 22–49. New Testament Theology. Cambridge: Cambridge University Press, 1995.

———. *The Gospel of Luke.* NICNT. Grand Rapids: Eerdmans, 1997.

———. "Healing and Healthcare." In *The World of the New Testament: Cultural, Social, and Historical Contexts*, edited by Joel B. Green and Lee M. McDonald, 330–44. Grand Rapids: Baker Academic, 2013.

———. "'In Our Own Languages': Pentecost, Babel, and the Shaping of Christian Community in Acts 2:1–13." In *The Word Leaps the Gap: Essays on Scripture and Theology in Honor of Richard B. Hays*, edited by J. Ross Wagner et al., 198–213. Grand Rapids: Eerdmans, 2008.

———. "Narrative Criticism." In *Methods for Luke*, edited by Joel B. Green, 74–112. Methods in Biblical Interpretation. Cambridge: Cambridge University Press, 2010.

———. "Salvation to the End of the Earth: God as Savior in the Acts of the Apostles." In *Witness to the Gospel: The Theology of Acts*, edited by I. Howard Marshall and David Peterson, 83–106. Grand Rapids: Eerdmans, 1998.

Gregory, Andrew. *The Reception of Luke and Acts in the Period before Irenaeus: Looking for Luke in the Second Century*. WUNT II 169. Tübingen: Mohr/Siebeck, 2003.

Gregory, Andrew F., and C. Kavin Rowe, eds. *Rethinking the Unity and Reception of Luke and Acts*. Columbia: The University of South Carolina Press, 2010.

Grundmann, Walter. "δύναμαι, δυνατός, δυνατέω, ἀδύνατος, ἀδυνατέω, δύναμις, δυνάστης, δυναμόω, ενδυναμόω." In *TDNT* 2:284–317.

Haenchen, Ernst. *Die Apostelgeschichte*. 13th ed. KEK. Göttingen: Vandenhoeck & Ruprecht, 1961.

———. "The Book of Acts as Source Material for the History of Early Christianity." In *Studies in Luke-Acts: Essays Presented in Honor of Paul Schubert*, edited by Paul Schubert et al., 258–78. Nashville: Abingdon, 1966.

Hamm, Michael Dennis. "Paul's Blindness and its Healing: Clues to Symbolic Intent (Acts 9; 22 and 26)." *Bib* 71 (1990) 63–72.

———. "This Sign of Healing, Acts 3:1–10: A Study in Lucan Theology." PhD diss., Saint Louis University, 1975.

Hannah, Darrell D. *Michael and Christ: Michael Traditions and Angel Christology in Early Christianity*. WUNT II 109. Tübingen: Mohr/Siebeck, 2000.

Hemer, Colin J. "First Person Narrative in Acts 27–28." *TynBul* 36 (1985) 79–109.

Hengel, Martin, and Anna Maria Schwemer. *Paul between Damascus and Antioch: The Unknown Years*. London: SCM, 1997.

Henrichs-Tarasenkova, Nina. *Luke's Christology of Divine Identity*. LNTS 542. London: Bloomsbury, 2016.

Henriksen, Jan–Olav, and Karl Olav Sandnes. *Jesus as Healer: A Gospel for the Body*. Grand Rapids: Eerdmans, 2016.

Herodotus. Translated by Alfred Denis Godley. 4 vols. LCL. London: Heinemann, 1920–1925.

Hesiod. *Theogony*. Translated by Glenn W. Most. LCL. Cambridge: Harvard University Press, 2006.

Hezser, Catherine. "The Torah Versus Homer: Jewish and Greco-Roman Education in Late Roman Palestine." In *Ancient Education and Early Christianity*, edited by Matthew Ryan Hauge and Andrew W. Pitts, 5–24. LNTS 533. London: Bloomsbury T. & T. Clark, 2016.

Hiebert, Theodore. "Theophany in the OT." In *ABD* 6:505–11.

Hiers, Richard H. "Day of the Lord." In *ABD* 2:82–83.

Holladay, Carl R. *Acts: A Commentary*. NTL. Louisville: Westminster John Knox, 2016.

Holmås, Geir Otto. *Prayer and Vindication in Luke-Acts: The Theme of Prayer within the Context of the Legitimating and Edifying Objective of the Lukan Narrative*. LNTS 433. London: T. & T. Clark, 2011.
Horn, Friedrich Wilhelm. "Entsetzen an der Schönen Pforte (Die Heilung des Gelähmten im Tempel)—Apg 3,1–10." In *Kompendium der frühchristlischen Wundererzäuhlungen*, edited by Ruben Zimmermann et al., 134–44. Band 2: Die Wunder der Apostel. Gütersloh, Germany: Gütersloher Verlagshaus, 2017.
———. "Holy Spirit." In *ABD* 3:260–80.
Humphrey, Edith M. "Collision of Modes? Self-Disclosure and the Question of Textual Indeterminacy in Rhetorical and Literary Design—Vision and Determining Argument in Acts 10:1—11:18." *Semeia* 71 (1995) 65–84.
Hur, Ju. *A Dynamic Reading of the Holy Spirit in Luke-Acts*. JSNTSup 211. Sheffield: Sheffield Academic, 2001.
Hurtado, Larry W. *God in New Testament Theology*. Library of Biblical Theology. Nashville: Abingdon, 2010.
———. "God or Jesus? Textual Ambiguity and Textual Variants in Acts of the Apostles." In *Texts and Traditions: Essays in Honour of J. Keith Elliott*, edited by Peter Doble and Jeffrey Kloha, 239–54. Leiden: Brill, 2014.
———. *Lord Jesus Christ: Devotion to Jesus in Earliest Christianity*. Grand Rapids: Eerdmans, 2003.
———. *One God, One Lord: Early Christian Devotion and Ancient Jewish Monotheism*. 3rd ed. London: Bloomsbury T. & T. Clark, 2015.
Jahn, Manfred. "Focalization." In *The Cambridge Companion to Narrative*, edited by David Herman, 94–108. Cambridge Companions to Literature. Cambridge: Cambridge University Press, 2007.
James, Henry. "The Art of Fiction, 1884." In *Henry James: Selected Literary Criticism*, edited by Morris Shapira, 49–57. Harmondsworth, UK: Penguin, 1963.
Jannidis, Fotis. "Character." In *The Living Handbook of Narratology*, edited by Peter Hühn et al. Rev. ed. Hamburg: Hamburg University. http://www.lhn.uni-hamburg.de/article/character.
Jervell, Jacob. *Die Apostelgeschichte*. 17. Aufl. KEK. Göttingen: Vandenhoeck & Ruprecht, 1998.
———. *Luke and the People of God: A New Look at Luke-Acts*. Minneapolis: Augsburg, 1972.
———. *The Theology of the Acts of the Apostles*. New Testament Theology. Cambridge: Cambridge University Press, 1996.
Johnson, Luke Timothy. *The Acts of the Apostles*. SP. Collegeville, MN: Liturgical, 1992.
———. *Prophetic Jesus, Prophetic Church: The Challenge of Luke-Acts to Contemporary Christians*. Grand Rapids: Eerdmans, 2011.
Josephus. *The Jewish Antiquities*. Translated by Henry St. J. Thackaray et al. 10 vols. LCL. Cambridge: Harvard University Press, 1926–1965.
———. *The Jewish War*. Translated by Henry St. J. Thackaray et al. 9 vols. LCL. Cambridge: Harvard University Press, 1926–1965.
Kartzow, Marianne B., and Halvor Moxnes. "Complex Identities: Ethnicity, Gender and Religion in the Story of the Ethiopian Eunuch (Acts 8:26–40)." *R&T* 17 (2010) 184–204.
Kee, Howard Clark. *Miracle in the Early Christian World: A Study in Sociohistorical Method*. New Haven: Yale University Press, 1983.

Keener, Craig S. *Acts: An Exegetical Commentary.* Vol. 2: *3:1—14:28.* Grand Rapids: Baker Academic, 2013.
———. *Acts: An Exegetical Commentary.* Vol. 3: *15:1—23:35.* Grand Rapids: Baker Academic, 2014.
———. *Acts: An Exegetical Commentary.* Vol. 4: *24:1—28:31.* Grand Rapids: Baker Academic, 2015.
Kennedy, George A. *New Testament Interpretation through Rhetorical Criticism.* Chapel Hill: University of North Carolina Press, 1984.
Kent, Benedict H. M. "Curses in Acts: Hearing the Apostles' Words of Judgment Alongside 'Magical' Spell Texts." *JSNT* 39 (2017) 412–40.
Kilgallen, John J. "Acts 13:38–39: Culmination of Paul's Speech in Pisidia." *Bib* 69 (1988) 480–506.
———. "The Function of Stephen's Speech (Acts 7:2–53)." *Bib* 70 (1989) 173–93.
———. "Paul before Agrippa (Acts 26:2–23): Some Considerations." *Bib* 69 (1988) 170–95.
———. *The Stephen Speech: A Literary and Redactional Study of Acts 7,2–53.* AnBib. Rome: Biblical Institute, 1976.
Kim, Ju-Won. "Explicit Quotations from Genesis within the Context of Stephen's Speech in Acts." *Neot* 41 (2007) 341–60.
Kingsbury, Jack Dean. *Matthew as Story.* Philadelphia: Fortress, 1986.
Klauck, Hans-Josef. *Judas—Ein Jünger Des Herrn.* QD 111. Freiburg, Germany: Herder, 1987.
Klein, Ralph W. *1 Samuel.* WBC. Waco, TX: Word, 1983.
Köster, Helmut. "φύσις, φυσικός, φυσικῶς." In *TDNT* 9:251–77.
Kraabel, A. Thomas. "The Disappearance of the 'God-Fearers.'" *Numen* 28 (1981) 113–26.
Krodel, Gerhard. *Acts.* ACNT. Minneapolis: Augsburg, 1986.
Kurz, William S. *Reading Luke-Acts: Dynamics of Biblical Narrative.* Louisville: Westminster John Knox, 1993.
Kucicki, Janusz. *The Function of the Speeches in the Acts of the Apostles: A Key to Interpretation of Luke's Use of Speeches in Acts.* BibInt 158. Leiden: Brill, 2018.
Kümmel, Werner Georg. *Introduction to the New Testament.* Translated by Howard Clark Kee. Rev. ed. Nashville: Abingdon, 1975.
Ladouceur, David J. "Hellenistic Preconceptions of Shipwreck and Pollution as a Context for Acts 27–28." *HTR* 73 (1980) 435–49.
Larsson, Edvin. *Apostlagärningarna 1–12.* Vol. 1. Stockholm: EFS-förlaget, 1983.
———. "Temple-Criticism and the Jewish Heritage: Some Reflexions on Acts 6–7." *NTS* 39 (1993) 379–95.
Lohfink, Gerhard. *Die Himmelfahrt Jesu: Untersuchungen zu den Himmelfahrts- und Erhöhungstexten bei Lukas.* München: Kösel-Verlag, 1971.
Lohse, Eduard. "προσωπολημψία, προσωπολήμπτης, προσωπολημπτέω, ἀπροσωπολήμπτως." In *TDNT* 6:779–80.
Lucian. Translated by Austin Morris Harmon, et al. 8 vols. LCL. Cambridge: Harvard University Press, 1913–1957.
MacDonald, Dennis Ronald. *Does the New Testament Imitate Homer? Four Cases from the Acts of the Apostles.* New Haven: Yale University Press, 2003.
———. "The Shipwrecks of Odysseus and Paul." *NTS* 45 (1999) 88–107.

Maddox, Robert. *The Purpose of Luke-Acts*. Studies of the New Testament and Its World. Göttingen: Vandenhoeck & Ruprecht, 1982.

Margolin, Uri. "Character." In *The Cambridge Companion to Narrative*, edited by David Herman, 66–79. Cambridge Companions to Literature. Cambridge: Cambridge University Press, 2007.

———. "The What, the When, and the How of Being a Character in Literary Narrative." *Style* 24 (1990) 453–68.

Marguerat, Daniel. *The First Christian Historian: Writing the "Acts of the Apostles."* SNTSMS 121. Cambridge: Cambridge University Press, 2002.

———. "Saul's Conversion (Acts 9; 22; 26)." In *Luke's Literary Achievement: Collected Essays*, edited by Christopher M. Tuckett, 179–204. Cambridge: Cambridge University Press, 2002.

Marguerat, Daniel, and Yvan Bourquin. *How to Read Bible Stories: An Introduction to Narrative Criticism*. London: SCM, 1999.

Marshall, I. Howard. *The Acts of the Apostles*. TNTC. Leicester: InterVarsity, 1980.

———. *Luke: Historian and Theologian*. 1st ed. Exeter: Paternoster, 1970.

Martín-Asensio, Gustavo. *Transitivity-Based Foregrounding in the Acts of the Apostles: A Functional-Grammatical Approach to the Lukan Perspective*. SNTG 8. JSNTSup 202. Sheffield: Sheffield Academic, 2000.

Maston, Jason S. "How Wrong Were the Disciples about the Kingdom? Thoughts on Acts 1:6." *ExpTim* 126 (2015) 169–78.

Matthews, Shelly. *Perfect Martyr: The Stoning of Stephen and the Construction of Christian Identity*. New York: Oxford University Press, 2010.

McCabe, David. *How to Kill Things with Words: Ananias and Sapphira under the Prophetic Speech-Act of Divine Judgement (Acts 4.32–5.11)*. LNTS 454. London: T. & T. Clark, 2011.

McConnell, James R., Jr. *The Topos of Divine Testimony in Luke-Acts*. Eugene, OR: Pickwick, 2014.

McWhirter, Jocelyn. *Rejected Prophets: Jesus and His Witnesses in Luke-Acts*. Minneapolis: Fortress, 2013.

Mead, Stephen. "Dressing up Divine Reversal: A Narrative-Critical Reading of the Death of Herod in Acts 12:19." *ResQ* 60 (2018) 227–34.

Meek, James A. *The Gentile Mission in Old Testament Citations in Acts: Text, Hermeneutic, and Purpose*. LNTS 385. London: T. & T. Clark, 2008.

Menzies, Robert P. *Empowered for Witness: The Spirit in Luke-Acts*. T. & T. Clark Academic Paperbacks. London: T. & T. Clark, 2004.

Merenlahti, Petri. *Poetics for the Gospels? Rethinking Narrative Criticism*. SNTW. Edinburgh: T. & T. Clark, 2002.

Metzger, Bruce M. *A Textual Commentary on the Greek New Testament: A Companion Volume to the United Bible Societies' Greek New Testament*. London: United Bible Societies, 1975.

Meyer, Rudolf, et. al. "προφήτης κτλ." In *TDNT* 6:829–61.

Miles, Gary B., and Garry W. Trompf. "Luke and Antiphon: The Theology of Acts 27–28 in the Light of Pagan Beliefs about Divine Retribution, Pollution, and Shipwreck." *HTR* 69 (1976) 259–67.

Miller, Chris A. "Did Peter's Vision in Acts 10 Pertain to Men or the Menu?" *BSac* 159 (2002) 302–17.

Miller, John B. F. *Convinced that God Had Called Us: Dreams, Visions, and the Perception of God's Will in Luke-Acts*. BibInt 85. Leiden: Brill, 2006.

———. "Exploring the Function of Symbolic Dream-Visions in the Literature of Antiquity, with Another Look at 1QapGen 19 and Acts 10." *PRSt* 37 (2010) 441–55.

Moberly, R. Walter L. "Miracles in the Hebrew Bible." In *The Cambridge Companion to Miracles*, edited by Graham H. Twelftree, 57–74. Cambridge Companions to Religion. Cambridge: Cambridge University Press, 2011.

Moessner, David P. "The Appeal and Power of Poetics (Luke 1:1–4)." In *Jesus and the Heritage of Israel: Luke's Narrative Claim Upon Israel's Legacy*, edited by David P. Moessner, 84–123. Vol 1 of *Luke the Interpreter of Israel*. Harrisburg, PA: Trinity, 2000.

———. "'The Christ Must Suffer': New Light on the Jesus–Peter, Stephen, Paul Parallels in Luke-Acts." *NovT* 28 (1986) 220–56.

———. *Lord of the Banquet: The Literary and Theological Significance of the Lukan Travel Narrative*. Harrisburg, PA: Trinity, 1989.

———. "Luke's 'Plan of God' from the Greek Psalter: The Rhetorical Thrust of 'the Prophets and the Psalms' in Peter's Speech at Pentecost." In *Scripture and Traditions: Essays on Early Judaism and Christianity in Honor of Carl R. Holladay*, edited by Patrick Gray and Gail R. O'Day, 223–38. Leiden: Brill, 2008.

Morgan-Wynne, John Eifion. *Paul's Pisidian Antioch Speech (Acts 13)*. Cambridge, UK: Clarke & Co., 2014.

Moule, C. F. D. "The Christology of Acts." In *Studies in Luke-Acts*, edited by Leander E. Keck and J. Louis Martyn, 159–85. Philadelphia: Fortress, 1980.

Mowery, Robert L. "Direct Statements Concerning God's Activity in Luke-Acts." In *Society of Biblical Literature 1990 Seminar Papers*, edited by David J. Lull, 196–211. SBLSP 29. Atlanta: Scholars, 1990.

———. "The Divine Hand and the Divine Plan in the Lukan Passion." In *Society of Biblical Literature 1991 Seminar Papers*, edited by Eugene H. Lovering Jr., 558–75. SBLSP 30. Atlanta: Scholars, 1991.

———. "Lord, God, and Father: Theological Language in Luke-Acts." In *Society of Biblical Literature 1995 Seminar Papers*, edited by Eugene H. Lovering Jr., 82–101. SBLSP 34. Atlanta: Scholars, 1995.

Nägele, Sabine. *Laubhütte Davids und Wolkensohn: Eine auslegungsgeschichtliche Studie zu Amos 9,11 in der jüdischen und christlichen Exegese*. AGJU XXIV. Leiden: Brill, 1995.

Najda, Andrzej Jacek. *Der Apostel als Prophet: Zur prophetischen Dimension des paulinischen Apostolats*. Frankfurt: Lang, 2004.

Navone, John S. J. "'Seeing God' in His Story." In *Seeking God in Story*, edited by John S. J. Navone, 205–8. Collegeville, MN: Liturgical, 1990.

Neagoe, Alexandru. *The Trial of the Gospel: An Apologetic Reading of Luke's Trial Narratives*. SNTSMS 116. Cambridge: Cambridge University Press, 2002.

Neirynck, Frans. "The Miracle Stories in the Acts of the Apostles: An Introduction." In *Les Actes Des Apôtres: Traditions, Rédaction, Théologie*, edited by Jacob Kremer, 169–213. BETL 48. Leuven: Leuven University Press, 1979.

Nestle, Eberhard, et al., eds. *Novum Testamentum Graece*. 28th ed. Stuttgart: Deutsche Bibelgesellschaft, 2012.

Nestle, Wilhelm. *Griechische Studien: Untersuchungen zur Religion, Dichtung und Philosophie der Griechen.* Stuttgart: Hannsmann, 1948.

Neudorfer, Heinz-Werner. "The Speech of Stephen." In *Witness to the Gospel: The Theology of Acts,* edited by I. Howard Marshall and David Peterson, 275–94. Grand Rapids: Eerdmans, 1998.

Oliver, Isaac W. "Simon Peter Meets Simon the Tanner: The Ritual Insignificance of Tanning in Ancient Judaism." *NTS* 59 (2013) 50–60.

O'Reilly, Leo. *Word and Sign in the Acts of the Apostles: A Study in Lucan Theology.* AnGr 243. Rome: Pontificia Universita Gregoriana, 1987.

Origen. *Contra Celsum.* Edited and translated by Henry Chadwick. Repr. with corr. ed. Cambridge: Cambridge University Press, 1965.

O'Toole, Robert F. "Acts 2:30 and the Davidic Covenant of Pentecost." *JBL* 102 (1983) 245–58.

Pao, David W. *Acts and the Isaianic New Exodus.* WUNT II 130. Tübingen: Mohr/Siebeck, 2000.

Park, Sejin. *Pentecost and Sinai: The Festival of Weeks as a Celebration of the Sinai Event.* LHBOTS 342. London: T. & T. Clark, 2008.

Parsons, Mikeal C. *Acts.* Paideia Commentaries on the New Testament. Grand Rapids: Baker Academic, 2008.

Penner, Todd C. *In Praise of Christian Origins: Stephen and the Hellenists in Lukan Apologetic Historiography.* ESEC 10. New York: T. & T. Clark, 2004.

Pervo, Richard I. *Acts: A Commentary.* Hermeneia. Minneapolis: Fortress, 2009.

———. *Profit with Delight: The Literary Genre of the Acts of the Apostles.* Philadelphia: Fortress, 1987.

Pesch, Rudolf. *Die Apostelgeschichte (Apg 1–12).* Vol. 1. EKKNT 5. Zürich: Benziger, 1986.

———. *Die Apostelgeschichte (Apg. 13–28).* Vol 2. EKKNT 5. Zürich: Benziger, 1986.

Peterson, David. "The Motif of Fulfilment and the Purpose of Luke-Acts." In *The Book of Acts in its Ancient Literary Setting,* edited by Bruce W. Winter and Andrew D. Clarke, 83–104. The Book of Acts in its First Century Setting 1. Grand Rapids: Eerdmans, 1993.

Petridou, Georgia. *Divine Epiphany in Greek Literature and Culture.* Oxford: Oxford University Press, 2016.

Phelan, James. "Narrative Theory, 1966–2006: A Narrative." In *The Nature of Narrative,* edited by Robert Scholes et al., 283–336. 40th anniversary rev. ed. Oxford: Oxford University Press, 2006.

Phillips, Thomas E. "The Genre of Acts: Moving toward a Consensus?" *CurBR* 4 (2006) 365–96.

Philo. Translated by George Herbert Whitaker, et al. 10 vols. LCL. Cambridge: Harvard University Press, 1929–1962.

Pietersma, Albert, and Benjamin G. Wright, eds. *A New English Translation of the Septuagint.* Oxford: Oxford University Press, 2007.

Plümacher, Eckhard. "Wirklichkeitserfahrung und Geschichtsschreibung bei Lukas. Erwägungen zu den Wir-Stücken der Apostelgeschichte." *ZNW* 68 (1977) 2–22.

Plutarch. *Plutarch's Lives.* Translated by Bernadotte Perrin. 11 vols. LCL. London: Heinemann, 1914–1926.

Plymale, Steven F. *The Prayer Texts of Luke-Acts.* AmUSt.TR 118. New York: Lang, 1991.

Porter, Stanley E. "Scripture Justifies Mission: The Use of the Old Testament in Luke-Acts." In *Hearing the Old Testament in the New Testament*, edited by Stanley E. Porter, 104-26. MNTS 8. Grand Rapids: Eerdmans, 2006.
Powell, Mark Allan. "Narrative Criticism." In *Hearing the New Testament: Strategies for Interpretation*, edited by Joel B. Green, 240-58. Grand Rapids: Eerdmans, 2010.
———. "Narrative Criticism: The Emergence of a Prominent Reading Strategy." In *Mark as Story: Retrospect and Prospect*, edited by Kelly R. Iverson and Christopher W. Skinner, 19-43. SBLRBS 65. Atlanta: Society of Biblical Literature, 2011.
———. "Salvation in Luke-Acts." *WW* 12 (1992) 5-10.
———. *What Are They Saying about Acts?* New York: Paulist, 1991.
———. *What is Narrative Criticism? A New Approach to the Bible*. London: SPCK, 1993.
Praeder, Susan Marie. "Acts 27:1—28:16: Sea Voyages in Ancient Literature and the Theology of Luke-Acts." *CBQ* 46 (1984) 683-706.
———. "The Problem of First Person Narration in Acts." *NovT* 29 (1987) 193-218.
Radl, Walter. *Paulus und Jesus im Lukanischen Doppelwerk: Untersuchungen zu Parallelmotiven im Lukasevangelium und in der Apostelgeschichte*. Europäische Hochschulschriften, Theologie 49. Frankfurt: Lang, 1975.
Rahlfs, Alfred, ed. *Septuaginta*. 8th ed. 2 vols. Stuttgart: Württembergische Bibelanstalt, 1965.
Reardon, Timothy W. "Cleansing through Almsgiving in Luke-Acts: Purity, Cornelius, and the Translation of Acts 15:9." *CBQ* 78 (2016) 463-82.
———. "Recent Trajectories and Themes in Lukan Soteriology." *CurBR* 12 (2013) 77-95.
Reimer, Andy M. *Miracle and Magic: A Study in the Acts of the Apostles and the Life of Apollonius of Tyana*. JSNTSup 235. London: Sheffield Academic, 2002.
Rhoads, David. *Reading Mark: Engaging the Gospel*. Minneapolis: Fortress, 2004.
Rhoads, David, and Donald Michie. *Mark as Story: An Introduction to the Narrative of a Gospel*. Philadelphia: Fortress, 1982.
Rimmon-Kenan, Shlomith. *Narrative Fiction: Contemporary Poetics*. 2nd ed. New Accents. London: Routledge, 2002.
Robbins, Vernon K. "By Land and Sea: The We-Passages and Ancient Sea Voyages." In *Perspectives on Luke-Acts*, edited by Charles H. Talbert, 215-42. PRSt. Edinburgh: T. & T. Clark, 1978.
———. *Jesus the Teacher: A Socio-Rhetorical Interpretation of Mark*. Philadelphia: Fortress, 1984.
———. "The Social Location of the Implied Author." In *The Social World of Luke-Acts: Models for Interpretation*, edited by Jerome H. Neyrey, 305-32. Peabody, MA: Hendrickson, 1991.
Roloff, Jürgen. *Die Apostelgeschichte*. NTD 5. Göttingen: Vandenhoeck & Ruprecht, 1981.
Røsæg, Nils Aksel. "The Blinding of Paul: Observations to a Theme." *SEÅ* 71 (2006) 159-85.
Rosner, Brian S. "Acts and Biblical History." In *The Book of Acts in Its Ancient Literary Setting*, edited by Bruce W. Winter and Andrew D. Clarke, 65-82. The Book of Acts in its First Century Setting 1. Grand Rapids: Eerdmans, 1993.
Rowe, C. Kavin. *Early Narrative Christology: The Lord in the Gospel of Luke*. BZNW 139. Berlin: de Gruyter, 2006.

———. "History, Hermeneutics and the Unity of Luke-Acts." *JSNT* 28 (2005) 131–57.
———. "Literary Unity and Reception History: Reading Luke-Acts as Luke and Acts." *JSNT* 29 (2007) 449–57.
Russell, Donald A. "On Reading Plutarch's Lives." *Greece and Rome* 13 (1976) 139–54.
Rydryck, Michael. "Miracles of Judgment in Luke-Acts." In *Miracles Revisited: New Testament Miracle Stories and Their Concepts of Reality*, edited by Stefan Alkier and Annette Weissenrieder, 23–32. SBR 2. Berlin: de Gruyter, 2013.
Sanders, Jack T. *The Jews in Luke-Acts*. Philadelphia: Fortress, 1987.
Sandnes, Karl Olav. "Beyond 'Love Language': A Critical Examination of Krister Stendahl's Exegesis of Acts 4:12." *ST* 52 (1998) 43–56.
———. *The Challenge of Homer: School, Pagan Poets and Early Christianity*. LNTS 400. London: T. & T. Clark, 2009.
———. "Omvendelse og gjestevennskap." In *Ad Acta: Studier til Apostlenes gjerninger og urkristendommens historie: Tilegnet professor Edvin Larsson på 70-årsdagen*, edited by Hans Kvalbein and Reidar Hvalvik, 325–46. Oslo: Verbum, 1994.
Savelle, Charles H. "A Reexamination of the Prohibitions in Acts 15." *BSac* 161 (2004) 449–68.
Savran, George W. *Encountering the Divine: Theophany in Biblical Narrative*. JSOTSup 420. London: T. & T. Clark, 2005.
———. "Theophany as Type Scene." *Proof* 23 (2003) 119–49.
Schmidt, Werner H. *The Faith of the Old Testament: A History*. Alttestamentlicher Glaube in seiner Geschichte. Oxford: Blackwell, 1983.
Schneider, Gerhard. *Die Apostelgeschichte: Einleitung: Kommentar zu Kap. 1,1—8,40*. Vol 1. HThKNT. Freiburg: Herder, 1980.
———. *Die Apostelgeschichte: Kommentar zu Kap. 9,1—28,31*. Vol 2. HThKNT. Freiburg: Herder, 1982.
———. "Gott und Christus als Κυριος nach der Apostelgeschichte." In *Begegnung mit dem Wort: Festschrift für Heinrich Zimmermann*, edited by Josef Zmijewski and Ernst Nellessen, 161–74. Bonn: Hanstein, 1980.
Segal, Alan F. *Paul the Convert: The Apostolate and Apostasy of Saul the Pharisee*. New Haven: Yale University Press, 1990.
Shauf, Scott. *The Divine in Acts and in Ancient Historiography*. Minneapolis: Fortress, 2015.
Shepherd, William H. *The Narrative Function of the Holy Spirit as a Character in Luke-Acts*. SBLDS 147. Atlanta: Scholars, 1994.
Skinner, Matthew L. *Intrusive God, Disruptive Gospel: Encountering the Divine in the Book of Acts*. Grand Rapids: Brazos, 2015.
———. *Locating Paul: Places of Custody as Narrative Settings in Acts 21–28*. AcBib 13. Atlanta: Society of Biblical Literature, 2003.
Sleeman, Matthew. *Geography and the Ascension Narrative in Acts*. SNTSMS 146. Cambridge: Cambridge University Press, 2009.
Smith, C. Drew. "The Theology of the Gospel of Mark: A Literary-Theological Investigation into the Presentation of God in the Second Gospel." PhD diss., University of Edinburgh, 2003.
Smith, Steve. *The Fate of the Jerusalem Temple in Luke-Acts: An Intertextual Approach to Jesus' Laments over Jerusalem and Stephen's Speech*. LNTS 553. London: Bloomsbury, 2017.

Soards, Marion L. *The Speeches in Acts: Their Content, Context, and Concerns.* Louisville: Westminster John Knox, 1994.

Spencer, F. Scott. *Journeying through Acts: A Literary-Cultural Reading.* Grand Rapids: Baker Academic, 2004.

———. "Scared to Death: The Rhetoric of Fear in the 'Tragedy' of Ananias and Sapphira." In *Reading Acts Today: Essays in Honour of Loveday C. A. Alexander,* edited by Steve Walton et al., 63–80. LNTS 427. London: T. & T. Clark, 2011.

Speyer, Wolfgang. "Gottesfeind." *RAC* 11 (1989) 996–1043.

Squires, John T. *The Plan of God in Luke-Acts.* SNTSMS 76. Cambridge: Cambridge University Press, 1993.

Stanton, Graham N. *Jesus of Nazareth in New Testament Preaching.* SNTSMS 27. New York: Cambridge University Press, 1974.

Steck, Odil Hannes. *Israel und das gewaltsame Geschick der Propheten: Untersuchungen zur Überlieferung des deuteronomistischen Geschichtsbildes im Alten Testament, Spätjudentum und Urchristentum.* WUANT 23. Neukirchen-Vluyn: Neukirchener, 1967.

Stendahl, Krister. *Paul among Jews and Gentiles and Other Essays.* Philadelphia: Fortress, 1976.

Sterling, Gregory E. *Historiography and Self-Definition: Josephos, Luke-Acts and Apologetic Historiography.* NovTSup 64. Leiden: Brill, 1992.

Strelan, Rick. *Strange Acts: Studies in the Cultural World of the Acts of the Apostles.* BZNW 126. Berlin: de Gruyter, 2004.

Sweeney, James P. "Stephen's Speech (Acts 7:2–53): Is it as 'Anti-Temple' as is Frequently Alleged?" *TJ* 23 (2002) 185–210.

Sylva, Dennis D. "The Meaning and Function of Acts 7:46–50." *JBL* 106 (1987) 261–75.

Talbert, Charles H. *Literary Patterns, Theological Themes, and the Genre of Luke-Acts.* SBLMS 20. Atlanta: Society of Biblical Literature, 1975.

———. *Reading Acts: A Literary and Theological Commentary on the Acts of the Apostles.* Rev. ed. Reading the New Testament. Macon, GA: Smyth & Helwys, 2005.

Talbert, Charles H., and John H. Hayes. "A Theology of Sea Storms in Luke-Acts." In *Jesus and the Heritage of Israel: Luke's Narrative Claim Upon Israel's Legacy,* edited by David P. Moessner, 267–83. Luke the Interpreter of Israel 1. Harrisburg, PA: Trinity, 1999.

Talbert, Charles H., and Perry L. Stepp. "Succession in Mediterranean Antiquity, Part 2: Luke-Acts." In *Society of Biblical Literature 1998 Seminar Papers,* edited by Mary E. Shields et al., 169–79. SBLSP 37. Atlanta: Scholars, 1998.

Tannehill, Robert C. *The Narrative Unity of Luke-Acts—A Literary Interpretation: Volume 1: The Gospel According to Luke.* Minneapolis: Fortress, 1986.

———. *The Narrative Unity of Luke-Acts—A Literary Interpretation: Volume 2: The Acts of the Apostles.* Minneapolis: Fortress, 1990.

———. "Israel in Luke-Acts: A Tragic Story." *JBL* 104 (1985) 69–85.

Tanner, J. Paul. "James's Quotation of Amos 9 to Settle the Jerusalem Council Debate in Acts 15." *JETS* 55 (2012) 65–85.

Thomas, John Christopher. "The Acts of the Apostles." In *The Devil, Disease and Deliverance: Origins of Illness in New Testament Thought,* 229–95. JPTSup 13. Sheffield: Sheffield Academic, 1998.

Thompson, Alan J. *The Acts of the Risen Lord Jesus: Luke's Account of God's Unfolding Plan.* NSBT 27. Downers Grove, IL: InterVarsity, 2011.

Thompson, Marianne Meye. *The God of the Gospel of John.* Grand Rapids: Eerdmans, 2001.

———. "'God's Voice You Have Never Heard, God's Form You Have Never Seen': The Characterization of God in the Gospel of John." *Semeia* 63 (1993) 177–204.

Thompson, Richard P. *Keeping the Church in its Place: The Church as Narrative Character in the Book of Acts.* New York: T. & T. Clark, 2006.

Thucydides. *History of the Peloponnesian War.* Translated by Charles Forster Smith. 4 vols. LCL. London: Heinemann, 1919–1923.

Tiede, David L. "'Glory to Thy People Israel': Luke-Acts and the Jews." In *Luke-Acts and the Jewish People: Eight Critical Perspectives*, edited by Joseph B. Tyson, 21–34. Minneapolis: Augsburg, 1988.

Treier, Daniel J. "The Fulfillment of Joel 2:28–32: A Multiple-Lens Approach." *JETS* 40 (1997) 13–26.

Trites, Allison A. *The New Testament Concept of Witness.* SNTSMS 31. Cambridge: Cambridge University Press, 1977.

Troftgruben, Troy M. *A Conclusion Unhindered: A Study of the Ending of Acts within its Literary Environment.* WUNT II 280. Tübingen: Mohr/Siebeck, 2010.

Turner, Max M. B. *Power from on High: The Spirit in Israel's Restoration and Witness in Luke-Acts.* JPTSup 9. 2000. Reprint, Eugene, OR: Wipf & Stock, 2015.

———. "The Spirit of Christ and Christology." In *Christ the Lord: Studies in Christology Presented to Donald Guthrie*, edited by Harold H. Rowdon, 168–90. Leicester: InterVarsity, 1982.

———. "The Spirit of Christ and 'Divine' Christology." In *Jesus of Nazareth: Lord and Christ. Essays on the Historical Jesus and New Testament Christology*, edited by Joel B. Green and Max M. B. Turner, 413–36. Grand Rapids: Eerdmans, 1994.

Twelftree, Graham H. *In the Name of Jesus: Exorcism among Early Christians.* Grand Rapids: Baker Academic, 2007.

———. "Introduction: Miracle in an Age of Diversity." In *The Cambridge Companion to Miracles*, edited by Graham H. Twelftree, 1–15. Cambridge Companions to Religion. Cambridge: Cambridge University Press, 2011.

Tyson, Joseph B. "The Implied Reader in Luke-Acts." In *Images of Judaism in Luke-Acts*, 19–41. Columbia: University of South Carolina Press, 1992.

———. "The Problem of Jewish Rejection in Acts." In *Luke-Acts and the Jewish People: Eight Critical Perspectives*, edited by Joseph B. Tyson, 21–34. Minneapolis: Augsburg, 1988.

van der Horst, Pieter W. "Hellenistic Parallels to the Acts of the Apostles 1:1–26." *ZNW* 74 (1983) 17–26.

van de Sandt, Hubertus Waltherus Maria. "The Quotations in Acts 13:32–52 as a Reflection of Luke's LXX Interpretation." *Bib* 75 (1994) 26–58.

Verheyden, Jozef. "The Unity of Luke-Acts. What are We Up To?" In *The Unity of Luke-Acts*, edited by Jozef Verheyden, 3–56. BETL 142. Leuven: Leuven University Press, 1999.

Via, E. Jane. "An Interpretation of Acts 7:35–37 from the Perspective of Major Themes in Luke-Acts." *PRSt* 6 (1979) 190–207.

Wahlen, Clinton L. "Peter's Vision and Conflicting Definitions of Purity." *NTS* 51 (2005) 505–18.

Walton, Steve. "The Acts — of God? What is the 'Acts of the Apostles' All about?" *EvQ* 80 (2008) 291–306.

———. "'The Heavens Opened': Cosmological and Theological Transformation in Luke-Acts." In *Cosmology and New Testament Theology*, edited by Jonathan T. Pennington and Sean M. McDonough, 60–73. LNTS 355. London: T. & T. Clark, 2008.

———. "A Tale of Two Perspectives? The Temple in Acts." In *Heaven on Earth: The Temple in Biblical Theology*, edited by T. Desmond Alexander and Simon J. Gathercole, 135–49. Carlile: Paternoster, 2004.

Warrington, Keith. "Acts and the Healing Narratives: Why?" *JPT* 14 (2006) 189–217.

Watt, Ian. "Realism and the Novel." In *Approaches to the Novel: Materials for a Poetics*, edited by Robert Scholes. San Francisco: Chandler, 1961.

Weaver, John B. *Plots of Epiphany: Prison-Escape in Acts of the Apostles*. BZNW 131. Berlin: de Gruyter, 2004.

Weinsheimer, Joel. "Theory of Character: Emma." *Poetics Today* 1 (1979) 185–211.

Wikenhauser, Alfred. "Doppelträume." *Bib* 29 (1948) 100–11.

Wilson, Benjamin R. "Jew-Gentile Relations and the Geographic Movement of Acts 10:1—11:18." *CBQ* 80 (2018) 81–96.

Wilson, Brittany E. "The Blinding of Paul and the Power of God: Masculinity, Sight, and Self-Control." *JBL* 133 (2014) 367–87.

———. "Hearing the Word and Seeing the Light: Voice and Vision in Acts." *JSNT* 38 (2016) 456–81.

———. *Unmanly Men: Refigurations of Masculinity in Luke-Acts*. Oxford: Oxford University Press, 2015.

Wilson, Stephen G. *The Gentiles and the Gentile Mission in Luke-Acts*. SNTSMS 23. Cambridge: Cambridge University Press, 1973.

Witherington III, Ben. *The Acts of the Apostles: A Socio-Rhetorical Commentary*. Grand Rapids: Eerdmans, 1997.

———. *New Testament Rhetoric: An Introductory Guide to the Art of Persuasion in and of the New Testament*. Eugene, OR: Cascade, 2009.

———. "Salvation and Health in Christian Antiquity: The Soteriology of Luke-Acts in its First Century Setting." In *Witness to the Gospel: The Theology of Acts*, edited by I. Howard Marshall and David Peterson, 145–66. Grand Rapids: Eerdmans, 1998.

Witherup, Ronald D. "Cornelius Over and Over and Over Again: 'Functional Redundancy' in the Acts of the Apostles." *JSNT* 15 (1993) 45–66.

Woods, David B. "Interpreting Peter's Vision in Acts 10:9–16." *Conspectus* 13 (2012) 171–214.

Zehnle, Richard F. *Peter's Pentecost Discourse: Tradition and Lukan Reinterpretation in Peter's Speeches of Acts 2 and 3*. SBLMS 15. Nashville: Abingdon, 1971.

Zwiep, Arie W. *Judas and the Choice of Matthias*. WUNT II 187. Tübingen: Mohr/Siebeck, 2004.

Author Index

Aalen, Sverre, 126–27
Abrams, Meyer Howard, 62
Alexander, Loveday C. A., 42, 202
Allen, O. Wesley, 220, 223, 225
Allison, Dale C., 136n66
Amundsen, Darrel W., and Gary B. Ferngren, 224–25
Anderson, Kevin L., 181–82
Aristotle, 62
Arterbury, Andrew E., 157n51

Bal, Mieke, 64
Barclay, John M. G., 151–52n33
Barrett, C. K., 89n73, 100–101
Bassler, Jouette M., 154
Bauckham, Richard, 48n77, 168, 241–43
Berlin, Adele, 60n128
Bibb, C. Wade, 84
Bietenhard, 103, 217
Bourquin, Yvan, 61n130, 63n139
Bovon, François, 5
Bowker, John, 129n39
Bennema, Cornelis, 25, 45n69, 66
Bock, Darrell L., 76n25, 81
Bockmuehl, Markus, 37n41
Bonz, Marianne Palmer, 39
Brawley, Robert L., 2, 6–7, 53n91
Bruce, Frederick Fyvie, 107, 178n8, 183n33, 195n11
Buckwalter, Douglas, 115n88
Burnett, Fred W., 19n93, 58, 59n126
Burridge, Richard A., 7

Chen, Diane G., 14, 15, 88n70, 178, 186n38
Cheng, Ling, 4, 14, 16, 17, 84–85n60, 107n47, 134n59
Cheung, Alex T. M., 161n70, 162

Chester, Andrew, 47
Chibici-Revneanu, Nicole, 115n89
Churchill, Timothy W. R., 121n4,, 129n39, 134n58
Cohen, Shaye J. D., 145n10
Conzelmann, Hans, 8, 9n38, 132n52, 213–14
Cosgrove, Charles H., 9, 10, 11–12, 163

Dahl, Nils Alstrup, 4, 6, 8, 19, 167
Darr, John A. 25n7, 33, 44, 65
Dennis, John A., 114
Dibelius, Martin, 95n4, 194n5
Dormeyer, Detlev, 222n71
Dunn, James D. G., 90, 114n82, 77n32, 145, 148n21, 157, 171, 182–83n26, 195n11

Eco, Umberto, 33
Elliott, J. H., 116–17n93, 133–34

Filtvedt, Ole Jakob, 34n32
Fitzmyer, Joseph A., 111n67, 182n26, 185, 198n95
Fletcher-Louis, Crispin H. T., 97n11
Foakes-Jackson, Frederick John, 95n6

Gathercole, Simon J., 151–52n33
Garrett, Susan R., 211n28, 226
Gaventa, Beverly R., 12, 82, 97n11, 105, 136, 137, 157n51, 162, 165n80, 168, 177, 183, 184, 196, 201, 226
Gempf, Conrad, 212n30
Gen, Raymond M., 220n62
Genette, Gérard, 64
Goldsmith, 182n25
Green, Joel B., 11–12, 14, 26, 77, 139n81, 144n3, 211, 214, 216

Gregory, Andrew, 35n35
Grundmann, Walter, 211n27

Haenchen, Ernst, 95n4, 120n2, 151, 186
Hamm, Michael Dennis, 123–24, 137, 215
Hannah, Darrell D., 217n53
Hayes, John H., 195
Henrichs-Tarasenkova, Nina, 24n1
Henriksen, Jan-Olav, 210
Hezser, Catherine, 43n64
Holladay Carl R., 132, 155
Holmås, Geir Otto, 147, 159
Humphrey, Edith M., 144–45
Hur, Ju, 54, 56, 159
Hurtado, Larry W., 48n77, 128n37

Jahn, Manfred, 64
James, Henry, 62
Jannidis, Fotis, 58
Jervell, Jacob, 128n36, 166
Johnson, Luke Timothy, 103, 146

Kartzow, Marianne B., 120n2
Kee, Howard Clark, 207n10
Keener, Craig S., 120n2, 145, 156, 159, 168n93, 169, 187, 197, 199, 201
Kennedy, George A., 176n1
Kilgallen, John J., 107n47n48
Kraabel, A. Thomas, 145n10
Krodel, Gerhard, 77n32, 89, 196n14
Kucicki, Janusz, 91n78
Kümmel, Werner Georg, 194n5

Ladouceur, David J., 202n35
Larsson, Edvin, 95n7
Lohfink, Gerhard, 52n88

McCabe, David R., 220–21, 223–24
MacDonald, Dennis R., 39n47, 195–96
Maddox, Robert, 188, 186n42
Margolin, Uri, 57, 59
Marguerat, Daniel L., 2–3, 27, 28, 29, 40, 138–39, 61n130, 63n139
Marshall, I. Howard, 8, 9, 213
Martín-Asensio, Gustavo, 87n65
Maston, Jason, 50n81
Matthews, Shelly, 113

Meek, James A., 187
Menzies, Robert P., 74–75, 157–58
Merenlahti, Petri, 25n7
Meyer, Rudolf, 96n9
Miller, Chris A., 145n7, 148–50
Moberly, R. Walter, 82
Moessner, David P., 41n57, 209n16
Morgan-Wynne, John Eifion, 191n59
Moule, C. F. D., 129n41
Mowery, Robert L., 5, 6, 8
Moxnes, Halvor, 120n2

Neirynck, Frans, 209n17

Pao, David W., 189–90n57
Park, Sejin, 76
Parsons, Mikeal A., 25, 72, 98n12, 112–13n61, 180n17
Penner, Todd C., 25n9, 41, 107–8, 114
Pervo, Richard I., 76–77, 135, 171, 195
Pesch, Rudolf, 117n94
Peterson, David, 13n65
Plymale, Steven F. 147n16
Porter, Stanley E., 79n37
Powell, Mark A., 32, 58, 60, 61n30, 75, 114, 214
Praeder, Susan Marie, 200

Reardon, Timothy W., 158n60, 213–14n38, 214
Reimer, Andy M., 210n20
Rimmon-Kenan, Shlomith, 58
Roloff, Jürgen, 116n91
Rowe, C. Kavin, 35n35, 37n41
Rydryck, Michael, 212, 220

Segal, Alan F., 139n81
Skinner, Matthew L., 14–15n67, 86, 155n48, 219
Sanders, Jack T., 186n40
Sandnes, Karl Olav, 126, 157n51, 210, 211
Savelle, Charles H., 171n111
Savran, George W., 121–22
Schneider, Gerhard, 100–101, 198n22
Shauf, Scott, 14, 17–18, 63, 99n16, 159, 232
Shepherd, William H., 53n92, 54, 56

AUTHOR INDEX

Sleeman, Matthew, 24, 52n86, 89n72, 123
Soards, Marion L., 167
Schmidt, Werner H., 72
Smith, Steve, 115–16n90
Spencer, F. Scott, 100, 133n55, 147, 223
Stendahl, Krister, 139n81
Strelan, Rick, 212
Squires, John T., 12, 13, 181
Steck, Odil Hannes, 105
Sweeney, James P., 108–9

Talbert, Charles H., 20–21n96, 38n43, 39n44, 115, 136, 195
Tannehill, Robert C., 10, 11, 12, 24–25, 94, 131n46, 132, 150, 160, 165n80, 171, 185, 187, 198
Tanner, J. Paul 169
Thompson, Alan J., 50, 71–72n4
Thompson, Marianne Meye, 59
Thompson, Richard P., 57
Tiede, David L., 187–89
Treier, Daniel J., 91
Troftgruben, Troy M., 188n55

Turner, Max M. B., 66, 74–75, 157–58
Twelftree, Graham H., 204n2
Tyson, Joseph B., 166, 188

Van de Sandt, Hubertus Waltherus Maria, 185n37
Verheyden, Joseph, 37n41
Via, E. Jane, 104n36

Walton, Steve, 7, 112, 239
Warrington, Keith, 211
Weaver, John B., 217n53, 218
Weinsheimer, Joel, 58, 59
Wilson, Benjamin R., 145n8
Wilson, Brittany E., 31, 103, 124
Wilson, Stephen G., 153n38
Witherington III, Ben, 95n4,5, 97, 105, 170n103, 176n1, 176n2, 195n11, 199, 214n43, 216n50
Witherup, Ronald D., 152n35

Zwiep, Arie W., 220

Ådna, Jostein, 169n101

Subject Index

Abraham, 95, 96, 98–102, 106, 111, 118, 233–34, 237
acts of restoration. *See* signs
acts of infliction. *See* signs
Ananias, 220, 222–24, 236
angel: 11, 27, 44, 46n70, 61, 69, 97, 99, 102–3, 115, 130, 144–49, 151, 172, 196–97, 202, 204–6, 217–25, 231–32, 236; of the Lord, 99, 103, 130, 146, 196, 206, 217, 218, 224
angelophany, 20, 102
apostolic council, 68, 143, 160–61, 171, 173, 232, 234
apostle meeting. *See* apostolic council
ascension, 3, 5, 8, 12, 23, 29, 36, 48, 51, 52, 61, 67, 70, 71–72n4, 88–89, 204, 230, 238

baptism, 55, 71, 90, 120, 133, 144, 158, 160, 225
Barnabas, 97, 161–62, 165–66, 185, 211, 222
biblical history, 38–44, 210, 231
blinding: of Paul, 225, 228; of Elymas, 226, 228
blindness: 235, 236; Paul's, 124–25, 127, 137, 204, 225

Christology, 46–48, 128, 239, 241–42
christophany, 88–89, 123, 125, 127
competent reader, 31–35, 45, 74, 178, 195–196, 236
Cornelius, 143–47, 150–54, 157n51, 158n60, 171–72, 237
covenant: 73, 76, 90; with Noah, 76; with Moses, 73, 76; with Abraham; 99; Davidic, 90, 92, 169, 182, 183, 191
cultural encyclopedia, 31, 33–34, 38, 43, 73, 81, 110–11, 196, 200, 216

day of judgment. *See* Day of the Lord
Day of the Lord, 79, 80–81, 85, 92, 166, 228–29, 233, 235–36
Day of Yahweh. *See* Day of the Lord
deeds of power, 78, 84, 206–8, 211, 227–228, 237

Elymas, 226–27, 236
ending, Acts', 186–189
enthronement: Jesus's, 86–89
Ethiopian eunuch, 120n2
exorcism. *See* signs

faithfulness, God's, 78–79, 86, 91–92, 106, 118, 138–40, 147, 175, 180, 182, 184–85, 189, 190–91, 233–34, 242–243
father, God as, 2, 15, 46, 49, 52, 58, 87–88, 140, 178, 182–83
forgiveness (of sins), 29, 90, 93, 117, 138n77, 156, 158n60, 172, 175, 184, 191, 213, 230, 234, 236

glory of God, 21, 72, 97–99, 110, 114–18, 239
god-language: explicit 27–29; implicit; 27–29; ambiguous 29–30, 180
Gospel of Luke, 18, 32, 34–38, 40, 42, 51–52, 81, 200

healing, 82, 125, 155n48, 156, 194, 206–16, 225, 227–28, 238

SUBJECT INDEX

heaven, 71, 103, 110, 111–12, 114–15, 118, 121–23, 127, 129, 146, 148, 172, 238–41
Herod, 218–20, 222, 224–25, 236

impartiality, 145, 148, 150, 153–57, 159, 160, 164–65, 171–72, 174, 190, 232, 235
Israel's Scriptures. *See* Scripture

James, 166–171
Jerusalem, 77, 95, 101, 131, 144n3, 162, 233
Jerusalem meeting. *See* Apostolic council
Judas, 28, 38, 205, 220–23, 236
judge: God as, 81, 105, 118, 154–55, 205n6, 222–26, 227–28, 232–33, 235–36; Jesus as, 47, 115–18, 125, 155–56, 172, 227, 240, 242

knower of hearts, 164

Law, 94, 104n37, 148–49, 161–63, 165–66, 171, 173–74, 184

miracles, 204n2, 210n20. *See* signs
mission: to the gentiles, 2, 3, 5, 11, 13, 50–51, 62, 68, 120, 125, 133, 142, 160–66, 168–69, 173, 186–87, 189–90; to the Jews; 186–89; universal, 50, 73, 80, 82, 91, 93, 133, 137, 215
mission to Jews and gentiles. *See* universal mission
Moses, 72n7, 74, 75, 94–95, 97–98, 100, 102–6, 118, 138, 207, 231
Most High, 111–12, 118

name: of God, 109–10, 126, 133, 169, 210–11, 240; of Jesus, 109–10, 125–26, 133, 156, 210–211, 215, 228, 234, 240; of the Lord, 81, 89, 166

Pentecost, 73–78, 80

plan of God, 6, 8–14, 21n98, 48, 51, 55–57, 63, 83–86, 88, 91–93, 132, 136, 144, 151–152, 159–164, 167, 169–170, 172–174, 177, 181, 190–192, 197–198, 201–3, 218, 221, 225–27, 234, 236, 239–240
portrayal of God, 3, 13–14, 20, 24–26, 27, 29, 30, 37, 44, 48, 50, 53, 59, 65, 66–68, 78, 84, 92, 99, 133–34, 143, 164, 171, 173, 196–97, 206, 224, 229–43
prayer, 109, 117–18, 133, 145–47, 151, 171, 209, 217–18, 239
preface: to Acts, 32, 38, 40, 42, 208–9; to Luke, 32, 38, 40, 42–43
prologue. *See* preface
providence. *See* plan of God
purpose. *See* plan of God
plot, 10, 36, 49, 54, 62–63, 67n150, 68–69, 79–80, 90–91, 125, 126, 145, 151, 159, 175, 179–80, 229
promise(s): of the Father. *See* promise of the Spirit; to David. *See* Davidic covenant; of land. *See* covenant with Abraham; to Israel, 1, 22, 56–57, 86, 88, 102, 138, 140, 141, 169, 175, 181, 183, 232–34, 242–43; of the Spirit, 57, 78, 70, 78, 87, 91

resurrection, 51, 84n58, 85n63, 86, 89–90, 92, 131n48, 135, 138–41, 168, 181–83, 191, 234, 238

Sapphira, 220, 222–24, 236
savior: God, 16, 81, 90–92, 101–2, 142–43, 156, 160, 161, 164, 165, 170–73, 191, 196–97, 201, 203, 205n6, 212, 216, 218, 220, 226–28, 231–33, 236–38, 240; Jesus, 135, 179–80, 191, 240, 242
Scripture, 10, 12, 14, 29, 34, 34n32, 43, 53, 71, 72, 76, 78–79, 91, 121, 123, 125–27, 139, 158–59, 164–66, 173–74, 181, 190–91, 224, 229, 232, 234, 242–43

shipwreck, 195–96, 202
signs, 71, 79, 82–84, 97, 98n13, 104n33, 123, 126, 131, 162, 165, 166, 173, 180, 204n3, 206–16, 227, 231, 237
signs and wonders. *See* signs
Stephen, 64, 82, 94–118, 133, 184, 231, 237

temple, 94–95, 100–101, 103, 105–13, 115–17, 133–34, 140, 168
theophany, 70–74, 78, 82, 88–89, 92, 102–3, 120–23, 127, 239
Torah. *See* the Law

vision(s), 10, 20, 27, 52, 62, 64, 71–72, 82–83, 96, 98n13, 103, 115–18, 120, 122, 125–26, 128–29n39, 133–34, 142–53, 155, 160, 171–72, 231, 239

witness (*n, v*), 54, 63, 96–97, 132–36, 137, 139, 158, 160, 164, 179, 180, 208–9, 218, 228
wonders. *See* signs
word of God, 21, 30, 109, 150, 175, 186, 189, 190, 191, 225, 234, 237
word of the Lord. *See* word of God

Scripture Index

New Testament

Gospel of Matthew

7:22	210n21
22:44	87

Gospel of Mark

3:29	222n70
9:38	210n21

Gospel of Luke

1	38, 195
1–2	143n2
1:1	40
1:1–4	32, 38, 40, 43
1:2	40, 132n53
1:3	25n9, 40
1:4	32, 38, 40
1:68	167n87
1:68–79	184
1:78	167n87
1:80	189n57
2:11	81
2:29–32	143n2
2:32	137
2:40	189n57
3:4	227
3:16	70, 78, 89
3:22	54n100
4:18	125n27
4:25–27	237n6
5:20–23	21n96
5:21	29n20
6:12	20n96
7:11–17	228n92
7:16	167n87
7:39–43	21n96
7:50	214n44
8:48	214n44
9:16	200
9:29	97
10:17	210n21
17:11	36n37
17:19	214n44
18:42	214n44
21:27	116
22	200
22:14–20	201n29
22:14–23	200
22:19	200
22:42	52
22:53	226
22:54–62	79
22:69	115
23:34	98n13, 117
23:46	98n13, 117
24:1–12	51
24:30	200
24:47	36n37, 213
24:49	70, 78
24:50–51	51
24:52	20n96

Gospel of John

5:22	236n5

Acts of the Apostles

1	71
1–8	218
1–12	11:5–10
1:1	209

Acts of the Apostles (continued)

1:1–2	52, 121
1:1–5	63
1:1–9	52
1:1–11	38
1:1–11	32, 51
1:2	53, 55, 70, 238
1:3	21, 132
1:4	15, 42, 49, 54, 55, 57, 70, 78, 88, 90, 162, 233
1:4–5	1, 30, 233
1:4–8	162
1:5	160, 185
1:5–8	160
1:6	21, 50, 81, 169, 229, 239
1:6–11	89n72
1:7	10n41, 15, 50, 70
1:7–8	51
1:8	42, 53, 55, 70, 96, 115, 133, 142, 143, 162, 164, 179, 189, 204n3, 208, 218, 233, 237
1:9	51, 70
1:9–11	51, 51n83, 146
1:10–11	52, 238
1:11	29, 51
1:13	79
1:15–26	79, 220
1:16	53, 221
1:16–20	28, 240
1:16–25	69, 124, 205, 220, 235
1:18	221
1:21	81
1:21–22	79
1:22	133, 238
1:24	20, 21n96, 81n45, 164, 239
1:24–26	70, 221
2	30, 74, 75
2:1	73
2:1–4	32n26, 30, 66, 70, 71, 73, 88, 89, 99
2:1–13	77
2:1–36	205n4
2:1–41	67, 70
2:1–47	162
2:2	71, 72, 121, 238
2:3	54, 71
2:4	53, 55, 77, 96, 97n9, 157n52
2:5	73
2:6–11	157
2:7–11	77
2:8	78
2:11	21, 78
2:14	79, 92
2:14–21	78
2:14–36	97n9
2:14–41	70, 73
2:15	79
2:16–21	99
2:17	2, 55, 60, 71, 78, 79, 80, 81, 82, 83, 88, 91, 96, 97n9, 143, 229, 230, 233, 237
2:17–18	54, 55m 82, 2:17–18, 240
2:17–21	55, 79, 80, 85, 87, 89, 142, 164, 228
2:17–36	73
2:18	83
2:19	82, 166, 207, 231
2:20	79, 81, 235
2:20–21	117, 233
2:21	50, 80, 82, 89, 90, 91, 117, 126, 143, 166, 194, 215, 234, 237, 240
2:21–22	20
2:22	23, 78, 84, 97, 98n13, 166, 190n57, 207, 209, 210, 211, 231
2:22–24	47, 71
2:22–28	36n39
2:23	12, 17, 21n98, 84, 85

SCRIPTURE INDEX

2:23–24	9	3:1–26	205n4
2:24	1, 51, 84, 85, 86, 168	3:1–4:22	133
2:24–28	85	3:6	210
2:25	71	3:6–8	212
2:25b–28	85, 86	3:7	72
2:25–36	123	3:8	207
2:27	86	3:8–9	20
2:28	218	3:12–26	104
2:29	86, 182	3:13	2
2:29–36	169, 182	3:14	103n31, 132
2:30	2, 71, 86, 86n4, 88, 182, 233	3:15	1, 30, 133, 218
		3:16	214, 215
2:30–31	182	3:18	9, 55
2:30–32	89, 182n24	3:19	137, 139n82, 236
2:30–36	75	3:21	55, 169
2:31	85, 86, 182, 213	3:23	89
2:31–33	51	3:25	99, 231
2:32	71, 133, 168, 182	3:26	168
2:32–33	87, 182	3:30	87
2:33	2, 15, 16, 53, 55, 57, 71, 78, 87, 88, 89, 89n73, 90, 231, 240, 239	4:3	217
		4:4	190n57
		4:7	211
		4:7–10	214, 215
		4:8	53, 83
2:33–34a	74	4:9	194, 214, 215, 238
2:34	71, 87, 89, 115, 182, 239	4:10	1
		4:11–12	215
2:34b–35	85, 89, 99	4:12	126, 194, 197, 215, 215n45, 240, 243
2:36	36n3, 47, 239, 71, 81, 88, 89, 90, 130, 183n26		
		4:16	206n8, 211
2:37	90	4:20	209
2:37–38	236	4:21	20, 207
2:37–40	184	4:22	206, 211
2:38	53, 55, 55n103, 138n77, 157, 213, 237	4:23–37	147
		4:24	20, 61
		4:24–30	20, 61n132
2:39	2, 71, 90, 93, 143	4:25	53, 54, 232
2:40	90, 194, 214	4:27–28	21n98
2:41	91	4:28	10, 12
2:42–47	208	4:29–30	210
2:43	82, 97, 208, 231	4:30	82, 166n82
2:46	201n29	4:31	21, 53, 99, 190n57, 217, 222
2:47	2, 20, 215		
3	211	4:32	222
3:1	146	4:32–37	224
3:1–10	208, 214	4:37	222
3:1–21	208	5	196n14

Acts of the Apostles (continued)

5:1–1	224
5:1–10	28n18
5:1–11	54n97, 69, 124, 205, 220, 222, 223, 235, 240
5:3	53, 222, 226
5:3–4	55
5:4	20, 222
5:5	190n57
5:9	54
5:10	72, 222, 224
5:11	223
5:12	82, 97, 166n82, 206, 231
5:12–16	208, 212, 223
5:12–42	133
5:16	212
5:17–20	97
5:17–21	61, 196, 206, 217
5:19	217, 219
5:19–20	103
5:20	218
5:21–42	133
5:29–30	2
5:30	1, 66
5:31	47, 138n77, 240
5:32	53, 54, 133
5:38	12
5:39	91
6:1–6	96
6:2	21, 190n57
6:5	53, 96
6:6	20
6:7	189
6:8	82, 97, 98n13, 208, 231
6:8—7:60	68
6:10	97
6:11	94, 97n11
6:13	97n11, 101, 103
6:13–14	94, 130n44
6:14	101
6:15	97, 97n11
7	30
7:1	95
7:1–8	96, 118
7:1–53	61n132
7:1–60	96
7:2	98, 102, 114
7:2–3	2, 100
7:2–7	100
7:2–8	99
7:2–34	95n4
7:2–45	7:2–45
7:2–53	108
7:3	99, 231
7:3–4	99
7:3–7	106
7:4	100
7:5	2, 99, 233
7:7	99, 100, 101, 231, 235
7:8	99
7:9	191
7:9–10	237
7:9–16	96
7:17	90, 102
7:17–43	96
7:20	102
7:20–43	177
7:25	102, 215, 237
7:30	102
7:30–38	118
7:31–33	99
7:32	99, 102
7:33	103
7:34	103, 104, 115
7:34–35	16
7:35	103, 104
7:35–36	237
7:35–37	104n36
7:35–38	104
7:35–43	104, 105
7:36	97, 104n33, 207, 231
7:37	104
7:38	104, 112, 184
7:39	112
7:39–41	105, 112
7:39–43	105
7:41	110
7:42	235

7:42b–43	105	8:21	20
7:44	106	8:22	213, 236
7:44–50	96, 101, 108	8:22–23	226
7:45	106, 234	8:25	21
7:46	106, 107	8:26	103, 146
7:47	106, 107	8:26–39	142
7:47–50	133	8:26–40	68, 120n2
7:48	5n19, 6, 96, 110, 111, 112, 115	8	143
		8:29	54, 232
7:48–50	107n47, 112	8:33	218
7:49	5n19, 238	8:39	54
7:49–50	107, 108, 111	9	119, 132, 141
7:49–59	109	9–10	121
7:50	20, 61, 111	9:1	122
7:51	53	9:1–2	121
7:51–53	95, 96, 104n36 105, 108, 112, 113	9:1–4	226
		9:1–19	68, 69, 119, 120, 121, 122, 130, 141, 142, 205, 220, 225, 235
7:52	10, 104, 112, 132		
7:53	97n11		
7:54	114	9:1–31	177
7:54–60	96	9:3	52n88, 122, 238
7:55	21, 52, 53, 64, 98, 112, 114, 238, 239	9:3–6	122, 123
		9:3–7	52
7:55–56	64, 96, 103, 115n90, 116n90, 118, 148	9:4	122, 121, 242
		9:5	122, 147
		9:8	123, 140
7:56	47, 64, 89n73, 115, 121, 238	9:8–19	122
		9:10	125
7:58–60	217	9:11	20
7:59	20n96, 81	9:14	126
7:59–60	98n13, 108, 117	9:15	120n2, 125n29, 132, 133, 141, 142, 144, 177, 189, 240
8:1	68, 95, 142		
8:3	121		
8:6	82		
8:6–7	208, 212	9:15–16	125, 126, 136
8:9–24	210n20	9:16	125n28, 126
8:10	21	9:17	53, 98n13, 123, 125
8:12	21		
8:12–16	55	9:17–19	55, 157n51
8:13	208	9:18	140, 225
8:14	21	9:19–22	140, 225
8:14–17	55n103	9:20	122, 127
8:15	53	9:20–22	47, 125
8:15–24	20	9:22	127
8:17	53, 203	9:23–25	138
8:19	53	9:27	123n15, 124
8:20	54	9:29–30	138

Acts of the Apostles (continued)

9:31	53
9:32–35	208
9:33–34	212
9:34	210
9:35	137
9:36–41	240
9:36–42	208
9:40	20
9:40–41	212
10	30, 154
10:1	145
10–15	56
10:1–23a	143
10:1–3	41n57
10:1–6	61
10:1–48	68, 142, 163, 164, 173
10:1—11:18	2, 68, 73, 126, 142, 142n1, 144, 145, 153, 154, 157n51, 160, 164
10:2	145, 152
10:2–4	20
10:2–5	145
10:3	146, 149
10:3–6	144, 145, 152, 153
10:3–16	144
10:4	102, 146, 147, 151
10:5	146
10:9	20
10:10–16	83, 120, 144, 159, 66, 238
10:13	148
10:13–16	99
10:15	148, 164
10:16	146, 148
10:17	149
10:19	54
10:20	151
10:22	151, 152, 153
10:23b–48	143
10:25	149
10:27	149
10:28	145, 149, 152, 153, 172
10:30	145
10:30–31	20
10:30–33	159
10:33	153
10:34	6, 91n78, 144, 146, 160, 164, 190, 235
10:34–35	153, 156, 172, 232
10:34–36	2
10:36	155
10:36–43	36n39, 158n60
10:38	53, 155n48, 156, 207, 209
10:38–41	155
10:40	1
10:41	526
10:41–42	10
10:42	47, 116, 155, 156, 235
10:42–43	15
10:43	29, 137n77, 155n48, 156, 158n60, 180n17
10:44	55, 83, 143, 157, 158n60, 172
10:44–45	53
10:44–47	233, 237
10:44–48	55, 55n103, 78, 82
10:46	157
10:47	53, 157
10:48	157n51
10:48—11:3	157n51
11:1	21n97
11:1–18	142, 143, 162
11:3	150
11:4	41n57
11:4–17	173
11:5	20, 147, 147n15, 149
11:5–10	41n57
11:10	146n12
11:12	149
11:14	142, 144, 160, 194, 215
11:15–16	53
11:15–17	82

11:16	21n97, 158, 160	13:9	53, 119n1, 226
11:16–17	55n103	13:10	226, 226n90
11:17	157, 160, 173	13:10–12	226
11:18	20, 142, 143, 160, 235	13:11	72, 226
		13:13–16a	176
11:19–24	161	13:13–52	68, 175, 176n1
11:19–26	173	13:14	173
11:21	137	13:15	176
11:24	53, 96	13:16	176, 177
11:28	55, 97n9	13:16–25	177
12:1	218	13:16–26	176
12:1–19	196	13:16–41	131, 175, 176
12:2	218	13:17	2, 177, 178
12:3–11	218	13:17–19	16, 179
12:4	225	13:17–25	176, 181, 182, 191
12:5	20, 218	13:18	178
12:6–11	61, 71, 217, 206	13:19	179
12:7–11	103	13:21	179
12:7	218, 219	13:21–22	179
12:10	219	13:22	179, 180
12:11	217, 218, 219	13:22–23	169, 233
12:12	20	13:23	2, 90, 135, 179, 180, 181
12:17	71, 166, 218, 219		
12:19	225	13:24	180
12:20–23	28n18, 97, 219, 221, 224, 240	13:25	180
		13:26	176, 177, 181, 183, 191, 215
12:21–23	69, 124, 205, 220, 235		
		13:27	181n21
12:22–23	224	13:27–31	181
12:23	72, 103, 218, 222, 224	13:27–37	176, 181, 183, 191
		13:29	181, 181n21
12:24	21, 189, 190n58, 223, 225	13:30	1, 51
		13:31	98n13
12:31	220	13:32	2, 90
13	178, 186, 234	13:32–33	135, 180, 233
13–14	71, 131, 162, 165, 167	13:32–39	140
		13:33	168, 181n21, 182, 182n22, 190
13–28	126		
13:2	53, 54, 131, 175, 177, 185, 232	13:33–34	51
		13:34	168, 183, 190
13:2–3	162	13:34–35	183
13:2—14:28	160	13:35	183
13:4	53, 83	13:36	21n98
13:4–12	69, 124, 205, 220, 235	13:37	1
		13:38	29, 138n77, 176
13:5	21, 190n58	13:38–39	184
13:6–12	226	13:38–41	176, 191
13:7	21	13:39	184

Acts of the Apostles (continued)

13:41	185, 189
13:41–42	185n37
13:42–50	185
13:42–52	176
13:43	177n5
13:44	21, 189
13:44–49	173
13:46	21, 186, 188, 189, 190
13:46–47	68, 162, 185
13:47	164, 187, 189, 190, 215, 237
13:48	21, 189n57, 190n57
13:48–49	190n58
13:49	21
13:52	53, 83
14	186
14:1	186
14:2	186
14:3	71, 82, 97, 166n82, 180, 208, 231
14:8–10	212
14:8–18	208, 211
14:8–20	212n30
14:9	194, 238
14:9–10	215
14:15	2, 20, 61, 137, 139n82
14:19–20	131, 138
14:22	21
14:27	161, 161n70, 165, 166, 166n81
15	62, 160
15:1	139n81, 161, 215
15:1–2	161
15:1–5	161
15:1–21	68, 73, 142, 143, 160, 161, 173
15:3	139, 162
15:4	71, 97, 162, 165, 166, 166n81
15:5	161, 162
15:6	163
15:6–9	142
15:6–21	143, 161
15:7	163, 164
15:7–9	2, 163
15:7–11	142n1
15:8	21n96, 53, 82, 158, 163, 164, 180
15:8–9	142, 149, 158, 158n60, 167
15:8–11	189
15:9	158, 164
15:10	165
15:10–11	184
15:11	142, 161, 163, 165, 165n80, 194, 215, 240
15:12	82, 163, 165, 231
15:13–21	163
15:14	167, 169
15:14–18	166
15:15–18	166, 167
15:16	168, 169
15:16–17	160, 168
15:16–18	234
15:17	169
15:17–18	169
15:19	137, 167
15:19–21	150, 146, 166
15:21	94, 171
15:27	219
15:28	53
15:29	170
15:30—18:22	160
15:35–36	21
16:6	53
16:6–7	83
16:6–10	46
16:7	54, 57, 87
16:9	98n13
16:10–17	63, 194, 194n4
16:14–15	157n51
16:16–18	208, 210, 212
16:17	215
16:22–23	131
16:23–40	217, 219
16:24–40	131
16:25–27	147

SCRIPTURE INDEX   277

16:25–34	206	20	201
16:25–40	138	20:5–15	63, 194, 194n4
16:26	72, 99	20:5—21:18	194n4
16:30	215, 219	20:7–12	208
16:30–31	194	20:9–12	212, 240
16:31	215	20:23	53
16:32	21	20:24	132
17:1–3	140	20:25	21, 197
17:13	21	20:26–27	21n98
17:13–14	138	20:27	12
17:22–24	2	20:28	10, 53
17:22–31	61n132, 238	20:42	189n57
17:23	46n71, 58	21:1–18	63, 194, 194n4
17:24	5n19, 61, 110, 239	21:11	53
17:24–25	110	21:20	21
17:24–26	20, 238	21:20–22	130n44
17:24–29	6	21:21	94n2
17:25a	5n19	21:25	170
17:27	5n19	21:26	133n55
17:29	5n19	21:28	133n55, 134n58
17:30	236	21:30	130
17:31	1, 10n41, 20, 47, 116, 235	22	119, 132, 141
		22:1	186
18:5	140	22:1–21	60, 68, 119, 120, 141
18:6	186, 188		
18:9	52n88	22:2	130n44
18:9–10	138	22:3	131, 223
18:11	21	22:3–4	186
18:17f	52n88	22:3–5	130n44
18:22	52n88	22:6	52n88, 238
18:26	21	22:6–16	123
19	212n30	22:8	134
19:1–6	55n103	22:10	10
19:1–7	55	22:11	52n88, 124
19:2	53	22:14	119, 125, 132, 133, 136, 139n81, 141, 240
19:6	53, 55, 83, 97n9		
19:8	21		
19:10	21	22:14–15	126
19:11	205n5, 207, 209	22:14–16	125, 131
19:11–12	131, 208, 209, 212	22:15	127, 132, 133, 134, 141
19:11–20	210n20		
19:13–15	210	22:17–18	134
19:15	210n20	22:17–21	133
19:20	189n57	22:18	134
19:21	192	22:19	134
19:26	212n30	22:21	132, 133, 136
19:28	212n30	23:6	135
19:34	212n30	23:11	192, 193, 197

Acts of the Apostles (continued)

24:15	135
25:19	135
26	141
26:1–23	60, 86, 120, 135, 141
26:2–3	135
26:4–7	186
26:4–8	135
26:6–7	2, 138
26:6–8	86, 138, 139, 233
26:8	135, 138
26:9–11	135
26:12–18	135, 136
26:13	52n88, 238
26:14	136
26:16	98n13, 132n53, 136, 141
26:16–18	136
26:17–18	137
26:18	29, 130, 137, 139, 226
26:19	52n88
26:19–23	135
26:20	137, 139n82, 236
26:22	140
26:22–23	138, 139
26:23	130, 137, 138
27	199, 200, 201
27:1–12	192
27:1–29	194n4
27:1–44	69, 192, 196, 202
27:1—28:16	63, 194, 194n4
27:4–8	193
27:5	195
27:8	195
27:9	193
27:9–10	195
27:10	193, 197
27:11	193, 195
27:12	193, 195
27:13	193, 195
27:13–20	192
27:13–44	238
27:14	193, 195
27:14–20	193
27:20	194, 196, 197
27:21–26	192
27:23	196
27:23–36	83
27:24	196, 197, 195n10
27:27–32	192
27:29	195
27:30	195
27:31	195n10
27:31–44	215
27:33	198
27:33–38	192, 200
27:34	198, 215
27:35	200
27:39–44	192
27:40	195
27:44	202
28	188
28:1–6	208, 211
28:3–5	212
28:7–8	208, 212
28:8	209
28:9	208, 208n13, 209, 212
28:23	21
28:24	188
28:24–28	186
28:25	54
28:25–28	188, 188n55
28:26–27	125n27
28:26–28	189, 229
28:27	137
28:28	186
28:30–31	188
28:31	21

Romans

4:13	90
4:16	90
4:20	90
9:8	90

1 Corinthians

1:23–25	85
15:24–28	236n5
15:25	87

Hebrews

1:13	87

James

5:14	210n21

Old Testament/Hebrew Bible/The Septuagint

Genesis

11:1–9	76
12	100n17
14:20	111
16:7–14	103, 217
21:1; 50:24;	167
22:10–18	103, 217
28:10–22	122
31:13	102n28

Exodus

3	217
3:1–6	102n26, 127
3:1–22	103, 217
3:2	218
3:2—4:17	122
3:8	218
3:12	100
4:1–9	207
4:11	125
6:1	178
6:6	178
6:6–7	218
7:3	207
7:4–5	218
7:8–11	207
9:3	227
11:9–10	207
12:17	218
12:42	218
12:51	218
13:3	218
13:9	218
13:14	218
13:16	218
14	102n28
14:19	218
15:26	211
16	65
16:6	218
16:10	114
16:32	218
18:1	218
19–24	73
19:16	121
19:17–18	72
19:18	217
20:2	218
23	154
23:16	76
23:20	218
23:23	218
24:9–10	72
24:16	98
24:16–18	114
24:17	72, 98
25:8	106
29:46	218
32:11	218
32:34	218
33:12–23	122
33.18–22	114n82
34:22	76
34:29	89

Leviticus

2:2	146
2:9	146
2:16	146
5:12	146
6:15	146
9:23–24	114
11	147
16	29n20
17–18	170
19:15	154
23:15–22	76

Numbers

11:25	159n63
16:31–32	217
20:14–16	103, 217
22:2–35	122
22:22—23:12	103, 217
28:26–31	76

Deuteronomy

1:31 LXX	178
4:11–40	72
4:12	72
4:31	65
4:34	82, 178, 207
5:15	178
6:22	82, 207
7:19	82, 207
9:26	178
16:9–12	76
26:8	82
29:2	82
32:8	111
32:2	111
34:10–12	207
34:11	82

Joshua

3:11	155
3:13	155
24:5	207n10

Judges

2:1–5	103
2:15	227
6:11–24	103, 217
13:2–25	122

Ruth

1:13	227

1 Samuel

2:21	167
5:6	227
5:9	227
7:13	227
8:7	179
12:15	227

2 Samuel

6:1–19	108
7:6–7	169
7:8–16	86
7:11–13	169
7:16	169
12:26–28	169n101
22:14	111
22:15	121
24:16f	103n29
24:16f	217n52

1 Kings

8:27	72
17:17–24	207
19:11	217

2 Kings

1:1–18	103, 217
5:1–14	207
5:7–15	211
6:18–23	207
8:27	108
1 Kgs 17—2 Kgs 13	207n11
17:7–20	105n40

3 Kingdoms

2:28	108
8:4	108

1 Chronicles

15:1–16:43	108

2 Chronicles

19:6–7	154
36:14–16	105n40

Ezra

9	29n20

Nehemiah

9:6–15	207n10
9:26	105n40

Book of Psalms

2	182
2:7	182
14:1	108n4
14:8–11 LXX	85
14:10 LXX	86
16:10	183
18:5	85n63
18:8	139
18:13	111, 18:14; 139
21:8–9	139
26:8	114
28:3 LXX	98n15
29:7	139
31:4	126
31:5	117
44:22	126
45:4	108n4
51:13 LXX	53n89
55:5 LXX	189n57
68:26 LXX	221
73:7	108n4
76:15	178n8
77:18–19	121
77:43 LXX	207
78:43	207n10
79:9	126
97:4	121
97:5	155
103:3	29n20
104:1–4	139
104:26–27 LXX	207
108:8 LXX	221
110	87, 89
110:1–2	87
110:5–6	88n69
135:8–12	207n10
135:9	82
136:11–16	178
139	164
144:6	121

Isaiah

2:2–4	81
3:18–4:1	81
4:5	114
6	127
6.1–4	114n82
6:1–13	122
7:18–23	81
10:3	81
11:10–16	81
12:1–4	81
19:18–25	81
22:5	81
24:21	80
25:6–9	81
40:3–5	227
42:1	158
42:6–7	137
42:8	126
43:10–11	126
43:21–22	126
44:3	158
45:20–22	168
45:23–25	185n37
48:9	126
49:6	186, 189
55:3	183, 185n37
55:6–11	185n37
57:19	211
63:10–11	53n89

Isaiah (continued)

66:1–2	107, 108, 109, 110
66:3–4	109
66:5	109, 126
66:6	109

Jeremiah

1:7–8	127
3:23	126
12:15–16	168
17:9–10	164
23:5–6	81
25:33	80
32:20	207n10

Ezekiel

1–2	136n66
1:1—3:14	122
1:4	121
1:7	121
1:13	121
1:26	129
1:28	114n82
2–3	127
2:1 LXX	136
7:7–12	81
20:44	126
30:3–5	80
36:26–27	158
37:14	158
37:29	158
39:13	81

Daniel

7:13–14	129

Hosea

1:4–5	81
3:5	168
5:9	81
13:4	126

Joel

1:15	81
2	81
2:28–29	159
2:32/3:5 LXX	126
	3:1–5a 79
3:1 LXX	80
3:11–16	80

Amos

2:13–16	81
3:14	81
5:25–27	105
8:3	81
8:9	81
9:2–4	72
9	169
9:11	168
9:11–12	168

Jonah

1:1–17	195n10

Micah

2:4	81
4:13	155
7:18–19	29n20

Habakkuk

1:5	185n37
1:5–11	185n37

Zechariah

4:14	155
6:5	155

Malachi

3:16–18	81

Early Extrabiblical Literature

Apocrypha

Baruch

2:16	207n10

2 Maccabees

2:27	178n12
9:5–12	224

Sirach

38:11	146
45:3	207n10
45:16	146

Pseudepigrapha

1 Enoch

14:8—16:4	136

Joseph and Aseneth

14.4–14	129

Jubilees

1:1	76
6:17–19	76

Other Ancient Authors and Writings

Aristotle

Poetics

6:15–30/1450a	62

Bede

Commentary on the Acts of the Apostles

2.4	77

Cyril of Jerusalem

Catechetical Lectures

17.17	76

Herodotus

History

4.205	224

Hesiod

Theogony

306–7	193n3

Josephus

Jewish Antiquities

3.252–54	75n21
4.55–56	112n65
13.252	75n21
14.337	75n21
17.168–169; 17.254	224
	75n21
15.324	112n65
19.343–52	224n83
19.345–50	28n17

Jewish War

1.253	75n21
1.419–20	112n65
1.656	224
2.42	75n21
4.614	112n65

Jewish War (continued)

6.299	75n12
7.175–77	112n65
7.294	112n65
7.451–53	28n17, 221

Justin Martyr

First Apology   67

Lucian of Samosata

How to Write History

9	40
47	41
48	41
51	41

Alexander

59	224

Origen

Contra Celsum

I.13	85n61
II.9	85n61

Philo

On the Life of Moses

2.88	111n65

On the Special Laws

2.179	75
2.179–87	75
2.181	76

Plutarch

Sulla

36.2–3	224

Thucydides

History of the Peloponnesian War

1.22.2	41
21.2	40

www.ingramcontent.com/pod-product-compliance
Lightning Source LLC
Chambersburg PA
CBHW061432300426
44114CB00014B/1655